GOVERNING EUROPE'S MARINE ENVIRONMENT

Corbett Centre for Maritime Policy Studies Series

The Corbett Centre for Maritime Policy Studies Series is the publishing platform of the Corbett Centre. Drawing on the expertise and wider networks of the Defence Studies Department of King's College London, and based at the Joint Services Command and Staff College in the UK Defence Academy, the Corbett Centre is already a leading centre for academic expertise and education in maritime and naval studies. It enjoys close links with several other institutions, both academic and governmental, that have an interest in maritime matters, including the Developments, Concepts and Doctrine Centre (DCDC), the Naval Staff of the Ministry of Defence and the Naval Historical Branch.

The centre and its publishing output aims to promote the understanding and analysis of maritime history and policy and to provide a forum for the interaction of academics, policy-makers and practitioners. Books published under the eagis of the Corbett Centre series reflect these aims and provide an opportunity to stimulate research and debate into a broad range of maritime related themes. The core subject matter for the series is maritime strategy and policy, conceived broadly to include theory, history and practice, military and civil, historical and contemporary, British and international aspects.

As a result this series offers a unique opportunity to examine key issues such as maritime security, the future of naval power, and the commercial uses of the sea, from an exceptionally broad chronological, geographical and thematic range. Truly interdisciplinary in its approach, the series welcomes books from across the humanities, social sciences and professional worlds, providing an unrivalled opportunity for authors and readers to enhance the national and international visibility of maritime affairs, and provide a forum for policy debate and analysis.

Governing Europe's Marine Environment

Europeanization of Regional Seas or Regionalization of EU Policies?

Edited by

MICHAEL GILEK
Södertörn University, Sweden

KRISTINE KERN
Leibniz Institute for Regional Development and University of Potsdam, Germany

Routledge
Taylor & Francis Group
LONDON AND NEW YORK

First published 2015 by Ashgate Publishing

Published 2016 by Routledge
2 Park Square, Milton Park, Abingdon, Oxon OX14 4RN
711 Third Avenue, New York, NY 10017, USA

Routledge is an imprint of the Taylor & Francis Group, an informa business

British Library Cataloguing in Publication Data
A catalogue record for this book is available from the British Library

The Library of Congress has cataloged the printed edition as follows:
A catalog record for this book is available from the Library of Congress

ISBN 9781409447276 (hbk)

Contents

Part 3: Marine Governance of Europe's Regional Seas

List of Figures and Tables

Figures

Tables

Notes on Contributors

Editors

Michael Gilek is Associate Professor in Ecology/Ecotoxicology at Södertörn University and has extensive research experience on chemical pollution and other ecological risks in the aquatic environment, as well as on associated science-policy interactions. In his current research Dr Gilek leads international interdisciplinary studies analysing marine spatial planning and environmental governance in the Baltic Sea.

Kristine Kern is Professor in Governance of Urban Infrastructure and Global Change, University of Potsdam and Leibniz Institute for Regional Development and Structural Planning (IRS). Her current research interests are in the areas of local and regional climate and energy policy, sustainable development of cities and regions, transnational networks of cities, European regional seas (Baltic Sea in particular) and the EU macro-regional strategies.

Contributors

Brita Bohman is a doctoral candidate in Environmental Law at Stockholm University. Her doctoral work is part of the transdisciplinary project Baltic Ecosystem Adaptive Management (BEAM) and focuses on prerequisites for effective ecosystem-based control of eutrophication in the Baltic Sea through international and EU law.

Ratana Chuenpagdee is Canada Research Chair in Natural Resource Sustainability and Community Development at the Memorial University of Newfoundland with a specialization on interdependencies between natural and human systems. Main current research topics include fisheries and ocean governance, small-scale fisheries sustainability, environmental stewardship, and community viability.

Elizabeth De Santo is Assistant Professor of Environmental Studies at Franklin & Marshall College. Her teaching and research focus on (1) the conservation and management of marine species and habitats, and (2) improving the science-policy interface in environmental decision-making. She is particularly interested in the challenges of effectively implementing Marine Protected Areas and biodiversity conservation worldwide.

Marion Dreyer is Deputy Scientific Director at DIALOGIK, which is a non-profit institute for communication and cooperation research. Her main fields of interest are risk governance and participation and cooperation processes in areas of societal controversy and conflict. In her ongoing research Dr Dreyer deals with water issues in terms of precaution-based strategies to deal with anthropogenic micro-pollutants in the water cycle.

Monica Hammer is Associate Professor in Natural Resource Management and Research leader at the Centre for Baltic and East European Studies at Södertörn University. Her research interests focuses on sustainability of integrated social-ecological systems and the services provided by ecosystems in the Baltic Sea region.

Björn Hassler is Associate Professor in Environmental Science at Södertörn University and has extensive experience from multidisciplinary research on environmental governance in the Baltic Sea region. His main focuses are on marine institutional structures in areas such as oil transportations, eutrophication and fisheries.

Svein Jentoft is a sociologist and a professor at the Norwegian College of Fishery Science, University of Tromsø. He specializes in social issues pertaining to fisheries and the marine environment such as their sustainable development, planning, and governance. He is currently engaged in a global research network ('Too Big to Ignore') focusing on the role and contribution of small-scale fisheries.

Mikael Karlsson is PhD in Environmental and Energy Systems. His research focuses on environmental governance, including risk management, science-policy studies, chemicals law and marine policy. Dr Karlsson is also President of the European Environmental Bureau.

Ståle Knudsen is Professor of Social Anthropology at University of Bergen. He specializes on Black Sea fisheries and environmental governance. His main current research interests include the political ecology of biodiversity and introduced species in the Black Sea, as well as social mobilization following energy plant constructions.

David Langlet is Associate Professor in Environmental Law at Stockholm University. His research spans a broad number of topics in the areas of environmental and energy law, law of the sea, and international economic law.

Judith van Leeuwen is Assistant Professor in Environmental Policy at Wageningen University. Her research interest lies in the changing authority and accountability relations between government and industry actors in polycentric environmental and marine governance settings.

Sebastian Linke is Assistant Professor in Theory of Science at the University of Gothenburg and studies the relationship between science, politics and society in fisheries and marine management focusing on the (changing) relations between scientists', fishers' and other stakeholders' knowledge in EU fisheries politics.

Juan Carlos Rodríguez Mateos is Professor of Human Geography at the University of Seville. His research focuses on the geography of the sea, ocean governance, marine spatial planning, as well as socio-economic and management aspects of fishing activities.

Piet Sellke has studied sociology and political science at the University of Stuttgart as well as sociology at the University of Oregon (USA). His main research interests are security studies, risk perception, risk governance, and technology assessment. Currently Piet Sellke is senior researcher and project manager with Dialogik non-profit institute for communication and cooperation research.

Sara Söderström is a PhD candidate in Environmental Science at Södertörn University. Her research interest rests within regional environmental governance having the Baltic Sea as a focal point, aligned with an emphasis on the ecosystem approach to management.

Jan P.M. van Tatenhove is Professor in Marine Governance at Wageningen University, the Netherlands. His research focuses on the institutionalization of marine governance arrangements at the level of EU regional seas and the Arctic.

Oksana Udovyk is PhD in Water and Environmental Studies. Her research interests include uncertainty, risk, and science-policy interactions in environmental governance.

Juan Luís Suárez de Vivero is Professor of Marine Geography at University of Seville. The research activity is centred on the field of maritime policy and geopolitics of the oceans, coastal management and maritime spatial planning.

List of Abbreviations

ACFA	Advisory Committee on Fisheries and Aquaculture
BAT	Best Available Technique
BSAP	Baltic Sea Action Plan
BSC	The Commission on the Protection of the Black Sea Against Pollution ('Black Sea Commission')
BSEC	Black Sea Economic Cooperation
BSERP	Black Sea Environmental Recovery Project
BS-SAP	Strategic Action Plan for the Black Sea
CBD	Convention on Biological Diversity
CBSS	Council of Baltic Sea States
CFCA	Community Fisheries Control Agency
CIS	Common Implementation Strategy
CFP	Common Fisheries Policy
COP	Conference of the Parties
CPMR	Conference of Peripheral Maritime Regions
DABLAS	Danube-Black Sea Task Force
DG	Directorate-General
DG MARE	Directorate General for Maritime Affairs and Fisheries
DIKE	Data, Information and Knowledge Exchange
EC	European Commission
ECJ	European Court of Justice
EEA	European Environmental Agency
EEZ	Exclusive Economic Zone
EMODNET	European Marine Observation and Data Network
EMSA	European Maritime Safety Agency
EP	European Parliament
ESA	Economic and Social Assessment
EU	European Union
EUSBSR	EU Strategy for the Baltic Sea Region
FEMIP	Facility for Euro-Mediterranean Investment and Partnership
GDP	Gross Domestic Product
GEF	Global Environmental Facility
GES	Good Environmental Status
GFCM	General Fisheries Council of the Mediterranean
HA	Horizontal Action
HELCOM	Helsinki Commission; Baltic Marine Environmental Protection Commission

ICES	International Council for the Exploration of the Seas
ICPDR	The International Commission for Protection of the Danube River
ICZM	Integrated Coastal Zone Management
IMP	Integrated Maritime Policy
IMO	International Maritime Organization
ICZM	Integrated Coastal Zone Management
IRBM	Integrated River Basin Management
JCP	Baltic Sea Joint Comprehensive Environmental Action Programme
LRIT	Long Range Identification and Tracking
MAP	Mediterranean Action Plan
MPAs	Marine Protected Areas
MCSD	Mediterranean Commission on Sustainable Development
MSCG	Marine Strategy Coordination Group
MSFD	Marine Strategy Framework Directive
MSP	Marine Spatial Planning
NATURA 2000	Habitats Directive and the Birds Directive
NGOs	Non-Governmental Organizations
NM	Nautical Miles
NSCOGI	North Seas Countries' Offshore Grid Initiative
NSMCs	North Sea Ministerial Conferences
NSRAC	North Sea Regional Advisory Council
OSPAR	Convention for the Protection of the Marine Environment of the North-East Atlantic
PA	Priority Area
RACs	Regional Advisory Councils
RBD	River Basin Districts
RBMP	River Basin Management Plans
SAR	Seas at Risk
SEA	Strategic Environment Assessment Directive
STECF	Scientific, Technical, and Economic Committee for Fisheries
TEU	Treaty on the European Union
TFEU	Treaty on the Functioning of the European Union
UNDP	United Nations Development Programme
UNEP	United Nations Environment Programme
UNECD	United Nations Conference on Environment and Development
UNCLOS	United Nations Convention on the Law of the Sea
WFD	Water Framework Directive
WWF	World Wide Fund for Nature (formerly World Wildlife Fund)

Preface

This volume presents research on current practices and challenges in the governance of Europe's marine environment – a complex, interdisciplinary and increasingly internationalized research field of high academic and societal concern.

The book grew out from two multidisciplinary workshops on 'Governing Europe's Marine Environment', which were organized to expand and contextualize findings gained in the multidisciplinary research project RISKGOV 'Environmental Risk Governance of the Baltic Sea', led by Michael Gilek at Södertörn University, Sweden. The RISKGOV project on environmental governance in the Baltic Sea and the subsequent workshops focussed also on other regional seas in Europe and Europe-wide research topics, involved international scholars and experts from social as well as natural sciences. Most of the contributions published in this book were, in draft form, first presented at the workshops. Many thanks to all project colleagues and workshop participants!

We are very grateful for the generous financial support received from The Foundation for Baltic and East European Studies (Östersjöstiftelsen), The Swedish Research Council Formas and The Centre for Baltic and East European Studies (CBEES) at Södertörn University. Without this support the present book would not have been possible.

Special thanks to all of our fellow contributors, all of whom have submitted topical papers based on high-quality research. Many thanks also to Ross Beveridge, who assisted us with technical as well as language editing. Finally, we are grateful for valuable comments received in the external peer review process as well as for the professionalism shown by our editors at Ashgate.

Michael Gilek, Södertörn University, Sweden

Kristine Kern, Leibniz Institute for Regional Development and University of Potsdam, Germany

Chapter 1
Governing Europe's Marine Environment: Key Topics and Challenges

Kristine Kern and Michael Gilek

Introduction

This book aims for a better understanding of the fragmented governance architecture of marine governance in Europe by combining in-depth analysis of marine governance structures and processes with development of analytical perspectives. In particular the tension between the Europeanization of regional seas and the regionalization of EU policies is in focus.

Although the EU has become the most important political player in Europe's regional sea areas, ecosystems as well as regional governance systems differ considerably across Europe's regional seas. The contributions to this edited volume show that marine governance differs among the various regional sea areas in Europe, depending on the environmental problems and the regional institutions. The Europeanization of Europe's regional seas may, therefore, lead to differing outcomes despite common objectives.

Moreover, the regionalization of EU marine governance has led to the emergence of new regional institutions. This trend can be observed in various areas, ranging from setting-up Regional Advisory Councils (RACs) for fisheries (Griffin 2007, Griffin 2009, Long 2010, Stör and Chabay 2010) to the introduction of a regional approach in EU directives (such as the Marine Strategy Framework Directive) and launching macro-regional strategies (such as the EU Strategy for the Baltic Sea Region 2009). This development points to a more regionalized approach to European integration, which may strengthen regional governance systems. Such an approach of more regionalization in marine governance provides flexibility for the development and implementation of regional sea conventions and macro-regional strategies.

Governing regional seas requires the establishment of a governance system for the entire region. Problems may occur because the boundaries of existing governance systems, the ecosystems, as well as various societal activities and impacts are not identical. Thus, the scope of regional conventions may be more appropriate than EU legislation because these regional institutions focus on the entire region, including non-member states (such as Russia and Norway). Decisions made in Brussels need to be adjusted to regional environmental institutions. However, marine governance in Europe can be characterized by a

North-South divide with respect to the degree of Europeanization. The North Sea and the Baltic Sea on the one side differ considerably from the Mediterranean and the Black Sea on the other side because the regional seas in the North of Europe are surrounded almost only by EU member states (with Norway and Russia as the only exceptions).

Multi-Sector Perspectives

The chapters of this book concentrate on the various aspects of multi-sector, multi-level and multi-actor marine governance. From a multi-sector perspective it can be asked as to how the various environmental risks (e.g. over-fishing, pollution, habitat loss, invasive species, shipping, climate change, etc.) that threaten Europe's coastal and marine environment can be governed? Traditionally, marine environmental management in Europe has focused primarily on handling particular sources of contamination (e.g. hazardous chemicals and nutrients) and extraction of resources (e.g. fish) in a polluter/extractor-oriented approach with a rather limited focus on protecting/restoring particular (valuable) marine areas (Karlsson et al. 2011). Gradually, however, an alternative and complementary environment-oriented approach, basing management of pollution and resource extraction on defined quality criteria and environmental objectives, has emerged. The Baltic Sea Action Plan (BSAP) is therefore based on an ecosystem approach (HELCOM 2007), i.e. the usual sectoral pollution reduction approach was replaced by a cross-sectoral approach that starts from the vision of a healthy sea with a good ecological status. Like HELCOM in its BSAP the EU developed an integrated approach for the protection of its marine environment based on an ecosystem approach. While the ecosystem approach has become the core approach in the Water Framework Directive and the Marine Strategy Framework Directive, in some areas such as chemicals (REACH) and fisheries management (Common Fisheries Policy) a polluter/extractor-oriented command-and-control type of management still prevails (Karlsson et al. 2011).

Science-policy interactions are crucial for the development and outcomes of marine environmental governance (e.g. Rice 2005). Scientific expertise serves as a basis for decision-making in most policy domains of industrialized societies. However, when social or political conflicts emerge, the primacy of science in politics is often put into question thus creating new demands and challenges for the science system (Bijker et al. 2009, Linke et al. 2014). This is not least the case when it comes to the governance of large-scale marine environmental risks such as overfishing, eutrophication and hazardous chemicals, where the demarcation between the two domains of science and policy is far from clear-cut due to scientific uncertainty and disagreements among stakeholders (Wilson 2009, Karlsson et al. 2011, Linke et al. 2014). Scientific uncertainties and stakeholder disagreements are particularly problematic for marine environmental governance when attempting to implement a holistic cross-sectoral ecosystem approach to management (Rice 2005, Wilson 2009, Linke et al. 2014).

Multi-Level Perspectives

Marine governance in Europe is affected by European multi-level governance. Increasing Europeanization of regional seas may cause coordination problems because the implementation of EU policies, such as the Marine Strategy Framework Directive, requires close cooperation not only with the member-states but also with already existing environmental organizations (such as HELCOM). Due to European integration and various waves of European enlargement, the governing systems of Europe's regional seas have undergone rapid changes since the 1970s and are now shaped by a fragmented governance architecture that combines national, international and European governance.

First, national environmental governance may vary considerably among the states surrounding regional seas. Thus, we find pronounced differences among the various regional seas in Europe. While the North Sea is bordered by founding members and countries that have long been members of the EU (except Norway) and exhibits well-developed national environmental governance systems, the group of Baltic Sea states includes old member states, new member states and Russia. While the Nordic countries and Germany can be considered as environmental pioneers, most of the new member states started to develop their environmental policy only recently. Like the Baltic Sea, the Black Sea has been directly affected by the end of the Cold War, and many of the riparian states, including Russia, are in transition from socialist states to market economies. However, in the Black Sea region only two countries (Bulgaria, Romania) are member states of the European Union, i.e. in the Black Sea region Europeanization is far less important than in the North Sea and the Baltic Sea regions. In the Black Sea and in the Mediterranean Sea regions the riparian countries seem to differ to a much higher degree than in the North Sea and Baltic Sea regions. Moreover, in these regions we find both *inter*state conflicts (for example between Ukraine and Russia in the Black Sea region) and *intra*state conflicts (such as the civil war in Syria). As national environmental governance systems are still the backbones of regional environmental governance, prospects for a sustainable development of Europe's regional seas varies considerable and seem to be better for the North Sea and the Baltic Sea than for the Black Sea and the Mediterranean Sea.

Second, regional seas are affected by global agreements (such as the IMO convention and UNCLOS), for example in the area of shipping (Suárez de Vivero and Rodriguez Mateos 2002), and by international treaties for regional sea areas. Initial efforts to improve the environmental situation in regional sea areas started relatively early. The Helsinki Convention on the protection of the marine environment of the Baltic Sea area was signed already in 1974. It was the first regional seas convention and triggered the creation of UNEP's Regional Seas

Programme. Today this program covers 18 regions in the world, including the Baltic Sea (Helsinki Convention), the Mediterranean Sea (Barcelona Convention 1976), the North-East Atlantic (OSPAR Convention 1992) and the Black Sea (Bucharest Convention 1992) (Doussis 2006, Hoballah 2006, Costa 2009). Regional sea conventions are implemented by guidelines and action plans such as the Baltic Sea Action Plan (BSAP) (HELCOM, 2007). It uses a multi-level approach and distinguishes between measures that can be implemented at national level, at EU level (e.g. Common Fisheries Policy, Common Agricultural Policy), and at international level (e.g. shipping control by the International Maritime Organization).

Third, the Europeanization of regional seas has developed very quickly. This is most prominent in the area of fisheries, which is dominated by the EU's Common Fisheries Policy (Princen 2010), but includes a proliferating body of EU legislation affecting various aspects of the marine environment such as the Water Framework Directive, REACH, Natura 2000, and the EU Recommendations for Integrated Coastal Zone Management. Moreover, the EU adopted a Marine Strategy Framework Directive in 2008 and is developing an Integrated Maritime Policy (see for example the Communication on Maritime Spatial Planning published in December 2010; COM(2010)771) (Suarez de Vivero 2006, Koivurova 2009, Queffelec et al. 2009, Borja et al. 2010, Fritz 2010, Juda 2010, Wakefield 2010, De Santo 2011). However, research shows a bifurcation between policies that aim at the use of ecosystem services such as the Common Agricultural Policy and the Common Fisheries Policy on the one hand and policies that are designed primarily for marine and coastal environmental protection such as the Water Framework Directive and the Marine Strategy Framework Directive on the other (De Santo 2010, Wenzel 2011). This points to the need for horizontal coordination of EU legislation because different directives may lead to contradictory and incompatible policies, for example between fisheries and nature conservation. At the implementation level Europeanization of national marine governance is supported by Common Implementation Strategies that have been developed, for example, for the Water Framework Directive and for the Marine Strategy Framework Directive.

Multi-Actor Perspectives

Vertical interplay within the region may strengthen the regional governance system and support the regionalization of EU policies. The multi-level systems of regional seas cannot be governed solely by hierarchical structures. Alongside horizontal interplay between regional environmental institutions and the EU, vertical interplay is of special interest for the development of regional governance systems. Vertical interplay in (regional) multi-level systems may result in a shift of competencies, for example from national governments to regions and cities.

In all regional seas governmental initiatives have been supplemented by initiatives of non-governmental and subnational organizations (Kern and Löffelsend 2004, Joas et al. 2007, 2008). Alongside subnational authorities, NGOs play an increasing role for vertical interplay in regional sea areas. Such forms of transnational governance range from the Black Sea NGO Network (BSNN) to the Union of the Baltic Cities. Moreover, transnational city networks have developed and thrived in Europe since the early 1990s (Kern and Bulkeley 2009).

Cross-level institutional arrangements such as transnational city networks or transnational networks of micro-regions may function as boundary or bridging organizations and play an intermediary role between different arenas and levels. In recent years, the transnationalization of regional seas transformed traditional international organizations such as HELCOM. Inclusion of subnational authorities at regional level (for example by granting observer status to city networks in regional sea conventions) strengthens the vertical coordination of regional sea areas and improves the implementation of regulations. Thus, the Baltic Sea Action Plan is the result of the active participation of all major stakeholder groups in the region, i.e. the shared vision of a healthy Baltic Sea has been defined together with all relevant stakeholders. The organization of regional stakeholder conferences has led to a transformation of decision-making at regional scale.

Structure and Content of the Book

The individual chapters of the book discuss various facets of marine governance in Europe from both the European and the regional perspective. Although various links exist between national, international and European governance arrangements, research has focused primarily on specific environmental institutions (such as HELCOM) or on EU policies, thereby neglecting the multi-level character of marine governance, the differences between Europe's regional seas, the interaction between EU legislation and regional sea conventions, and the transferability of regional best practice.

Consequently, in response to the above outlined key challenges and critical research gaps the analysis of European marine governance presented in this book is organized in three parts. In the *first part* key *analytical perspectives on marine governance* are discussed with the aim of contributing to the development of more comprehensive and multi-disciplinary analytical approaches for studying marine governance and its challenges. This includes general theoretical ideas about governance, governing, and governability which serve as a starting point for analysing the development of marine governance in Europe from the perspective of different disciplines, in particular on political, social, legal aspects as well as the ecosystem approach. This includes chapters on new forms of marine governance, institutional capacity building in multi-level systems, the role of law in marine governance, and the implications of the ecosystem approach for marine governance.

In the second chapter Jentoft and Chuenpagdee argue, based on examples of marine protected areas (MPA) and marine spatial planning (MSP) initiatives, that the appropriateness of marine governance strategies depend on the marine social and ecological system, as well as the capability of the governing system to implement them. A critical assessment of the system that is being governed, the governing system, and the governing interactions in their natural, socio-cultural and political environments, is therefore required. They assume that it is in the systems and their contexts that the means to enhance governability would be found. They contend that the governing system must somehow reflect the diversity, complexity, dynamics and scale of the marine social and ecological system. Enhancing governability will therefore require critical assessment of these systems and considerable institutional adaption and, in many instances, innovation.

In the following chapter, Van Tatenhove develops a conceptual model to understand and analyse institutional capacity building in a multi-level governance setting. It is shown that institutional capacity building is required to design and implement integrated marine governance arrangement at the level of, for example, regional seas, in a complicated multi-level institutional setting. The chapter concludes that capacity building is influenced by marine governance arrangements, power dynamics, as well as negotiations and the translation to formal decision-making. It is also hypothesized that institutional capacity building in marine governance will differ for the European seas because every sea has a different institutional setting. This will affect the involvement of stakeholders, the possibility to mobilize knowledge and relational resources and the possibility to define rules at the regional sea level. Consequently, comparison of institutional capacity building in various governance contexts such as in different regional seas is therefore identified as an important focus for future research.

The next analytical perspective added to the analysis of marine governance is the role of law. In their chapter Bohman and Langlet provide a conceptual basis for analysing the multi-levelled web of rules and processes that make up the legal aspect of marine governance in Europe. They argue that much of the pertinent legislation is ambitious and promising, providing a ground for a more coordinated and compound implementation, and introducing new judicial tools and mechanisms. However, several factors that may counteract successful governance are also identified (e.g. linked to the far-reaching coordination between policy areas envisioned in the ecosystem approach). Consequently, it is concluded that continued political commitment to marine governance is a prerequisite for law to serve as the strong floater that it ought to be.

Finally, in the last chapter of the first part of the book, Monica Hammer contributes with a state-of-art review and analysis of various perspectives and framings of ecosystem management, as well as the implications and challenges of this holistic management approach for the governance of Europe's marine environment. She concludes that, despite many severe implementation challenges, the present policy framework within the EU is promoting a shift towards a more comprehensive ecosystem management of marine systems acknowledging the interconnections within ecosystems as well as links between ecosystems and humans. However, processes such as stakeholder participation, learning and innovation are identified as being in need of more research in relation to ecosystem management and its possibilities and challenges.

The *second part* focuses on rigorous analysis of *marine governance of the European Union*, in particular the Marine Strategy Framework Directive and the Common Fisheries Policy. Marine governance in Europe is still characterized by a bifurcation between policy areas that are dominated by a polluter/extractor-oriented approach (such as the Common Fisheries Policy) and policy areas that have incorporated the ecosystem approach (such as the MSFD). This part focuses on the internal dimension and institutional tensions of the MSFD, on the stakeholder involvement in European fisheries and the science-policy interfaces in European marine governance. The studies in this part also show faster developments in the North and the Baltic Seas on the one hand and the Mediterranean and Black Seas on the other.

Chapter 6 by De Santo examines the potential of the MSFD as a catalyst for Marine Spatial Planning in the European Union focusing, first, on the institutional tensions and their implications within the European Union (in particular between DG Environment and DG MARE) and beyond EU borders (regional sea conventions, non-EU members); and second on the integration of a wide range of legislative instruments at the national and regional levels. The analysis of the Common Implementation Strategy shows that the member states, in particular in the Mediterranean and the Black Seas face difficulties to agree on a common understanding for defining Good Environmental Status and setting specific targets and indicators. The article also examines the architecture of 'Good Environmental Status', the compliance with EU Directives and the capacities in regional sea areas for the implementation of the MSFD. As some member states are a party to more than one regional sea convention it can be hoped that the experiences from the North and Baltic Seas will spread to the Mediterranean and Black Seas.

In chapter 7 Dreyer and Sellke discuss the importance and challenges of regional-level stakeholder involvement in EU marine governance. They do so by examining the challenges linked to 'inclusion' and 'closure', which have been identified as critical to processes of participation in environmental governance. While inclusion refers to the contents of the debate and the included actors, closure means the choice of the decision-making principle and the criteria for decision-making. It is concluded that setting up an inclusive marine advisory body implies addressing demanding issues related to inclusion and closure. These issues are particularly critical when the advisory body is to provide input on how to design and/or implement a holistic ecosystem approach. This requires consideration and representation of various economic, social and environmental aspects and interests – leading to a major 'dilemma of numbers'; in other words it bears the risk that appropriately broad participation is achieved at the expense of quality of deliberation and effectiveness of reaching joint products.

Finally, in chapter 8 Gilek et al. use the development and implementation of the MSFD to investigate how Europeanization, regionalization and the ecosystem approach influence science and policy and their interactions in European marine governance. It is concluded that the MSFD fits well to a modernized understanding of the blurred nature of science-policy interfaces, thus opening opportunities for enhancing trust in the relationship between science, policy and stakeholders. Furthermore, the analysis indicates that the three processes of Europeanization, regionalization and implementation of EAM facilitate marine environmental governance, in a rather co-evolutionary manner, by helping to develop credibility of the knowledge base, legitimacy of science-based advice and, thereby, preventing tensions and conflicts. These developments in science-policy interactions and marine governance are shown to be progressing at a faster pace in the Baltic and North Seas compared to the Mediterranean and Black Seas and it is suggested that a way forward could be to stimulate learning between different regional seas.

The chapters in the *third part* provide in-depth analyses of *marine governance of Europe's regional Seas*, namely the Baltic Sea, the North Sea, the Mediterranean Sea and the Black Sea. They discuss the key environmental problems, the governance architecture in these regional sea areas, in particular the development of regional institutions, the growing influence of the EU in the region and the trends towards regionalization of EU marine governance in these regional sea areas.

Based on a description of the key environmental threats (eutrophication, over-fishing, chemical pollution, invasive alien species, pollution from marine transportation and climate change), chapter 9 by Söderström, Kern and Hassler describes and analyses the changing governance arrangements and their problem solving capacities in the Baltic Sea region. It concentrates on HELCOM and the European Union and two parallel trends: the emergence of a Baltic Sea macro-region with own institutions and an increasing Europeanization of the region since the end of the Cold War. The chapter analyses three phases: (i) regionalization through the Helsinki Convention; (ii) Europeanization through EU legislation; and (iii) macro-regionalization through the EU Strategy for the Baltic Sea Region. It is asked how horizontal interplay between EU institutions and HELCOM, vertical interplay including subnational authorities and civil society and the relations with non-EU countries, have developed during these three phases. It is argued that institutional interplay between EU legislation, the EU Strategy for the Baltic Sea Region and HELCOM (with its BSAP) has led to remarkable synergies, that vertical interplay has increased over time and that Russia has become 'socialized' into the region.

In chapter 10 Van Tatenhove and Van Leeuwen analyse the patterns of regionalization in the North Sea. This chapter aims at a better understanding of the recent developments in marine governance of the North Sea as different patterns of regionalization. The authors discuss the main environmental and spatial problems in the North Sea, the governance initiatives which have been taken to deal with these problems and three patterns of regionalization that have emerged in the region: (i) regionalization through cooperation of governmental actors; (ii) regionalization through the empowerment of non-governmental actors and (iii) regionalization as an organizing principle for activities and planning on the North Sea. Environmental problems in the North Sea have been dealt with by legal conventions on marine pollution, the North Sea Ministerial Conferences and the European Union. Europeanization of marine governance has caused a high level of regionalization. The authors suggest that the regional dynamics has resulted in institutional ambiguity, i.e. a mismatch between the institutional setting of the EU and the North Sea, and argue that different patterns of regionalization should be combined.

Marine governance in the Mediterranean Sea is described in chapter 11 by Juan Luís Suárez de Vivero and Juan Carlos Rodríguez. Governance in the Mediterranean Sea is marked by regionalization of marine governance and Europeanization of marine policies. The key elements of marine governance in the Mediterranean Sea are the Mediterranean Action Plan (Convention and Protocols) and the European Union. In the Mediterranean Sea exists an adequate legal-institutional structure alongside weak political integration and marked economic differences. Mediterranean marine governance should be multilateral and concerted because of the basin's peculiar geographical constraints and the nature and size of the problems. Environmental issues are regulated by the states, UNCLOS and an intricate regional web that revolves around the Mediterranean Action Plan and complemented by national initiatives. The EU is driving the Europeanization of the Mediterranean's regional system due to its leading role and also because many coastal states often concur with its legal approaches and take them on board as their own. However, the North-South imbalance strongly limits the implementation of the management of marine affairs, with only a small number of states having enough financial and technical capacity to solve the problems.

Finally, Ståle Knudsen discusses Marine Governance in the Black Sea. This chapter reviews the environmental problems in the Black Sea; discusses processes of regionalization, in particular intergovernmental structures and NGO cooperation; studies the EU influence on Black Sea environmental policies; analyses the geopolitical tensions in the region and introduces a case-study on transboundary Black Sea fisheries management. International agreements such as the Bucharest Convention resulted in some significant achievements, especially with respect to the identification of issues, agenda setting, regional networking, monitoring etc. Despite a progressive environmental agenda, e.g. a holistic approach to environmental governance, there is a lack of compliance, even if national action plans exist. There seems to be a significant lack of capabilities to implement policies that would significantly improve the environmental situation of the Black Sea. EU initiatives seem to constitute the soundest and most realistic road towards effective regional cooperation. However, there are major geopolitical challenges because in the Black Sea region three major political powers meet: the EU, Russia and Turkey. Since both Russia and Turkey claim stronger and more independent roles in the region and Russia tends to resist EU influence around the Black Sea, transboundary cooperation depends on changes of the geopolitical situation and the priorities of national governments.

In the final concluding chapter we subsequently revisit the key topics and challenges identified in this introduction and explore what has been learnt in terms of problems and opportunities associated with the governance of Europe's marine environment.

References

Backer, H., Leppänen, J-M., Brusendorff, A.C., Forsius, K., Stankiewicz, M., Mehtonen, J., Pyhälä, M. et al. 2010. HELCOM Baltic Sea Action Plan – A regional programme of measures for the marine environment based on the Ecosystem Approach. *Marine Pollution Bulletin*, 60, 642-649.

Bijker, W.E., Bal, R. and Hendriks, R. 2009. *The Paradox of Scientific Authority*. Cambridge, MA: The MIT Press.

Borja, A., Elliott, M., Carstensen, J., Heiskanen, A.-S., van de Bund, W. 2010. Marine management – towards an integrated implementation of the European Marine Strategy Framework and the Water Framework Directives. *Marine Pollution Bulletin*, 60, 2175-2186.

Costa, O. 2009. *From Rivalry to Convergence: Environmental Cooperation in the Mediterranean*, EU4seas Working Paper.

De Santo, E. 2010. Whose science? Precaution and power-play in European marine environment decision-making. *Marine Policy*, 34, 414-420.

De Santo, E. 2011. Environmental justice implications of maritime spatial planning in the European Union. *Marine Policy*, 35, 34-38.

Doussis, E. 2006. Environmental protection of the Black Sea: a legal perspective, *South East European and Black Sea Studies*, 6(3), 355-369.

Fritz, J-S. 2010. Towards a 'New form of governance' in science policy relations in the European maritime policy. *Marine Policy*, 34, 1-6.

Gehring, T. and Oberthür, S. (eds). 2006. *Institutional Interaction in Global Environmental Governance: Synergy and Conflict among International and EU Policies*. Cambridge, MA and London: The MIT Press.

Griffin, L. 2009. Scales of knowledge: North Sea fisheries governance, the local fisherman, and the European scientist. *Environmental Politics*, 18(4), 557-575.

Griffin, L. 2007. All aboard: power, participation, and governance in the North Sea Regional Advisory Council. *International Journal of Green Economics*, 1(3-4), 478-493.

Hoballah, A. 2006. Sustainable development in the Mediterranean region. *Natural Resources Forum*, 30, 157-167.

Joas, M., Kern, K., and Sandberg, S. 2007. Actors and arenas in hybrid networks: implications for environmental policy-making in the Baltic Sea Region. *Ambio*, 35(3), 237-242.

Joas, M., Jahn, D., and Kern, K. (eds) 2008. *Governing a Common Sea: Environmental Policies in the Baltic Sea Region*. London/Sterling: Earthscan.

Juda, L. 2010. The European Union and the Marine Strategy Framework Directive: continuing the development of European ocean use development. *Ocean Development and International Law*, 41(1), 34-54.

Karlsson, M., Gilek, M. and Udovyk, O. 2011. Governance of complex socio-environmental risks: the case of hazardous chemicals in the Baltic Sea. *AMBIO*, 40, 144-157.

Kern, K. and Löffelsend, T. 2004. Sustainable development in the Baltic Sea region. Governance beyond the nation state. *Local Environment*, 9(5), 451-467.

Kern, K. and Bulkely, H. 2009. Cities, Europeanization and multi-level governance: governing climate change through transnational municipal networks. *JCMS-Journal of Common Market Studies*, 47(1), 309-332.

Kern, K. 2011. Governance for sustainable development in the Baltic Sea region. *Journal of Baltic Studies*, 42(1), 67-81.

Koivurova, T. 2009. A note on the European Union's integrated maritime policy. *Ocean Development and International Law*, 40, 171-183.

Linke, S., Gilek, M., Karlsson, M. and Udovyk, O. 2014. Unravelling science-policy interactions in environmental risk governance of the Baltic Sea: comparing fisheries and eutrophication. *Journal of Risk Research*, 17(4), 505-523.

Long, R. 2010. The role of Regional Advisory Councils in the European Common Fisheries Policy: legal constraints and future options. *International Journal of Marine and Coastal Law*, 25(3), 289-346.

Princen, S. 2010. Venue shift and policy change in EU fisheries policy. *Marine Policy*, 34, 36-41.

Queffelec, B., Cummins, V., and Bailly, D. 2009. Integrated management of marine biodiversity in Europe: perspectives from ICZM and the evolving EU Maritime Policy Framework. *Marine Policy*, 33, 871-877.

Rice, J.C. 2005. Implementation of the ecosystem approach to fisheries management – asynchronous co-evolution at the interface between science and policy. *Mar. Ecol. Prog. Ser.*, 300, 265-70.

Suárez de Vivero, J.L. and Ridriguez Mateos, J. 2001. The Mediterranean and Black Sea: regional integration and maritime nationalism. *Marine Policy*, 26, 383-401.

Suárez de Vivero, J.L. 2006. The European vision for oceans and seas – social and political dimensions of the green paper on maritime policy for the EU. *Marine Policy*, 31(4), 409-414.

Stöhr, C. and Chabay, I. 2010. Science and participation in governance of Baltic Sea fisheries. *Environmental Policy and Governance*, 20, 350-363.

Van Leeuwen, J. and Van Tatenhove, J. 2010. The triangle of marine governance in the environmental governance of Dutch offshore platforms. *Marine Policy*, 34, 590-597.

Wakefield, J. 2010. Undermining the integrated maritime policy. *Marine Pollution Bulletin*, 60, 323-333.

Wenzel, B. 2011. *Environmental Governance and Institutional Interaction in the Baltic Sea Region: Effective Governance System or Institutional Entanglement?*, M.Sc. thesis, University of Marburg.

Wilson, D.C. 2009. *The Paradoxes of Transparency: Science and the Ecosystem Approach to Fisheries Management in Europe*. Amsterdam: Amsterdam University Press.

Young, O. 2002. *The Institutional Dimensions of Environmental Change: Fit, Interplay, and Scale*. Cambridge, MA and London: The MIT Press.

PART 1:
Analytical Perspectives on Marine Governance

Chapter 2
The 'New' Marine Governance: Assessing Governability

Svein Jentoft and Ratana Chuenpagdee

Introduction

Marine governance is a major concern of coastal states in Europe and elsewhere as marine ecosystems are exposed to ongoing pressures, including overfishing, pollution, new industries and other users competing for marine space (e.g. off-shore oil and gas exploration, marine aquaculture, wind farms, shipping, recreational users). Indeed, these multiple uses and their complex relationships and interaction create 'wicked' problems (Rittel and Webber 1973), with no easy technical solutions, for marine governance (Jentoft and Chuenpagdee 2009). Current efforts to rectify the problems take many forms that are generally more integrative and holistic than previous attempts. Popular among them are place-based instruments such as marine protected areas (MPAs), including their networks, and most recently marine spatial planning (MSP). Both have been widely promoted, albeit for different reasons and with sometimes poor results due to various factors, such as lack of legitimacy and stakeholder involvement (Bogaert et al. 2009). MPAs, for instance, appeal to conservation groups as they are meant to drastically reduce extractive activities causing pressure on habitats and natural resources. MPAs can contribute to building local capacity for fisheries management, but may thus also be seen as a tool to help increase fishery yield (Hilborn et al. 2004). Generally referred to by the World Conservation Union (IUCN) as 'any area of intertidal or subtidal terrain, together with its overlying water and associated flora, fauna, historical and cultural features, which has been reserved by law or other effective means to protect part or all of the enclosed environment' (Kelleher 1999: xi), MPAs vary in design, purpose and degree of protection. MPAs have been used by many coastal nations for decades although their implementation has never been straightforward, and not always successful. Experiences from the California Channel Islands and the Great Barrier Reef Marine Park suggest that their establishment can take 10 to 20 years, respectively (see Davis 2005, Guénette et al. 2000). Several examples of failed attempts and unsuccessful MPAs have also been noted (Kelleher et al. 1995, Alder 1996, Mora et al. 2006, Jameson et al. 2002). Our own experience from researching MPAs in the case of Spain suggests that implementation challenges result, for the most part, from the ambiguity about their goals and the lack of attention to stakeholders' perceptions and images about what these MPAs were intended for (Jentoft et al. 2011, 2012).

Similar to MPAs, MSP is a spacially-based tool designed to support ecosystem-based and holistic management of oceans and coasts (Gilliland and Laffoley 2008). While MPAs aim mainly at conservation on limited geographical scales, MSP more broadly seeks to integrate the ecological, social, economic and political elements of human activities into the planning process. In fact, MSP can be seen as a means to compensate for the weaknesses of MPAs. Thus Agardy et al. (2011: 231) observe: 'Marine spatial planning, fully utilizing ocean zoning within which strategically planned MPAs are embedded, allow MPA shortcomings to be overcome in order to better safeguard the ocean worldwide and the lives of those who depend on it' (see also Cicin-Sain and Belfiore 2005). According to the United Nations Educational, Scientific, and Cultural Organization, MSP is mainly a 'public process of analysing and allocating the spatial and temporal distribution of human activities in marine areas to achieve ecological, economic, and social objectives that usually have been specified through a political process' (see Douvere and Ehler 2009: 78).

Because of its integrative and proactive nature, and due to the increasing usage of marine areas, coupled with the anticipation of new challenges posed by climate change, many countries, including those in Europe, are now incorporating these tools in their management planning. The MSP process generally begins with identifying goals, objectives and issues, followed by data collection, analysing information, generating and evaluating options, and preparing and examining the plan (Gilliland and Laffoley 2008). It also typically involves a search for consensus through stakeholder consultation or more direct forms of participation, as in the case of the European Union (Suárez de Vivero et al. 2009). MSP, as a zoning tool, has been used widely; for instance, in Australia's Great Barrier Reef Marine Park, the US Florida Keys National Marine Sanctuary, the Canada Eastern Scotian Shelf Management Initiative and the Philippines Provincial Resource Management Plan. It is the European countries, however, that seem to be taking the lead in the design and implementation of MSP (Douvere and Ehler 2009). The implementation of the Natura 2000 network of marine protected areas under the European Habitats Directive (92/43/EEC) is an important initiative in this respect (Fock 2011).

Both 'zoning' approaches resemble comprehensive land-use planning and integrated coastal management, which have long been practiced worldwide. Proponents of the present zoning efforts emphasize the potential contributions of these tools to minimize conflicts among multiple ocean and coastal users as a result of their focus on acquiring and synthesizing different types of data and knowledge, and on supporting cross-sector participatory and consultative processes (Crowder et al. 2006, Young et al. 2007, Douvere 2008, Dahl et al. 2009, Sanchirico et al. 2010, Calado et al. 2012). Others argue, however, that these approaches insufficiently integrate human considerations, and thus propose methodological refinements to zoning that better reflect social and cultural realities (St. Martin and Hall-Arber 2008, Dalton et al. 2010). Moreover, concerns regarding the use of tools and zoning approaches as technical fixes have been raised (Degnbol et al. 2006, Brady and Waldo 2009). The appropriateness of the scope, scale and boundary choices in ocean zoning (Mahon et al. 2008, Cumming et al. 2006), as well as the ability of these initiatives to cope with uncertainty and change in linked social-ecological systems, including climate-related change (Young et al. 2007), are some of the key issues facing MSP, rendering it with difficulties in implementation. As Suárez de Vivero et al. (2009: 625) observe, 'In the European context, marine spatial planning initiatives … still do not define in detail what the most appropriate geographical scope or scopes should be for the formulation and execution of plans.'

Another concern with zoning approaches relates to the nature of stakeholder participation and consultation processes (Pomeroy and Douvere 2008, Ritchie and Ellis 2010). While involving stakeholders in resource management and decision-making is favourably viewed, several obstacles have been identified, such as cost and time investment (Rutherford et al. 2005, Foster et al. 2005); learning capacity (Armitage et al. 2008); representation and legitimacy (Jentoft 2000, Jentoft et al. 2003); and power and marginality (Jentoft 2007a, Jupp 2008). The lack of clarity and transparency about stakeholder selection and the negotiations between people with unequal power can generate mistrust and frustration and discredit the zoning efforts. Compared to other natural resources, oceans and coasts are heavily regulated and most have already been zoned for many purposes, including conservation, jurisdiction and safety. Numerous informal and formal institutions are present at the state, market and civil society levels, serving regulatory, normative and cognitive functions (Scott 2001). Legal pluralism, where several laws and rules, including official and traditional, often overlap without full knowledge of those concerned (Blacket 2001, Jentoft et al. 2009), is likely to occur in oceans and coastal areas. As Bavinck (2005) suggests, conflicts among actors in the marine realm not only reflect differences in material interests (e.g. access to resources) but have also important symbolic and discursive dimensions framed in law, as well as in culture and social organization.

The above suggests that although tools like MPAs and MSP are promising for marine governance, they come with challenges that may hinder goals from being fully attained. As Wood (2011: 526) notes: 'Although large-scale conservation targets may provide overarching frameworks for, and motivate action at smaller scales … in the context of marine conservation and protected areas, this has met with variable success.' Similarly, in the social sphere, such zoning tools may help to contain conflicts, but may not eradicate them once and for all. Thus, with reference to the Great Barrier Reef, Sanchirico et al. (2010) maintain that comprehensive zoning does not make conflicts and allocation disputes vanish but it serves to expand the set of mechanisms for addressing them. This is also what Christensen and Peters (1999: 167) see as the essential quality of governance, which they consider to be about the very 'capacity of the governing system to minimize internal conflict and organize the system to mediate conflicts in a manner that will permit the system to persist.'

In what follows, we describe the interactive turn in fisheries governance, which, inspired by Rhodes (1996), we discuss as the 'new' marine governance – one that draws on the capacities and capabilities of industry stakeholders and civil society in governance, planning and decision-making. In this context, capacity is about having resources or mandates for action whereas capability is the sum of expertise and capacity to perform these actions as it applies to human and institutional capital, in a particular governance situation. We further introduce the interactive governance perspective and the governability concept (Kooiman 2003, Kooiman and Chuenpagdee 2005, Bavinck et al. 2013), as they apply to the marine sphere. Using the governability assessment framework, we examine factors that may determine the success of MPAs and MSP, and formulate some of the key research questions that need to be explored in order to secure the knowledge base necessary for enhancing performance of these marine governance tools and to provide a better fit between the system-to-be-governed and the governing system that these tools are part of (Mayntz 1994).

Interactive Governance and Governability

Governance as a concept has long been used to mean pilot or steer, typically associated with governments or corporate entities (Kjær 2004). In contemporary usage, governance has also come to imply forms and processes of steering involving non-state actors like those of civil society. Definitions of this 'new' governance (Rhodes 1996) have flourished, but all emphasize its inclusive and cooperative nature and the involvement of public-private partnerships (Stoker 1998, Berkhout et al. 2002, Ansell and Gash 2007, Offe 2009, Berkes 2011). They are also applied to the marine sphere, phrased as 'the sharing of policy making competences in a system of negotiation between governmental institutions at several levels (international, supranational, national, regional and local) on the one hand, and state actors, market parties and civil society organizations on the other hand in order to govern activities at sea and their consequence' (Van Leeuwen and Van Tatenhove 2010: 591). Interactive governance is a particular perspective which highlights various forms and qualities of interactions between governing actors and stakeholders. As defined by Kooiman et al. (2005: 17), interactive governance is about 'the whole of public as well as private interaction taken to solve societal problems and create societal opportunities. It includes the formulation and application of principles guiding those interactions and care for institutions that enable them.' A key concept in interactive governance is 'governability,' which refers to the quality of the overall system for successful governance, measured against key concerns and stated goals (Chuenpagdee and Jentoft 2013). Since not all conditions are conducive to the enhancement of governability, careful examination is required to determine what properties of the social-ecological systems contribute positively to improving governance and what are receptive to intervention (Bavinck et al. 2013).

Although not explicit in its definition, power and power relations are central to interactive governance with its acknowledgment of how interactive governance arrangements work and whose interests they serve. The role that power plays and how power is shared, as well as the recognition that power may have both restricting and enabling functions are key issues in the governability assessment (Jentoft 2007b, Jentoft et al. 2012). Governance may also involve the delegation of power from government to stakeholder organizations, as when the latter have certain responsibilities for monitoring and controlling access within MPAs or MSP boundaries. This transfer of power represents a shift from a reactive to a proactive role of industry and civil society stakeholders in governance, resulting thus in a more open and potentially more democratic form of governance. Whether this is actually happening within new forms of marine governance is an intriguing empirical research question (Van Leeuwen and Van Tatenhove 2010). The multi-faceted dimensions associated with new governance concepts, such as interactive governance, undoubtedly have operational challenges, which need to be dealt with since 'new' governance does not automatically guarantee 'good' governance, as defined by the World Bank and others (see Williams 2009). The blurring of institutional boundaries that occurs within public-private partnership arrangements involves several risks, such as overlapping functional responsibilities and hence the possibility of reduced coherence and accountability. It may also increase the danger of powerful interests taking advantage of governing opportunities 'to usurp genuinely public tasks' or to 'outright corrupt practices' that follow in their new role (Offe 2009: 553). Again, whether this is what is actually happening, where, how, why, and what can be done to prevent it are researchable questions.

Interactive governance, as defined above, is not necessarily an exact representation of how societal sectors are steered. From a research point of view it should be regarded more as an 'ideal type' – as Max Weber (see Schils and Finch 1997) stated with respect to the bureaucratic model – than as a precise description of how governance works in the real world. In this way the definition of interactive governance would work as a yardstick, a heuristic to be used for comparison and contrast. Interactive governance does, then, invite researchers to find out how far reality is from the ideal model and what might possibly explain the discrepancy. Ultimately, how interactive governance takes place is an empirical question that needs to be researched in particular contexts. For instance, a comparative study of fisheries governance in Europe showed great variations among countries with regard to government-industry interaction (Van Hoof and Van Tatenhove 2009, Mikalsen and Jentoft 2009). Whereas some countries display more hierarchical modes of governance, others are regionalized and decentralized. In Scandinavia, consultative arrangements between government and industry are commonly found, while in Spain regions are granted considerable autonomy in fisheries as well as in other sectors. The move as part of the new common fisheries policy within the European Union – which Degnbol and Wilson (2008: 189) describe as traditionally 'perhaps the most top-down fisheries-management system on the planet' – towards a greater role for the Regional Advisory Councils suggests that we will see a more regionalized and interactive mode of fisheries governance in the future (Degnbol and Wilson 2008, Long 2010, Linke et al. 2011).

Nevertheless, interactive governance is expected to broaden the information base, induce mutual learning, and make governance more sensitive to the specificities of local contexts. A more interactive and cooperative form of governance should make governing systems more capable to employ a broader set of tools, such as MPAs and MSP, or at least use tools already at their disposal more effectively. It is reasonable to assume that interactive governance would have a greater chance of producing rules with a greater degree of legitimacy and hence compliance than top-down modes of governance (Jentoft 2000). If so, governability would increase. From a governability perspective, how these outcomes in the end add up and balance out is another intriguing question.

Governability Assessment Framework and Application to MPA/MSP

In any governance setting, including the marine realm, there is a system-to-be-governed, made up of the natural and the social-cultural sub-systems. In connection to this, there is a governing system, made up of institutions and organizations with a functional responsibility to steer the system-to-be-governed towards a set of goals. For governance to take place, some forms of interactions between the two systems are required. According to the interactive governance perspective, these interactions determine the degree to which a system is governable. In the 'new' governance, such interactions operate bi-directionally, and in principle, the larger the area of overlap, the stronger the interactions, whether they are positive or negative in producing desirable outcomes. Interactive governance therefore is concerned with understanding how these interactions contribute to governability, taking into account the particular characteristics of both the system-to-be-governed and the governing system, and their contexts. Figure 2.1 illustrates the target of the governability assessment: any limitations and opportunities for governance are to be found in the two systems and within the overlapped area. From an instrumental perspective, creating such an overlap area for MPAs and MSP is a major challenge with the increasing uses and activities in the oceans and coastal zones. The process is further complicated by the high diversity, complexity, dynamics, and, in the MSP case in particular, the scale issues, of both the system-to-be-governed and the governing systems.

As far as the interactive governance perspective is concerned, the natural system-to-be-governed of the marine realm includes water bodies, ocean surface and sea floor, as well as all organisms living in and using these habitats, including how they interact with each other and how they form trophic chains. The social system refers to different categories of resource users, other stakeholders and their relationships and interactions within and across sectors, and how they form value chains. In both systems, issues related to multiple jurisdictions arise, as is expected in the case of Europe where marine systems frequently cut across national borders (Gilliland and Laffoley 2008). Actions and decisions taken to manage these interactions on a daily basis is the substance of what Kooiman (2003) calls 'first order' of governance. With respect to the governing system, interactive governance considers formal and informal institutions and steering mechanisms, including legislation, rules and norms, which are designed to address concerns and facilitate interactions within the system-to-be-governed and between systems. The formation, design and arrangements of institutions aimed at governing the interactions within and between systems is the focus of governance at the second order. The third key feature of interactive governance is the focus on the 'meta order', which deals with values, images and principles underlying institutions and activities (Kooiman and Jentoft 2009). Deliberation and decision-making on good governance criteria, such as those ascribed by the World Bank, belong here, but they may occur at all scales, including at the local community level. So do principles such as the precautionary approach and subsidiarity, dexterity, accountability and the like frequently referred to in marine ecosystem governance, and in human development, respectively (Suárez de Vivero et al. 2009). In fisheries, the Code of Conduct for Responsible Fisheries (FAO 1995) is a set of governance principles that are supposed to have global application and have now been embraced by countries worldwide. Operationalizing and implementing meta-order governance in oceans and coastal management is complicated given the many viewpoints, diverse, and often competing, interests and aspirations of multiple stakeholders, including governments, environmental groups and other civil society organizations, as is the case with MSP. The more decentralized the system, the greater the number of management agents and stakeholders tend to become. This, according to Suárez de Vivero et al. (2009: 631), is the 'paradox of scale'. Thus, decentralization is not always the answer to governability problems.

As the implementation of MPAs and MSP emerge in a growing number of jurisdictions because of their broad appeal in addressing ocean crises, so does the need for a proper assessment of these marine governance tools. We propose that the suitability of these tools as new forms of marine and ocean governance must be examined through a series of empirical questions, such as those suggested in Table 2.1. Following the interactive governance system scheme (Figure 2.1), these

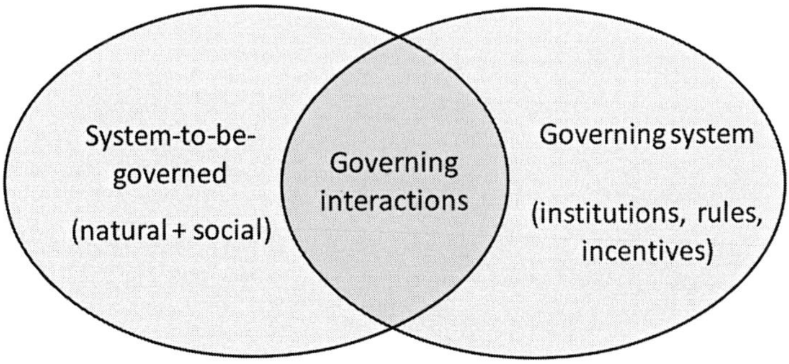

Figure 2.1 Interactive governance relating system-to-be-governed with governing system through interactions

Table 2.1 Examples of questions related to MPA and MSP governability

Analysis	Governability questions
Step 1: System properties (Diversity, complexity, dynamics and scale)	What bio-physical and ecological characteristics of marine areas are known and which are unknown? What actors are included in, or excluded, from zoning decisions and boundary-making processes? What institutions currently exist and how do they function, individually and collectively?
Step 2: Capabilities (fit, responsiveness and performance)	Do scale and boundary choices effectively match uncertain and dynamic system conditions and their multiple scales? How robust and resilient is the proposed governance tool to social-ecological change, including climate-related change? To what extent is the proposed governance tool appropriate in multi-dimensional and linked social-ecological systems and compatible with the existing legal system?
Step 3: Interactions (presence and quality)	What mechanisms promote and enhance the quality of interactions among stakeholders? Are normative aspects – such as values, images and principles, guiding behaviours and decisions of stakeholders – understood, discussed, communicated and incorporated in the governance process? Are power relations among stakeholders well understood and addressed and how do they affect interactions?

questions cover key features of the social and natural system-to-be-governed, the governing system and their interactions. They also reflect the three steps in the governability assessment framework (Figure 2.2).

The governability assessment framework as proposed here aims to evaluate the extent to which oceans and coastal systems are governable and, in this case, whether or not MPAs and MSP make a difference in this respect. It involves three levels of analysis. First, governability is related to the diversity, complexity, dynamics and scale of the natural and social systems-to-be-governed, as well as those of the governing system (Figure 2.2). These properties increase in the context of MSP as more stakeholders, organizations, institutions and actions are involved in the process, thus potentially increasing transaction costs and lowering the system's governability. Another governability challenge lies in the decision about inclusion and exclusion of some stakeholder groups at certain stages in the planning and decision-making process. No matter how well justified, such decisions are likely to create some level of animosity as they inevitably involve the inclusion of some and the exclusion of others.

Acknowledging concerns with legal pluralism, the governability assessment would involve the identification of the types of formal and informal institutions that exist prior to the implementation of these tools, and in step 2 (Figure 2.2), their compatibility with the system's properties. In the context of MPAs and MSP, the question is related to whether zoning and planning approaches match the characteristics of the natural environment, the range of user groups and their issues. Further, through an institutional analysis, an examination of the behaviour and function of these institutions and of how they may change with the demands of zoning practice is required. Step 2 is also related to the capability of the MPA/MSP, in their role as a governing system, to respond to natural and anthropogenic changes. Given the high level of uncertainty in the ocean ecosystem, the demand is high for the MPA/MSP to perform and deliver as intended.

The third step in assessing governability is to determine the presence and absence of various types of interactions. Further, the quality of interactions between the system-to-be-governed and the governing system also determines the MPA/MSP governability. Stakeholders' hostility and system incompatibility, referred to in the previous steps, can be reduced when attention is paid to the normative aspects of the system. Here, we posit that how the values, images and principles of marine and ocean actors guide and influence their behaviours and decisions must be explored using a combination of qualitative and quantitative methods available in social science research. For instance, the governability of the MPA and MSP depends partly on the images that stakeholders have about what they are and what they do, and the degree to which these images are compatible among stakeholders. Images may be influenced at the initial stage before the MSP is implemented, as suggested by Jentoft et al. (2012). In addition to images, principles and values, which are parts of the meta-order governance, need to be properly understood and formulated to guide the MPA/MSP process. Positive interactions can be facilitated to potentially enhance the implementation success of the MPA/MSP with the understanding of the underlying values, images and principles that people hold about marine social and ecological systems and about the governing system. Linked to these normative aspects are power relations among stakeholders, which are critical to identify and address when they prohibit flows of information, create inequities, affect cooperation and in the final instance impede governance.

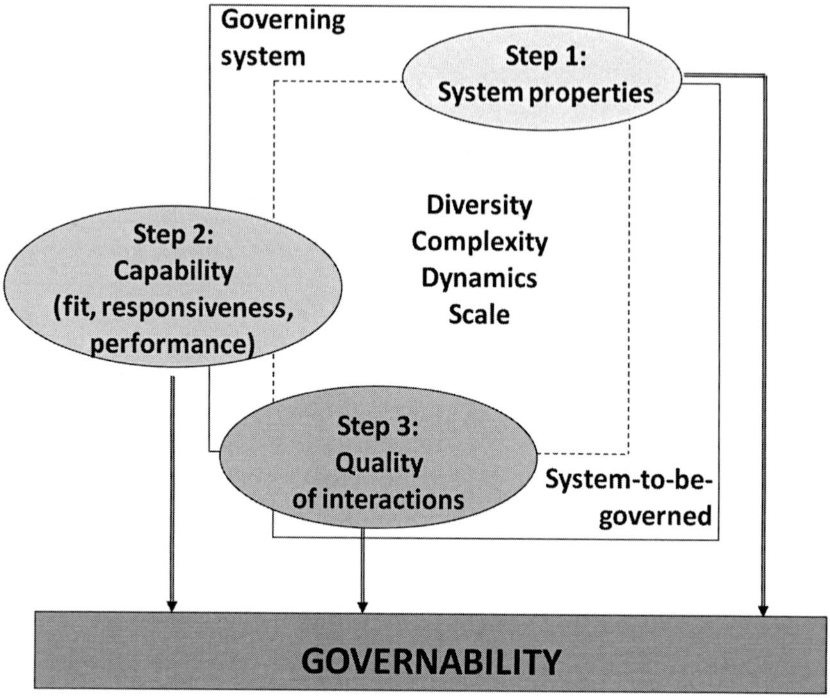

Figure 2.2 Governability of the MPA/MSP depends on the properties of the system-to-be-governed, the capability of the governing system and the quality of governing interactions

Key Factors Affecting MPA/MSP Governability

The following summarizes key factors affecting governability of MPA and MSP, areas where governing actors need to pay close attention, and where opportunities for governability enhancement may be found, and where governability research efforts should be directed. When applicable, we offer questions and methodological suggestions to help navigate these issues.

System Characteristics and Scale Compatibility

Coasts and oceans are non-equilibrium systems characterized by multiple states and continuous change. Cross-scale effects (e.g. local, global, lag-times), non-linearity observed through thresholds, sudden phase shifts in ecosystem properties, and path dependency, make governability of ocean and coastal systems profoundly challenging (Bavinck et al. 2013). Ocean zoning strategies that seek stability, control, simplification or optimization of these systems (e.g.

dampening of disturbance or focusing management on high-value species) may catalyse longer-term governance challenges by undermining variation, diversity and ecosystem processes that foster adaptability and renewal. Indeed, empirical studies highlight the negative consequences of strategies that seek to optimize or control for a limited set of ecosystem goods (Berkes 2010) and institutions that fail to match the scalar complexity of marine ecosystems (Crowder et al. 2006, Chapin et al. 2009, Mahon et al. 2009). An examination of the properties of these social-ecological systems and of how they correspond with ocean zoning schemes is the first key step in assessing governability. Further, factors determining governability, such as the critical system conditions, scale influences and boundary issues, need to be characterized (Armitage and Johnson 2006) in order to provide necessary insights into the appropriateness of the MPA/MSP scheme. For instance, we need to explore the interconnectedness of these social-ecological systems that are subjected to ocean zoning. An ecosystem modelling tool (e.g. Bundy and Fanning 2005) is helpful in exploring the complexity and dynamics of the natural system-to-be-governed. Similarly, stakeholder analysis (Mitchell et al. 1977) can be employed to understand the current composition, relationships and interactions of the social system-to-be-governed, with a particular emphasis on power disparities and dynamics. As well, we need to assess the attributes of the governing system in directing attention to the importance of flexible, interactive governance arrangements and learning institutions (Kooiman et al. 2005, Armitage et al. 2009).

Institutional Structure, Properties and Qualities

Marine governance institutions, be they MPAs or MSP, typically work under external and internal pressures. As they try to accommodate environmental and global adaptation and change, such as climate change, dwindling resources, trade barriers and political regimes, they also need to effectively address conditions and demands that stem from within the governing system itself, including legal norms and principles, budget limitations, knowledge requirements and decision-making procedures (Jentoft 2004, Acheson 2006). These demands require institutions that are resilient and robust: while they need to be flexible and elastic, which are essential qualities for adaptation and learning, they also need to be principled, firm and instrumentally effective and predictable. Although there is some overlap between robustness and resilience, and both impact the stability, endurance, and effectiveness of institutions (Young 2010), they are analytically distinct concepts that give rise to different research questions (Janssen and Andriese 2007). What are the characteristics and capabilities of governing institutions such as MPAs and MSP to balance robustness and resilience? What are their weak spots, limitations and constraints? From an interactive governance perspective, the values, images and principles are more deeply structured than governing institutions (Kooiman 2003), but they should not inhibit institutional change if appropriate. Therefore, what normative properties underpin these institutions and make them stable and predictable, while allowing rules and incentives to be adaptive with experiential learning, needs to be examined. Methods such as discursive-institutional analysis (Arts and Buizer 2009) are suitable to employ as they emphasize the role of ideas, concepts and narratives in understanding institutional dynamics. Network analysis (Brandes and Wagner 2004) is another tool that can be used to examine the relationships and interactions among institutions and within the governing system.

Values, Images and Principles

Coasts and oceans provide a wide range of non-use values (e.g. aesthetic, moral, cultural) and use values (both consumptive and non-consumptive), encompassing all dimensions of importance, including social, cultural, spiritual, political, economic, ecological and environmental. But what do these values mean to different ocean actors and how are they expressed? What images do stakeholders have when thinking about the oceans and in expressing such values? Do these images influence how they relate to the oceans or are there other guiding principles? These are difficult but critical questions that must be answered before initiating governance tools such as MPAs and MSP. A mixture of qualitative and quantitative methods is available for this investigation. For the valuation study, methods such as choice experiments (Holmes and Adamowicz 2003) and contingent valuation (Haab and McConnell 2002) questionnaires, specially designed to account for respondent uncertainty (Akter et al. 2008) and to differentiate individual preferences from those of citizens (Martínez-Espiñeira 2006) are available. Coupled with these methods are the non-monetary valuation approaches such as damage schedules (Chuenpagdee et al. 2001) and other deliberative methods such as verbal protocol (Vatn 2009) and citizen workshops (Timotijevic and Raats 2007). These latter approaches can be used, along with the Q-sort method (Ten Klooster et al. 2008), to examine images that stakeholders have of the oceans and the principles that underpin their behaviours and decisions about the oceans.

Conceptual Clarification, Deliberation and the Initial Planning Stage

When governance instruments such as MPAs and MSP fail to deliver, an assessment of their design (including size and location), types and implementation, is required. Also there is a need to examine whether such poor performance is related to the conditions and the characteristics of the ecosystem and the social system before these tools are implemented. We argue that a 'step zero' analysis (Chuenpagdee and Jentoft, 2007) is necessary to fully understand the possible causes of shortfalls and the potential for adaptation and governability advancement, thus avoiding the band-aid approach to improving effectiveness. Essentially, we believe that the pre-implementation of the MPAs and the MSP, including the initial conceptualization, is as important as the actual operation, and considerations about the institutions involved are as important as those about the ecosystem. It is reasonable to assume that there is path-dependency involved here (Evans 2008), where what is determined initially in the process and then acted upon creates a trajectory that at a later stage may be difficult to deviate from, even when reorientation is required and performed. The interactive governance framework provides a conceptual toolbox for identifying the window of opportunity that step zero involves. This means that attention must be given to how these MPA and MSP concepts are introduced, defined and communicated among affected stakeholders and to society at large. Asking questions about the pre-implementation stage is as important, if not more, in helping us understand the success and failure of any management system. For instance, we should explore why MPAs and MSP are employed in the first place and what the conditions and needs of the ecological and social systems are when the idea about the MPA and MSP are conceived. Related to this are questions about who brings up the idea, how they try to convince others to support them, and how goals are deliberated (Jentoft et al. 2011).

Conclusions

The 'new' governance, as initially coined by Rhodes (1996), is apparent in the marine realm (Van Hoof and Van Tatenhove 2009). In both MPAs and MSP, there is an increasing appreciation of the need to open up the governing system to allow for broader participation, inspection and power sharing. A case has been made for a stronger role and involvement of environmental organizations in the MPAs and MSP process, as embodied within a European Habitat Directive and the new Common Fisheries Policy (Fock 2011, Calado et al. 2012). There is also a normative argument to support this move towards new marine governance, most prominently captured by the concept of good governance, promoted by the World Bank and the European Union.

For the purpose of analysing the trend, we have offered the interactive governance as a conceptual framework. The argument underpinning this approach is that the road towards new marine governance is littered with potholes. Although potential for improving the governability of social and ecological marine systems certainly exists, the new marine governance still involves risks and pitfalls that need to be examined as part of a rational and comprehensive spatial planning process. The interactive governance framework offers suggestions on where to look for these potholes, what to look for, and what to look at, as well as some key issues that must be explored.

The idea that marine governance problems tend to be 'wicked' in the sense that Rittel and Webber (1973) proposed, would indicate that the MPA and MSP processes are less linear and synchronized than textbook planning models suggest. Defining what the problem is, what the challenges are and what solutions should be prescribed, and in what order, is not straightforward and is largely influenced by preconceived images and world views. In essence, defining the problem *is* the problem. Goals are, for instance, not just set initially in the process but negotiated all the way, after plans have been implemented and experiences have been gained, when stakeholders discover how they are affected, and whether promises and expectations are fulfilled. It is more meaningful to think of MPAs and MSP as tools that trigger interactive learning, but where power may distort the adaptive process. Lessons learned are therefore not always implemented or stored for later use. Stakeholders strive to secure their interests even when they go against those of other groups and the collective interest. As a consequence, social conflict and disorder often occur that sometimes lead the process of MPA and MSP implementation into stalemate. These are factors that would naturally reduce the governability of marine social and ecological systems to the extent that goals may need to be levelled to account for what is realistically attainable. Governance failure is a real possibility, suggested also by the fact that ocean ecosystem health continues to deteriorate so that stakeholder groups and coastal communities are suffering the consequences.

In line with the new marine governance concept, bringing stakeholders and the human dimensions into the equation, as also promoted by the interactive governance approach discussed in this chapter, makes a lot of sense. But they also need a critical assessment, one that the interactive governance theory offers. How to involve stakeholders and account for their differences is indeed a wicked problem (Ritchie and Ellis 2010), suggesting that there are no quick fixes, no technical or scientific solutions to many if not most of the challenges that marine governance faces. MPAs and MSP can only bring us a step closer to good marine governance, but hardly all the way. This is because marine governance does not exist in isolation from other sector policies that may or may not align with what is at stake in the marine area. Also, the problems that marine governors are confronted with are inherently political and must be dealt with interactively and in accord with good governance principles. Somehow, consensus must be reached as to what these principles are and how they apply to marine governance. Knowing what stakeholders think about MPAs and MSP, encouraging interactions among stakeholders in determining norms and principles underlying the MPA and MSP process, and recognizing that both instruments are not only about solving problems, but also about creating opportunities are the basics of new marine governance.

References

Acheson, J.M. 2006. Institutional failure in resource management. *The Annual Review of Anthropology*, 35, 117-134.

Agardy, T., Notarbartolo de Sciara, G. and Christie, P. 2011. Mind the gap: addressing the shortcomings of marine protected areas though large scale marine spatial planning. *Marine Policy*, 35, 26-232.

Akter, S., Bennett J. and Akhter, S. 2008. Preference uncertainty in contingent valuation. *Ecological Economics*, 67(3), 345-351.

Alder, J. 1996. Have tropical marine protected areas worked? An initial analysis of their success. *Coastal Management*, 24(2), 97-114.

Ansell, C. and Gash, A. 2007. Collaborative governance in theory and practice. *Journal of Public Administration Research and Theory*, 18, 543-571.

Armitage, D. and Johnson, D. 2006. Can resilience be reconciled with globalization and the increasingly complex conditions of resource degradation in Asian coastal regions? *Ecology and Society* [online] 11(1), 2. Available at: http://www.ecologyandsociety.org/vol11/iss1/art2/ [accessed: 13 July 2014].

Armitage, D., Berkes, F. and Doubleday, N. 2008. *Adaptive Co-Management: Collaboration, Learning, and Multi-Level Governance*. Vancouver: University of British Columbia Press.

Armitage, D., Plummer, R., Berkes, F., Arthur, R., Charles, A., Davidson-Hunt, I., Diduck, A., Doubleday, N., Johnson, D., Marschke, M., McConney, P., Pinkerton, E. and Wollenberg, L. 2009. Adaptive co-management for social-ecological complexity. *Frontiers in Ecology and the Environment*, 7(2), 95-102.

Arts, B. and Buizer, M. 2009. Forests, discourses, institutions: a discursive-institutional analysis of global forest governance. *Forest Policy and Economics*, 11, 340-347.

Bavinck, M. 2005. Understanding fisheries conflict in the south – a legal pluralist perspective. *Society and Natural Resources*, 18, 805-820.

Bavinck, M., Chuenpagdee, R., Jentoft, S. and Kooiman, J. (eds) 2013. *Governability of Fisheries and Aquaculture: Theory and Applications*. Dordrecht: Springer.

Berkes, F. 2012. Implementing ecosystem-based management: evolution or revolution? *Fish and Fisheries*, 13(4), 465-476.

Berkes, F. 2010. Shifting perspectives on resource management: resilience and redefinition of 'natural resources' and 'management'. *MAST / Maritime Studies*, 9(1), 13-40.

Berkhout, F., Hertin, J. and Jordan, A. 2002. Socio-economic futures in climate change impact assessment: using scenarios as 'learning machines'. *Global Environmental Change*, 12, 83-95.

Blacket, A. 2001. Global governance, legal pluralism and the decentered state: a labour law critique of codes of corporate conduct. *Indiana Journal of Global Legal Studies*, 8(2), 401-447.

Bogaert, D., Cliquet, A. and Maes, F. 2009. Designation of marine protected areas in Belgium: a legal an ecological success? *Marine Policy*, 33, 878-886.

Brady, M. and Waldo, S. 2009. Fixing problems in fisheries – integrating ITQs, CBM and MPAs in management. *Marine Policy*, 33, 258-263.

Brandes, U. and Wagner D. 2004. Vision-analysis and visualization of social networks, in *Graph Drawing Software*, edited by M. Junger and P. Mutzel. Berlin: Springer Verlag, 321-340.

Bundy, A., and Fanning, P. 2005. Can Atlantic cod (Gadus morhua) recover? Exploring trophic explanations for the non-recovery of the cod stock on the eastern Scotian Shelf, Canada. *Canadian Journal of Fisheries and Aquatic Sciences*, 62(7), 1474-1489.

Calado, H., Bentz, J., Ng, K., Zivian, A., Schaefer, N., Pringle, C., Johnson, D., and Phillips, M. 2012. NGO involvement in marine spatial planning: A way forward? *Marine Policy*, 36, 382-388.

Chapin III, S., Kofinas, G. and Folke, C. (eds) 2009. *Principles of Ecosystem Stewardship: Resilience-based Resource Management in a Changing World*. New York: Springer-Verlag.

Christensen, T. and Peters, B.G. 1999. *Structure, Culture, and Governance: A Comparison of Norway and the United States*. Lanham: Rowman & Littlefield Publishers Inc.

Chuenpagdee, R. 2011. Interactive governance for marine conservation: an illustration. *Bulletin of Marine Science*, 87(2), 197-211.

Chuenpagdee, R. and Jentoft, S. 2013. Assessing governability: What's next?, in *Governability of Fisheries and Aquaculture: Theory and Applications*, edited by J.M. Bavinck, R. Chuenpagdee, S. Jentoft and J. Kooiman. Dordrecht: Springer Science, 335-350.

Chuenpagdee, R. and Jentoft, S. 2009. Governability assessment for fisheries and coastal systems: A reality check. *Human Ecology*, 37, 109-120.

Chuenpagdee, R. and Jentoft, S. 2007. Step zero for fisheries co-management: what precedes implementation. *Marine Policy*, 31(6), 657-668.

Chuenpagdee, R., Knetsch, J.L. and Brown, T.C. 2001. Environmental damage schedules: community judgments of importance and assessment of losses. *Land Economics*, 77(1), 1-11.

Cicin-Sain, B. and Belfiore, S. 2005. Linking marine protected areas to integrated coastal and ocean management: a review of theory and practice. *Ocean & Coastal Management*, 48, 847-868.

Crowder, L.B., Osherenko, G., Young, O.R., Airamé, S., Norse, E.A., Baron, N., Day, J.C., Douvere, F., Ehler, C.N., Halpern, B.S., Langdon, S.J., McLeod, K.L., Ogden, J.C., Peach, R.E., Rosenberg, A.A. and Wilson, J.A. 2006. Resolving mismatches in U.S. ocean governance. *Science*, 313, 617-618.

Cumming, G.S., Cumming, D.H.M. and Redman, C.L. 2006. Scale mismatches in social-ecological systems: causes, consequences, and solutions. *Ecology and Society*, 11(1), 14-34.

Dahl, E.E. Moksness, E. and Støttrup, J. (eds) 2009. *Integrated Coastal Zone Management*. Oxford: Wiley and Blackwell Publishing.

Dalton, T., Thompson, R. and Jin, D. 2010. Mapping human dimensions in marine spatial planning and management: an example from Narragansett Bay, Rhode Island. *Marine Policy*, 34, 309-319.

Davis, G.E. 2005. Science and society: marine reserve design for the California Channel Islands. *Conservation Biology*, 19(6), 1745-51.

Degnbol, P., Gislasson, H., Hanna, S.S., Jentoft, S., Raakjær Nielsen, J., Sverdrup-Jensen, S. and Wilson, D.C. 2006. Painting the floor with a hammer: technical fixes in fisheries management. *Marine Policy*, 30, 534-543.

Degnbol, D. and Wilson, D.C. 2008. Spatial planning on the North Sea. A case of cross-scale linkages. *Marine Policy*, 32, 189-200.

Douvere, F. 2008. The importance of marine spatial planning in advancing ecosystem-based sea use management. *Marine Policy*, 32, 762-771.

Douvere, F. and Ehler, C.N. 2009. New perspective on sea use management: initial findings from European experience with marine spatial planning. *Journal of Environmental Management*, 90(1), 77-88.

Evans, L.S. 2008. *Governing resilience: inclusion, knowledge and complexity in marine social-ecological systems in Kenya*. PhD thesis, University of East Anglia, UK.

FAO 1995. 2009. *Code of conduct for responsible fisheries*. Rome: Food and Agricultural Organization of the United Nations.

Fock, H.O. 2011. Natura 2000 and the European Common Fisheries Policy. *Marine Policy*, 35, 181-188.

Foster, E., Haward, M. and Coffen-Smout, S.S. 2005. Implementing integrated oceans management: Australia's south east regional marine plan (SERMP) and Canada's eastern Scotian shelf integrated management (ESSIM) initiative. *Marine Policy*, 29, 391-405.

Gilliland, P.M. and Laffoley, D. 2008. Key elements and steps in the process of developing ecosystem-based marine spatial planning. *Marine Policy*, 32, 787-796.

Guénette, S., Chuenpagdee, R. and Jones, R. 2000. Marine protected areas with an emphasis on local communities and indigenous peoples: a review. *Fisheries Centre Research Reports*, 8(1), 1-55.

Haab, T.C. and McConnell, K.E. 2002. *Valuing Environmental and Natural Resources*. Cheltenham, UK: Edward Elgar.

Hilborn, R., Stokes, K., Maguire, J.J., Smith, T., Botsford, L.W., Mangel, M., Orensanz, J., Parma, A., Rice, J. and Bell, J. 2004. When can marine reserves improve fisheries management? *Ocean & Coastal Management*, 47(3-4), 197-205.

Holmes, T. and Adamowicz, W. 2003. Attribute-based methods, in *A Primer on Non-market Valuation*, edited by K.J. Boyle and P.A. Champ. Boston: Kluwer Academic Publishers, 171-219.

Jameson, S.C., Tupper, M.H. and Ridley, J.M. 2002. The three screen doors: Can marine 'protected' areas be effective? *Marine Pollution Bulletin*, 44(11), 1177-83.

Janssen, M.A. and Anderies, J.M. 2007. Robustness trade-offs in social-ecological systems. *International Journal of the Commons*, 1(1), 43-65.

Jentoft, S. 2000. Legitimacy and disappointment in fisheries management. *Marine Policy*, 24(2), 141-148.

Jentoft, S. 2004. Institutions in fisheries: what they are, what they do, and how they change. *Marine Policy*, 28, 137-149.

Jentoft, S. 2007a. In the power of power: the understated aspect of fisheries and coastal management. *Human Organization*, 66(4), 426-437.

Jentoft, S. 2007b. Limits of governability? Institutional implications for fisheries and coastal governance. *Marine Policy*, 31, 360-370.

Jentoft, S. and Chuenpagdee, R. 2009. Fisheries and coastal governance as a wicked problem. *Marine Policy*, 33, 553-560.

Jentoft, S., Mikalsen, K.H. and Hernes, H-K. 2003. Representation in fisheries co-management, in *The Fisheries Co-management Experience: Accomplishments, Challenges and Prospects*, edited by D. Wilson, J.R. Nielsen and P. Degnbol. Dordrecht: Kluwer Academic Publishers, 281-292.

Jentoft, S., Bavinck, M., Johnson, D. and Kaleekal, T. 2009. Co-management and legal pluralism: how an analytical problem becomes an institutional one. *Human Organization*, 68(1), 27-38.

Jentoft, S., Chuenpagdee, R. and Pascual-Fernandez, J. 2011. What are MPAs for: On goal formation and displacement. *Ocean & Coastal Management*, 54, 75-83.

Jentoft, S., Pascual-Fernandez, J.J., De la Cruz Modino, R., Gonzalez-Ramallal, M. and Chuenpagdee, R. 2012. What stakeholders think about marine protected areas: Case studies from Spain. *Human Ecology* DOI 10.1007/s10745-012-9459-6.

Jupp, E. 2008. The feeling of participation: everyday spaces and urban change. *Geoforum*, 39, 331-343.

Kelleher, G. (ed.) 1999. *Guidelines for Marine Protected Areas*. Gland, Switzerland and Cambridge, UK: IUCN, xxiv, 107 pp.

Kelleher, G., Bleakley, C. and Wells, S. (eds) 1995. *A Global Representative System of Marine Protected Areas*. Gland, Switzerland: IUCN, World Conservation Union.

Kjær, A.M. 2004. *Governance*. Cambridge: Polity Press.

Kooiman, J. 2003. *Governing as Governance*. London: Sage Publications.

Kooiman, J. 2008. Exploring the concept of governability. *Journal of Comparative Political Analysis*, 10(2), 171-190.

Kooiman, J., Bavinck, M., Jentoft, S. and Pullin, R. (eds) 2005. *Fish for Life: Interactive Governance for Fisheries*. Amsterdam: Amsterdam University Press.

Kooiman, J. and Chuenpagdee, R. 2005. Governance and governability, in *Fish for Life: Interactive Governance for Fisheries*, edited by J. Kooiman, M. Bavinck, S. Jentoft and R.S.V. Pullin. Amsterdam: Amsterdam University Press, 325-350.

Kooiman, J. and Jentoft, S. 2009. Meta-governance: values, norms and principles and the making of hard choices. *Public Administration*, 87(4), 818-836.

Linke, S., Dreyer, M. and Sellke, P. 2011. The Regional Advisory Councils: what is their potential to incorporate stakeholder knowledge into fisheries governance? *AMBIO*, 40(2), 133-43.

Long, R. 2010. The role of Regional Advisory Councils in the European common fisheries policy: legal constraints and future options. *International Journal of Marine and Coastal Law*, 25, 289-346.

Mahon, R., Fanning, L. and McConney, P. 2009. A governance perspective on the large marine ecosystem approach. *Marine Policy*, 33(2), 317-321.

Mahon, R., McConney, P. and Roy, R. 2008. Governing fisheries as complex adaptive systems. *Marine Policy*, 32(1), 104-112.

Martínez-Espiñeira, R. 2006. A Box-Cox Double-Hurdle model of wildlife valuation: the citizen's perspective. *Ecological Economics*, 58(1), 192-208.

Mayntz, R. 1994. Governing failures and the problem of governability: some comments on a theoretical paradigm, in *Modern Governance: New Government – Society Interactions*, edited by J. Kooiman. London: Sage Publications Ltd., 9-20.

Mikalsen, K.H and Jentoft, S. 2009. Participatory practices in fisheries across Europe: making stakeholders more responsible. *Marine Policy*, 32(2), 169-177.

Mitchell, R.K., Agle, B.R. and Wood, D.J. 1977. Towards a theory of stakeholder identification: defining the principle of who and what really counts. *Academy of Management Review*, 22(4), 853-886.

Mora, C., Andréfouët, S., Costello, M.J., Kranenburg, C., Rollo, A., Veron, J., Gaston, K.J. and Myers, R.A. 2006. Coral reefs and the global network of marine protected areas. *Science*, 312, 1750-1751.

Offe, C. 2009. Governance: an 'Empty Signifier'? *Constellations*, 16(4), 550-562.

Pomeroy, R. and Douvere, F. 2008. The engagement of stakeholders in the marine spatial planning process. *Marine Policy*, 32, 816-822.

Rhodes, R.A. 1996. The new governance: governing without government. *Political Studies*, XLIV, 652-667.

Ritchie, H. and Ellis, G. 2010. A system that works for the sea? Exploring stakeholder engagement in Marine Spatial Planning. *Journal of Environmental Planning and Management*, 53(6), 701-723.

Rittel, H.W.J. and Webber, M.M. 1973. Dilemmas in a general theory of planning. *Policy Sciences*, 4, 155-169.

Rutherford, R.J., Herbert, G.J. and Coffen-Smout, S.S. 2005. Integrated ocean management and the collaborative planning process: the Eastern Scotian Shelf Integrated Management (ESSIM) Initiative. *Marine Policy*, 29, 75-83.

Sanchirico, J.N., Eagle, J., Palumbi, S. and Thompson, B.H. Jr. 2010. Comprehensive planning, dominant use-zones, and user rights: a new era in ocean governance. *Bulletin of Marine Science*, 86(2), 249-259.

Schills, E.A. and Finch, H.A. 1997. *The Methodology of the Social Sciences*. New York: Free Press.

Scott, W.R. 2001. *Institutions and Organizations*. London: Sage Publications.

St. Martin, K. and Hall-Arber, M. 2008. The missing layer: geo-technologies, communities and implications for marine spatial planning. *Marine Policy*, 32, 779-786.

Stoker, G. 1998. Governance as theory: five propositions. *International Social Science Journal*, 50, 17-28.

Suárez de Vivero, J.L., Rodríguez Mateos, J.C. and Florido del Corral D.F. 2009. Geopolitical factors of maritime policies and marine spatial planning: state, regions and geographical planning scope. *Marine Policy*, 33, 624-634.

Ten Klooster, P.M., Visser, M. and de Jong, M.D.T. 2008. Comparing two image research instruments: the Q-sort method versus the Likert attitude questionnaire. *Food Quality and Preference*, 19, 511-518.

Timotijevic, L. and Raats, M.M. 2007. Evaluation of two methods of deliberative participation of older people in food-policy development. *Health Policy*, 82, 302-319.

Van Hoof, L. and Van Tatenhove, J. 2009. EU marine policy on the move: the tension between fisheries and maritime policy. *Marine Policy*, 33, 726-732.

Van Leeuwen, J. and Van Tatenhove, J. 2010. The triangle of marine governance in the environmental governance of Dutch offshore platforms. *Marine Policy*, 34, 590-597.

Vatn, A. 2009. An institutional analysis of methods of environmental appraisal. *Ecological Economics*, 68(8-9), 2207-2215.

Williams, G. 2009. Governance, Good. *International Encyclopedia of Human Geography*, 606-614.

Wood, L. 2011. Global marine protection targets: How S.M.A.R.T. are they? *Environmental Management*, 47, 525-535.

Young, O. 2010. Institutional dynamics: resilience, vulnerability and adaptation in environmental and resource regimes. *Global Environmental Change*, 20(3), 378-385.

Young, O.R., Osherenko, G., Ekstrom, J., Crowder, L.B., Ogden, J., Wilson, J.A., Day, J.C., Douvere, F., Ehler, C.N., McLeod, K.L., Halpern, B.S. and Peach, R. 2007. Solving the crisis in ocean governance: place-based management of marine ecosystems. *Environment*, 49, 20-32.

Chapter 3
Marine Governance: Institutional Capacity-building in a Multi-level Governance Setting

Jan P.M. van Tatenhove

Introduction

In 2007, the EU launched its vision of an Integrated Maritime Policy[1] to establish an all-embracing marine policy aimed at developing a 'thriving maritime economy in an environmentally sustainable manner'. This integrated maritime policy will encompass all aspects of the European oceans and seas in an integrated manner. It is expected that the Integrated Maritime Policy (IMP) will create a new playing field. The integration discourse and ecosystem-based management will not only set new rules and resources, but also result in new coalitions of actors across the different maritime activities, such as fisheries, oil and gas extractions, offshore wind parks, shipping and tourism. This playing field will be different for each of the regional sea basins in Europe (Baltic Sea, the North East Atlantic Ocean, the Mediterranean and the Black Sea).

Based on the policy arrangement approach and the concept of institutional capacity-building the aim of this paper is to understand which marine governance arrangements are needed to develop and implement an EU Integrated Maritime Policy, given the specific institutional setting of EU multi-level governance. The central questions of this paper are:

- What kind of marine governance arrangements are needed for the development and implementation of an Integrated Marine Policy?
- How does the multi-level setting of the EU enable or constrain these novel forms of marine governance?

---

1 In general, marine refers to the marine environment and marine ecosystems, while maritime refers to the activities on seas and oceans. In its policy documents the EU uses maritime, while in the USA marine is more common. In this chapter I use marine, apart from when I refer to official EU documents (when maritime is used).

- What are the possibilities of institutional capacity-building within this setting?
- What are the enabling and constraining conditions to develop integrated marine governance arrangements at the regional sea level?

This paper develops a conceptual model to understand the possibilities of institutional capacity-building in (integrated) marine governance projects at the level of the regional seas, in a complicated multi-level institutional setting. Core concepts of this model are marine governance arrangements, the power dynamics of marine governance and institutional capacity-building.

In the following section the institutional framework of EU marine governance is introduced. Within this EU institutional setting a diversity of marine governance arrangements develops. Thereafter the third section starts with the introduction of the analytical concept of marine governance arrangement. Because these arrangements do not develop in a political and societal vacuum, the power dynamics of the multi-level setting is subsequently outlined as three constitutive phases: the establishment of a power architecture, negotiations and the translation to formal decision-making circuits. In the fourth section, the concept of institutional capacity-building is discussed. Institutional capacity-building is the ability of actors to get involved in processes of policy-making and to change the rules of the game, in order to develop institutional rules at the regional sea level to overcome environmental and spatial problems. Dimensions of institutional capacity building are, mobilizing resources, relational resources and mobilizing capacities. These dimensions are related to the different stages in the exercising of power. Central to the fifth section is the development of marine governance in the EU, especially the development of EU Integrated Maritime Policy. The central question of the sixth section is how to develop integrated marine governance arrangements at the level of the regional sea by a process of institutional capacity-building. In the final section key conclusions are presented.

The EU Governance Framework

The EU does not fit into any accepted category of government; it is not an international organization, a federal state nor is it replacing member states. On the contrary, 'the European Union is a fundamental instrument for the survival of existing nation-states on the condition of conceding shares of sovereignty in exchange for a greater say in the world, and domestic, affairs in the age of globalization' (Castells 1998: 330). According to Castells '(...) the image illustrates powerfully the new form of state epitomized by European institutions: the network state. It is a state characterized by the sharing of authority (that is, in the last resort, the capacity to impose legitimized violence) along a network' (Castells 1998: 332).

Three characteristics make the European Union a unique political and policy system (Van Tatenhove et al. 2006). Firstly, the institutional setting of the EU is in constant flux. With several Treaty revisions within a few decades the pace and scope of institutional change in the EU is unprecedented. Secondly, the Union is the result of the interplay of both intergovernmental decisions taken by the heads of states and day-to-day politics made by a large number of governmental and non-governmental actors at the supranational, national and sub-national levels. Thirdly, the EU is a fragmented system with differentiated competences according to policy area and layer of governance. Policy-making takes place in a diversity of formal and informal settings.

To understand the dynamics and unique character of the EU a diversity of governance concepts has been developed over the years, such as network governance (Kohler-Koch 1999, Sbragia 2000), informal governance (Christiansen and Piatonni 2003, Mak and Van Tatenhove 2006), committee governance (Christiansen and Kirchner 2000), and the policy pendulum (Wallace 2000). According to Héritier (1999), European policies present themselves as a 'patchwork': a complex mixture of different policy-making styles, instruments and institutions. The process at work is less one of intentional and detailed harmonization but of 'regulatory competition'.

Characteristic of all these forms of governance is their ability to grasp the dynamics of policy-making in the EU as the interplay between different actors at different levels, sharing decision-making competencies; i.e. multi-level governance (Marks 1993, Hooghe and Marks, 2001). In this chapter, the focus is on marine governance as a specific form of MLG. Marine governance involves a process of negotiation between nested general institutions at several levels, on the one hand, and state actors, market parties and civil society organizations, on the other. This process leads to a sharing of policy making competences to govern activities at sea and control their consequences (Van Tatenhove 2013). Considering the EU as being in constant flux, fragmented, balancing somewhere between intergovernmental bargaining and multi-level governance, the institutional structure of marine governance should, then, be understood as the interconnection of intergovernmental, supranational and transnational arenas (Van Tatenhove 2013).

In the intergovernmental and supranational arenas the role of codified institutions such as national governments and EU institutions is dominant. Only Member States play a role in the European Council and the Council of Ministers. At the same time, the supranational arena, consisting of the European Commission (EC), the European Parliament (EP) and the European Court of Justice (EJC), has gained more and more independent influence on collective decision-making, resulting in a significant loss of control for individual national governments (Hooghe and Marks 2001, Van Tatenhove 2013). DG MARE and DG ENV initiate policies and regulations in the maritime domain, such as the Common Fisheries Policy (CFP), NATURA 2000, the Marine Strategy Framework Directive (MSFD), and the Integrated Maritime Policy.

The transnational arena consists of a diversity of formal and informal institutions and organizations. Examples of formal transnational institutions are the diversity of committees and European agencies. The institutionalization of a variety of committee structures in all stages of the policy process gave in to the need to establish forums in which policy ideas could be deliberated upon, policy proposals could be discussed and policy implementation could be monitored (Christiansen and Kirchner 2000). European Agencies are also an example of formal transnational institutions. Important Agencies in the maritime domain are the European Environmental Agency (EEA), the Community Fisheries Control Agency (CFCA) and the European Maritime Safety Agency (EMSA). Agencies, with their information gathering, product-licensing and monitoring tasks, have a significant influence on regulation in the EU: they improve the Community's monitoring capacity and fulfil regulatory functions in administrative practices outside the Commission's direct control (Keleman 2002). An example of a transnational institution (both formal and informal) is the Committee structure to achieve the Common Implementation Strategy (CIS), consisting of the meetings of the Marine Directors, the Marine Strategy Coordination Group (MSCG), the Committee of MS representatives and Working Groups (on Good Environmental Status, Economic and Social Analysis and on Information Exchange). The Marine Directors meet twice a year. These meetings take place back-to-back with the meetings of the Water Directors, because of the overlap between defining Good Environmental Status (MSFD) and Good Ecological Status (WFD) and because the directors attend both meetings (Van Leeuwen et al. 2012). The Marine Strategy Coordination Group consists of MS, neighbouring countries, international organizations and stakeholders. The working groups consist of representatives of MS, the Regional Sea Conventions, the Commission and NGOs. For example, Seas at Risk (SAR) is member of the MSCG and the working groups on GES and Economic and Social Analysis.

Marine Governance: The Staging and Power Dynamics of Marine Governance Arrangements

To understand processes of policy-making and decision-making at seas by different public and private actors from different levels I use the concept of marine governance. Marine governance is about the negotiations between public and private actors at several levels to share policy-making competencies in order to govern activities at sea and to control their consequences. More specifically, marine governance is about marine policy-making and decision-making, which take place in different marine governance arrangements. In the following section the concept of marine governance will be introduced and thereafter the focus is put on the power dynamics of marine governance.

Marine Governance Arrangements

A marine governance arrangement is a temporary stabilization of the content and organization of a marine policy domain. In a marine governance arrangement different more or less stable coalitions of governmental actors at several levels, representatives of maritime activities (fisheries, oil and gas winning, off shore wind parks, navigation and shipping), environmental NGOs and representatives of other interest groups try to influence the activities and processes that occur at sea and aim to design legitimate and accountable governing initiatives based on shared discourses, managing resources and defining the rules of the game (on different levels). The structure of a marine governance arrangement can be analysed along four dimensions:

- The actors and their coalitions. Which actors are involved in policy-making and decision-making and how are they selected?
- The division of resources between these actors, leading to differences in power and influence, where power refers to the mobilization and deployment of the available resources, and influence to who determines policy outcomes and how. What are the power relations between the actors and how do power balances between actors within a coalition influence their participation (inclusion and exclusion)?
- The rules of the game (institutional setting) currently in operation, in terms of formal procedures of decision making and implementation as well as informal rules and 'routines' of interaction within institutions.
- The current policy discourses, where discourses entail the views and narratives of the actors involved (norms, values, definitions of problems and approaches to solutions). How do actors mobilize discourses and how do these discourses influence the definition of problems, the selection of legitimate solutions and which rules are negotiable?

Because these four dimensions are inextricably interwoven, change in one of the dimensions may induce change in other dimensions, which in turn alters the arrangement as a whole (Van Tatenhove et al. 2000, Liefferink 2006, Van Tatenhove 2013).

Marine policy-making and decision-making takes place in different marine governance arrangements. Maritime activities, such as shipping, fishing, and offshore wind parks are regulated by different governance arrangements. In fisheries (an exclusive EU competence) supranational governance arrangements are dominant, along with different intergovernmental and transnational governance arrangements, while shipping is governed mainly by intergovernmental governance arrangements. Table 3.1 summarizes the characteristics of three types of governance arrangements: intergovernmental, supranational and transnational.

Table 3.1 Types of governance arrangements

Dimensions	Coalitions	Power/ resources	Rules	Discourses (of cooperation)
Intergovernmental	Coalitions of states	Dominance of (big) Member states	Sovereign states are the locus of formal authority and legitimacy; also informal authority and legitimacy for non-state actors	Confrontational, integrative and consensual.
Supranational	Supranational institutions	Diffusion of power between states and supranational institutions	Supranational institutions are the locus of authority and legitimacy	Integrative, confrontational, and consensual
Transnational	Flexible coalitions of governments and stakeholders in formal and informal institutions	Diffusion of power among stakeholders	Coalitions of states and stakeholders are the locus of authority and legitimacy	Integrative, confrontational and consensual

In integrated marine policy, (inter)governmental, supranational and transnational arrangements come together. In intergovernmental governance arrangements coalitions of states are dominant. This is the case in the regional sea commissions, in IMO and in the Council. In supranational governance arrangements the supranational institutions play a dominant role. The Treaties provide the rules, competences and responsibilities of these institutions. Depending on the issues at stake and the actors involved, the nature of negotiations could vary from consensus-oriented problem solving to confrontational bargaining. An example of consensual cooperation is the MASPNOSE project to find solutions for spatial conflicts at the Dogger Bank (see the North Sea chapter), an example of a confrontational cooperation is the demarcation of responsibilities in Marine Spatial Planning (MSP).

The Power Dynamics of Marine Governance

To understand the power dynamics of marine governance arrangements I first introduce the concept of power and then turn to unravelling the power dynamic of marine governance arrangements in three stages.

Power is 'the organizational and discursive capacity of agencies, either in competition with one another or jointly, to achieve outcomes in social practices, a capacity which is however co-determined by the structural power of those social institutions in which these agencies are embedded' (Arts and Van Tatenhove 2004: 347). Power is a multi-layered concept and is more than just the mobilization of bias and resources in interaction. Besides forms of relational power, which focuses on the influence of actors in policy and politics, and the capacity of these actors to achieve outcomes through interactions, we also have to take into account the institutional and structural context in which actors operate (Arts and Van Tatenhove 2004, Van Tatenhove et al. 2010). This is reflected in dispositional and structural power. Dispositional power shapes an agency's capacity to act. Organizational rules and an unequal distribution of resources define and position the actors vis-à-vis each other on the level of governance arrangements. These positions co-determine what agents may achieve in terms of relational power. The unequal distribution and use of resources, the positioning of actors in an arrangement and the nature of negotiations in the face of external constraints are all the outcome of structural power. Structural power refers to the way in which macro-societal structures shape the nature and conduct of agents.

To understand the multi-layered power dynamics of marine governance arrangements I distinguish three stages in integrated marine planning processes. These stages are: (1) establishing the power architecture of a marine governance arrangement; (2) the negotiations and processes of capacity-building within marine governance arrangements; and (3) the way outcomes of negotiations in these arrangements are translated into formal decision-making circuits (Van Tatenhove et al. 2010).

The power architecture of a marine planning project provides the context in which negotiations take place. In this sense the architecture of a marine planning project is a form of dispositional power; as the positioning of actors vis-à-vis each other determines what actors may achieve in terms of relational power (Van Tatenhove et al. 2010: 7). Establishing the power architecture of a marine spatial planning project firstly involves defining the borders of a marine region. Secondly, establishing the power architecture sets the playing field for negotiations by defining the integrative frame of reference, the organizational rules and the rules through which participants are included and excluded. This involves dispositional power, the positioning of actors vis-à-vis each other based on an unequal distribution of resources.

The second stage is about the capacity of actors to mobilize resources and to realize desired outcomes in negotiations within an institutionalized power architecture. How does relational power develop during a project and to what outputs? Power within negotiations refers to the actual use of resources by actors in interactions, the mechanisms of participation (who is included and who is excluded) and issues of diversity and representativeness. In other words, the relational power of the participants is played out within the specific dispositional power structure (the architecture), results in specific outcomes and outputs.

The third stage is the translation of the results of negotiations into the formal decision-making and implementation circuits of the EU and Member States. How do politicians and civil servants of the different Member States deal with the outcomes of, for example, integrated (trans-boundary) marine planning projects? Are they willing to transfer competences to the EU? How do these outcomes relate to already existing policy initiatives in the different countries?

Institutional Capacity-Building

Crucial to understand the dynamics of processes of marine governance, especially the ability of public and private actors to define problems and to formulate solutions by mobilizing resources to change the rules of the game, the concept of institutional capacity building could be helpful. Because institutional capacity-building as a concept is used in different settings, we discuss these different roots to define institutional capacity building in marine governance arrangements.

One of the roots of the concept is the United Nations Development programme (UNDP 1970). They defined capacity-building as 'the creation of an enabling environment with appropriate policy and legal frameworks, institutional development, including community participation (of women in particular), human resources development and strengthening of managerial systems, adding that, UNDP recognizes that capacity-building is a long-term, continuing process, in which all stakeholders participate (ministries, local authorities, non-governmental organizations and water user groups, professional associations, academics and others)' (www.undp.org). By 1992, capacity-building became a central concept in Agenda 21 and the United Nations Conference on Environment and Development (UNCED). However, capacity-building is not limited to international aid or development work. More recently, governments used the concept to transform community and industry approaches to social and environmental problems.

Also in planning theory there is a long tradition of institutional capacity-building. Amin and Thrift (1995) used the term, to find positive qualities of territorial innovation milieu. According to them a plethora of civic associations, a high level of interaction among social groups, coalitions which crossed individual interests, and a strong sense of common purpose, generated 'institutional thickness', within which firms and households were embedded, and institutional capacity to mobilize to sustain supportive conditions for both. Healey and colleagues (Healey et al. 2003) developed a relational view of institutional capacity. Building on the concept of institutional capital Healey (1998) makes a distinction between three forms of capital: intellectual capital (knowledge resources), social capital (trust and social understanding which build up through face to face encounters) and political capital (the capacity to act collectively to develop local qualities and capture external attention and resources). Healey et al. (2003: 63-67) analyse institutional capacity-building processes in terms of the knowledge resources, relational resources and mobilization capabilities they draw upon and generate (see Table 3.2). Although Healey and colleagues focus on local governance processes, their concept of institutional capacity-building is a useful starting point to develop a framework to analyse marine governance processes at regional seas.

Table 3.2 The dimensions of institutional capacity-building, in Healey et al. 2003: 65

DIMENSIONS OF INSTITUTIONAL CAPACITY-BUILDING	
Knowledge resources	– The *range* of knowledge resources; – The *frames* of reference; – The extent to which range and frames are shared among stakeholders, *integrating* different spheres of policy development and action; – The capacity to absorb new ideas and learn from them (*openness and learning*);
Relational resources	– The *range* of stakeholders involved; – The *morphology* of their network (density of network interconnections); – The extent of *integration* of the various networks; – The location of the power to act (relations of power between the actors and the interaction with wider authoritative, allocative and ideological structuring forces;
Mobilization capacity	– The *opportunity structure*; – The institutional *arena* used and developed by stakeholders to take advantage of opportunities; – The *repertoire* of mobilization techniques which are used to develop and to sustain momentum; – The presence or absence of critical *change agents* at different stages.

Institutional capacity is the ability of coalitions consisting of public and private actors in governance arrangements to get involved in policy processes and decision-making processes by using specific discourses and mobilizing knowledge resources and relational resources (Buunk 2003, Healey et al. 2003). More particularly, institutional capacity-building is about the capacity of actors in a specific institutional setting to mobilize knowledge and relational resources, in order to change the rules of the game, to (re)define problem definitions of a policy domain, to change policy and political agendas and translate and implement the outcomes of negotiations to decision-making arrangements. Improving the institutional capacity of governance arrangements refers to the ability of coalitions to redefine and change the rules of the game by using discourses, and mobilizing knowledge and relational resources in order to change the pathways of policy-making. As we shall see, institutional capacity-building will differ for the three stages of the power dynamics of marine governance arrangements. Before discussing the possibilities of institutional capacity-building to design integrated marine governance arrangements, the next section discusses the development of EU integrated maritime policy (IMP). Integrated Maritime Policy, and especially one of its tools, Maritime Spatial Planning, is an illustration of an EU policy initiative to deal with conflicts between users and conflicts between users and the marine environment.

Integrated Marine Governance

The development of integrated marine governance is high on Europe's policy and political agendas. With regard to the marine environment, the EC's Strategic Objectives for 2005-2009 state that: 'in view of the environmental and economic value of the oceans and the seas, there is a particular need for an all-embracing maritime policy aimed at developing a thriving maritime economy and the full potential of sea-based activity in an environmentally sustainable manner' (COM (2005) 12 final).

This commitment resulted in the Green Paper in June 2006 (EC 2006) and after a consultation round of one year with stakeholders in the Blue Paper, in October 2007 (EC 2007b). In the Blue Paper, the EC proposes an Integrated Maritime Policy for the European Union, 'based on the clear recognition that all matters relating to Europe's oceans and seas are interlinked, and that sea-related policies must be developed in a joined-up way if we are to reap the desired results' (EC 2007b: 2). According to the EC, a more collaborative and integrated approach is needed to deal on the one hand with the 'increasing competition for marine space and the cumulative impact of human activities on marine ecosystems' (EC 2007b: 4) and on the other hand to overcome the inefficiencies, incoherencies and conflicts of use caused by fragmented decision-making in maritime affairs.

The Integrated Maritime Policy (IMP) aims to cover a wide range of issues and seeks to bring together actors from a diversity of sectors, such as shipbuilding and shipping, ports, fisheries, offshore energy (including oil, gas and renewables), coastal and maritime tourism, exploitation of mineral resources, aquaculture, blue biotech and emerging sub-sea technologies. Further, it aims to find common ground between the recreational, aesthetic and cultural uses and the ecosystem services provided. The IMP forms an integrative discourse, one including the entire marine and maritime field of activities, sectors and stakeholders' (Van Hoof and Van Tatenhove 2009: 730).

According to the EC, an Integrated Maritime Policy requires a governance framework that applies the integrated approach at every level as well as horizontal and cross-cutting policy tools, such as maritime spatial planning, an integrated approach to data collection processing and delivery, and the coordination of surveillance and monitoring activities and processes (EC 2007a). In the next sub-sections the three tools of integrated maritime policy will be introduced with special attention paid to MSP.

A European Network for Maritime Surveillance

Maritime surveillance is needed to ensure safe use of the seas and to secure Europe's maritime borders, especially with regards to the challenges and threats relating to safety of navigation, marine pollution, law enforcement, and overall security. Member States carry out surveillance activities (concerning fisheries, the environment, policing of the seas, immigration), but most of the activities and threats that they address are transnational in nature. The EC therefore advocates the need for a higher degree of coordination on maritime surveillance through deeper cooperation within and among the Members States' coastguards and other appropriate agencies. One of the suggested policy instruments is an integrated network of vessel tracking and e-navigation systems for European coastal waters and the high seas, including satellite monitoring and Long Range Identification and Tracking (LTIR). A guiding principle of the integration of maritime surveillance is that 'an integrated approach to maritime surveillance should improve the effectiveness of the authorities responsible for maritime activities by making available more tools and more information necessary for the performance of their duties. This should result in more efficient operations and reduced operating costs' (EC 2009b: 12).

Data and Information

The availability and access to a wide range of natural and human activity data on the oceans is the basis for strategic decision-making on maritime policy. Data are collected and stored all over Europe for a wide variety of purposes. The establishment of an appropriate marine data and information structure is of utmost importance. 'This data should be compiled in a comprehensive and compatible system, and made accessible as a tool for better governance, expansion of value – added services and sustainable maritime development' (EC 2007). The Commission wants to take steps towards a European Marine Observation and Data Network (EMODNET) and promote the multi-dimensional mapping of Member States' waters, in order to improve access to high quality data.

Marine Spatial Planning

Marine Spatial Planning (MSP) is 'a process of analysing and allocating parts of the three-dimensional spaces to specific uses, to achieve ecological, economic and social objectives that are usually specified through the political process; the MSP process usually results in a comprehensive plan or vision for a marine region' (Ehler and Douvere 2007, Douvere 2008). Specific for MSP is the balancing and integration of sectoral activities in a three dimensional marine space; (a) on the surface (fisheries, shipping, dredging, oil and gas platforms, windmill parks and recreation); (b) in the water column (fisheries (pelagic gear), dredging, recreation and oil and gas production; (c) on the seabed (pipelines, fisheries (benthic gear), dredging, oil and gas winning).

In November 2008, the European Commission published its Roadmap for Maritime Spatial Planning (MSP) (EC, 2008). MSP – as a key instrument for IMP – 'helps public authorities and stakeholders to coordinate their action and optimize the use of marine space to benefit economic development and the marine environment' (EC, 2008: 2). The rationale for developing MSP is that the increased activity on Europe's seas leads to competition between sectoral interests, such as shipping and maritime transport, offshore energy, ports development, fisheries and aquaculture and environmental concerns. 'MSP is a tool for improved decision-making. It provides a framework for arbitrating between the competing human activities and managing their impact in the marine environment. Its objective is to balance sectoral interests and achieve sustainable use of marine resources in line with the EU Sustainable Development Strategy. MSP should be based on the specificities of individual marine regions or sub-regions. It is a process that consists of data collection, stakeholder consultation and the participatory development of a plan, the subsequent stages of implementation, enforcement, evaluation and revision' (EC 2008: 2-3).

Implementation of MSP is the responsibility of the Member States. In its roadmap, the Commission formulated the following benefits for MSP. (1) Joint work on MSP provides a framework for coordinating sectoral approaches. It increases the effectiveness and coherence of EU and national policies, reducing economic costs of non-coordination. (2) Maritime activities have a cross-border dimension. The role of the EU is to promote a common approach among Member States that takes account of cross-border impacts. (3) For the Internal market, MSP provides a basis for simplified permit systems and reducing the costs of regulatory and administrative procedures, ensuring a transparent and reliable planning framework. (4) Work on MSP at the EU level provides an appropriate forum for Member States to discuss and develop a holistic approach to the management of maritime activities in line with ecosystem requirements.

Realizing Integrated Marine Governance Arrangements at the Level of the Regional Seas

Europe's regional seas are confronted with a variety of environmental, economic, spatial and biodiversity problems. To find solutions for these problems a patchwork of policies has been developed by the Member States, EU and the Regional Sea Conventions. A complicating factor is that sectoral maritime activities have different dynamics and are regulated at different governmental levels. In the section above, the tools of Integrated Maritime Policy as introduced by the EC were discussed so as to detail with some of these problems. Each of these tools suggests an integrated approach which needs a common approach between Member States. In the following the focus will be on MSP.

Marine Spatial Planning is one way of dealing with conflicts between users and between users and the environment and to integrate sectoral policies at the level of regional seas (Van Tatenhove 2011). Because implementation of MSP is the responsibility of the Member States, the role of the European Commission is to facilitate cooperation (for example when there are cross-border conflicts) and to develop a common approach. Of the 11 key principles of MSP[2] formulated by the EC, especially the 'ecosystem approach' and 'cross-border cooperation and consultation' refer to the tension between implementing MSP at the member state level or at the regional (sea-basin) level. Most countries are developing their own Marine Spatial Plans, but ecosystems and (some) maritime activities do not end at the political and administrative borders of countries. However, cross-border cooperation is not yet a success and, further, a common approach has not been developed. In its Communication about achievements and future developments in EU MSP (EC, 2010), the EC draws three main conclusions:

- There is a broad agreement on the need for a common approach on MSP and a confirmed interest in further developing MSP at the EU level.
- A more coherent common approach would enhance the potential value of MSP for the EU as a whole, as well as in sea-basin contexts.
- The increased need for coordinated planning of sea-basins would benefit strongly from MSP, as this policy would set out parameters that facilitate cross-border cooperation on MSP among Member States.

For the further development of MSP it is important to understand the possibilities of capacity-building at the regional sea level. The key question of this section is therefore: what conditions enable and constrain the development of integrated marine governance arrangements which can deal with environmental, economic, spatial and nature conservation problems at the regional sea level? To answer

2 The EC formulated the following key principles of MSP: (1) ecosystem approach; (2) using MSP according to area and type of activity; (3) defining objectives to guide MSP; (4) developing MSP in a transparent matter; (5) stakeholder participation; (6) coordination within Member States – simplifying decision-making processes; (7) ensuring the legal effect of national MSP; (8) cross-border cooperation and consultation; (9) incorporating monitoring and evaluation in the planning process; (10) achieving coherence between terrestrial planning and MSP – relationship with ICZM; (11) a strong data and knowledge base (EC 2008 and EC 2010).

this question we make use of the power dynamics of governance arrangements and institutional capacity-building to gain an insight to the possibilities of collaborative marine spatial planning (compare Healey 1998, Innes and Booher 2003: 36). To develop and implement integrated marine governance arrangements for specific marine regions which are tailored to particular problems in particular contexts (Healey 1998, Arts and Van Tatenhove 2004), knowledge is needed on the possibilities of institutional capacity-building within integrated marine governance arrangements, given the specific power dynamics of these governance arrangements in a specific institutional setting.

In theory, integrated marine governance arrangements consist of coalitions of governmental representatives from several levels, representatives of sectoral maritime activities (fisheries, shipping, renewable and non-renewable energy-production, nature conservation, tourism), a diversity of NGOs and other interest groups. These coalitions should have the ability to change the rules of the game and to mobilize resources to develop, for example, an integrated spatial plan for a specific (sub-) marine region. The definition of problems and the formulation of problems is an active social process, one in which social meanings are constructed through discourse and language, and in which social practices are shaped and given legitimacy (cf. Healey 1998: 1543).

When we look at EU initiatives to develop a common approach, facilitate cross-border cooperation and to stimulate coordinated planning, a future direction could be the development and design of EU integrated marine governance arrangements (IMGA). IMGAs could have the characteristics of intergovernmental, supranational and transnational governance arrangements. In these arrangements, coalitions of public actors (politicians and civil servants of MS, EC) and private actors (market parties from the different maritime sectors, NGOs, scientists, etc.) negotiate the development of integrated initiatives for the sea-basin level. Ecosystem-based management and regionalization are the leading discourses affecting the rules and resources (compare Van Hoof et al. 2012).

The possibilities for institutional capacity-building are different for the different stages of the power dynamics of marine governance arrangements. In the remainder of this section, I will focus on capacity-building for each of the three stages.

The *establishment of the power architecture* of an integrated marine governance arrangement concerns the mobilization capacity to define the borders of the marine region, and to mobilize knowledge and relational resources to define legitimate problems and to select the stakeholders. Setting the borders of a marine region could be done according to the marine ecosystems. A starting point for selecting marine regions might be the division of marine regions and sub-regions as defined in the Marine Strategy Framework Directive. However, the size of marine regions depends not on biological and ecological factors alone, but also on the interests and problem definitions of the involved actors, their frame of reference, the conflicts between different sectoral activities, and the institutional setting. This could result in a redefinition of the boundaries of a marine region. What are the problems, which activities cause them and who has the power to define those problems? Defining the environmental, economic, nature conservation and spatial problems for a marine region is a collaborative task for the relevant actors, one in which, for example, the European Commission (DG MARE) could take the lead. As a possible initiator of IMGAs, the European Commission should play a key role in designing the architecture by selecting participants and formulating the initial definition of the problems. Stakeholder participation will increase the legitimacy of these processes of balancing and integrating sectoral activities.

The second stage is about the capacity of actors to mobilize resources to realize desired outcomes in *negotiations* within the existing power architecture. The aim of marine spatial planning projects is to find solutions for both conflicts between users and conflicts between the environment and different maritime activities. The formal rules of the multi-level institutional setting and the involved (maritime) policy domains and activities influence the negotiations within integrated marine governance arrangements. The formal rules and regulations of the multi-level institutional setting (compare Maes 2008) vary from rules set by UNCLOS (United nations Convention on the Law of the Sea), the Convention on Biological Diversity and IMO (International Maritime Organization), to regulations of the Regional Sea Conventions (OSPAR; HELCOM; Barcelona Convention and the Bucharest Convention). Besides these rules, sectoral marine policies and other EU regulations, such as the Marine Strategy Framework Directive (MSFD), the Water Framework Directive (WFD), the Habitats Directive and the Birds Directive (NATURA 2000), the Strategic Environment Assessment Directive (SEA), the Common Fisheries Policy (CFP) and the EU ICZM Recommendation influence the negotiations.

The third stage concerns the way the outcomes of negotiations in integrated marine governance arrangements are *translated into the formal decision-making and implementation practices of the EU and the Member States* (compare Edelenbos et al. 2009: 130).

Conclusions

This chapter introduced a conceptual model to understand the possibilities of institutional capacity-building in integrated marine governance projects at the level of the regional seas, in a complicated multi-level institutional setting (EU, MS, non-Member States, Regional Sea Conventions). Core concepts of this model are marine governance arrangements, the power dynamics of marine governance and institutional capacity-building. Integrated marine policy is high on the agenda of DG MARE and EU Maritime Spatial Planning (MSP) is seen as a tool that allows public authorities and stakeholders to coordinate their actions and optimize the use of marine space to benefit economic development and the marine environment. However, the responsibility for developing marine spatial plans rests with the Member States. The EC can only promote a common approach between member states, one that takes account of cross-border impacts and ecosystem requirements. To find solutions for cross-border conflicts between users and/or users and the environment, institutional capacity-building is required to design and to implement integrated marine governance arrangement. This will be a key challenge for the future. As this chapter showed, capacity-building is influenced by different stages in the exercising of power; the establishment of a power architecture, negotiations and the translation to formal decision-making circuits. Earlier research (Van Leeuwen et al. 2012) showed a difference in institutional ambiguity for the North Sea, the Baltic Sea, the Black Sea and the Mediterranean Sea. Based on these findings an important assumption is that institutional capacity-building in processes of marine governance will differ for the European seas because every sea has a different institutional setting. This will affect the selection of stakeholders, the possibility to mobilize knowledge and relational resources and the possibility to define rules at the regional sea level. Because the implementation of IMP and processes of regional cooperation have just started, it is too early to elaborate upon the differences of institutional capacity-building for the different seas This will be an important focus for future research.

References

Arts, B. and Van Tatenhove, J. 2004. Policy and power: a conceptual framework between the 'old' and 'new' policy idioms. *Policy Sciences*, 37(3-4), 339-356.

Arts, B., Leroy, P. and Van Tatenhove, J. 2006. Political modernisation and policy arrangements: a framework for understanding environmental policy change. *Public Organization Review: A Global Journal*, 6(2), 93-106.

Arts, B. and Van Tatenhove J. 2006. Political modernisation, in *Institutional Dynamics in Environmental Governance*, edited by B. Arts and P. Leroy. Dordrecht: Springer, 21-43.

Christiansen, T. and Kirchner, E. (eds) 2000. *Committee Governance in the European Union*. Manchester: Manchester University Press.

Douvere, F. 2008. The importance of marine spatial planning in advancing ecosystem-based sea use management. *Marine Policy*, 32(2008), 762-771.

EC. 2006. *Towards a future maritime policy for the Union: A European vision for the oceans and seas*, Green Paper, Brussels, 7.6.2006 [COM(2006)275final, Volume II – ANNEX].

EC. 2007a. *An integrated maritime policy for the European Union*, Brussels, 10.10 2007 [SEC(2007)1278].

EC. 2007b. *An integrated maritime policy for the European Union*. Blue Paper, Brussels, 10.12. 2007 [COM(2007)575final].

EC. 2008. *Roadmap for Maritime Spatial Planning: Achieving Common Principles in the EU*, Brussels, 25.11.2008 [COM(2008)791final].

EC. 2009a. *Progress report on the EU's Integrated Maritime Policy*, Brussels, 15.10.2009 [COM(2009)540final].

EC. 2009b. *Towards the integration of maritime surveillance: A common information sharing environment for the EU maritime domain*, Brussels, 15.10.2009 [COM(2009)538final]

EC. 2010. *Maritime Spatial Planning in the EU – Achievements and Future development*. Brussels, 17.12.2010 [COM(2010) 771final]

Edelenbos, J., Klok, P.J. and Van Tatenhove, J. 2009. The institutional embedding of interactive policy making. Insights from a comparative research based on 8 interactive projects in the Netherlands. *The American Review of Public Administration*, 39(2), 125-148.

Ehler, C. and Douvere, F. 2007. *Visions for a Sea Change Report of the first international workshop on Marine Spatial Planning: Intergovernmental Oceanographic Commission and Man and the Biosphere Programme*. IOC manual and guides no. 48, IOCAM Dossier no. 4 Paris: UNESCO.

Hajer, M.A. and Wagenaar, H. (ed.) 2003. *Deliberative Policy Analysis: Understanding Governance in the Network Society*. Cambridge: Cambridge University Press.

Healey, P., De Magalhaes, C., Madanipour, A. and Pendlebury, J. 2003. Place, identity and local politics: analyzing initiatives in deliberative governance, in *Deliberative Policy Analysis: Understanding Governance in the Network Society*, edited by M.A. Hajer and H. Wagenaar. Cambridge: Cambridge University Press, 60-87.

Héritier, A. 1999. *Policy-making and Diversity in Europe*. Cambridge: Cambridge University Press.

Hooghe, L. and Marks, G. 2001. *Multi-Level Governance and European Integration*. Lanham/Oxford: Rowman & Littlefield Publishers.

Innes, J.E. and Booher, D.E. 2003. Collaborative policymaking: governance through dialogue, in *Deliberative Policy Analysis: Understanding Governance in the Network Society*, edited by M.A. Hajer and H. Wagenaar. Cambridge: Cambridge University Press, 33-59.

Kelemen, R.D. 2002. The politics of 'Eurocratic' structure and the New European Agencies. *West European Politics*, 25(4), 93-118.

Kohler-Koch, B. and Eising, R. (eds) 1999. *The Transformation of Governance in the EU*. London and New York: Routledge/ECPR Studies in European Political Science.

Liefferink, D. 2006. The dynamics of policy arrangements: turning round the tetrahedron, in *Institutional Dynamics in Environmental Governance*, edited by B. Arts and P. Leroy. Dordrecht: Springer, 45-68.

Maes, F. 2008. The international legal framework for marine spatial planning. *Marine Policy*, 32(5), 797-810.

Van Hoof, L. and Van Tatenhove, J. 2009. EU Marine policy on the move: the tension between fisheries and maritime policy. *Marine Policy*, 33(4), 726-732.

Van Hoof, L., Van Leeuwen, J. and Van Tatenhove, J. 2012. All at sea: regionalization and integration of marine policy in Europe. *Maritime Studies*, 11, 9.

Van Leeuwen, J. 2010. *Who Greens the Waves? Changing Authority in the Environmental Governance of Shipping and Offshore Oil and Gas Production.* Wageningen: Wageningen Academic Publishers.

Van Leeuwen, J., and Van Tatenhove, J. 2010. The triangle of governance: the interplay of polity, policy and politics in marine governance. *Marine Policy*, 34, 590-597.

Van Leeuwen, J., Van Hoof, L. and Van Tatenhove, J. 2012. Institutional ambiguity in implementing the European Union Marine Strategy Framework Directive. *Marine Policy*, 36(3), 636-643.

Van Tatenhove, J., Arts, B. and Leroy, P. (eds). 2000. *Political Modernisation and the Environment: the Renewal of Environmental Policy Arrangements.* Dordrecht/Boston/London: Kluwer Academic Publishers.

Van Tatenhove, J. and Leroy, P. 2003. Environment and participation in a context of political modernisation. *Environmental Values*, 12, 155-74.

Van Tatenhove, J., Mak, J. and Liefferink, D. 2006. The inter-play between formal and informal practices. *Perspectives on European Politics and Society*, 7(1), 8-24.

Van Tatenhove, J. 2008. Innovative forms of marine governance: a reflection. Presentation at the Symposium: *On Science and Governance*, 7 March 2008, Wageningen University.

Van Tatenhove, J., Edelenbos, J. and Klok, P.J. 2010. Power and interactive policy-making: A comparative study of power and influence in 8 Interactive projects in the Netherlands. *Public Administration*, 88(3), 609-626.

Van Tatenhove, J. 2011. Integrated marine governance: questions of legitimacy. *Maritime Studies (MAST)*, 10(1), 87-113.

Van Tatenhove, J. 2013. How to turn the tide: developing legitimate marine governance arrangements at the level of the regional seas. *Ocean & Coastal Management*, 71, 296-304.

Wallace, H. 2000. The policy process. A moving pendulum, in *Policy-Making in the European Union*, edited by H. Wallace and W. Wallace, Fourth Edition. Oxford: Oxford University Press, 39-64.

Chapter 4

Float or Sinker for Europe's Seas? The Role of Law in Marine Governance

Brita Bohman and David Langlet

Introduction – Law and the Environment

Marine environmental governance is hugely challenging. This follows both from the multitude of human activities within and beyond the marine area which affect the quality of the environment and from the complexity, variability and interconnectedness of the marine ecosystems themselves and their inhabitants. In addition, each marine region or sub-region has its own particular conditions that call for specific measures. Is the law pertaining to marine governance in Europe up to meeting this challenge?

A key task of law is to provide structures for coordinated measures that are needed over time to achieve certain goals. Core values of any legal system aiming for legitimacy are legal certainty and stability, which allow actors to predict how the system will affect them in the future and adapt their behaviour accordingly. This holds true in the field of marine governance, which requires coordination between various states and sub-state actors in tackling multifaceted phenomena. Many stakeholders, from states to companies and individuals are also expecting the rules to be transparent and the outcomes of future measures within the legal framework to be reasonably foreseeable. At the same time the effectiveness of any piece of legislation addressing ecosystems and the interaction between human societies and those systems hinges on its ability to utilize scientific information and enable appropriate responses to changes in the environmental situation. Successful marine governance thus needs to build on legal structures that provide both stability and a high degree of flexibility and responsiveness to change in ecosystems, our understanding of those systems, and the human behaviour that affects them.

If these two requirements can be successfully balanced within the legal system – without crossing those lines that may constitute breaking points for functioning ecosystems – and the required measures can be effectively implemented, then law may serve as a 'floater', helping to maintain a sustainable relationship between human societies and their ecological foundations. If, however, the law fails to be sufficiently adaptive or if its responses to scientific data are too heavily compromised by competing objectives – either due to systemic flaws in the law itself, or because its implementation or enforcement are ineffectual – then law may rather act as a 'sinker', entrenching unsustainable action, while projecting an image of purposeful measures being taken. Attempts at flexibility can also render the system so complex and supple as to make it unable to provide sufficient steering force.

The prevalence of, inter alia, overfishing, eutrophication, and the spread of toxic substances in marine ecosystems certainly casts doubts on the ability of current legal structures to achieve marine sustainability, despite the multitude of partly overlapping legal rules and mechanisms in existence.

The challenge of combining stability with adaptability – without sacrificing effectiveness – on the regional level is made so much greater by the perceived weakness of many international legal structures, and by the complexity of multilevel regulation, which is particularly prevalent in the European context. At the same time, the unique regional structure of the EU provides unparalleled opportunities for policy-making and enforcement on a regional scale.

This chapter charts the web of rules and processes that make up the legal aspect of marine governance in Europe. In doing so it focuses on pertinent international law – both global and regional – and the particular legal system established by the EU. The extent to which individual states retain a policy space of their own – and whether that is positive or negative from a sustainability perspective – follows from the characteristics and operation of these international and supranational legal structures.

Having set the regulatory scene, the chapter aims to assess to what extent law – in the particularly multileveled form it takes in Europe – currently serves as the reliable floater it ought to be for marine environmental governance, and what may be needed to bolster its buoyancy. At the heart of the analysis will be the ecosystem approach, which has come to play an ever more central role in the attempts to fine-tune the legal system to the demands of ecological and societal realities.

The Role of International Law

Background

The regulation of human activities at sea is one of the oldest tasks of international law, well-represented in international legal writing at least since the seminal works of Hugo Grotius in the early 17th century. The evolution of a comprehensive regulation of the sea has often been spurred by competing claims regarding the right to exercise control over parts of the oceans and the activities that may be carried out there. The fundamental tension has been between claims by coastal states to regulate ever larger areas of the sea adjacent to the coasts and opposing demands by states with a strong navy or commercial fleet for an extensive 'freedom of the seas'. Although the trend during the 21st century was clearly towards extending the rights of coastal states,[1] the jurisdiction that these states may exercise remains significantly circumscribed, particularly with respect to the passage of ships in the vicinity of their coasts. Beyond any coastal state's jurisdiction, on the so-called high seas, the classical freedoms still reign.

Given the openness and interconnectedness of the seas it is obvious that any meaningful preservation of the environment and resources of the seas has to be a joint or at least coordinated effort undertaken by many actors, not least coastal states and flag states.[2] However, coordination presupposes the existence of distinct competences and thus the ability to allocate rights and responsibilities between the actors concerned.

International Legal Structures and Frameworks

UNCLOS/International Law

The fundamental rules on activities at sea or otherwise directly relating to the seas were laid down in the 1982 United Nations Convention on the Law of the Sea (UNCLOS), to which the EU as well as the member states are all parties. Large parts of the Convention are considered to reflect customary international law, meaning that they are binding also on states, such as the USA, that are not parties.

UNCLOS establishes a 'legal infrastructure' by determining what competences – primarily legislative and executive jurisdiction in relation to various activities – different categories of states may exercise in different areas. On the high seas, where the so-called freedoms of the seas apply, all states (and thus their citizens) enjoy freedom of navigation, fishing, the laying of submarine cables and pipelines, and over-flight of aircraft. An old principle reaffirmed by UNCLOS is flag state jurisdiction meaning that the state whose flag a ship carries always has jurisdiction over the actions or omissions of that ship. On the high seas this principle reigns almost exclusively. An important implication of this is that any effort at regulating e.g. fishing at the high seas must involve virtually all states whose ships engage in fishing in a particular area.

However, it is only on the high seas that the flag state is the sole wielder of regulatory power. The closer a ship comes to the shore of a foreign country the more extensive the legitimate claims of that country for exercising jurisdiction will be. For example, by regulating what kind of activities – such as fishing, carrying nuclear arms, or disgorging oil sludge – it may engage in. Already 200 nautical miles (nm) from the coast, or more exactly the baseline,[3] the exclusive

1 Compared to the previous century that is. The 15th and 16th centuries, however, had seen claims of exclusive rights over very large areas.

2 The notions of 'coastal state' and 'flag state' are discussed under 'UNCLOS/International law' below.

3 The 'baseline' is the low-water line along the coast as marked on large-scale charts officially recognized by the coastal state (normal baseline). Where the coastline is deeply

economic zone, or EEZ, commences (provided it is physically possible and the coastal state has claimed such a zone). Here the coastal state has sovereign rights for the purpose of exploring and exploiting, conserving and managing the living as well as non-living natural resources and with regard to other activities for the economic exploitation and exploration of the zone, such as the production of energy from the water, currents and winds. In this area it also has jurisdiction with regard to the protection and preservation of the marine environment; marine scientific research; and the establishment and use of artificial islands, installations and structures (UNCLOS, article 56). That, inter alia, protection and preservation of the marine environment are subject to the coastal state's jurisdiction rather than its sovereign rights signals that the state's powers may be subject to significant restrictions as defined in UNCLOS itself. To the extent that the freedoms of the seas are not affected by the specific rights of the coastal state in the EEZ they also apply in the EEZ.

Where geography allows, the so-called territorial sea begins at a distance of 12 nm from the coast. Here the coastal state in most respects enjoys competences similar to those that apply on land. The significant exception is the right to so-called innocent passage, which guarantees that ships from other states may navigate in this area as long as their passage is continuous and expeditious and they don't engage in activities prejudicial to the peace, good order or security of the coastal state. This precludes any fishing activities, any act of wilful and serious pollution contrary to UNCLOS, as well as the carrying out of research or survey activities (UNCLOS, articles 17-19).

Accordingly, coastal states have far-reaching rights to regulate potentially environmentally harmful or hazardous activities in the vicinity of their coasts. But that does not mean that coastal states necessarily have the ability to actually protect and preserve the environment within this area. This follows both from the fact that the environment is affected by various activities carried out outside the coastal area, and from the problem of effectively enforcing applicable rules even within the territorial sea or the EEZ. Common standards that apply to all actors who may affect the environmental quality and resources of any particular area are thus needed.

In addition to defining competences UNCLOS sets out substantive rules in many areas, including protection of the marine environment and management of its living resources. The overall obligation incumbent on states in this respect is to protect and preserve the marine environment (article 192). States shall, individually or jointly, take all measures necessary to prevent, reduce and control pollution of the marine environment from any source. Using for this purpose the best practicable means at their disposal and measures necessary to protect and

indented and cut into or, if there is a fringe of islands along the coast in its immediate vicinity, so-called straight baselines may be drawn by joining appropriate points on the coast or on certain elevations. On the drawing of such baselines see further UNCLOS, article 7.

preserve rare or fragile ecosystems as well as the habitat of depleted, threatened or endangered species and other forms of marine life. States shall also take all measures necessary to ensure that activities under their jurisdiction or control are conducted so as not to cause damage by pollution to other states and their environment (article 194). However, these provisions are far from detailed and in many cases serve more as a platform for further elaboration than as operative rules for actual activities. Part IX of UNCLOS also establishes that states bordering an enclosed or semi-enclosed sea should cooperate in the management and conservation of marine living resources, if appropriate through regional organizations (articles 122-123). It is hence appropriate that UNCLOS has been complemented by many other international agreements establishing more specific rules and procedures, either for a certain activity or subject matter (such as dumping, vessel source pollution, fishing) or for a region, such as the Baltic Sea or the Mediterranean. The global agreements addressing different forms of polluting activities have mostly been developed and continue to be administrated by the International Maritime Organization (IMO), which is the United Nations specialized agency responsible for the safety and security of shipping and the prevention of marine pollution by ships.

As regards regional measures the United Nations Environment Programme (UNEP) launched a special Regional Seas Programme already in 1974. The programme aims to address the marine environmental degradation by engaging states that share a common body of water in comprehensive protection actions. In some cases this has also led to the adoption of regional treaties.

These agreements, like UNCLOS itself, are all part of international law, which is based on the notion of consent. States may not be subjected to international obligations without having, at least tacitly, consented to being so. The mere weight of an objective or urgency of an action cannot per se create binding obligations on states. Also adjudication rests on consent, meaning that in cases of diverging views on the nature of law or facts, there may not be any organ competent to provide an authoritative answer. Nor are states typically enthusiastic about having recourse to legally binding means of dispute resolution. Even when breaches of international obligations can be established, it is common that international law does not offer very strong mechanisms for enforcement, but largely relies on the concerned states' loyalty to the system, their perceived self-interest, 'naming and shaming', and incentives such as financial support to enable future compliance. This characteristic is quite salient in the field of environmental protection.

The EU

In a European context the European Union (EU) plays an increasingly central role in marine governance. It not only has a direct impact on the domestic legal orders of the now 28 member states, but it is also an important actor in the creation and implementation of international law. According to the Treaty on the European Union (TEU), one of the EU's founding documents, the union shall contribute to 'the strict observance and the development of international law' as well as to the 'sustainable development of the Earth' (article 3 (3) TEU).

The EU is party to many international and regional agreements of relevance for marine governance, including UNCLOS, the global London Convention on dumping (with its 1996 protocol), the 1992 Helsinki Convention on the Protection of the Marine Environment of the Baltic Sea Area, the OSPAR Convention for the Protection of the marine Environment of the North-East Atlantic, and the Barcelona Convention for the Protection of the Mediterranean Sea Against Pollution. Furthermore the EU has observer status – and some of the member states are parties – to the Convention on the Protection of the Black Sea Against Pollution (the Bucharest Convention).

When the EU becomes party to an international agreement it acquires an independent obligation – parallel to that of the member states who are themselves parties – to enforce the agreement. The Union therefore regularly transforms its international obligations into provisions of EU law which, in many cases, are directly applicable in the member states' legal orders (in the form of so called EU regulations). This is particularly important since the EU also has mechanisms for compliance control and adjudication more resembling those of a state than those found in traditional international law.

A pivotal principle of EU law is that the powers of the EU only go so far as the member states have transferred – through the EU treaties – the required competence to the union (article 5(1) of the TEU). All legislative acts adopted by the EU based on this competence are collectively referred to as secondary EU law, whereas the treaties that establish the Union and define its competences and institutions are known as primary law.

Several policy areas, among them international trade, the internal market, fisheries, and environmental protection are largely subject to supranational decision-making, meaning that individual member states have relinquished the ability to block legislation that attracts support by a qualified majority of member states representing a qualified majority of the EU citizens.

When the EU legislates on a particular matter the EU rules may constitute total harmonization, barring – with little room for exceptions – national legislation that goes beyond mere implementation. However, it may also constitute minimum harmonization, which is an important feature of EU environmental legislation, meaning that the member states are allowed to take more, but not less, protective measures compared to the EU rules.

Since legislation based on the EU's environmental policy only entails minimum harmonization individual member states may opt in favour of more far-reaching protective measures as long as they are compatible with the aim of the secondary EU law, are proportional and not arbitrarily discriminatory in their effects on trade between the member states.[4] Important legislation relating to

4 To be precise, such measures adopted by an individual member state have to be consistent with the EU treaties, not least the rules on free movement of goods set out in articles 34 to 36 TFEU and the case law of the EU Court.

marine governance, such as the Marine Strategy Framework Directive (2008/56/EC) belong to this category, whereas other pieces of legislation with significant implications for the marine environment, such as the chemicals regulation 1907/2006 'REACH', or Directive 2005/35/EC on ship-source pollution belong to other policy areas and thus generally entail full harmonization. There is, however, a strong tendency among member states to also regard EU environmental legislation as setting a standard which national legislation should not go beyond for fear of harming the individual states' economic interests (Jans et al. 2009).

In a few policy areas, among them conservation of marine biological resources under the common fisheries policy, the EU enjoys exclusive competence. In these areas the member states are barred from adopting any legislation unless given such a right by specific EU secondary law. This follows from the Treaty on the functioning of the European Union (TFEU), which sets out the competences of the different organs of the EU (article 3).

The implementation and enforcement of EU legislation are the responsibility of the member states. The EU legal order provides for (in comparison to international law) relatively strong monitoring and enforcement instruments to ensure compliance by individual member states.

Against this backdrop it is no surprise that EU law stands a better chance of being effectively enforced than purely international agreements do. At the same time EU legislation, particularly that based on the rationale of the internal EU market,[5] has much more potential to restrain individual states that want to take protective measures of their own than international law does.

Ecosystems, Law and Adaptability

The EU policy on the environment shall contribute, inter alia, to pursuit of the objectives of preserving, protecting and improving the quality of the environment, protection of human health, and rational utilization of natural resources (article 191 TFEU). This is also reflected in the EU framework directives on water and marine environmental policy (2000/60/EC and 2008/56/EC), which both aim at achieving good ecological and environmental water status, taking as their point of departure the environmental conditions and the ecosystems (see further the sections 'The Water Framework Directive' and 'Marine Strategy Framework Directive' below).

One concept that has increasingly become a guiding principle for environmental agreements, and which plays a prominent role in these directives, is the so-called *ecosystem approach.*

This concept signifies a view on management that takes the ecosystem, its functions and dynamics, as the departure point for regulation. The state of the ecosystem itself is used as an indicator by which to identify the measures and

5 I.e. secondary legislation based on article 113 TFEU or its predecessor article 95 in the previous EC Treaty.

actions needed for proper management. The importance of this approach should also be seen in contrast to earlier legislation addressing each sector separately.

Although this concept already started to take shape at the time of the Stockholm Conference on the Human Environment in 1972 (the Stockholm Conference) there is still no universal definition. However, the parties to the Convention on Biological Diversity (CBD) have agreed on the first definition of global applicability. According to that the ecosystem approach ' ... *is a strategy for the integrated management of land, water and living resources, promoting conservation and sustainable use in an equitable way* ...' (CBD, COP 5, Decision V/6). This definition has been complemented by twelve principles on how to apply the concept to management as well as guidance for the CBD parties on how to interpret and integrate the approach has also been developed.[6] Neither the definition nor the principles are formally binding but may provide important guidance.

Similar formulations are found in the frameworks of all of the regional agreements on marine governance in Europe (or in their amendments), all of which endorse an ecosystem approach. When applied to the marine environment, it will include a dimension of coordination between all states in the relevant drainage basins and measures taking into account all kinds of sources and activities that may negatively affect the marine environment.

The ecosystem approach is challenging since it necessitates a broad knowledge base, deep and systematic understanding of the environment, and the ability to address complex environmental problems in a new way – not least from a legal point of view. A major challenge is how to adapt the often rigid and linear structures of the legal system to meet the needs of diverse and non-linear natural systems.

Attempts at translating the ecosystem approach into functional substantive law are described in the next subsection.

Marine Regional Agreements and EU Law

Regional Agreements

As mentioned above the EU is party to many international and regional agreements that are of relevance for marine governance, and that complement UNCLOS.

Both the Helsinki Convention for the protection of the Baltic Sea and the OSPAR Convention, protecting the North Sea and the North-East Atlantic, trace their roots to the 1970s and were forerunners of and important to the development of marine protection of today. They are crucial for regional cooperation, both between the parties to these agreements themselves and for the wider cooperation within the EU's regional seas. Together with the Barcelona Convention for the protection of the Mediterranean these regional conventions have been promoting good environmental status for many years and will, not least due to their institutional structures, play a crucial role in the implementation of EU marine legislation.

6 The so-called *Malawi Principles* adopted at the CBD, COP 5 (Decision V/6) and *Operational Guidance* in accordance with CBD COP 7, Decision VII/11.

Today all of the regional seas agreements to which the EU is party profess to the ecosystem approach in one way or another, and most of them have adopted quite progressive action plans or protocols to complement the provisions found in the conventions. The Helsinki Convention covers the whole of the Baltic Sea area, including inland waters as well as the water of the sea itself and the seabed. Measures are to be taken in the whole catchment area of the Baltic Sea to reduce land-based pollution. The Helsinki Convention and its administrative body the Helsinki Commission (HELCOM) take a holistic view on the marine environment, and the Convention regulates all kinds of activities and forms of pollution. The definition of ecosystem approach applied by HELCOM is:

> The comprehensive integrated management of human activities based on the best available scientific knowledge about the ecosystem and its dynamics, in order to identify and take action on influences which are critical to the health of marine ecosystems, thereby achieving sustainable use of ecosystem goods and services and maintenance of ecosystem integrity.[7]

Furthermore the Helsinki Convention has recently adopted a specific action plan (BSAP) with four main focus areas. These are areas that are considered to be specifically crucial for the environmental status of the Baltic. The plan, which was adopted in 2007, contains specific regulations for measures to be taken by the contracting parties within these areas and aims to implement an ecosystem approach. The BSAP is even presented as a regional implementation of the EU Marine Strategy Framework Directive (MSFD) (HELCOM 2011). As the vast majority of the parties to the Helsinki Convention are EU member states, this region has a good potential for successful integration of the different regulatory regimes and thus effective implementation of the MSFD (see further 'Marine Strategy Framework Directive' below). To a large extent HELCOM, as well as other international river and regional seas commissions, have actually changed position and are increasingly focused on implementing European law and policy rather than developing their own international obligations to be implemented by their respective parties and the EU (Hey 2009).

The OSPAR Convention for the protection of the North Sea and the North East Atlantic was originally two Conventions (the 1972 Oslo Convention and the 1974 Paris Convention) that were merged to become the OSPAR Convention in 1992. It is an agreement with fifteen parties. Unlike the other regional agreements addressed here OSPAR does not cover an enclosed or semi-enclosed sea but rather aims to regulate activities in a significant part of the Atlantic Ocean. However, the OSPAR-area also includes more confined bodies of water such as the English Channel and the Kattegat Bay.

---

7 Statement on the Ecosystem Approach to Management of Human Activities 'Towards an Ecosystem Approach to the Management of Human Activities', First Joint Ministerial Meeting of the Helsinki and OSPAR Commissions (JMM), Bremen 2003, Agenda item 6, Annex 5, paragraph 5.

The main tasks of OSPAR has been to provide monitoring structures and, through the OSPAR Commission, to be an organ for cooperation in the region. A large number of the parties are also members of the EU. In 2010 the OSPAR Convention adopted a special Environmental Strategy for the North East Atlantic with a number of focus areas important for the environmental status of the sea. This strategy emphasizes the ecosystem approach as a basic concept and makes references to the MSFD. OSPAR intends to take an active role in facilitating a coherent and coordinated implementation of the MSFD. However, considering the geographical scope of the convention and the number of member states this will be a challenging task.

Within the Black Sea area the Bucharest Convention for the protection of the Black Sea from 1992 is applicable. The catchment area of the Black Sea is about six times larger than the surface area of the sea itself. Hence the Black Sea is particularly sensitive to land-based pollution. The runoff districts, however, include a large number of countries that are not Black Sea coastal states and hence not parties to the Convention. This makes it more difficult to effectively control pollution discharges.

In addition to the Bucharest Convention, the 1994 Danube River Protection Convention also applies to part of the Black Sea area and complements the rather narrow geographical application of the Bucharest Convention. Like most river basin conventions, and in parallel to the WFD's river basin approach, the Danube Convention takes a *hydrological basin approach,* applied to the Danube river catchment area. The protocols to the Bucharest Convention in some cases have a wider area of application than the Convention itself. The general feature of regional agreements for ocean management is otherwise to only include the coastal states. A likely explanation is that generally only the coastal states have a genuine and not least an economic interest in the status of the marine waters. Of all regional agreements only the OSPAR Convention has among its parties non-coastal states: Luxembourg, Switzerland and Finland[8] (Vinogradov 2007: 589-597). These states are parties due to the fact that their territories lie within the catchment areas of the region, and thus contribute to the land-based pollution of the sea.

The Bucharest Convention, which is a framework convention with very few precise regulations, derives much of its substance from in total four protocols focusing on different sectors of activities. This approach to regulation is common to all agreements adopted within the UNEP Regional Seas Programme (also see 'UNCLOS/International law' above). Of all the regional agreements in Europe the Bucharest Convention itself appears as the least modern instrument, with far too general provisions and traditionally lacking most of the environmental principles, such as the *precautionary principle* and the principle of *best available technique* (BAT), that are central to comparable instruments (Vinogradov 2007:

8 Finland is a coastal state but not of the North Sea or the North East Atlantic. However, some of its rivers flow to the Barents Sea, and historically it was involved in efforts to control the dumping of hazardous waste in the Atlantic and the North Sea.

598). However, the parties to the Bucharest Convention have agreed on a strategic action plan to further the implementation of the Convention mechanisms and the regional compliance with ecosystem quality objectives. The action plan was revised in 2008. With the revision of the action plan principles like *sustainable development practices*, *the precautionary principle* and *public participation* was adopted (Strategic Action Plan for the Black Sea 2009, BS-SAP). This action plan also includes principles and mechanisms such as integrated coastal zone management (ICZM); the ecosystem approach; and integrated river basin management (IRBM).

To establish a system for observation of the marine conditions in the Black Sea region, the Black Sea Integrated Monitoring and Assessment Programme was set up by the UNEP Regional Seas Programme in collaboration with the Black Sea Commission. Only two of the Black Sea Coastal states are member states to the EU and thus bound by EU law. However this has triggered an initiative by the EU to increase cooperation with the whole region. (DiMento and Hickman 2012).

For regional geopolitical reasons the legal division of the Mediterranean into coastal zones, EEZ and high seas has been debated ever since UNCLOS was signed in 1982. This complicates coastal and marine governance in the area. However, in recent years several protocols that further the objectives of the Barcelona Convention have been adopted to combat the deterioration of the environment of the Mediterranean, not least the increasing loss of biodiversity. The Barcelona Convention, which was first adopted in 1976, was comprehensively amended, expanded and re-named in line with Agenda 21 in 1995.

Unlike for example the Helsinki and OSPAR Conventions, which contain some quite precise requirements, the Barcelona Convention, like the Bucharest Convention, is a framework treaty adopted within the UNEP Regional Seas Programme. It lays down general rules that have subsequently been supplemented by more detailed protocols. Although this means that the convention as such has little steering power this model creates a structure for cooperation and for continuously addressing areas or activities that are in need of better regulation. It has enabled new topics to be dealt with without necessitating amendments to the convention. The latest addition, a protocol on ICZM, entered into force in 2011. This protocol itself takes the form of a framework agreement with six aims; sustainable development of coastal zones by rational planning of activities; preservation of coastal zones; sustainable use of natural resources; preservation of ecosystems and coastlines; prevention and reduction of natural disasters and climate change; and improvement of cooperation. With the protocol on ICZM the Mediterranean area claims to step beyond the problems of traditional state jurisdiction and instead develop new tools for environmental protection. As with the Black Sea the effective implementation of EU marine law in this region is challenged by the large number of Mediterranean coastal states that are not EU member states, some of which are also in a state of political uncertainty (Del Vecchio Capotosti 2008, Gavouneli 2008, Birnie et al. 2009: 395-396).

All the regional agreements are important, not least for providing a legal and political frame, and all aim for cooperation towards environmental protection across geographical, ecological and political differences. The efforts taken so far under these agreements have seen varying results. It continues to be a great challenge in all these regional contexts to effectively implement the measures needed to combat serious and complex environmental problems. This follows from the nature of the problems but also from the diversity of states involved and the complex institutional structures that these differences both create and demand. Effective legal control is hard to achieve on an international or regional level. The ecosystem approach is a promising instrument if effectively operationalized. The MSFD will also have an important coordinating role in this work. As mentioned the MSFD has also become an important driver for law creation within these international organizations, particularly with respect to the Baltic Sea and the North-East Atlantic. This adds to the effect of the EU directive and related legal acts. However the number of non-EU member states in the marine regions complicates coordination and implementation and is therefore an obstacle that will have to be managed.

The Water Framework Directive

The aquatic environment has been the subject of extensive EU regulation, to a degree as a result of the EU being party to many agreements in the field of water protection and marine governance. Since emissions of all kinds have a tendency to eventually end up in watercourses and oceans the marine environment is in fact affected by many pieces of EU legislation. For reasons of space, however, we focus here on legal acts directly dealing with the marine environment.

The Water Framework Directive (WFD) was the first and most significant step within the EU towards a more coupled and holistic view of water management. This directive is now complemented by the Marine Strategy Framework Directive (MSFD). Together they cover the complete water regimes of the EU. They both embrace an ecosystem-based approach and aim to guarantee that certain environmental quality goals are reached for each area concerned. The directives are also devised to embrace and take into account the regional differences existing between the different European seas. Furthermore, an important purpose of these directives is to enforce regional agreements to which the EU is party.

In the WFD the environmental water quality goals are assessed specifically for every river basin, river basin district or coastal area, and are based on the specific biology and aquatic ecosystem conditions found within that area, i.e. a river basin approach (articles 2(13) and 3(1)). What protection measures to take depends on the actual conditions in these run off districts (article 2(15)). The scope of the WFD is limited mainly to inland waters. However, it is also applicable to the surface waters on the landward side of the baseline and one nautical mile on the seaward side of this line (articles 2(3) and 2(7)).

The purpose of the WFD is to provide a framework for protection of these waters and prevent further deterioration, protect the marine environment, enhance the status of aquatic ecosystems, and generally improve the aquatic environment (article 1). The directive regulates surface water, groundwater, inland water, transitional water[9] and coastal water and calls for 'good ecological and chemical status' of freshwater (see definitions in article 2 of the directive). Hence its role for marine areas is fundamental in so far as coastal waters and transitional waters inevitably end up in, and are interconnected with, the marine ocean basins. Land based pollution even contributes the vast majority of all marine pollution according to UNEP.[10] The aim is to enhance the protection and the improvement of the aquatic ecosystems through the establishment of measures for progressive reduction of discharges and emissions of some priority substances. This is done through a complex system of reference elements and quality standards and characteristics set for different types of waters and ecological aspects. The member states are required to establish monitoring programs in order to establish a coherent and comprehensive overview of the water status within each river basin district and to determine whether the water status is high, good or moderate, and what measure to take to improve it. The WFD also emphasizes the need for achieving the objectives of relevant international agreements, and establishes innovative principles for water management, including public participation in planning and economic approaches (article 1).

One important feature of the WFD is the coordination of administrative arrangements. As the WFD obligates the member states to identify and assign special river basin districts as ecologically suitable, the states are also to assign a governmental body or appropriate competent authority to govern the area (article 3), and hence be responsible for measuring, monitoring and data sampling in that district. Hence the directive takes a holistic approach also in this regard, as it emphasizes the environmental and ecological boundaries rather than the geographical or political ones.

The WFD is to be evaluated in 2015, when all quality goals set out in the directive and by the river district authorities are to be fulfilled. It is a very ambitious piece of legislation, which has attracted a lot of criticism. Some has claimed that the quality indicators are contra-productive to the ecosystem approach since they once again imply a fragmentation rather than an integrated approach and cause difficulties for appropriate and coherent implementation in-between different member states (see for example Grimeaud 2001: part 3, Keessen et al. 2010, Josefsson and Baaner 2011). However it is also argued that much of the complexities are due to the many exceptions found in the

9 'Transitional waters' are bodies of surface water in the vicinity of river mouths which are partly saline in character as a result of their proximity to coastal waters but which are substantially influenced by freshwater flows. WFD, article 2(6).

10 http://www.unep.org/regionalseas/issues/landactivities/default.asp [14 February 2014].

directive (Lee 2009: 34, Jans and Vedder 2012: 395). Another critique is that the actual goals are too unclear, although some numerical standards are set by the directive many of the factors to be taken into account are only mentioned in very general terms as a result of the need for flexibility. The directive's reporting and information requirements might also be a problem in terms of implementation since absence of knowledge will affect the assessments and decisions (Lee 2009: 31 and 36 ff). Hence, although the aims are ambitious there are several obstacles and uncertainties to be overcome.

Marine Strategy Framework Directive

Unlike the WFD, the MSFD is applicable to the EU's marine waters, beyond the baseline. According to the MSFD the states concerned within each area of the European regional seas are to evaluate the conditions and make a plan for their marine region. The MSFD is applicable to coastal zones with respect to issues not already addressed by the WFD, and also to the seabed and subsoil in the coastal zones (article 3(1)). Furthermore the directives correlate in the sense that the results of the monitoring under the WFD are to be taken into account when assessing the marine waters according to the MSFD (article 8). Just as the WFD, the MSFD focuses on natural geographical and ecological boundaries, the regional specifics and the drainage areas rather than on national borders. The MSFD aims at achieving 'good environmental status' of the EU's marine waters until 2020. The term 'good environmental status' is defined as '... the status of marine waters where these provide ecologically diverse and dynamic oceans and seas which are clean, healthy and productive within their intrinsic conditions, and the use of the marine environment is at a level that is sustainable ...' (article 3(5)). This definition is similar to the definition of 'ecological status' in the WFD. Hence what signifies good environmental status varies, and is specific to each region, decided on the basis of specific quality descriptors.

An initial assessment of the marine areas was to be made by July 2012. By the same time member states were to determine what conditions represent 'good environmental status' and establish the environmental targets and associated indicators. A monitoring program for ongoing assessment and regular updating of targets is required to be established and implemented by 2014 by each state. Thereafter, the states should develop and enter into operation a program of measures designed to achieve or maintain 'good environmental status'. This programme of measures is to be developed by 2015.

The aim of the MSFD is to more effectively protect the marine environment across Europe. It is based, and focuses specifically, on the four maritime regions of the EU: the Mediterranean Sea, the Baltic Sea, the Black Sea and the North-east Atlantic Ocean, including the waters surrounding the Azores, Madeira and the Canary Islands. The purpose of this is that the states in these regions shall cooperate and take into account the specific regional conditions when developing the plans for how to implement the directive. Furthermore the member states are encouraged to also seek cooperation with third party countries and base this cooperation on existing regional agreements. In the area of the Black Sea for example, this implies cooperation primarily with Georgia, the Russian Federation, Turkey and Ukraine (which are not members of the EU) and to consolidate the MSFD implementation with the work done in the Bucharest Convention and the Black Sea Commission, as well as under the Strategic Action Plan for the Black Sea. However, seen in the light of the ecosystem approach, cooperation with third party countries could probably also imply cooperation with non-coastal states that are part of a run off district which causes discharges in one of the regional seas. If relevant non-member states and non-coastal states are not actively involved in the work it could be difficult for the member states to reach the environmental objectives and thus comply with their obligations. As an example, the run off districts of the Black Sea include about twenty countries (BS-SAP, p. 2).

The encouragement to cooperate and incorporate regional agreements is important as an attempt to apply an ecosystem approach. It is also of value by enabling knowledge already gathered on the problems and of the environmental status in a specific area to be used within the EU framework. Hence the MSFD encourages the member states to work progressively to incorporate all the efforts already made by regional organs like HELCOM and the OSPAR Commission (the administrative organs of the Helsinki Convention and the OSPAR Convention) and the administrative structures, for example for monitoring of the water status, already set up. It furthermore allows for more effective and consistent interpretation of these agreements through the legal regime of the EU. Through the adoption of the MSFD the EU has initiated a new kind of transboundary public governance (Hey 2009).

Both HELCOM and the OSPAR Commission have been valuable to marine protection as regards their monitoring structures. Within the frames of its work the OSPAR Convention has tried to identify threats to the marine environment and organized programmes and measures for national action. As a consequence of its efforts to do so it has also been a successful example of how to ensure monitoring and assessment of the quality status of the seas by setting internationally agreed goals, and by making sure that participating states deliver what is needed to keep this up. This latter task falls on the OSPAR Commission. These kinds of monitoring structures are today adopted by most regional seas conventions in one way or another.

The OSPAR Commission and HELCOM have also initiated cooperation in developing strategies on how to implement the ecosystem approach and especially the pertinent EU directives, within their regions and with respect to the non-EU member states. This is a requirement and a prerequisite for achieving good environmental status in the whole region. OSPAR and HELCOM are similar also in this regard since both conventions have very few non-EU member states (Iceland and Norway, and the Russian Federation respectively). This is a much more challenging task for the other regional agreements where the EU member states are a minority and thus have less basis for pushing the EU regime as a model for the region.

According to the MSFD each member state – cooperating with other member states and non-EU countries within a marine region – is required to develop strategies for its marine waters (article 5(1)). The core idea of the directive is for each country to cooperate within its marine region to create a marine strategy with the aim of reaching good environmental status. This work shall be coordinated to attain coherence between the states in the area, so that all countries in the area endeavour to find a common approach. However the evaluations or assessments of the water quality needed to fulfil the aim of the directive are still to be made individually rather than jointly within each sub-region. The same is true for evaluating measures to be carried out. It could be questioned whether it would not be more effective if these assessments and evaluations of measures were made and implemented in cooperation.

Remaining Challenges

Despite the very promising features of recent EU action, particularly the increasing emphasis on coordination, science-based governance, and the ecosystem approach, there remain several challenges, which may undermine the ability to actually deliver on the environmental goals. Prominent among these is the far-reaching coordination needed. It will be challenging in practice to apply the requirement for 'good environmental status' in a consistent manner over regions and sub-regions. Not least due to the need for evaluating and deciding on appropriate measures. In an attempt to come to terms with this the EU has created an implementing strategy developed by the European Commission (EC). This strategy, the Common Implementation Strategy provides instructions on what to take into account in developing a marine strategy and is to be coordinated further with both the WFD and the work pursued within regional agreements.

Still, the criteria provided to determine 'good environmental status' range from the general and vague to the very complex. There is also an inherent conflict between exactness and comparability on the one hand and flexibility on the other which may leave member states with very significant discretion (Markus et al. 2011: 79). That discretion is further increased by the exceptions that member states may legitimately apply in order not to take measures otherwise prescribed by the MSFD or the WFD. Taken together this can allow member states to act – or fail to act – in a manner that is counter to the objectives of sustainable governance without there being any transgression of the legal requirements, and thus no clear case for using legal remedies to correct the situation.

One should also remember that the MSFD contains very little in terms of concrete measures that directly affect the environmental situation. It sets goals and establishes processes but relies heavily on other (more fragmented) EU-law and international agreements for substantive instruments to effect change. This also means that individual member states are left to strike the balance between stability and legal certainty on the one hand and adaptability and responsiveness on the other in concrete cases. The struggle between competing interests is thus likely to play out once more – as it did at EU level when the directives were drafted – at member state level when specific measures are to be devised and implemented. This situation can also potentially create another problem in regard to compliance control and enforcement procedures. Since the obligations incumbent on the states are rather vague enforcement is of great importance, not least as a means of coordination and by generating authoritative interpretations. At the same time the line where enforcement action may be triggered is blurred by that same vagueness. And while the EU at least formally has a far-reaching competence to act on non-compliance, most of the regional organizations have very little such competence and are thus unlikely to contribute significantly to filling the functions of an effective enforcement mechanism.

Furthermore, while the member states are largely responsible for achieving the environmental goals, important measures remain outside their control and may only be taken at the EU level or in international forums. The first applies e.g. to fisheries and marine conservation, which is tightly regulated by the EU, but also to a large extent to agriculture and transport. The latter applies to numerous measures in regions where action by non-EU member states is vital for achieving the goals.

Conclusions

The legal rules and procedures applicable to the governance of Europe's seas are plentiful and complex. They include measures at global-, regional-, EU- and national levels. In many cases they are over-lapping and synergetic, and support regional marine governance, or at least provide a good structure for governance measures. Much of the pertinent legislation is ambitious and promising, providing a ground for a more coordinated and compound implementation, and introducing new judicial tools and mechanisms.

Although it is difficult to devise legislation that fits all marine regions in Europe, the EU framework directives in particular are of vital importance, not least politically. They raise the issue of marine governance, but also set quality standards for the marine environment. The EU also has the potential to function as a node, distributing creative forms of regulation devised in regional agreements to other regions within the EU. The EU commission and the EU Court play important roles in enhancing the implementation of these regional agreements. With more resources directed towards technical support, monitoring and enforcement, that role could be even greater.

However, there is no lack of factors that may counteract successful governance. It will, inter alia, be quite interesting to see whether the EU's member states and institutions can manage the far-reaching coordination between policy areas and regional legal regimes envisioned by the MSFD. Clearly, that will require considerable effort and commitment. To promote the achievements and potential of regional agreements for the attainment of the MSFD's goals without suffering setbacks caused by conflicting interests, fragmentation and requirements for unanimity in decision-making will also be a toll order. Eventually, even stronger regional and/or supranational mechanisms might be necessary to reach the environmental quality goals.

Undoubtedly, continued and effective integration of environmental considerations in all relevant policy areas of the EU – including agriculture, fisheries, transport and certain aspects of the internal market – will be indispensable. Otherwise these policies risk hamstringing the member states, and may in some cases bar necessary action. Also international agreements can sometimes restrict the ability to take effective measures, particularly with respect to pollution from ships and other sea-based activities. This will necessitate continued and increased commitment from member states and the EU alike to press for raising the protective level of pertinent international standards.

The ecosystem approach has been instrumental for placing scientific knowledge about the ecosystems and their variability at the heart of marine governance. But the ecosystem approach is not only hard to define with precision but might also get into conflict with traditional legal requirements for legal certainty and coherence. Such conflicts are seldom addressed in substance in international or EU law, but rather left to individual states to manage in the concrete circumstances. It remains to be seen how the MSFD's objectives will be reconciled with competing objectives at member state level. Further clarification of what measures EU member states are expected to take – and will be allowed to take considering harmonizing EU policies – when needed to meet environmental quality standards might be necessary, although it can conflict with the desired far-reaching flexibility.

Although much of the critique directed at the frameworks implementing the ecosystem approach is justified, these frameworks constitute an important step towards putting environmental quality and ecosystem dynamics, rather than administrative or activity specific boundaries, at the centre of governance.

A major hurdle to achieving good environmental status is deficiencies in implementation. When criticizing the applicable regulation it is, however, important to realize that many of the legal structures and regimes governing our seas, although beginning to take shape already in the seventies, have only been in force for a decade or less. One needs to have some patience with the fact that it takes time for new structures and regulations to be fully incorporated and made to operate to their full potential.

Obviously, good implementation and enforcement is a continuous endeavour that requires commitment and resources. And the legal framework can over time never be better than the policies it is devised to effectuate – as the common fisheries policy of the EU has so prominently shown. Continued political commitment to marine governance is thus a prerequisite for the law to serve as the strong floater that it ought to be, and which it shows promising signs of becoming.

References

Birnie, P., Boyle, A. and Redgwell, C. 2009. *International Law and the Environment*. Third edition. Oxford: Oxford University Press.

Black Sea Commission. 2009. Strategic Action Plan for the Environmental Protection and Rehabilitation of the Black Sea (SAP-BS), Adopted in Sofia, Bulgaria, 17 April, 2009.

Del Vecchio Capotosti, A. 2008. *In Maiore Stat Minus*: a note on the EEZ and the zones of ecological protection in the Mediterranean Sea. *Ocean Development and International Law*, 39(3), 287-297.

DiMento, J F.C. and Hickman, A.J. 2012. *Environmental Governance of the Great Seas – Law and Effect*. New Horizons in Environmental and Energy Law. Cheltenham/Northampton, MA: Edward Elgar Publishing.

Gavouneli, M. 2008. Mediterranean challenges: between old problems and new solutions. *The International Journal of Marine and Coastal Law*, 23(3), 477-497.

Grimeaud, D. 2001. Reforming EU Water Law: towards sustainability? Part 1, 2 and 3, *European Environmental Law Review*, 10 (issue 2, 41-51, issue 3, 88-97, and issue 4, 125-135).

HELCOM 32/2011, Communiqué of the high-level segment of the 32nd meeting, Doc 2/1/Rev.2, 8.3.2011.

Hey, E. 2009. Multi-dimensional public governance arrangements for the protection of the transboundary aquatic environment in the European Union: the changing interplay between European and Public International Law. *International Organizations Law Review*, 6, 191-223.

Jans, J.H., Squintani, L., Aragão, A., Macrory R. and Wegener, B.W. 2009. 'Gold plating' of European Environmental Measures? *Journal for European Environmental & Planning Law*, 6(4), 417-435.

Jans, J.H., and Vedder, H.H.B. 2012. *European Environmental Law after Lisbon*. Fourth edition. Groningen: Europa Law Publishing.

Josefsson, H., and Baaner, L. 2011. The Water Framework Directive – A Directive for the Twenty-first century? *Journal of Environmental Law*, 23(3), 463-486.

Keessen, A., van Kempen, J., van Rijswick, M., Robbe, J. and Backes, C. 2010. European River Basin Districts: are they swimming in the same implementation pool? *Journal of Environmental Law*, 22(2), 197-221.

Lee, M. 2009. Law and governance of water protection policy, in *Environmental Protection: European Law and Governance*, edited by J. Scott. Oxford: Oxford University Press, 27-55.

Markus, T., Schlacke, S. and Maier, N. 2011. Legal implementation of integrated ocean policies: the EU's Marine Strategy Directive. *The International Journal of Marine and Coastal Law*, 26(1), 59-90.

Vinogradov, S. 2007. Marine pollution via transboundary watercourses – an interface of the 'Shoreline' and 'River-Basin' regimes in the wider Black Sea region. *The International Journal of Marine and Coastal Law*, 22(4), 585-620.

List of Conventions and EU Legal Acts

International Conventions

Convention on Cooperation for the Protection and Sustainable use of the Danube River, Sofia, 29 June 1994 (Danube Convention).
Convention for the Protection of the Marine Environment of the North-East Atlantic, Paris, 22 September 1992 (OSPAR Convention).
Convention Biological Diversity, Rio de Janeiro, 5 June 1992 (CBD).
Convention on the Protection of the Black Sea against Pollution, Bucharest, 21 April 1992 (Bucharest Convention).
Convention on the Protection of the Marine Environment of the Baltic Sea Area, Helsinki, 9 April 1992 (Helsinki Convention).
United Nations Convention on the Law of the Sea, Montego Bay, 10 December 1982 (UNCLOS).
Convention for the protection of the Mediterranean Sea against Pollution, Barcelona, 16 February 1976 (Barcelona Convention).
Convention for the Prevention of Marine Pollution from Land-Based Sources, Paris, 4 June 1974 (Paris Convention).
Convention on the Prevention of Marine Pollution by Dumping of Waste and Other Matter, London, 13 November 1972, with its 1996 protocol (London Convention and London Protocol).
Convention for the Prevention of Marine Pollution by Dumping from Ships and Aircraft, Oslo, 15 February 1972 (Oslo Convention).

EU Legal Acts

Treaty on European Union (Consolidated version), [2010] OJ C 83/13.
Treaty on the Functioning of the European Union (Consolidated version), [2010] OJ C 83/47.
Directive 2008/56/EC of the European Parliament and of the Council of 17 June 2008 establishing a framework for community action in the field of marine environmental policy (Marine Strategy Framework Directive), [2008] OJ L 164/19.
Regulation (EC) No 1907/2006 of the European Parliament and of the Council of 18 December 2006 concerning the Registration, Evaluation, Authorization and Restriction of Chemicals (REACH), establishing a European Chemicals Agency, amending Directive 1999/45/EC and repealing Council Regulation (EEC) No 793/93 and Commission Regulation (EC) No 1488/94 as well as Council Directive 76/769/EEC and Commission Directives 91/155/EEC, 93/67/EEC, 93/105/EC and 2000/21/EC, [2006] OJ L 396/1.
Directive 2005/35/EC of the European Parliament and of the Council of 7 September 2005 on ship-source pollution and on the introduction of penalties for infringements, [2005] OJ L 255/11.

Directive 2000/60/EC of the European Parliament and of the Council of 23 October 2000 establishing a framework for Community action in the field of water policy, [2000] OJ L327/1

Chapter 5

The Ecosystem Management Approach: Implications for Marine Governance

Monica Hammer

Introduction

Large marine ecosystems, including the four regional seas in Europe, provide an array of ecosystem services important to human well-being, such as fish production, nutrient cycling and recreation (Daily 1997, MA 2005). However, the effective functioning of marine ecosystems required to sustain these services is challenged by a range of human activities resulting in a complex mix of effects on the ecosystem (Costanza et al. 1998, Duda and Sherman 2002). To meet these challenges, natural resource management of marine ecosystems has changed considerably throughout the twentieth century. The oceans and seas were long considered to be vast and inexhaustible frontiers (Regier and Baskerville 1984, Hanna 1997). However, the post-war development with the intensive use of natural resources resulting in overexploitation and degradation of marine systems altered this view. For example, dramatic decline in some marine species as a result of over fishing provide striking examples of failed management, which partly result from a lack of knowledge, but also from inadequate governance institutions (Hammer et al. 1993, Pauly et al. 1998).

In the latest decades, new perspectives in ecological science, such as the recognition of the importance of periodic natural disturbances in ecosystems, along with changing social and economic conditions has altered governance perspectives. The traditional 'command-and-control' management approaches aim primarily for technical-economic organization and rely on good knowledge of the system and a high probability of regulating its behaviour (Holling and Meffe 1996). However, these approaches are not tailored to cope with the processes and dynamics of complex marine social-ecological systems (Scheffer et al. 2001, Folke et al. 2004).

At least three main reasons can be identified for the failure of traditional management: a focus on individual sectors or objectives, mismatches of administrative and ecological scales and boundaries, and overlooking the significance of ecosystem services and their life-supporting ecosystems in decision-making. The scope of what constitutes an environmental problem has broadened from a relatively narrow framing of management problems to ecosystem-based, multi-dimensional approaches which include ecological as well as social and economic dimensions. An illustrative example of this development is the Helsinki Commission Joint Action Plan (JCP) from 1992 and the recent HELCOM Baltic Sea Action Plan (BSAP) from 2007. While the key part of the first Helsinki Action plan in 1992 was a list of hot spots, typically consisting of pollution point sources, the Baltic Sea Action Plan formulated fifteen years later instead focuses on sustainability and an ecosystem approach to management, involving stakeholders and adaptive management (Hassler et al. 2011). Hence, ecosystem management has slowly evolved by integrating an increasing understanding of the dynamics of ecosystems, including the role of humans, as well as changing societal priorities. Ecosystem management approaches can be seen as a bridging concept linking human and ecological systems, where the combination of ecological understanding and knowledge of human systems provide a common governance framework for the integrated social-ecological system (Berkes et al. 2003, Walker et al. 2004, Chapin III et al. 2010).

The scientific base for an ecosystem approach to management is now strong enough to be widely accepted in polices for governing marine systems (CBD 1998, Garcia et al. 2003, Rice 2005, Backer et al. 2010, Österblom et al. 2010). Rationales for ecosystem management include the need to jointly address complex environmental problems, risks, and uncertainty in marine systems such as fish stock depletion, hazards emanating from mixtures of different chemicals and the long-term effects of nutrient overload. It provides a framework to address interdependencies between a targeted natural resource, the ecosystems providing the resource, and the trade-offs made by a complex human society. For example, the EU Marine Strategy Framework Directive (MSFD) aims to minimize pollution and protect marine life, while at the same time recognizing that society's use of the natural resources provided by the marine system must be sustainable. Effective management decisions to deliver these disparate objectives requires an integrated systems analysis that could be facilitated by an ecosystem approach to management as described in the MSFD marine strategies (EU 2008).

Ecosystem management approaches are now also featured in a number of other marine policy and legal documents in the EU and elsewhere (European Commission 2002, CBD 1998, 2004, EU 2008, HELCOM 2008). However, the MSFD does not define the concept and there can be different views of what ecosystem management encompasses and how it should be made operational.

Hence, there are still challenges regarding how ecosystem management should be interpreted and implemented in practice. In this chapter, based on a review of selected scientific literature and policy documents, I present an overview of ecosystem management perspectives and analyse how ecosystem management of marine systems is understood. Further, I examine and exemplify how ecosystem management plays out in European marine governance and discuss the main future challenges for implementation and development of this approach.

What is Ecosystem Management of Marine Systems?

Since the early 1990s, many definitions of ecosystem management, ecosystem-based management, or the ecosystem approach, both marine (e.g. Pikitch et al. 2004) and generic (Christensen et al. 1996, CBD 1998, 2004), have emerged. The definitions vary in their focus and comprehensiveness (Arkema et al. 2006, Meffe et al. 2002, Pitcher et al. 2008, Curtin and Prellezo 2010). For example, a narrow definition of the concept focuses on the effects of fishing on non-target species or other food web related issues (Pickitch et al. 2004). A broader view of ecosystem management includes both sustainability of natural resources, the recognition that these resources depend on a functioning ecosystem and the interdependencies with human society. For example, the UN Convention on Biodiversity (CBD) has adopted the ecosystem approach as the main framework for conserving biodiversity. The ecosystem approach in CBD is defined as, 'a strategy for integrated management of land, water, and living resources that promotes conservation and sustainable use in an equitable way', whilst also emphasizing the economic and social aspects of the human system (CBD 2004).

A set of twelve principles, the Malawi principles, has been developed to further define the ecosystem approach according to CBD (CBD 1998: Table 5.1). These principles stress a management focus on functional relationships and processes in ecosystems, where benefit sharing should be enhanced, in particular among stakeholders. Adaptive management practices, including flexibility and learning are called for as change and uncertainties are inherent in social-ecological systems. The CBD guidelines also underline that ecosystem management needs to recognize the diversity of social and cultural factors affecting natural resource use. Further, management actions should be carried out at the scale appropriate to the issue at hand: including increased inter-sectoral communication and cooperation at a range of levels with decentralization to the lowest appropriate level. Stakeholder involvement, adaptive management and decentralization, when necessary, are key to the successful and sustainable management of social-ecological systems in this framework (CBD 1998, 2004). In systems such as the EU regional seas, where there are multi-level management arrangements as well as significant interdependences between resource users, joint management approaches involving stakeholders in some form of collaborative management is called for in the MSDF, the WFD, as well as HELCOM and OSPAR (Pinkerton 2009, Wilson et al. 2003, Hammer et al. 2011).

The concept, ecosystem approach, as used by CBD has been taken up by, inter alia, the Regional Seas Conventions, OSPAR, for the North East Atlantic and HELCOM for the Baltic Sea. The EU Marine Strategy Framework Directive uses the term ecosystem based approach and under the EU Common Fisheries Policy (CFP) both the terms ecosystem approach and ecosystem-based approach are used and seemingly inter-changeable (European Commission, 2009, 2011). Further, Arkema et al. (2006), reviewed the terminology used in 18 selected definitions of ecosystem management and evaluated the overlap and differences in how the

Table 5.1 The Malawi principles for the ecosystem approach in the UN Convention on biodiversity (CBD, 1998, 2004)

1. The objectives of management of land, water and living resources are a matter of societal choices.
2. Management should be decentralized to the lowest appropriate level.
3. Ecosystem managers should consider the effects (actual or potential) of their activities on adjacent and other ecosystems.
4. Recognizing gains from management, there is usually a need to understand and manage the ecosystem in an economic context. Any such ecosystem management programme should:
   a. Reduce those market distortions that adversely affect biological diversity;
   b. Align incentives to promote biodiversity conservation and sustainable use;
   c. Internalize costs and benefits in the given ecosystem to the extent feasible.
5. Conservation of ecosystem structure and functioning, in order to maintain ecosystem services, should be a priority target of the ecosystem approach.
6. Ecosystems must be managed within the limits of their functioning.
7. The ecosystem approach should be undertaken at the appropriate spatial and temporal scales.
8. Recognizing the varying temporal scales and lag-effects that characterize ecosystem processes, objectives for ecosystem management should be set for the long term.
9. Management must recognize that change is inevitable.
10. The ecosystem approach should seek the appropriate balance between, and integration of, conservation and use of biological diversity.
11. The ecosystem approach should consider all forms of relevant information, including scientific and indigenous and local knowledge, innovations and practices.
12. The ecosystem approach should involve all relevant sectors of society and scientific disciplines.

concepts ecosystem management, ecosystem-based management and ecosystem-based fisheries management were defined and found no principle differences regarding how the terms were used.

The ecosystem approach does not preclude other management approaches, such as the conservation of biosphere reserves or integrated coastal management, but could rather integrate them to deal with complex situations and trade-offs on a local, regional or global scale. A concept used in relation to ecosystem management literature is 'integrated management' (Garcia et al. 2003, de la Mare 2005). The ecosystem management and integrated management concepts can be seen as complementary in that they share many similar principles even though they have different emphases. Integrated management has typically focused on accommodating multiple sector activities to sustainably develop coastal and ocean areas. Ecosystem management, on the other hand, has its focus on the maintenance of ecosystem services and functions in complex marine ecosystems.

Marine Ecosystems as Complex Adaptive Systems

Ecosystem management ideas have a strong foundation in ecological research, and have been discussed since at least the early 1950s (Jansson 1972, Grumbine 1994, Elmgren 2001). From an ecological perspective, ecosystem management as a systems approach takes into account the full array of organisms and processes that characterize and comprise the ecosystem. It treats a target resource, such as a commercial fish species as an inseparable component of a complex network of processes and functions at different spatial and temporal scales (Christensen et al. 2003, Dale et al. 2003). It focuses on the capacity of ecosystems to sustain the delivery of natural resources and ecosystem services for human well-being and the capacity of society to cope with, adapt to and shape change (Holling 1973, Folke 2006).

In particular, the development of systems ecology and the theory of ecosystems as complex adaptive systems with inherent uncertainty and possibilities of threshold effects and multiple equilibrium states have been important (Holling 1973, Levin 1998, Levin and Lubchenco 2008). The understanding of how to address resilience, referring to the capacity of a system to absorb disturbance and reorganize while undergoing change, does then become key to sustainable governance (Gunderson and Holling 2002, Walker et al. 2004). The external conditions of particular ecosystems (e.g. climate, inputs of nutrients or toxic substances, harvesting of fish and shellfish and habitat fragmentation) often change gradually over time and decrease system buffer capacity or resilience (Scheffer et al. 2001, Folke et al. 2004). As a result of such gradual long-term loss of resilience, ecosystems may shift abruptly to alternative states. In the Central Baltic Sea for example, an ecological regime shift was considered to have taken place in the late 1980s. Overfishing, eutrophication and climate change diminished the cod fish stocks leading to a change in ecosystem structure from a cod to a sprat dominated food web in the Central Baltic Sea which resulted in decreasing cod fish catches (Möllmann et al. 2009, Österblom et al. 2010). Hence, ecosystem management for large marine ecosystems requires a consideration of the food web and how this in turn affects ecosystem functioning, as well as the role of human activities.

In large marine ecosystems such as the regional seas in Europe, a number of environmental problems and risks involving uncertainty and ecological complexity can be identified such as the complex pattern connected to fisheries as exemplified above, even though the character of the individual problems varies substantially (see e.g. Gilek et al. 2011). Eutrophication, risks of chemical pollution and overfishing can be found in all European regional seas. Uncertainty exists in all these problems to various degrees and implies that future consequences cannot be fully predicted. In such cases, adaptive and flexible management practices are needed. Adaptive management is an approach designed to address inherent uncertainties in a system's response to different management changes. It emphasizes management as a process of learning through monitoring the response from the ecosystem of a particular human action (Holling 1978, Folke et al. 2005). Adaptive governance in turn describes the governance process whereby feedbacks are addressed through collaboration and cooperation between different levels of government, non-governmental actors and individuals. In particular, adaptive governance is a process of resolving trade-offs and identifying a vision and direction forward (Boyle et al. 2001, Folke et al. 2005).

Marine ecosystems simultaneously produce a number of different ecosystem services that interrelate in various ways. A key challenge in ecosystem management is determining how to manage multiple ecosystem services and trade-offs between different management priorities across sectors (Bennett et al. 2009, Raudsepp-Hearne et al. 2010). For example, Atlantic salmon (*Salmo salar*) spawn in several rivers tributary to the Baltic Sea and are composed of numerous, genetically distinct local populations. The salmon migrate hundreds of kilometres in the Baltic Sea, during which time both offshore, coastal commercial as well as recreational fisheries exploit them. During the 20th century, most of the wild salmon populations in the Baltic Sea disappeared and the remaining ones were greatly depleted. This was mainly a result of over fishing and freshwater habitat degradation, in particular as a result of hydropower development limiting the salmon migration up the rivers to their spawning areas (Karlsson and Karlström 1994). In addition, high dioxin levels in salmon, has resulted in national dietary advisories for human consumption of Baltic salmon in several coastal countries (ICES 2006). Also, the trade-off between the interests of salmon fisheries and conservation policies directed towards Baltic seal populations has led to an increase in the seal population, which, in turn, has increased predation on coastal fish including salmon (Lunneryd et al. 2004). Wild salmon in the Baltic Sea contribute to a range of ecosystem services but are also affected by a number of different factors. Some of these are directly related to salmon fisheries, but also to other land-based human activities or changes in the supporting ecosystem affecting the fish stocks (which are more or less anticipated by managers) (Hammer 2009). Hence, in order to manage marine ecosystems services, their interrelations and the linkages between terrestrial and aquatic ecosystems in the drainage basins needs to be considered. This is apparent in, for example, the EU Water Framework Directive that adopts a drainage basin perspective to water management (European Commission 2000).

In summary, key aspects of ecosystem management relevant to the governance of marine ecosystems in Europe would include: a broader system-wide perspective, integrating ecological and human systems and boundaries, emphasis on the functioning of ecological systems, acknowledgement of uncertainties and risks in complex systems, integration across various spatial and temporal scales, and adaptive, flexible management processes and decision-making.

Institutional Frameworks for Ecosystem Management

The ecosystem approach puts new demands on management institutions at local, national and regional levels in Europe. These challenges consist of moving from governance based on geopolitical boundaries to governance based on ecosystem boundaries, which necessitates coordination, and multi-level collaboration across states and sectors, increased stakeholder participation and a capacity for adaptive co-management (Olsson et al. 2004, Nilsson and Langaas 2006, Hammer et al. 2011).

Over the last three decades, a number of steps consistent with moving towards a broader ecosystem approach in governance of marine resources can be identified in various policy frameworks and legal agreements as exemplified in Table 5.2.

Recent international legislation at the EU level, in particular the EU Marine Strategy Framework Directive (MSFD) (European Parliament, 2008) and the EU Water Framework Directive (WFD) (European Parliament, 2000) are important regulating factors in developing sustainable ecosystem governance of marine systems at the regional level. Prior to the MSFD and the WFD, legislation tended to focus primarily on a single activity or issue and national environmental policies dominated. Currently, there is a transformation towards the dominance of cross-border cooperation and transnational networking reinforced by the recent enlargement of the EU (Kern and Löffelsend 2004).

The MSFD is the first piece of legislation applied across Europe's regional seas that requires assessment of the range of issues that should encompass overall marine environmental sustainability (Breen et al., 2012). The Marine Strategy Framework Directive aims to achieve a 'good environmental status' in the marine environment by 2020. In the MSFD, in addition to ecosystems, the concept marine region is used, defined as 'taking into account hydrological, oceanographic and biogeographic features' (MSFD 2008/56/EC, art 3(2)).

Table 5.2 Steps towards the development of ecosystem management approach

Year		
1982	The UN Law of the Sea Convention	Framework that requires coastal states to take into account effects on associated or dependent species in the marine ecosystem.
1992	The UN Rio Declaration and Agenda 21	Emphasizes multi-species management in marine systems.
1992	The Helsinki Convention, Baltic Sea	9 coastal countries, EU. Protection of the Marine Environment.
1992	The OSPAR Convention, North East Atlantic	15 countries. Protection of the marine environment.
1992	The Bucharest Convention	6 countries. Protection of the Black Sea against pollution.
1995	The Barcelona Convention	22 countries. Protection of the Marine Environment and the Coastal Region of the Mediterranean. Action plan adopted (MAP II).
1995	FAO Code of Conduct for Responsible Fisheries, UN Fish Stocks Agreement	Requires conserving, protecting and safeguarding ecosystems, calls for implementing an ecosystem approach.
1998	UN Convention on Biodiversity (CBD)	Issues the Malawi principles for the ecosystem approach.
2000	EU Water Framework Directive	Europe's waters should be managed according to ecological boundaries, good ecological water status by 2015.
2002	The Johannesburg Plan of Implementation, World Summit on Sustainable Development	Calls for an application of the ecosystem approach to management by 2010.
2003	Joint Ministerial Meeting of OSPAR and HELCOM 'The Bremen Statement'	Defines the ecosystem approach and sets detailed plans for HELCOM and OSPAR to implement the ecosystem approach.
2007	HELCOM Baltic Sea Action Plan	Restore the Baltic Sea's environmental status by 2021, ecosystem approach framework.
2008	EU Marine Strategy Framework Directive	Good environmental status for Europe's marine waters by 2021.
2008	Barcelona Convention	Adopted the ecosystem approach for the Mediterranean Sea.
2010	OSPAR The NEA Environment Strategy	OSPAR Integrated assessment.
2010	HELCOM	HELCOM, Initial holistic assessment.

In Europe, there are also four cooperation structures originally dating back to the 1970s that underpin the Regional Seas Conventions (RSC). They include the OSPAR convention for the North-East Atlantic, the Helsinki Convention for the Baltic Sea, the Barcelona Convention for the Mediterranean Sea and the Bucharest Convention for the Black Sea. In the regional seas in Europe, ecosystem services and the ecosystems they depend on are shared by a number of coastal nations. In order to operationalize the MSFD, the member states are required to coordinate at the regional level, using the existing Regional Seas Conventions. The Member States must cooperate closely on developing marine strategies both in the preparatory assessment stage that determines targets and indicators (by 2012), in the monitoring programme and soon (2015-16) the Programme of Measures (PoM) in the identified marine regions. However, there is no single governance structure for any of Europe's regional seas.

Also, a healthy marine ecosystem is to a large part dependent on what happens in the drainage basin. The Baltic Sea, with a drainage basin four times the size of the sea itself, is a large heterogeneous socio-economic region. 14 countries, of which nine are coastal states and ten are EU members, share the Baltic Sea.

The EU Water Framework Directive (WFD), adopted in 2000, provides a common framework for water policy. For the first time land-use planning is linked to water resources in all member states and new administrative boundaries have been introduced based on the larger river basin districts (RBD). The WFD aims for more integration in water management and encompasses different water resources, such as surface waters, groundwater, estuaries and adjacent coastal waters to 1 nautical mile from the coast. Hence, the possibilities for achieving environmental objectives in the regional seas, such as no eutrophication, are largely dependent on altered activities on land within the framework of the WFD (see e.g. Wulff et al. 2007).

River basins often extend across national borders requiring international cooperation in these RBDs, also with states outside the EU. According to Nilsson and Langaas (2006) 33% of the RBDs are international and cover ca. 70% of the total district area. Since both the WFD and the MSFD are framework directives, they are further shaped by the national legislation developed for their implementation. The transnational governance cooperation requirements are, however, significant. The regional seas and the RBDs necessitate the further development of links between the Directive frameworks, the regional level and the national implementation processes. The main disparity in the EU governance framework is the allocation of competencies. Certain issues are the competence of the EU while others are the competence of the Member States and some are joint competence. The MSFD is an EU Directive adopted under EU competence, but many of the specifics of implementation are the competence of Member States. The way in which coordination should take place to ensure an effective system of multi-level governance to implement the directives is uncertain. This leads to institutional ambiguity, which is perhaps most noticeable in the Mediterranean Sea with its large number of bordering (and non EU) states (Van Leeuwen et al. 2012).

Further, in complex social-ecological systems such as regional seas, risks and uncertainties are inherent and there is a need to build a capacity for adapting to change, and to frame and handle risks. The regional seas can be characterized as common-pool resources often at risk, where different priorities and conditions make sustainable governance more complex (Ostrom et al. 2002, Dietz et al. 2003). Systemic risks, in contrast to traditional risks, require particular attention. Systemic risks are characterized by a high degree of complexity and uncertainty and are usually not confined to a single sector or nation state – this necessitates more holistic, reflexive and adaptive approaches (Olsson et al. 2004, Voss et al. 2006, Renn et al. 2011).

Systemic risks also often cause ambiguity, i.e. there are different legitimate views on how to evaluate the risk at hand. For example, oil discharges can be seen as a quite simple environmental risk in terms of the range of causes and sources. Eutrophication on the other hand combines complex changes in the ecosystem, involving an array of nutrient sources (e.g. agriculture, municipal and industrial waste water), with high scientific uncertainty in terms of long-term ecosystem outcomes. Still, despite large differences between various types of environmental problems and risks examined in the Baltic Sea, assessment and management interactions were found to apply a rather traditional view of risks, one assuming low uncertainty (Gilek et al. 2011).

A major issue in sustainable ecosystem management is how to handle trade-offs between bundles of ecosystem services. Differences among stakeholders may lead to considerable controversy and differences of priorities. In such cases participatory management involving stakeholders is recommended, in line with ecosystem management (Klinke and Renn 2002). The WFD, for example, emphasizes an integrated, iterative process with co-governance between different stakeholders and the responsible water management authority within the different river basin districts (European Parliament 2000). Member states are obliged to make information outlined in the river basin management plans available to the public, and to organize public consultation, while active involvement should be encouraged. In ecosystem management, a wider range of knowledge sources including local knowledge is important to manage ecosystem functions and respond to feedback signals from the ecosystems in an adaptive way. For example, suggested mitigation measures for reducing nutrient discharges into the Baltic Sea require trade-offs and decisions to be made among multiple actors. A suitable location for the creation of a wetland might mean loss of land for agricultural production—an issue that requires detailed local ecological knowledge, but one that can also lead to considerable conflict among local actors.

Further, the implementation of the WFD in, for example, Sweden, implies that some of the water issues are moved up to a regional RBD level. While the RBD aims for water governance with a better spatial fit between administrative and ecological boundaries, the cross-scale interactions and linkages are still unclear.

Challenges for the Practical Implementation of Ecosystem Management in Marine Systems

The utility of ecosystem management approaches ultimately depends on whether they actually inform and influence practical management decisions and actions. A number of frameworks for implementing ecosystem management have been developed in recent years to include empirically based insights to strategies that make transitions to such a form of management possible, whilst highlighting challenges (see e.g. Rosenberg and McLeod 2005, Murawski 2007, Levin et al. 2009, Tallis et al. 2010). Cury et al. (2005), for example, identified three main problems with implementation of an ecosystem approach to fisheries. First, to define proper long-term ecosystem related objectives; second, to define meaningful indicators and reference values for desirable and undesirable states; and finally to develop proper data collection, analytical tools, and models. Further, Arkema et al. (2006) found that management objectives and interventions in ecosystem management often tend to miss critical ecological and human factors emphasized in the scientific literature. Although ecosystem management represents a multidisciplinary approach to resource management, single objectives often miss connectivity between ecological concepts and the human dimension. For example, Österblom et al. (2011) analysed existing incentives in European fisheries and their role in stabilizing governance systems in sustainable or unsustainable trajectories. In European fisheries overcapacity of the fishing fleet, aggravated by subsidies, has resulted in pressure for short-term decision-making, which has, in turn, led to continued overcapacity and unsustainable fishing quotas. High biological uncertainty has contributed to the low status of the science meant to inform management (Wilson 2009, Österblom 2011). A governance system not tailored to address this uncertainty, combined with low transparency and resulting lack of legitimacy of decisions, may also contribute to reducing the incentives for compliance. In comparison, Österblom et al. (2011) found a different social-ecological feedback structure in the Norwegian and North American fisheries, where the decision-structure had a stronger focus on ecological sustainability and an emphasis on reducing subsidies and overcapacity. Improved scientific legitimacy also created a strong argument for a decision-making process focusing on ecological sustainability.

The ecosystem approach is relatively knowledge intensive and requires an understanding of the panarchy of an ecosystem's structure and function, as well as the dynamics of ecosystem services and their driving forces in the integrated social-ecological system. Implementation of the EU Water Framework Directive by Member States entails routine data collection covering various information needs including the collection of comprehensive data covering the characteristics and state of water bodies, the various pressures caused by human activities and the resulting impacts as well as governance aspects such as public participation activities. In a case study on Sweden, Hammer et al. (2011) identified a number of challenges with respect to information and public participation including: problems in classifying the status of water bodies; a need to improve and co-ordinate monitoring within River Basin Districts; and the development of means to tackle and control diffuse sources of pollutants.

Ecosystem management as an integrated approach considers entire ecosystems including humans. However, management has relied on a number of different assessment and management techniques (such as total allowable catch quota systems in fisheries) that needs to be reconciled within an ecosystem approach to management. Hence, integrated assessments directed at ecosystem functioning and feedbacks between human uses and ecosystems are needed. Frameworks for aiding the ecosystem management process by integrated ecosystem assessment have been developed recently (see e.g. Curtin and Prellezo 2010). Levin et al. (2009), for example, use a case study from the Puget Sound to spell out a five-step process to inform management decisions in marine ecosystem management across sectors and at multiple scales: scooping, developing indicators, risk analysis, management strategy and ecosystem assessment. The MSFD requires a comprehensive set of indicators and related objectives to measure progress towards a good environmental status. The OSPAR Convention for the North-East Atlantic, applying the ecosystem approach, has worked towards an integrated assessment of ecosystem health. As early as 1992, the OSPAR Joint Assessment and Monitoring Program (JAMP) addressed the issue of how to assess ecosystem health and human impact. In collaboration with ICES, Ecological Quality Objectives (EcoQOs) have been developed for an integrated assessment and to provide a link between human activities and the impacts of biodiversity (Heslenfeld and Enserink 2008, OSPAR 2010). This process was initiated as a learning-by-doing activity that was relatively non-committal for the Member States, but has recently turned into a potentially legally binding set of objectives with the adoption of the MSFD in 2008.

A central challenge in practical ecosystem management is developing useful and straightforward approaches for balancing a range of, sometimes conflicting, human uses of ecosystems. Implementing the Marine Strategy Directive in EU Member States with extensive maritime domains, such as Spain demands a significant effort. Marine spatial planning (MSP) as a tool to allocate space to a range of ecosystem services provided by marine ecosystems is developing as a means to implement the EU Marine Strategy Directive. In Europe, MSP is promoted by the EU Integrated Maritime Policy (European Commission, 2007, 2008). MSP can, for example, provide an opportunity for comprehensive goal-setting and may resolve potential human use conflicts in a proactive and future oriented way. Further potential benefits from MSP as identified by Gilliland and Laffoley (2008) include more efficient use of available marine space and resources. However, the success of marine spatial planning relies to a large extent on its ability to achieve integration of activities and sectors (Ehler and Douvere 2009). A critical step in an MSP process is defining the scale and scope (Portman, 2011).

Conclusions

Even though many governance and scientific challenges to practical implementation of ecosystem management in marine systems are yet to be resolved, the present policy framework within the EU is promoting a shift towards a more comprehensive ecosystem management of marine systems. This acknowledges the interconnections within ecosystems as well as links between ecosystems and humans. A challenge to the implementation of EU Directives such as the MSFD and the WFD (one experienced in other externally initiated programmes that often involve top-down structures) is that they are too rigid in structure and allow local actors such as farmers or fishermen less scope to adapt the systems to meet their needs. Even so, top-down enabling EU legislation can help to stimulate innovation and re-organize governance structures at the drainage basin level to the regional seas, as well as in their catchments as a whole. Further, an emphasis on stakeholder participation could encourage bottom-up, pilot initiatives from local to regional levels that can lead to a diffusion of innovation critical for a transition to ecosystem management.

References

Arkema, K.K., Abramson, S.C. and Dewabury, M. 2006. Marine ecosystem-based management: from characterization to implementation. *Frontiers in Ecology and the Environment*, 4, 525-532.

Bennett, E.M., Peterson, G.D. and Gordon, L. 2009. Understanding relationships among multiple ecosystem services. *Ecology Letters*, 12, 1394-1404.

Berkes, F., Colding, J. and Folke, C. (eds) 2003. *Navigating Social-Ecological Systems: Building Resilience for Complexity and Change*. Cambridge: Cambridge University Press.

Boyle, M., Kay, J. and Pond, B. 2001. Monitoring in support of policy: an adaptive ecosystem approach, in *Encyclopedia of Global Environmental Change, Volume 4*, edited by T. Munn. London: Wiley, 116-137.

Breen, P., Robinson, L.A., Rogers, S.I., Knights, A.M., Piet, G., Churilova, T., Margonski, P., Papadopoulou, N., Akoglu, E., Eriksson, A., Finenko, Z., Fleming-Lehtinen, V., Galil, B., Goodsir, F., Goren, M., Kryvenko, O., Leppanen, J.M., Markantonatou, V., Moncheva, S., Oguz, T., Paltriguera, L., Stefanova, K., Timofte, F. and Thomsen, F. 2012. An environmental assessment of risk in achieving good environmental status to support regional prioritisation of management in Europe. *Marine Policy*, 36, 1033-1043.

Chapin III, F.S., Kofinas, G.P. and Folke, C. (eds) 2009. *Principles of Ecosystem Stewardship: Resilience-Based Natural Resource Management in a Changing World*. New York: Springer-Verlag, 241-258.

Costanza, R., Andrade, F., Antunes, P., den Belt, M., Boersma, D., Boesch, D.F., Catarino, F., Hanna S., Limburg, K., Low, B., Molitor, M., Pereira,

J.G., Rayner, S., Santos, R., Wilson, J. and Young, M. 1998. Principles for sustainable governance of the oceans. *Science*, 281, 198-199.

Christensen, N.L., Bartuska, A.M., Brown, J.H., Carpenter, S., d'Antonio, C., Francis, R., Franklin, J.F., MacMahon, J.A., Noss, R.F., Parsons, D.J., Peterson, C.H., Turner, M.G. and Woodmansee, R.G. 2003. The report of the Ecological Society of America on the scientific basis for ecosystem management. *Ecological Applications*, 6, 665-691.

Convention on Biodiversity (CBD). 1998. Report of the workshop on the Ecosystem Approach. Lilongwe, Malawi. 26-28 January, 1998. UNEP/COP/4/Inf.9.

Convention on Biodiversity (CBD). 2004. The ecosystem approach. Secretariat of the Convention on Biodiversity. Montreal. Canada.

Cury, P.M., Mullon, C., Garcia, S.M. and Shannon, L.J. 2005. Viability theory for an ecosystem approach to fisheries. *ICES Journal of Marine Science*, 62, 577-584.

Curtin, R. and Prellezo, R. 2010. Understanding marine ecosystem-based management: A literature review. *Marine Policy*, 34, 821-830.

Daily, G. (ed.). 1997. *Nature's Services: Societal Dependence on Natural Ecosystems*. Washington, DC: Island Press.

Dale, V.H., Brown, S., Haeuber, R.A., Hobbs, N.T., Huntley, N., Naiman, R.J., Ribesame, W.E., Turner, M.G. and Valone, T.J. 2000. Ecological principles and guidelines for managing the use of land. *Ecological Applications*, 10, 639-670.

de la Mare, W.K. 2005. Marine ecosystem-based management as a hierarchical control system. *Marine Policy*, 29, 57-68.

Dietz, T., Ostrom, E. and Stern, P.C. 2003. The struggle to govern the commons. *Science*, 302, 1907-1912.

Duda, A.M. and Sherman, K. 2002. A new imperative for improving management of large marine ecosystems. *Ocean & Coastal Management*, 45, 797-833.

Ehler, C. and Douvere, F. 2009. *Marine Spatial Planning: A Step-by-step Approach Towards Ecosystem-based Management*. Paris: UNESCO.

Elmgren, R. 2001. Understanding human impact on the Baltic ecosystem: changing views in recent decades. *Ambio*, 30, 222-231.

European Parliament, Council 2000. *Directive 2000/60/EC* (Water Framework Directive).

European Parliament, Council 2008. *Directive 2008/56/EC* (Marine Strategy Framework Directive).

Folke, C., Carpenter, S., Walker, B., Scheffer, M., Elmqvist, T., Gunderson, L. et al. 2004. Regime shifts, resilience and biodiversity in ecosystem management. *Annual Review of Ecology, Evolution, and Systematics*, 35, 557-581.

Folke, C., Hahn, T., Olsson, P. and Norberg, J. 2005. Adaptive governance of social-ecological systems. *Annual Review of Environment and Resources*, 30, 441-473.

Folke, C. 2006. Resilience: the emergence of a perspective for social-ecological systems analyses. *Global Environmental Change*, 16, 253-267.

Garcia, S.M., Zerbi, A., Aliaume, C., Do Chi, T. and Lasserre, G. 2003. The ecosystem approach to fisheries. Issues, terminology, principles, institutional foundations, implementation and outlook. FAO Fisheries Technical Paper. No. 443. Rome, FAO.

Gilek, M., Lundberg, C., Renn, O., Wolowicz, M., Jönsson, A.M., Hassler, B., Boström, M., Karlsson, M., Hammer, M., Udovik, O., Södertström, S., Linke, S., Bonsdorff, E., Grönholm, S., Haahti, B.-M., Joas, M., Kern, K., Dreyer, M., Sellke, P., Zgrundo, A. and Lemke, P. 2011. Environmental risk governance of the Baltic Sea (RISKGOV). Riskgov Final report. Deliverable 12, RISKGOV project. Available online at http://www.sh.se/riskgov [accessed: 13 July 2014].

Gilliland, P.M. and Laffoley, D. 2008. Key elements and steps in the process of developing ecosystem-based marine spatial planning. *Marine Policy*, 32, 787-796.

Grumbine, R.E. 1994. What is ecosystem management? *Conservation Biology*, 8, 1-12.

Hammer, M., Jansson, AM. and Jansson, B-O. 1993. Diversity, change and sustainability – implications for fisheries. *Ambio*, 22, 97-105.

Hammer, M. 2009. Whose fish? Managing salmonidae and humans in complex social-ecological systems. – Examples from the Baltic Sea Region, in *Challenges for Diadromous Fishes in a Dynamic Global Environment*, edited by A.J. Haro, K.L. Smith, R.A. Rulifson, C.M. Moffitt, R.J. Klauda, M.J. Dadswell, R.A. Cunjak, J.E. Cooper, K.L. Beal and T.S. Avery. Symposium 69, Betsheda. Maryland, American Fisheries Society, 663-676.

Hammer, M., Balfors, B., Mörtberg, U., Petersson, M. and Quin, A. 2011. Governance of water resources in the phase of change: a case study of the implementation of the EU Water Framework Directive in Sweden. *Ambio*, 40, 210-220.

Hanna, S. 1997. The new frontier of American fisheries governance. *Ecological Economics*, 20, 221-233.

Hassler, B., Boström, M. and Grönholm, S. (2011). Environmental risk governance in the Baltic Sea – A comparison among five key areas. Deliverable 8, RISKGOV project. Available online at http://www.sh.se/riskgov [accessed: 13 July 2014].

HELCOM (Helsinki commission). 2008. Convention on the protection of the marine environment of the Baltic Sea area. Including the amendments to its Annexes adopted by the Helsinki Commission in 2000, 2001, 2003 and 2007. Helsinki Commission, Baltic Marine Environment Protection Commission.

Heslenfeld, P. and Enserink, E.L. 2008. OSPAR Ecological Quality Objectives: the utility of health indicators for the North Sea. *International Council for the Exploration of the Seas*, 65(8), 1392-1397.

Hilborn, R. 2007. Moving to sustainability by learning from successful fisheries. *Ambio*, 36, 296-303.

Holling, C.S. 1973. Resilience and stability of ecological systems. *Annual Review of Ecology and Systematics*, 4, 1-23.

Holling, C.S. (ed.) 1978. *Adaptive Environmental Assessment and Management*. London: Wiley.

Holling, C.S. and Meffe, G.K. 1996. Command and control and the pathology of resource management. *Conservation Biology*, 10, 328-337.

Holling, C.S. and Gunderson, L. (eds) 2002. Panarchy: understanding transformations in human and natural systems. Washington, DC: Island Press.

ICES. 2006. Report of the Baltic salmon and trout assessment working group (WGBAST), 28 March-6 April 2006. ICES Headquarters ICES CM 2006/ ACFM: 21. Copenhagen: The International Council for the Exploration of the Sea, 209 pp.

Jansson, B.O. 1972. The ecosystem approach to the Baltic Problem. *Bulletins* from the *Ecological Research Committee*, NFR 16, 1-82.

Karlsson, L. and Karlström, Ö. 1994. The Baltic salmon (*Salmo salar L.*): its history, present situation and future. *Dana*, 10, 61-85.

Kern, K. and Löffelsend, T. 2004. Governance beyond the nation-state: Transnationalization and Europeization of the Baltic Sea region. Discussion Paper SP IV 2004-105. Social Science Research Center, Berlin.

Klinke, A. and Renn, O. 2002. A new approach to risk evaluation and management: risk-based, precaution-based, and discourse-based management. *Risk Analysis*, 22, 1071-1094.

Levin, P.S., Fogarty, M.J., Murawski, S.A., Fluharty, D. 2009. Integrated ecosystem assessments: developing the scientific basis for ecosystem-based management of the ocean. *PLoS*, 7, 1-6.

Levin, S.A. 1998. Ecosystems and the biosphere as complex adaptive systems. *Ecosystems*, 1, 431-436.

Levin, S. and Lubchenco, J. 2008. Resilience, robustness, and marine ecosystem-based management. *Bioscience*, 58, 27-32.

Lunneryd, S., Königson, S. and Sjöberg, N. 2004. By-catch of seals, harbour porpoises and birds in Swedish commercial fisheries. *Finfo*, 8. (In Swedish with English summary.)

Meffe, G.K., Nielsen, L.A., Knight, R.L. and Schenborn, D.A., 2002. *Ecosystem Management: Adaptive Community-based Conservation*. Washington, DC: Island Press.

Millennium Ecosystem Assessment (MA). 2005. *Ecosystems and Human Well-being: Synthesis*. Washington, DC: Island Press.

Murawski, S.A. 2007. Ten myths concerning ecosystem approaches to marine resource management. *Marine Policy*, 31, 681-690.

Möllman, C., Diekmann, R., Müller-Karulis, B., Kornilovs, G., Plikshs, M. and Axe, P. 2009. Reorganization of a large marine ecosystem due to atmospheric and anthropogenic pressure: a discontinuous regime shift in the Central Baltic Sea. *Global Change Biology*, 15, 1377-1399.

Nilsson, S. and Langaas, S. 2006. International river basin management under the EU Water Framework Directive: An assessment of cooperation and water quality in the Baltic Sea Drainage Basin. *Ambio*, 35, 304-311.

Odum, E.P. 1969. The strategy of ecosystem development. *Science*, 164, 262-270.
Olsson, P., Folke, C. and Berkes, F. 2004. Adaptive co-management for building resilience in socio-ecological systems. *Environmental Management*, 34, 75-90.
OSPAR. 2010. OSPAR Quality Status Report. OSPAR Commission.
Ostrom, E., Dietz, T., Dolšak, N., Stern, P.C., Stonich, S. and Weber, E.U. (eds) 2002. *The Drama of the Commons*. Washington, DC: National Academy Press.
Österblom, H., Gårdmark, A., Bergström, L., Müller-Karulis, B., Folke, C., Lindegren, M., Casini, M., Olsson, P., Diekmann, R., Blencker, T., Humborg, C. and Möllman, C. 2010. Making the ecosystem approach operational – Can regime shifts in ecological and governance systems facilitate the transition? *Marine Policy*, 34, 1290-1299.
Österblom, H., Sissenwine, M., Symes, D., Kadin, M., Daw, T. and Folke, C. 2011. Incentives, social-ecological feedbacks and European fisheries. *Marine Policy*, 35, 568-574.
Ounanian, K., Delaney, A., Raakjaer, P. and Ramirez-Monsalve, P. 2012. On unequal footing: Stakeholder perspectives on the marine strategy framework directive as a mechanism of the ecosystem-based approach. *Marine Policy*, 36, 658-696.
Pauly, D., Christensen, V., Dalsgaard, J., Froese, R. and Torres Jr., F. 1998. Fishing down marine food webs. *Science*, 279, 860-863.
Pickitch, E., Santora, C., Babcock, E., Bonfil, R., Conover, D., et al. 2004. Ecosystem based fishery management. *Science*, 305, 346-347.
Pinkerton, E. 2009. Partnerships in Management, in *A Fishery Manager's Guidebook*, edited by K. Cochrane and S. Garcia. Second Edition. Oxford: FAO and Wiley-Blackwell, 283-300.
Pitcher, T.J., Kalikoski, D., Short, K., Varkey, D. and Pramod, G. 2009. An evaluation of progress in implementing ecosystem-based management of fisheries in 33 countries. *Marine Policy*, 33, 223-232.
Portman, M.E. 2011. Marine spatial planning: achieving and evaluating integration. *ICES Journal of Marine Science*, 68, 2191-2200.
Raudsepp-Hearne, C., Peterson, G.D. and Bennet, E.M. 2010. Ecosystem service bundles for analyzing tradeoffs in diverse landscapes. *PNAS*, 107, 5242-5247.
Regier, H.A. and Baskerville, G.L. 1984. Sustainable redevelopment of regional ecosystems degraded by exploitive development, in *Sustainable development of the biosphere*, edited by W. Clark and R. Munn. Cambridge: Cambridge University Press, 75-103.
Renn, O., Klinke, A. and van Asselt, M. 2011. Coping with complexity, uncertainty, and ambiguity in risk governance: a synthesis. *Ambio*, 40, 231-246.
Rosenberg, A.A. and McLeod, K.L. 2005. Implementing ecosystem-based approaches to management for the conservation of ecosystem services. *Marine Ecology Progress Series*, 300, 241-296.
Ruckelshaus, M., Klinger, T., Knowlton, N. and DeMaster, D.P. 2008. Marine ecosystem-based management in practice: scientific and governance challenges. *Bioscience*, 58, 53-63.

Scheffer, M., Carpenter, S., Foley, J.A., Folke, C. and Walker, B. 2001. Catastrophic shifts in ecosystems. *Nature*, 413, 591-596.

Tallis, H., Levin, P.S., Ruckelshaus, M., Lester, S.E., McLeod, K.L., Fluharty, D.L. and Halpern, B.S. 2010. The many faces of ecosystem-based management: making the process work today in real places. *Marine Policy*, 34, 340-348.

Van Leeuwen, J., Van Hoof, L. and Van Tatenhove, J. 2012. Institutional ambiguity in implementing the European Union Marine Strategy Framework Directive. *Marine Policy*, 36, 636-643.

Walker, B., Holling, C.S., Carpenter, S.R. and Kinzig, A. 2004. Resilience, adaptability and transformability in social-ecological systems. *Ecology and Society* [online] 9, 2, 5 URL: http/www.ecologyandsociety.org/vol9/iss2/art5 [accessed: 13 July 2014].

Wilson, D.C. (ed.) 2009. *The Paradoxes of Transparency: Science and the Ecosystem Approach to Fisheries Management in Europe*. MARE Publication series No 5. Amsterdam: Amsterdam University Press.

Voss, J.-P., Kemp, R. and Bauknecht, D. 2006. Reflexive governance: A view on an emerging path, in *Reflexive Governance for Sustainable Development*, edited by J-P. Voss, D. Bauknecht and R. Kemp. Cheltenham: Edward Elgar, 419-437.

Wulff, F., Savchuk, O., Sokolov, A., Humborg, C. and Mörth, C.M. 2007. Management options and effects on a marine ecosystem: Assessing the future of the Baltic. *Ambio*, 36, 243-249.

PART 2:
Marine Governance of the European Union

Chapter 6
The Marine Strategy Framework Directive as a Catalyst for Maritime Spatial Planning: Internal Dimensions and Institutional Tensions

Elizabeth De Santo

Introduction

Bordered by two oceans and four seas, and with a coastline stretching 70,000 kilometres, the European Union's (EU) marine regions play a pivotal role in its economy, contributing 40% of its GDP and population (European Commission 2007a). The increasing importance of the maritime environment in the EU's political economy is evident in the recent development of legislation aimed at harmonizing the economic uses and environmental health of European seas. With the 2007 launch of an Integrated Maritime Policy (IMP), the EU began moving towards Maritime Spatial Planning (MSP)[1] as a way forward for reconciling economic development and environmental management. The IMP is built on two pillars, economic and environmental. The Marine Strategy Framework Directive (MSFD), released in January 2008, comprises the environmental pillar and is the key piece of European legislation aimed at formalizing an ecosystem-based approach to marine environmental management in European marine waters, on both the national and regional levels. It requires Member States to achieve 'Good Environmental Status' (GES) in European seas by 2020, which will necessitate harmonizing their implementation of several pieces of EU legislation. Member States had until 15 July 2012 to determine targets and indicators for GES, and they were required to establish monitoring programs by July 2014 and programs of measures by 2015 (Van Leeuwen et al. 2012). The MSFD also requires Member States to manage human activities in marine areas in accordance with the ecosystem approach and ensure that 'the collective pressure of such activities is kept within levels compatible with the achievement of GES' (Article 1). Whilst not explicitly requiring MSP, the MSFD

1 A generally accepted international definition of MSP is 'a public process of analysing and allocating the spatial and temporal distribution of human activities in marine areas to achieve ecological, economic and social objectives' (Ehler and Douvere 2009). NB This chapter was written before the July 2014 release of the EU's MSP Directive.

does indicate that in developing their marine strategies, Member States should undertake spatial measures (Article 13(4)) and spatial and temporal distribution controls and management coordination measures, including management measures that influence when and where an activity is allowed to occur (Annex VI).

However, it is worth noting that the European approach to MSP is focused on 'maritime' rather than 'marine' spatial planning, a choice of terminology that emphasizes the human use and thus economic importance of the marine environment (De Santo 2010).[2] The EU has released two Communications on MSP (European Commission 2008, 2010a), but no firm guidelines on how Member States should utilize MSP to implement the MSFD. It is worth reflecting on whether it would be better for MSP to be driven by conservation and environmental lines through the MSFD, versus along a maritime and economic sector driven approach. A recent analysis of the implementation of the MSFD in Spain (de Vivero and Mateos 2012) argued that the MSFD's environmental goals are playing a more important role, precluding Member States from taking a proactive planning approach for developing their maritime sectors. This perceived imbalance may be responsible for the observation that there is some impetus towards developing a new MSP Directive to harmonize economic activities in the marine environment (Qiu and Jones 2013). Indeed, whilst the MSFD provides the foundation for a more ecosystem-based MSP through the mechanism of achieving GES, the IMP arguably focuses more on economic development, thus arguably the MSFD and IMP prescribe two different paths towards MSP (Qiu and Jones 2013).

However there is strong opposition towards creating a separate MSP Directive from the European NGO community[3] as well as from some Member States. In an informal meeting of EU Water and Marine Directors held in December 2010 in Spa as part of the Common Implementation Strategy[4] for the MSFD, several Marine Directors emphasized that 'MSP should be a tool to support policy and not affect existing policy objectives of substance, such as achieving GES' (European Commission 2010b). At this meeting, France and the UK, in particular, were unconvinced of the need to create a new Directive for MSP, with some agreement

2 According to the Oxford English Dictionary (online edition www.oed.com) the adjective *maritime* indicates something 'connected, associated, or dealing with shipping, naval matters, navigation, seaborne trade etc.' as a primary definition, whilst *marine* indicates the sea more generally and/or the branch of science concerned specifically with the sea. Whilst a subsequent, less used definition of *marine* includes 'relating to military or commercial use of the sea', it is worth noting that 'the branch of international law dealing with shipping, ocean fishery, territorial and international waters etc. [and] body of laws applying to the territorial waters of a particular country' is called *maritime* law, not *marine*. The same holds true for *maritime* power and a *maritime* state: these terms imply naval power and human use of the environment.

3 The joint NGO position paper (from May 2011) is available online: http://www.mio-ecsde.org/_uploaded_files/article_file_244_S1V18GIL9LNPN.pdf.

4 The Common Implementation Strategy is discussed in more depth below in the section on 'Tensions between the European Commission and Member States'.

from Denmark, Greece, Spain and the Netherlands. Several of these Member States emphasized the need for the environmental pillar of the IMP to be 'meaningful' and 'clearly upheld' and indicated that their own internal implementation of the MSFD was linked to MSP approaches, hence a new Directive could present an overlap and complicate the progress they are already making on the national level. In addition, given the timeline for implementing the MSFD and its 2012 deliverables, it was acknowledged that articulating a legislative proposal for an MSP Directive in such a tight timeframe would be difficult. In a subsequent meeting held in May 2011 in Budapest, most of the Marine Directors stated explicitly that they were not in favour of a legislative initiative on MSP, emphasizing that MSP 'can be a useful tool to support the implementation of the MSFD and should be approached in that perspective' (European Commission 2011). Some Marine Directors called for developing common approaches to MSP in a similar approach to that of the Common Implementation Strategy for the MSFD, and others mentioned the potential for a partial amendment to the MSFD to address MSP more explicitly. These discussions notwithstanding, it can be argued that further complicating the already complex legal architecture of EU legislation applicable in the marine environment will unnecessarily complicate the process for implementing MSP (cf. Bohman and Langlet 2015 in this volume).

This chapter examines the potential of the MSFD as a catalyst for MSP in the European Union, focusing on (1) tensions within the internal institutional framework of the European Commission and between the Commission, Member States, regional seas conventions, and non-EU members, and (2) the challenges posed by integrating a wide array of legislative instruments on both the national and regional levels. A fundamental tension exists between fisheries management and nature conservation in the EU, with the former falling under the jurisdiction of the Commission whilst Member States are responsible for the latter (Churchill 1987, De Santo and Jones 2007). This tension poses a significant challenge for the achievement of GES as required under the MSFD, and this issue plays an important role not only in each Member State's implementation of the array of legislation required to achieve GES, but also on the Commission level with regard to internal tensions between the Directorate General for the Environment (DG Environment) and the Directorate General for Maritime Affairs and Fisheries (DG MARE). The legal complexity and institutional tensions examined in this analysis have implications for the science-policy interface in environmental decision-making, and the implementation of MSP in the EU more widely.

Internal Dimensions and Institutional Tensions

Before delving into the national and regional implementation challenges of implementing the MSFD, it is worth examining underlying tensions within the European Commission that affect the potential effectiveness of the MSFD and its role in catalysing MSP in the EU. These tensions are a product of relations within the internal institutional framework of the European Commission (i.e. between Directorate Generals) as well as between the Commission and Member States, regional seas conventions, and non-EU members.

Tensions within the European Commission

As mentioned earlier, the MSFD represents the environmental pillar of the wider Integrated Maritime Policy (IMP), released by the EU in 2007. How and whether the economic pillar will require a separate directive to implement MSP specifically remains to be determined, but as discussed above, this idea lacks both merit and full support from Member States. Given the fact that fisheries management falls under the Commission's jurisdiction whilst Member States are responsible for nature conservation within their territories (as well as in shared regional seas, as required by the MSFD), it is worth exploring tensions within the Commission (i.e. between Directorates General) as well as between the Commission and Member States at the interface between environmental protection and fisheries management.

A brief explanation of the EU's governmental structure may benefit readers less well acquainted with its unique nature. The EU has a Council, a Parliament and a Court of Justice, which can be seen as representing, respectively, the executive, legislative, and judiciary components of governance, but there is some overlap in their responsibilities. The Council is comprised of ministers from Member States' governments and shares legislative authority with the Parliament, which is composed of directly elected members. The Court of Justice is comprised of judges appointed by Member States and includes a lower court (the Court of First Instance). In addition to these three bodies, there is the European Commission, a multinational civil service comprised of members appointed by Member States but acting in the EU's interests. With the exclusive right to initiate legislation and functioning in a quasi-executive role, the Commission 'epitomizes supranationalism and lies at the centre of the EU system' (Dinan 1999: 205). The Commission is currently divided into 33 departments, known as Directorates General, and several services (e.g. a central library, anti-fraud office, archives etc.). The Directorates General address a wide range of issues, from Agriculture and Rural Development to the EU Budget and Justice.

In examining the role and responsibilities of the Directorates General, it is important to acknowledge the imbalance in power and perceived importance between these bodies, and the resulting tensions. Whilst the Directorate General for the Environment (DG Environment) is tasked with 'protecting, preserving and improving the environment for present and future generations',[5] focusing on the application of more than 200 pieces of EU environmental law with a staff of approximately 500, the Directorate General for Maritime Affairs and Fisheries (DG MARE) 'works to develop the potential of the European maritime economy and to secure a safe and stable supply of seafood, sustainable fisheries, healthy

5 DG Environment website: http://ec.europa.eu/dgs/environment/index_en.htm.

seas and prosperous coastal communities, for today's Europeans and for future generations'[6]. DG MARE is responsible for managing two policy areas, the CFP and IMP, with a staff of approximately 400, and is clearly more economically focused. There is also a general perception by European environmental policy experts that DG MARE is viewed as the more powerful of the two Directorates General, whilst DG Environment is viewed as relatively weak among the DGs (Knill and Liefferink 2007, De Santo 2008).

DG Environment began as a team of five people in a branch of DG Industry in 1973; the establishment of a separate DG to deal with environmental issues did not occur until 1981, in recognition of the growing importance of environmental policy in the European Community (Dinan 1999). However DG Environment's reputation for activism in its early years and as a means for environmental groups to pressure the Commission often put DG Environment at odds with its more powerful, economically-focused counterparts (Dinan 1999). DG MARE has a longer formal history, albeit under a different identity. Founded in 1975 as the Directorate General for Fisheries, it formally encompassed Maritime Affairs in March 2008. This transformation included the creation of three new geographic directorates within the DG responsible for managing the CFP and IMP in the EU's maritime regions, namely the Atlantic, outermost regions and Arctic (Directorate C); the Mediterranean and Black Sea (Directorate D); and the Baltic Sea, North Sea and landlocked Member States (Directorate E). The other three Directorates within DG MARE cover policy development and coordination (Directorate A); international affairs and markets (Directorate B); and resources (Directorate F). In contrast, DG Environment's Directorates are distinguished by themes rather than geography: legal affairs and cohesion (Directorate A); nature, biodiversity and land use (Directorate B); sustainable resource management, industry and air (Directorate C); water, the marine environment, and chemicals (Directorate D); international affairs, LIFE and eco-innovation (Directorate E); and a sixth directorate on strategy (Directorate F). Given the MSFD's focus on a regional implementation of GES, coordination between the thematic Directorates of DG Environment with the geographical Directorates of DG MARE will be essential.

Tensions between the European Commission and Member States

In addition to the differing perceptions of DG Environment and DG MARE and their relative standing and roles within the Commission, there is another aspect of institutional tension that will affect the implementation of GES: the role of advisory bodies in providing advice to the Commission, and the DGs in particular. Previous research on the disconnect within the European Commission with respect to the bifurcation between fisheries management and nature conservation (De Santo and Jones 2007, De Santo 2010) examined the different

6 DG MARE website, mission statement: http://ec.europa.eu/dgs/maritimeaffairs_fisheries/about_us/mission_statement/index_en.htm.

outcomes of two cases that used the Common Fisheries Policy emergency closure mechanism to protect a habitat and/or species of concern. In the case of the Darwin Mounds area of cold-water coral located in Scotland's offshore waters, advice recommending this closure was provided by the International Council for the Exploration of the Sea (ICES) to the Commission. ICES is viewed as an impartial and independent scientific advisory body, and its advice was implemented, resulting in the Darwin Mounds area becoming the first offshore marine protected area in the EU as well as the first successful use of the Common Fisheries Policy emergency closure mechanism. A subsequent attempt by the UK to use the same legal tool to close the English Channel to pair-trawl fishing methods for sea bass, which are associated with by-catch of small cetaceans, was not successful. The information on bottlenose dolphin and harbour porpoise strandings on UK beaches presented by the UK's Sea Mammal Research Unit to the Commission was arguably less well-received than the evidence used in the Darwin Mounds closure, presented by an impartial and independent scientific advisory body rather than a Member State's own research unit. Other factors were also responsible for this difference in outcome, particularly given the fact that one case involved protecting a sessile, benthic organism whilst the other involved an economically lucrative fishery, and there was a degree of uncertainty regarding cetacean population estimates. However this comparison does highlight an issue about the relative value and importance of national versus community data that may be of concern to Member States as they implement GES and report to the Commission.

The Commission has set up a Common Implementation Strategy for the MSFD as an informal coordinating programme. The Strategy is comprised of Marine Directors, a Marine Strategy Coordination Group, and working groups. Figure 6.1 shows the organizational hierarchy of the Strategy. There are currently three working groups, focused on: Data, Information and Knowledge Exchange (DIKE); GES; and Economic and Social Assessment (ESA); as well as two technical subgroups focusing on underwater noise and litter. This structure may help overcome the imbalance in advice received by the DGs. For example, DG Environment receives advice from the Habitats Committee to aid its implementation of the Habitats Directive, whilst DG MARE receives input for implementing the Common Fisheries Policy from two expert bodies on fisheries, ICES and the Scientific, Technical and Economic Committee for Fisheries (STECF) as well as stakeholder input from the Advisory Committee for Fisheries and Aquaculture (ACFA) and from Regional Advisory Councils (De Santo 2010). The Common Implementation Strategy appears to strengthen the advice and input DG Environment will receive in implementing the MSFD, and the topical areas of its working groups are well-suited to providing a foundation for compiling information required for implementing a spatial approach to regional marine management. However, Member States have had some challenges to date with developing a common understanding to approaches for defining GES and developing targets, indicators and a common terminology.

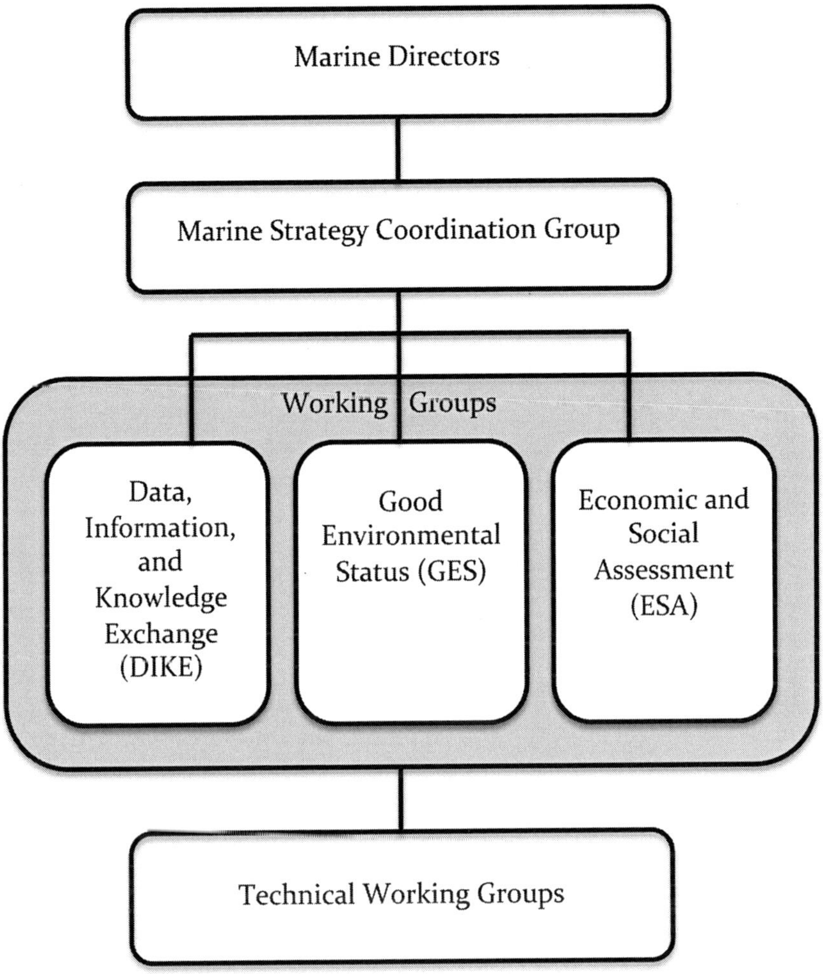

Figure 6.1 Common Implementation Strategy (CIS) for the MSFD (adapted from the European Commission website: http://ec.europa.eu/environment/marine/eu-coast-and-marine-policy/implementation/index_en.htm)

Hopefully the Common Implementation Strategy process will be harmonized with the regional seas approaches and will assist Member States in the Black and Mediterranean Seas to achieve GES (as OSPAR and HELCOM are more in line than the Barcelona and Bucharest Conventions at the moment). In addition, the Common Implementation Strategy process is well-positioned to supporting the development of MSP in European regional seas, which would be aided by an amendment to that effect to the MSFD.

Tensions between the European Commission, Regional Seas Conventions, and Non-EU Members

The EU has had long-standing involvement in regional agreements with the Mediterranean and Baltic states, providing technical and financial assistance and expertise. However this assistance may have been driven largely by an interest in minimizing the possibility of transboundary and in particular nuclear contamination (Vogler 2005). It has been argued that the MSFD's requirement for reporting on indicators of GES shifts the focus of responsibility from the Commissions of the Regional Seas Conventions to the European Commission, which means that standards developed within OSPAR, for example, may be subject to scrutiny by the European Commission (Kropelien 2007). The OSPAR and HELCOM conventions have followed the model of the MSFD in requiring their Parties to achieve GES within close timeframes to those proposed by the Commission, which may have prevented a perception of ceded authority. The CIS structure explained above and illustrated in Figure 6.1 also poses a potential for some overlap in terms of information feeding into the working groups. How the information flow will be harmonized between the Regional Seas conventions' reporting process and that of the CIS remains to be seen.

With regard to neighbouring countries not bound by European legislation (and/or new Member States), Norway adopts most EU environmental legislation as a member of the European Economic Area, and Iceland will be required to implement the MSFD as part of its candidacy to the EU. Russia's relationship with the EU with respect to environmental issues is currently defined within (1) the EU-Russia Environmental Dialogue and (2) the Northern Dimension Environmental Partnership, focusing on North-west Russia, the Baltic Sea and the Arctic Sea, in partnership with several EU Member States, Norway and international financial institutions. These initiatives include water and marine issues, which in addition to Russia's commitment to HELCOM should help bring it in line with targets for GES. Russia borders two regional seas, the Baltic and Black Sea; if it follows HELCOM's standards in the former, it may be able to help foster a similar approach for the Bucharest Convention. A few EU Member States are also Parties to multiple regional seas conventions. As shown in Table 6.1, Denmark, Finland, Germany and Sweden are all Parties to both OSPAR and HELCOM, whilst France and Spain are Parties to both OSPAR and the Barcelona Convention. For all of these countries, including Russia, it can be hoped that their acceding to standards for one regional sea can provide a basis for implementing similar standards in another. This would be particularly beneficial in the Mediterranean and Black Seas.

In addition to the institutional and regional tensions discussed here, Member States also face obstacles for achieving the key goal of the MSFD, i.e. GES. The next section goes into some detail on the required aspects and potential challenges Member States are confronting.

Table 6.1 **Status of EU and non-EU membership bordering European regional seas and/or Parties to regional seas conventions (as of November 2014)**

Country	EU Membership Status	Bordering North-east Atlantic	OSPAR Members	HELCOM Members	Bordering Mediterranean Sea (Barcelona Convention Members)	Bordering Black Sea (Bucharest Convention Members)
Albania	Candidate				X	
Algeria	Non-member				X	
Belgium	Member	X	X			
Bosnia-Herzegovina	Potential candidate				X	
Bulgaria	Member					X
Croatia	Member				X	
Cyprus	Member				X	
Denmark	Member	X	X	X		
Egypt	Non-member				X	
Estonia	Member			X		
Finland	Member		X	X		
France	Member	X	X		X	
Georgia	Non-member					X
Germany	Member	X	X	X		
Greece	Member				X	
Iceland	Candidate	X	X			
Ireland	Member	X	X			
Israel	Non-member				X	
Italy	Member				X	
Kosovo	Potential candidate					
Latvia	Member			X		

Table 6.1 *Continued*

Country	EU Membership Status	Bordering North-east Atlantic	OSPAR Members	HELCOM Members	Bordering Mediterranean Sea (Barcelona Convention Members)	Bordering Black Sea (Bucharest Convention Members)
Lebanon	Non-member				X	
Libya	Non-member				X	
Lithuania	Member			X		
Luxembourg	Member		X			
Macedonia	Candidate					
Malta	Member				X	
Monaco	Non-member				X	
Montenegro	Candidate				X	
Morocco	Non-member				X	
Netherlands	Member	X	X			
Norway	Non-member	X	X			
Poland	Member			X		
Portugal	Member	X	X			
Romania	Member					X
Russian Federation	Non-member			X		X
Slovenia	Member				X	
Spain	Member	X	X		X	
Sweden	Member	X	X	X		
Switzerland	Non-member		X			
Syria	Candidate				X	
Tunisia	Non-member				X	
Turkey	Candidate				X	X
UK	Member	X	X			
Ukraine	Non-member					X

The Architecture of 'Good Environmental Status'

Annex I of the MSFD outlines eleven qualitative descriptors that Member States are required to use in determining their progress towards GES, but it does not refer specifically to which legal instruments should be used to monitor these environmental goals. Table 6.2 outlines the most applicable legislative instruments (on the EU and international level) for each descriptor, as well as relevant programs and committees of the regional seas initiatives.

Table 6.2 MSFD Annex I qualitative descriptors for achieving GES, relevant EC instruments, and global/regional conventions

MSFD Annex I qualitative descriptor	Relevant EC legislation and initiatives	Global and regional conventions addressing issues relevant to MSFD GES
(1) Biological diversity is maintained. The quality and occurrence of habitats and the distribution and abundance of species are in line with prevailing physiographic, geographic and climatic conditions.	Habitats Directive (92/43/EEC) Water Framework Directive (2000/60/EC) EU Discards Policy Birds Directive (2009/147/EC) Port Waste Reception Facilities Directive (2000/59/EC)	Convention on Biological Diversity Bern Convention Bonn Convention Ramsar Convention
(2) Non-indigenous species introduced by human activities are at levels that do not adversely alter the ecosystems.	EU strategy on invasive species (in development)	IMO Ballast Water Management Convention
(3) Populations of all commercially exploited fish and shellfish are within safe biological limits, exhibiting a population age and size distribution that is indicative of a healthy stock.	Common Fisheries Policy (Regulation 2371/2002)	International Convention for the Conservation of Atlantic Tunas (ICCAT) North East Atlantic Fisheries Commission (NEAFC) General Fisheries Commission for the Mediterranean (GFCM)
(4) All elements of the marine food webs, to the extent that they are known, occur at normal abundance and diversity and levels capable of ensuring the long-term abundance of the species and the retention of their full reproductive capacity.	Common Fisheries Policy Habitats Directive (92/43/EEC) EU Discards Policy	Convention on Biological Diversity

Table 6.2 *Continued*

MSFD Annex I qualitative descriptor	Relevant EC legislation and initiatives	Global and regional conventions addressing issues relevant to MSFD GES
(5) Human-induced eutrophication is minimized, especially adverse effects thereof, such as losses in biodiversity, ecosystem degradation, harmful algae blooms and oxygen deficiency in bottom waters.	Water Framework Directive (2000/60/EC) Urban Waste Water Treatment Directive (91/271/EEC) Nitrates Directive (91/676/EEC) Integrated Pollution Prevention Control (IPPC) Directive (2008/1/EC) Rural Development Regulation (1698/2005)	Long-Range Transboundary Air Pollution (LRTAP) Convention Protocol on Nitrogen Oxides MARPOL 73/78 Convention
(6) Sea-floor integrity is at a level that ensures that the structure and functions of the ecosystems are safeguarded and benthic ecosystems, in particular, are not adversely affected.	Habitats Directive (92/43/EEC)	
(7) Permanent alteration of hydrographical conditions does not adversely affect marine ecosystems.	Strategic Environmental Assessment (SEA) Directive (2001/42/EC), Environmental Impact Assessment (EIA) Directive (85/337/EEC)	
(8) Concentrations of contaminants are at levels not giving rise to pollution effects.	Water Framework Directive (2000/60/EC) and daughter Directive on Priority Substances (2008/105/EC) Bathing Water Quality Directive (76/160/EEC) Dangerous Substances Directive (76/464/EEC) EC and regional legislation on marine pollution (various) IPPC Directive (2008/1/EC) REACH Regulation (on chemicals and their safe use) (1907/2006) EU Chemicals Strategy and Directives on Cosmetics (76/768/EEC), Pesticides (91/414/EEC), Biocides (98/8/EC), Pharmaceuticals (75/319/EEC) and Veterinary Medicine (81/851/EEC)	LRTAP Convention UNEP Stockholm Persistent Organic Pollutants (POPs) Convention MARPOL 73/78 Convention Convention on the Control of Harmful Anti-fouling Systems on Ships UN Framework Convention on Climate Change (UNFCCC)

Table 6.2 *Continued*

MSFD Annex I qualitative descriptor	Relevant EC legislation and initiatives	Global and regional conventions addressing issues relevant to MSFD GES
(9) Contaminants in fish and other seafood for human consumption do not exceed levels established by Community legislation or other relevant standards.	Dangerous Substances Directive (76/464/EEC) REACH Regulation (1907/2006)	
(10) Properties and quantities of marine litter do not cause harm to the coastal and marine environment.	Dangerous Substances Directive (76/464/EEC) Packaging and Packaging Waste Directive (94/62/EEC) REACH Regulation (1907/2006)	
(11) Introduction of energy, including underwater noise, is at levels that do not adversely affect the marine environment.	Environmental Noise Directive (2002/49/EC) Renewable Energy Directive (2009/28/EC)	

In 2010 the Commission released detailed criteria and methodological standards for assessing GES (European Commission 2010b), which must be met on both the Member State and regional level (i.e. within the Baltic Sea, North-east Atlantic Ocean, Mediterranean Sea, and the Black Sea). The MSFD requires Member States to build upon existing regional cooperation structures, including those within the relevant regional seas conventions, in developing their marine strategies (Article 6). The marine environment of each of these regions is governed by multiple international environmental instruments, as illustrated in Table 6.3. Consequently, as Member States are accountable not only to several EU Directives, but also to regional seas environmental instruments, a major challenge posed by the MSFD is harmonizing marine environmental governance from the national to the European and wider regional seas level. Arguably, if Member States are to achieve GES they are not only meeting EU standards, but also helping the EU meet global standards. It is also worth noting that whilst Directives are implemented by Member States through the creation of national legislation, Regulations are directly applicable at the national level as published. Consequently the Common Fisheries Policy is applicable once released, i.e. in the latest iteration from January 1 2014, whilst the MSFD and all of the other Directives Member States will need to harmonize in order to achieve GES are being implemented more slowly and with some risk of misinterpretation and/or other issues of compliance, as discussed in more detail below.

Table 6.3 European marine regions and relevant environmental legislation

Marine Region	Institutions	Protocols	EU Implementation Instruments
Baltic Sea	Helsinki Convention (HELCOM) (1974, revised 1992)		Council Decisions 94/156/EC and 94/157/EC (1994) Council Decision 95/308/EC (1995)
	HELCOM Baltic Sea Action Plan (2007)		
	Baltic Sea Joint Comprehensive Environmental Action Programme (1992)		
North-east Atlantic Ocean	OSPAR Convention (1992)		Council Decision 98/249/EC (1997)
Mediterranean Sea	Barcelona Convention (1976, amended 1995)	Dumping Protocol (1976)	Council Decision 77/585/EEC (1977)
		Protocol concerning Co-operation in Combating Pollution of the Mediterranean Sea by Oil and Other Harmful Substances in Cases of Emergency (1976)	Council Decision 81/420/EEC (1981)
		LBS Protocol (1980)	Council Decision 81/101/EEC (1983)
		SPA and Biodiversity Protocol (1982)	Council Decision 84/132/EEC (1984)
		Offshore Protocol (1994 – ***Not yet entered into force***)	

Marine Region	Institutions	Protocols	EU Implementation Instruments
		Hazardous Wastes Protocol (1996 – ***Not yet entered into force)***	
		Prevention and Emergency Protocol (2002)	Council Decision 2004/575/EC (2004)
		ICZM Protocol (2011)	Council Decision 2010/631/EU (2010)
Black Sea	Bucharest Convention (1992)	Protocol on the Protection of the Black Sea Marine Environment Against Pollution from Land Based Sources (1992)	(***EU is not a party***)
		Protocol on Cooperation in Combating Pollution of the Black Sea Marine Environment by Oil and Other Harmful Substances in Emergency Situations (1992)	
		Protocol on the Protection of the Black Sea Marine Environment Against Pollution by Dumping (1992)	
	Revised Strategic Action Plan for the Environmental Protection and Rehabilitation of the Black Sea (2009)		
	Revised Protocol on the Protection of the Marine Environment of the Black Sea from Land-Based Sources and Activities (2009 – ***Not ratified yet***)		

Challenges for Implementing the Qualitative Descriptors

Whilst guidance on harmonizing national and regional approaches to GES is lacking, some recent studies shed light on strengths and weaknesses of the MSFD's approach. A recent analysis (Van Leeuwen et al. 2012) of the implementation of the MSFD in European regional seas assessed 'institutional ambiguity', i.e. the mismatch between institutions of different policy making settings, and concluded that the Baltic Sea exhibits the lowest institutional ambiguity whilst the Mediterranean exhibits the highest (and the North and Black Seas fall in between). Another recent study (Borja et al. 2011) examined how the Basque Country in Spain (southern Bay of Biscay) is developing an integrated environmental status assessment approach to address the eleven qualitative descriptors for GES and the detailed criteria and methodological standards outlined by the Commission (European Commission 2010c). This analysis drew on methods, tools, indicators and targets implemented in the WFD as a model (including using mean values for descriptors, to avoid the risk of failing to attain GES based upon the failure of a single indicator or descriptor), an approach which the authors suggest 'provides an easier and reliable way to implement this complex directive' and which is in line with an earlier analysis conducted by the lead author on integrating the implementation of the MSFD and the WFD (Borja et al. 2010).

Examining the criteria for GES listed in the MSFD more closely (see Table 6.2), several challenges are apparent, on both the national and regional scales. As mentioned above, whilst directives are implemented in Member States through the creation of new national legislation, regulations are binding 'as is'. With fisheries governed by a regulation whilst most[7] of the other EU legislation applicable for achieving GES is comprised of Directives (see Table 6.2), the MSFD provides an opportunity to improve the ecosystem-based management of fisheries and it may strengthen Member State competencies and responsibilities to do so (Rätz et al. 2010). However, the MSFD does not provide advice regarding how Member States are to harmonize the implementation of a complex network of legislation. By including fisheries within GES, the MSFD may result in better harmonization of fisheries and environmental protection, but this is as yet unproven and will depend largely on the way in which the directive is implemented not only nationally but also regionally. In addition, it will be important to see how the revised CFP, released in 2014, has evolved from its last iteration ten years ago.

Moving from the Member State level to the regional sea level, key challenges for successfully implementing the MSFD will be integrating different pieces of legislation that have had varied levels of success, as well as cooperating effectively with non-EU members bordering regional seas (cf. Bohman and Langlet 2015 in this volume). Table 6.1 shows the relevant EU members, candidate countries, potential candidate countries, and non-members, in the context of their participation

7 The exception being the REACH Regulation, which deals with the registration, evaluation, authorization, and restriction of chemical substances.

in regional seas environmental conventions. Before going into each of the regional seas in more depth, it is worth exploring the challenges of implementing European legislation on the national level and the risks of non-compliance, especially with regard to newer Member States.

European Enlargement and Compliance with European Directives

In examining the effects of European enlargement on Member States and their capacity for complying with Directives, there are some aspects of Europeanization, i.e. the emergence and development of distinct governance structures at the European level (Risse et al. 2001), that are applicable. Research in this area has outlined conditions that produce domestic changes in response to Europeanization, namely that (1) the process of adapting to European-level measures must be inconvenient (i.e. there must be some degree of misfit or incompatibility between European-level processes and those on the domestic level), and (2) facilitating factors such as actors or institutions may aid domestic adaptation (Börzel and Risse 2000). As mentioned above, the role of advisory bodies can have mixed results, and may depend on how they are viewed at the Commission level. In addition to these factors, it is also worth focusing on the issue of compliance, specifically within the context of European Directives. Compliance can be defined as whether or not 'countries adhere to the provision of the accord and to the implementing measures that they have instituted' (Jacobson and Brown-Weiss 1995) and is conceptually distinct from effectiveness, which addresses whether or not the goals of the commitments are met, which may occur independently of compliance (Haas 1998).

Previous research on non-compliance with European Directives in other issue areas has pointed to several issues that can affect Member State interpretation and implementation of European legislation on the national level. In their examination of six labour law directives in fifteen Member States, Falkner et al. (2002) uncovered four avenues for non-compliance: direct opposition, administrative reasons, issue linkage, and interpretation problems. In the first, non-compliance as direct opposition, a Member State that disagreed with a directive may fight against it at the Commission level, and upon losing, try to fight it again in the implementation stage. Alternatively opposition can be due to a desire to defend existing rules and regulations on the national level, without significant protest having occurred at the European level. In the second form of non-compliance, due to administrative reasons, Falkner et al. (2002) found in several cases that even where national governments are not un-willing to transpose European legislation, there may still be delays and/or incorrect transposition of directives due to administrative shortcomings (including sufficient financial and personnel resources). The third form of non-compliance, a result of issue linkage, occurs when a Member State transposes a directive in connection with other issues, which may or may not be thematically related to the subject of the directive. This approach can lead to delays in implementation, especially if the subject is contentious and results in substantive debates on the national level. The fourth and final form of non-compliance examined in this analysis was due to interpretation problems. In this case, there may be uncertainty as to what is actually required, and the authors indicate that this uncertainty can also be a way in which Member States hide what is essentially direct opposition.

At first glance, the problems posed by administrative shortcomings and issue linkages seem particularly relevant for the implementation of the MSFD in European regional seas, especially in new Member States. The most recent waves of European enlargement took place in 2004 with the inclusion of the Czech Republic, Estonia, Cyprus, Latvia, Lithuania, Hungary, Malta, Poland, Slovakia, and Slovenia, and in 2007 with the addition of Romania and Bulgaria. As of 2014, candidates to join the EU include Albania, Iceland, Macedonia, Montenegro, Serbia, and Turkey, and potential candidates include Bosnia and Herzegovina, and Kosovo. A recent comparative project (Falkner and Treib 2008) that examined the transposition, enforcement and application of EU labour legislation in the Czech Republic, Hungary, Slovakia and Slovenia in 2005-2006 found better performance at the transposition stage than later in the implementation cycle. The key impediments to compliance uncovered in this analysis were due not to a lack of political will or administrative shortcomings, but rather to strained economies with high unemployment and worker-unfriendly conditions, court systems lacking resources and knowledge concerning EU law, and an inadequate organization of labour inspectorates (Falkner and Treib 2008).

Consequently, if we consider the potential for new Member States to contribute to achieving GES in regional seas, it is important to examine not just how well they comply with the MSFD, but also the wider picture of their economic health and capacity for monitoring and enforcement. Within the context of the MSFD's potential to achieve GES and its implications for MSP, it is also worth examining the mechanisms in place for monitoring and enforcing the range of legislation necessary for implementing GES in each of Europe's regional seas, as well as the existing provisions for stakeholder engagement.

European Regional Seas' Capacity for Implementing the MSFD

Article 4 of the MSFD sets out the marine regions and sub-regions in which Member States are required to implement the directive as follows: the Baltic Sea, the North-east Atlantic Ocean (including the North Sea), the Mediterranean Sea and the Black Sea. Each of these areas is governed by a regional seas body: the OSPAR convention in the North-east Atlantic, HELCOM in the Baltic Sea, the Barcelona Convention in the Mediterranean, and the Bucharest Convention in the Black Sea. See Table 6.1 for a listing of the countries bordering these seas and their membership in the relevant Conventions. The North-east Atlantic (including the North Sea) is bordered by nine EU members (Belgium, Denmark, France, Germany, Ireland, the Netherlands, Portugal, Spain, Sweden and the UK), one non-member (Norway), and one candidate country (Iceland). The OSPAR

Convention includes these and three additional countries as members (Finland, Luxembourg, and Switzerland). In 2010 the OSPAR Commission released a Regional Implementation Framework for the EU MSFD (OSPAR Commission 2010) that set out a timetable for Member States to deliver initial assessments of their marine waters by mid-2012, including establishing environmental indicators and targets to guide the progress towards GES by 2020. This framework takes a stepwise and comprehensive approach to helping OSPAR Parties achieve regional cooperation, responding to the timeframe set out for EU Member states under the MSFD. Consequently it is clear that there is a mechanism in place for implementing the MSFD in the North-east Atlantic on the regional level, via OSPAR, which appears to be well-organized and transparent given clear targets and timeframe set out in the Regional Implementation Framework (cf. Van Tatenhove and Van Leeuwen 2015 in this volume).

The Baltic Sea is bordered by eight EU members (Denmark, Sweden, Finland, Estonia, Latvia, Lithuania, Poland and Germany) and one non-member, Russia. All of these countries (with the addition of the EU) are Parties to HELCOM. Like OSPAR, HELCOM has also provided its Parties with a roadmap to implementing the MSFD in the Baltic Sea with timelines and targets (HELCOM 2011). Like the MSFD, the Baltic Sea Action Plan also aims for GES of the Baltic Sea, by 2021 (a year later than the MSFD), and HELCOM's activities have been aligned to synergistically implement both the Action Plan and the MSFD. Consequently, it seems likely that given eight out of nine coastal countries in the Baltic are EU members and Parties to HELCOM, achieving GES on the regional level will be straightforward, assuming the newer EU Member States are on track with their implementation of the directive on the national level (cf. Söderström et al. 2015 in this volume).

The Mediterranean Sea is surrounded by a mix of states in varying stages of EU accession. In addition to the eight Member States (Croatia, Cyprus, France, Greece, Italy, Malta, Slovenia and Spain), there are nine non-members (Algeria, Egypt, Israel, Lebanon, Libya, Monaco, Morocco, Syria and Tunisia), one candidate country (Turkey), and four potential candidates (Albania, Bosnia-Herzegovina, Macedonia and Montenegro). Whilst this geography presents a significant challenge for monitoring and enforcing EU legislation, it also provides an opportunity for improving the candidate countries' environmental behaviour, as accession to the EU requires states to *inter alia* implement existing environmental legislation. These twenty-one countries plus the EC comprise the Contracting Parties to the Barcelona Convention (cf. Suárez de Vivero and Rodríguez 2015 in this volume). However unlike OSPAR and HELCOM, the Barcelona Convention has not produced guidance or a timeline for implementing the MSFD or GES in the Mediterranean Sea. As shown in Table 6.3, there are relevant protocols within the Convention, but not all are in force.

The Black Sea is bordered by two EU Member States (Bulgaria and Romania), one candidate country (Turkey) and three non-members (Georgia, the Russian Federation, and Ukraine). These six nations comprise the Contracting Parties to the Bucharest Convention. Following the accession of Bulgaria and Romania to the EU in 2007, the European Commission declared EU membership to the Bucharest Convention to be a priority. In its communication on Black Sea Synergy (European Commission 2007b), the Commission outlines the following maritime policy (emphasis in original):

Black Sea synergy provides an opportunity for *dialogue on the emerging holistic maritime policy* of the Union which aims to maximize sustainable growth and job creation in sea related sectors and coastal regions. This would include building a network of clusters of maritime cross-sectoral co-operation among services, industries and scientific institutions and also *improving cooperation and integration on the surveillance of the sea,* with a view to safety and security of shipping and environmental protection (European Commission 2007b: 6).

The Bucharest Convention is to provide the regional forum for implementing the MSFD in the Black Sea, which may be more straightforward if Turkey joins the EU and if the EU becomes a party to the Convention. The participation of Georgia, Russia, and the Ukraine in achieving standards comparable to those required by the MSFD will be much more likely to occur if the Bucharest Convention adopts similarly stringent standards and if it provides effective coordination between Black Seas countries' marine protection policies. As discussed elsewhere in this volume (see Knudsen 2015 in this volume), cooperation among Black Sea states has been much more difficult than might have been expected in the new geopolitical climate following the collapse of the Soviet Union.

Another important component for implementing the MSFD, and eventually MSP in European regional seas is the provision for stakeholder participation. The MSFD encourages the use of existing management bodies for stakeholder engagement (Article 19), including Regional Advisory Councils, Scientific Advisory Bodies and Regional Seas Conventions. With the advent of the last version of the Common Fisheries Policy in 2002, seven Regional Advisory Councils were created for the Baltic, Mediterranean, and North Seas, north-western waters, south-western waters, pelagic stocks, and the high seas/long distance fleets. These bodies are in various stages of development and there may be some danger in relying too heavily on RACs as the primary platform for stakeholder consultation, as they only address fishing and provide a potential stage for intra-industry power relations that can complicate policy-making (Griffin 2007, De Santo 2011). A key lesson that can be learned from the Baltic Sea RAC experience to date is the need for earlier inclusion of stakeholders in the governance process (i.e. during the science advisory process) to provide information on the state and dynamics of the resource under consideration grounded in reality (Linke et al. 2011). Including this kind of information is important for ecosystem-based management, and is factored into the Common Implementation Strategy's current working group structure, discussed below. Bringing together different industries and other marine uses within appropriate stakeholder forums through the MSFD will be an important step towards MSP in European regional seas. The MSFD consequently provides an opportunity to lay the groundwork for MSP by providing transparent and open stakeholder involvement in the process leading up to assessing GES; this groundwork can subsequently be expanded to include other sectors and issue areas, within a framework of ecosystem-based management.

Conclusions

Whilst the GES targets for the MSFD provides a foundation for ecosystem-based approach to MSP (Katsanevakis et al. 2011), there are significant challenges to implementing the Directive both in terms of harmonizing a plethora of legislation, and in dealing with inherent tensions on different scales ranging from the Commission to the European marine regions. Continued European expansion adds a challenge but also an opportunity to improve areas that have not had the benefits of the EU's environmental governance to date as well as improve the environmental behaviour of non-EU members. It can be hoped that the regional approach espoused by the MSFD will not only help 'laggard' countries benefit from the example of 'leaders' within the EU, but also aid the implementation of better environmental standards in non-EU members whilst helping strengthen the Barcelona and Bucharest conventions.

As the implementation process for the MSFD moves forward in European marine regions, there is an opportunity for better harmonization between fisheries management and environmental conservation. However, there are also a lot of moving parts in play, including a new version of the Common Fisheries Policy out in 2014 that still must improve its approach towards ecological sustainability, otherwise this could become a thorn in the side of Member States trying to achieve GES. It is no secret that the Common Fisheries Policy is widely viewed as a failure (Payne 2000, Daw and Gray 2005), and without serious and committed reform, the EU risks undermining its own legal architecture for sustainable ocean management.

The Common Implementation Strategy process provides some resolution to the imbalance between DG Environment and DG MARE, but it is still unclear how well these two Directorates General will cooperate in attaining GES. Given DG Environment is structured around themes whilst DG MARE is structured along geographic regions, better coordination between these two bodies will be necessary not only for implementing the MSFD, but for achieving effective ecosystem-based MSP. Granted, the Common Implementation Strategy puts in place a better advisory process for DG Environment to implement the MSFD than it has had in the past, but whether this process is really on equal footing with DG MARE's focus on the IMP and Common Fisheries Policy will become clear when these issues overlap. Sustainable fisheries is one of the eleven qualitative descriptors for GES, and both flawed fisheries management and the economic 'maritime' focus of the IMP still have potential to derail the process. To some degree, it will come down to Member States to ensure that effective ecosystem-based MSP will proceed, but in regional seas with less stringent standards and/ or where non-EU members are numerous and not held to the same standards, the individual actions of 'leader' Member States could be diluted.

In examining whether the MSFD provides a catalyst for MSP, this analysis has shown how overwhelming the complex legal architecture can be, especially for new Member States. It has also drawn attention to institutional tensions within and beyond the Commission, which should be taken into consideration as the process towards achieving GES evolves. If ecosystem-based drivers can be the foundation for MSP in Europe, the underlying ecosystem services that provide for the economic uses of the European marine environment, from fisheries to tourism, will have a greater chance at being maintained for years to come.

References

Bohman, B. and Langlet, D. 2015. Float or Sinker for Europe's Seas? The role of law in marine governance, in *Governing Europe's Marine Environment: Europeanization of Regional Seas or Regionalization of EU Policies*?, edited by M. Gilek and K. Kern. Farnham, UK: Ashgate Publishing.

Borja, À., Elliot, M., Carstensen, J., Heiskanen, A.S. and van de Bund, W. 2010. Marine management – towards an integrated implementation of the European Marine Strategy Framework and the Water Framework Directives. *Marine Pollution Bulletin*, 60, 2175-2186.

Borja, À., Galparsoro, I., Irgoien, X., Iriondo, A., Menchaca, I., Muxika, I., Pascual, M., Quincoces, I., Revilla, M., Rodrígues, J.G., Santurtún, M., Solaun, O., Uriarte, A., Valencia, V. and Zorita, I. 2011. Implementation of the European Marine Strategy Directive: A methodological approach for the assessment of environmental status, from the Basque Country (Bay of Biscay). *Marine Pollution Bulletin*, 62, 889-904.

Börzel, T.A. and Risse, T. 2000. When Europe hits home: Europeanization and domestic change. *European Integration online Papers (EIoP)* 4(15). Available at: http://eiop.or.at/eiop/texte/2000-015a.htm [accessed: 13 July 2014].

Churchill, R. 1987. *EEC Fisheries Law*. Dordrecht: Martinus Nijhoff Publishers.

Daw, T. and Gray, T. 2005. Fisheries science and sustainability in international policy: a study of failure in the European Union's Common Fisheries Policy. *Marine Policy*, 29, 189-197.

De Santo, E.M. and Jones, P.J.S. 2007. Offshore marine conservation in the North East Atlantic: emerging tensions and opportunities. *Marine Policy*, 31, 336-347.

De Santo, E.M. 2008. Offshore marine conservation in the North East Atlantic: opportunities and challenges for the developing regime. Unpublished PhD thesis, University College London, Department of Geography.

De Santo, E.M. 2010. 'Whose science?' Precaution and power-play in European marine environmental decision-making. *Marine Policy*, 34, 414-420.

De Santo, E.M. 2011. Environmental justice implications of Maritime Spatial Planning in the European Union. *Marine Policy*, 35, 34-38.

de Vivero, J.L.S. and Mateos, J.C.D. 2012. The Spanish approach to marine spatial planning. Marine Strategy Framework Directive vs. EU Integrated Maritime Policy. *Marine Policy*, 36, 18-27.

Dinan, D. 1999. *Ever Closer Union*, Second Edition. Houndmills: Palgrave.

Ehler, C. and Douvere, F. 2009. Marine Spatial Planning: a step-by-step approach toward ecosystem-based management. Intergovernmental Oceanographic Commission and Man and the Bisophere Program. IOC Manual and Guides No. 53, ICAM Dossier No. 6. Paris: UNESCO.

European Commission 2007a. Communication from the Commission to the European Parliament, the Council, the European Economic and Social Committee and the Committee of the Regions: an Integrated Maritime Policy for the European Union. COM(2007) 575 final, Brussels, 10 October 2007.

European Commission 2007b. Black Sea Synergy – a new regional cooperation initiative. Communication from the Commission to the Council and the European Parliament, COM(2007) 160 final, Brussels, 11 April 2007.

European Commission 2008. Roadmap for Maritime Spatial Planning: Achieving Common Principles in the EU. Communication from the Commission COM(2008) 791 final, Brussels, 25.11.2008.

European Commission 2010a. Maritime Spatial Planning in the EU – Achievements and Future Development. Communication from the Commission COM(2010) 771 final, Brussels 17 December 2010.

European Commission 2010b. Fourth Marine Directors Meeting, 2-3 December 2010, Spa, Belgium. MSFD Common Implementation Strategy Meeting Documents. Available at: http://ec.europa.eu/environment/marine/eu-coast-and-marine-policy/implementation/index_en.htm [accessed: 13 July 2014].

European Commission 2010c. Commission Decision of 1 September 2010 on criteria and methodological standards on good environmental status of marine waters (notified under document COM(2010) 5956). OJ L 232, 2.9.2010, p. 14.

European Commission 2011. Fifth Marine Directors' Meeting, 26-27 May 2011, Budapest, Hungary. MSFD Common Implementation Strategy Meeting Documents. Available at: http://ec.europa.eu/environment/marine/eu-coast-and-marine-policy/implementation/index_en.htm [accessed: 13 July 2014].

Falkner, G., Hartlapp, M., Leiber, S. and Treib, O. 2002. Opposition through the backdoor? The case of national non-compliance with EU Directives. *Political Science Series*, 83, Institute for Advanced Studies, Vienna.

Falkner, G. and Treib, O. 2008. Three worlds of compliance or four? The EU-15 compared to new Member States. *Journal of Common Market Studies*, 46(2), 293-313.

Griffin, L. 2007. All aboard: power, participation and governance in the North Sea Regional Advisory Council. *International Journal of Green Economics*, 1(3-4), 478-493.

Haas, P. 1998. Compliance with EU directives: insights from international relations and comparative politics. *Journal of European Public Policy*, 5(1), 17-37.

HELCOM 2011. A coordination platform for the implementation of the EU Marine Strategy Framework Directive in the Baltic Sea region.

Jacobson, H.K. and Brown-Weiss, E. 1995. Compliance with international environmental accords. *Global Governance*, 1(1), 119-148.

Katsanevakis, S., Stelzenmüller, V., South, A., Sørensen, T.K., Jones, P.J.S., Kerr, S., Badalamenti, F., Anagnostou, C., Breen, P., Chust, G., D'Anna, G., Duijin, M., Filatova, T., Fiorentino, F., Hulsman, H., Johnson, K., Karageorgis, A.P., Kröncke, I., Mirto, S., Pipitone, C., Portelli, S., Qiu, W., Reiss, H., Sakellariou, D., Salomidi, M., Van Hoof, L., Vassilopoulou, V., Fernández, T.V., Vöge, A., Weber, A., Zenetos, A. and ter Hofstede, R. 2011. Ecosystem-based marine spatial management: review of concepts, policies, tools and critical issues. *Ocean and Coastal Management*, 54, 807-820.

Knill, C. and Liefferink, C. 2007. *Environmental Politics in the European Union*. Manchester: Manchester University Press.

Knudsen, S. 2015. Marine Governance in the Black Sea, in *Governing Europe's Marine Environment: Europeanization of Regional Seas or Regionalization of EU Policies?*, edited by M. Gilek and K. Kern. Farnham, UK: Ashgate Publishing.

Kroepelien, K.F. 2007. The Norwegian Barents Sea management plan and the EC Marine Strategy Directive: some political and legal challenges with an ecosystem-based approach to the protection of the European marine environment. *Review of European Community International Environmental Law*, 16(1), 24-35.

Linke, S., Dreyer, M. and Sellker, P. 2011. The Regional Advisory Councils: what is their potential to incorporate stakeholder knowledge into fisheries governance? *Ambio*, 40, 133-143.

OSPAR Commission 2010. OSPAR regional implementation framework for the EU Marine Strategy Framework Directive (MSFD road map). Available at: http://www.ospar.org/documents/dbase/publications/p00501/p00501_msfd%20roadmap.pdf [accessed: 13 July 2014].

Payne, D.C. 2000. Policy-making in nested institutions: explaining the conservation failure of the EU's Common Fisheries Policy. *Journal of Common Market Studies*, 38(2), 303-324.

Qiu W. and Jones P.J.S. 2013. The emerging policy landscape for marine spatial planning in Europe. *Marine Policy*, 39, 182-190.

Rätz, H.J., Dörner, H., Scott, R. and Barbas, T. 2010. Complementary roles of European and national institutions under the Common Fisheries Policy and the Marine Strategy Framework Directive. *Marine Policy*, 34, 1028-1035.

Risse, T., Caporaso, J., and Cowles, M.G. 2001. Europeanization and domestic change. Introduction, in *Transforming Europe: Europeanization and Domestic Change*, edited by M. Cowles, J. Caporaso and T. Risse. Ithaca, NY: Cornell University Press, 1-20.

Suárez de Vivero, J.L. and Rodríguez, J.C. 2015. Marine Governance in the Mediterranean Sea, in *Governing Europe's Marine Environment: Europeanization of Regional Seas or Regionalization of EU Policies*?, edited by M. Gilek and K. Kern. Farnham, UK: Ashgate Publishing.

Söderström, S., Kern, K. and Hassler, B. 2015. Marine governance in the Baltic Sea: current trends of Europeanization and regionalization, in *Governing Europe's Marine Environment: Europeanization of Regional Seas or Regionalization of EU Policies*?, edited by M. Gilek and K. Kern. Farnham, UK: Ashgate Publishing.

Van Leeuwen, J., Van Hoof, L. and Van Tatenhove, J. 2012. Institutional ambiguity in implementing the European Union Marine Strategy Framework Directive. *Marine Policy*, 36, 636-643.

Van Tatenhove, J. and Van Leeuwen, J. 2015. Marine Governance of the North Sea: patterns of regionalization, in *Governing Europe's Marine Environment: Europeanization of Regional Seas or Regionalization of EU Policies*?, edited by M. Gilek and K. Kern. Farnham, UK: Ashgate Publishing.

Vogler, J. 2005. The European contribution to global environmental governance. *International Affairs*, 81(4), 835-850.

Chapter 7
The Regional Advisory Councils in European Fisheries: An Appropriate Approach to Stakeholder Involvement in an EU Integrated Marine Governance?

Marion Dreyer and Piet Sellke

Regional-level Stakeholder Involvement in EU Marine Governance: An Emerging Issue

The question of how to involve stakeholders in the future governing of the EU marine environment and resources is an emerging topic. Increasingly, the regional sea is mentioned as one level (besides the local, national and EU-level) at which stakeholder involvement is required. This reference to the regional level is mainly found in scholarly contributions dealing with the current reform of the EU's Common Fisheries Policy (CFP) (Symes 2009, Raakjær et al. 2010) and/or the relationship between the CFP and the novel EU marine policies (Van Hoof and Van Tatenhove 2009, De Santo 2011).

'Better governance through regionalization' (COM 2011a: 7) is one of the objectives that the European Commission proposes to pursue through the current reform of the CFP, and also the EU's Marine Strategy Framework Directive (MSFD; EC 2008), the environmental pillar of the EU's developing Integrated Maritime Policy (IMP; COM 2007), has a regional focus. The rationale underlying this focus is that the diversity of Europe's regional seas requires management approaches that are tailored to the specificities of the different sea-basins. A recurrent note in the recent literature on the future prospects of EU fisheries governance is that the ecological and integration objectives of the new EU marine initiatives require a critical review of the existing regional-level stakeholder involvement system in the EU: the Regional Advisory Councils (RACs). The RACs were established under the 2002 reform of the CFP. They present a *sectoral* approach of regional-level stakeholder involvement insofar as they are confined to groups and organizations from or specifically concerned with the fisheries sector. They do not include other marine sectors such as energy production or maritime transport. Recent papers point out that the new EU marine policies, particularly the MSFD which has at its core the cross-sectoral ecosystem approach to management (EAM), create, however, a need for much broader, multi-interest *and* cross-sector stakeholder involvement (Van Hoof and Van Tatenhove 2009, De Santo 2011: 34).

The MSFD's focus on regions and EAM and the cross-sector approach of the IMP have made regional-level cross-sector stakeholder involvement a topic of significance. If it was to become part of an integrated EU marine governance, it would require devising appropriate structures and processes through which such broad-based involvement could occur. Efforts on analysing the challenges associated with this task have only started (cp. Van Tatenhove 2011).

This chapter seeks to unfold some of the central issues that one faces when trying to involve a wide diversity of stakeholders through an advisory body for regional-level marine governance. We refer to this notional regional-level body as Inclusive Marine Advisory Body. We examine the challenges of extending the RACs into such broader-based bodies through an analytical lens centred on 'inclusion' and 'closure'. Inclusion and closure have been identified as critical to processes of participation in environmental (risk) governance (Renn and Schweizer 2009). Following Renn and Schweizer (2009),[1] *inclusion* refers to the question of what to make the subject of consultation among the advisory body members (e.g. single policy options or a set of options for comparative evaluation) and whom to include (e.g. relevant stakeholders and/or knowledge experts). By *closure* we refer to the question of which decision-making principle to choose (e.g. consensus principle or majority principle) and what to base the decision-making on (e.g. different kinds of knowledge and/or a wide diversity of interests and value preferences). By *marine governance* we refer to collective decision-making on marine uses as a multi-actor and multi-level process involving new modes of collaboration (cp. Van Tatenhove 2011, Jentoft and Chuenpagdee 2015 in this volume). We define *stakeholders* as socially organized groups who are affected by or have a strong interest in the policy actions or management activities that are up for discussion and resolution in marine governance (cp. Renn 2008: 273).

The structure of the chapter is as follows. In the next section we present the RACs as an innovative approach to stakeholder involvement in EU fisheries governance. We then highlight the pressures to change that follow for the RACs from the new EU marine policies. Our main argument here is that the RACs are likely to come to be increasingly criticized as insufficiently inclusive advisory institutions. Thereafter we discuss multi-interest *and* cross-sector marine advisory bodies as a possible future model of stakeholder involvement at the regional level. We refer to this model as Inclusive Marine Advisory Body and highlight what we consider as important challenges in relation to inclusion and closure facing the establishment of such a broad-based body. This discussion takes account of the experiences so far with the RACs as a multi-stakeholder regional-level participatory mechanism. Information on

1 See also Hajer and Wagenaar (2003) and Stirling (2008).

experiences was drawn from literature review and interviews and round table exchanges with relevant stakeholders (Dreyer et al. 2011[2]).

In the last section we offer reflections on what could be possible ways of addressing some of the specified challenges. We point to the need to account for the 'dilemma of numbers' through structural design and to facilitate the development of trustful relationships and constructive deliberation within and across socio-economic sectors and related civil society organizations. Hitherto there is little experience of organizing multi-interest, cross-sectoral, cross-national stakeholder involvement in natural resource or environmental governance. In large parts of the Western World, including Europe, there is some expertise and practical experience in stakeholder involvement at local and national levels (Webler and Wiedemann 1995, Beierle and Cayford 2002). At the global (Steffek and Ferretti 2009, Willets 2011) and international (Linnerooth-Bayer et al. 2001) levels, both research and practice are only in a nascent state. Participatory structures have traditionally developed within the national state system. For these reasons, the reflections in the final section are informed mainly by general insights into requirements for organising stakeholder participation (Renn 2006, 2008). They are also informed by round table discussions among academics and practitioners of fisheries governance on whether and how to redesign the RACs for more integrated regional-level marine governance (Dreyer, et al. 2011).[3]

The Regional Approach to Stakeholder Involvement under the CFP: The Regional Advisory Councils

The Regional Advisory Councils are an important outcome of the 2002 reform of the Common Fisheries Policy, the European Union's instrument for the management of fisheries and aquaculture. The formal mandate of the 'stakeholder-led organizations' (EC 2004, Recital (3)) is to advise the European Commission in respect of proposals for fisheries management measures such as multi-annual recovery or management plans (EC 2002, Art. 31(4)). They are intended to serve two main purposes: first, to satisfy stakeholders' demands for better involvement and thereby reduce deficits in regulatory compliance and enforcement (COM 2001a); second, to enrich the decision-making process in EU fisheries policy and management by the knowledge and experience of the fishermen and fishing industry concerned and also of other stakeholders, such as environmental protection and consumer groups (EC 2002, Recital (27)).

2 Interviews and round table exchanges were part of the interdisciplinary ERANET BONUS project RISKGOV in which the authors of this chapter carried out a case study on fisheries. The case study was concerned with overfishing as a Baltic Sea environmental risk governance issue (Sellke et al. 2010).

3 These discussions were part of the RISKGOV project.

Five of the seven existing advisory bodies cover particular sea areas (see Table 7.1).[4] These are the Baltic Sea RAC, the Mediterranean RAC, the North Sea RAC, the North-western Waters RAC and the South-western Waters RAC. The five RACs are intended to add a source of regionally sensitive advice to the CFP (Long 2010). Their work is considered complementary to that of the Advisory Committee on Fisheries and Aquaculture (ACFA), which operates at the European level and provides advice largely on horizontal matters.

Table 7.1 RACs with a regional limitation

RACs with a regional character	Established	Members from
North Sea RAC	1 November 2004	Belgium, Denmark, France, Germany, Netherlands, Poland, Spain, Sweden, United Kingdom
North-western waters RAC	26 September 2005	Belgium, Spain, France, Ireland, the Netherlands, UK
Baltic Sea RAC	13 March 2006	Estonia, Denmark, Finland, Germany, Latvia, Lithuania, Poland, Sweden
South-western waters RAC	9 April 2007	Belgium, France, Portugal, Netherlands, Spain.
Mediterranean waters RAC	August 2008	Spain, France, Italy, Greece, Malta, Cyprus, Slovenia
Black Sea RAC (European Commission proposal)	to be established by 2015	

Information source: Fact Sheet – Regional Advisory Councils.

The RACs were not intended as a step in an incremental move towards a regionalized CFP (Sissenwine and Symes 2008: 66). However, in the context of the current reform of the CFP,[5] the European Commission has attached special importance to their regional structure, which is highlighted as a possible indication of how Europe's future fisheries management might look:

> And their regional structure, which prefigures recent developments in both the CFP (technical measures) and environmental policy (Marine Strategy

4 The other two RACs are defined by exploitation of specific stocks: pelagic stocks in Community waters (except in the Mediterranean and Baltic Seas) and high-sea fisheries outside Community waters (COM 2009: 2).

5 The reformed CFP has entered into force on 1 January 2014; this chapter was produced some time before the new CFP became effective.

> Directive), may provide one clue as to how Europe's fisheries could be managed more effectively in the future (COM 2009: 9).

Under the regionalization model that the European Commission proposes as part of the current CFP reform it is envisaged to maintain and extend the role of the RACs in advising on conservation policy (COM 2011a: 7). In view of the specificities of the Black Sea the Commission proposes further to set up a Black Sea Advisory Council by 2015.[6] There are no proposals in regard to changing the RACs' basic structure and membership (established in EC 2004), although these are not uncontroversial. It is a distinctive feature of the RACs that they have a broad constituency. They are composed of organizations representing the fisheries sector (fishermen, vessel owners, processors, traders, fish farmers, women's fisheries groups) and so-called 'other interest groups' affected by the CFP, groups with environmental, conservation, consumer or other concerns.

> RACs were in fact the first formal attempt to generate a network of multi-national, multi-interest organizations with a strong regional focus (Sissenwine and Symes 2007: 66).

The inclusion of parties not having an economic stake in fisheries management decisions was a response and contribution to a 'new societal/political context of fisheries management' in Europe (Varjopuro et al. 2008: 151) in which fisheries policy and management were increasingly defined as an environmental challenge and an issue of public interest (Jentoft et al. 2003). Among the main drivers of this new view of fisheries management were:

- several international agreements which endorsed the need to complement the traditional approach to fisheries management with environmental policy principles and objectives as a basis for management action (Varjopuro et al. 2008: 147);
- the EU's emerging policy of moving towards an ecosystem approach to marine management (Berghöfer et al. 2008);

6 The Council Decision establishing RACs (EC 2004) does not explicitly mention the Black Sea. According to the law and policy analyst Ronan Long (2011: 458) the absence of a Black Sea RAC is an 'obvious institutional weakness'. Until only recently, the European Commission has had a different view. In its 2008 review of the functioning of the RACs it still pointed to the possibility that the Mediterranean RAC could deal with the Black Sea through a specific working group, as the General Fisheries Commission for the Mediterranean does. Only in its 2011 Communication does the Commission propose to set up a specific RAC for the Black Sea. It also proposes to establish a new Advisory Council for Aquaculture. It points out that the RACs would need to be renamed Advisory Councils because not all of them have a 'regional character or limitation' (COM 2011b: 10).

- the increasing pressure exerted by environmental non-governmental organizations (NGOs) to switch to such an approach and not damage the marine ecosystem beyond repair (Gray 2005);

- the persistent problems of overfishing and resource depletion.

In the EU and globally, fisheries became tainted by the image of 'an ecological crisis in the making' (Mikalsen and Jentoft 2001: 286). Under these context conditions resource users came to be increasingly recognized as only one part of the entirety of affected and interested parties of EU fisheries management (ibid.: 282).

However, while the RACs are more inclusive in terms of stakeholder representation than established stakeholder advisory mechanisms such as ACFA,[7] they are still dominated by economic interests. EC regulation determines that in both the General Assembly and the Executive Committee a majority (two thirds) of the seats shall be allotted to representatives of the fisheries sector and only one third to representatives of other interest groups (EC 2004, Art. 5(3)). Environmental NGOs such as the World Wide Fund for Nature (WWF) have challenged the privileged role of the fisheries sector claiming that it was over-represented (Raakjær et al. 2010: 41, Linke et al. 2011: 134).

Critical Reflection on the RAC System in the Light of the New EU Marine Policies

Since the 2002 CFP reform, through which the RACs were established, the regulatory and political context of EU fisheries management has continued to change. With these changes the question of what constitutes a fair and balanced representation of stakeholders in EU fisheries and marine governance has become increasingly the subject of attention by academic and policy circles.

The most important change is that fisheries management has become a constituent of the European Integrated Maritime Policy (IMP) and the Marine Strategy Framework Directive (MSFD), which is classified as the environmental pillar of the EU's new maritime policy (Van Hoof and Van Tatenhove: 2009). Since the CFP's 2002 reform, a progressive implementation of an eco-system-based approach to fisheries management is a stated objective under the EU fisheries policy (EC 2002 Art. 2(1)). With this last revision of the CFP and the enactment of the MSFD, environmental and ecological objectives have turned into an integral part of EU fisheries management. The holistic approach of the IMP calls for fisheries management to be sensitive and responsive to the concerns, interests and impacts associated with the operations, management and policy of

7 It has been noted that in ACFA economic interests are even more dominant than in the RACs (Wilson 2009: 96).

other marine sectors (e.g. shipping, energy production or tourism). This is the main rationale for more collaborative and coordinated development of sectoral marine policies and management strategies as envisioned by the IMP: the need to tackle the 'increasing competition for marine space and the cumulative impact of human activities on marine ecosystems' (EC 2007: 4) and to deal with 'the inefficiencies, incoherencies and conflicts of use caused by fragmented decision-making in maritime affairs' (Van Tatenhove 2011: 87).

The RACs under Adaptation Pressure: Extension of Activities?

Scholars of fisheries governance have highlighted the pressures on the RACs to adapt to these recent changes in the political context and regulatory conditions of fisheries management (Sissenwine and Symes 2007, Raakjær et al. 2010). Such pressures for adjustment have been a prominent issue in debates around a 'regionalized' CFP which have taken place in the context of the current CFP reform process in academic and also in policy and fisheries sector circles. Here the idea has gained currency that RACs should have some involvement in the emerging broad-ranging debate around integrated marine and maritime management.

The CFP's reform package which the European Commission proposed in mid-2011 includes the proposal that the Advisory Councils extend their activities to other areas of marine management that affect fishing activities (COM 2011a: 7). The 2009 Inter-RAC Conference highlighted the challenges in terms of resource implications for RAC members if the RACs were to deal with a wider range of tasks. At the same time the importance of RACs engaging with broader maritime and marine issues was emphasized (Inter-RAC Conference 2009: 7). The European Commission's 2008 review of the functioning of the RACs found that some RACs were 'showing an interest in discussing maritime policy issues' (COM 2008: 8); these RACs engaged in discussions on the Nord Stream project in the Baltic Sea[8] (COM 2008). The preparedness to engage with broader maritime and marine issues is likely to vary among the different RACs and be influenced by factors such as capacity development challenges, duration and membership composition. A progressive stance towards such engagement has been stated by the North Sea RAC, the longest existing RAC to have benefited from an existing regional initiative.[9] The North Sea RAC assumes a key role in the development and implementation of the IMP and ensures that implementation of the CFP at regional level is compliant with the MSFD.[10]

8 The objective of the project is to construct a direct gas pipeline between Russia and Germany.

9 The North Sea Commission Fisheries Partnership.

10 To facilitate fulfilment of this role the North Sea RAC has established a Spatial Planning Working Group (Symes 2005a: 4-5) and claims to act already now as a 'focal point for discussions on maritime spatial planning' (Andersson NSRAC: 3).

Merging the RACs into an Inclusive Marine Stakeholder (Advisory) Structure at the Regional Level?

The debate on the current CFP reform has also brought forth ideas to conduct more wide-ranging change of the structures for stakeholder involvement in fisheries governance at the regional level. One vision of a regionalized governance system as embodied in the current reform debates is that the RACs are extended into cross-sector bodies to advise (or co-manage) marine/maritime (and not just fisheries) matters relating to the regional sea areas (cp. Raakjær et al. 2010). Scholars of marine (environmental) governance have highlighted the creation of a regional-level stakeholder involvement mechanism that is multi-national, multi-interest *and* cross-sectoral as a promising option to facilitate implementation of the new EU marine policies (De Santo 2011: 38, Van Tatenhove 2011: 99). The IMP's cross-sectoral approach and the MSFD's regional approach are considered complementary (De Santo 2010: 416) and requiring an 'integrated regional approach' (Van Hoof and Van Tatenhove 2009: 730), and this approach is seen as demanding more comprehensive structures of stakeholder involvement. It is highlighted that the IMP incorporates fisheries within much broader concerns for marine and maritime development and therefore brings many more stakes and stakeholders into play. In this view, the new EU marine policies demand the creation of 'new partnerships where different sectors will feel they are on equal footing' (De Santo 2011: 38). In these cooperative structures, the fisheries sector would only be one grouping of stakeholder interests among many others.

The European Commission's CFP reform package proposal (COM 2011a, 2011b) has made it clear that the RACs will continue to exist as fisheries sector-based bodies. It is unclear if the Commission's proposal to develop a new approach to stakeholder involvement on horizontal issues not covered by the RACs (COM 2011a: 7-9) aims at cross-sectoral exchanges between the fisheries sector and other marine sectors. The content of this recommended measure remains vague and tentative. However, as stressed by the literature on marine environmental governance, cross-sectoral stakeholder exchanges could facilitate implementation of the eco-system based approach to marine environmental management (the application of which is a central pillar of the MSFD; McLeod and Leslie 2009) and also of the IMP as both require management across sectors. Against this backdrop, the RACs are likely to be increasingly challenged as a manifestation of insufficiently inclusive advisory institutions. Growing attention should be devoted to the prospects of cross-sector marine advisory councils operating at the regional level to become the model of the future.

In the following sections we deal with this question by pointing out some of the key challenges that would need to be faced in the setting up of such an innovative stakeholder involvement mechanism. This account considers experiences with the RACs thus far, which themselves constitute a novel participatory mechanism in marine (fisheries) governance. We confine the discussion to the main issues linked to devising a stakeholder body with a purely *advisory* function (as the

RACs are). Establishment of a co-management stakeholder body would pose formidable legal challenges and require separate analysis.

Inclusion and Closure: Particular Challenges in Devising Regional-level Stakeholder Involvement

Analysts of governance processes in the fields of risk and environment have noted that devising a stakeholder involvement process requires addressing difficult issues of 'inclusion' and 'closure' (Renn and Schweizer 2009). Inclusion and closure constitute essential parts of any decision or policy-making activity. With the advent of innovative participatory processes, issues of inclusion and closure have, however, 'become more complex and sophisticated' than purported in conventional strategies of decision-analysis' (Renn and Schweizer 2009: 175, see also Webler 1999). Focussing on the challenges of inclusion and closure the following sections highlight this complexity with respect to establishing a marine advisory body that is aimed at corresponding to the integrated regional-level approach as called for by the new EU marine policies. Table 7.2 provides an overview of main issues related to these design elements of the process of advice production.

Whom to Include?

An integrated approach to marine/maritime governance acknowledges that all uses of Europe's seas and oceans need to be reconciled with each other and managed as part of wider marine ecosystems. A regional marine advisory body would thus need to work across the neighbouring coastal states of the respective marine region. The countries required to cooperate at this level depends on the definition of the regions and the criteria used to establish them; criteria likely to be included are hydrological, oceanographic and biogeographic features. The body would also need to work across the key sectors in the region (such as fisheries, maritime transport, energy production, tourism) with environmental protection and nature conservation as cross-cutting issues. Considering that the sectors do not constitute homogeneous entities but comprise actors with often very different interests and agendas (such as small-scale fishermen and producer and other market organizations in fisheries) this means a large number of possible members of the advisory body. The real challenge then is to define the boundaries of stakeholder involvement such that the membership's composition is acknowledged within and outside the advisory body as a true reflection of the range of relevant stakeholders in the region while ensuring at the same time efficient working processes which help to make participation attractive to the target groups (cp. Mikalsen and Jentoft 2001: 284). This challenge, emphasized with regard to representation of national, fisheries sector and other interests in the RACs, is aggravated substantially with such a broad-ranging advisory body.

The question of who qualifies as a legitimate stakeholder is a particularly sensitive issue considering the risk of an unmanageable membership size. Furthermore, the issue of what constitutes a balanced representation of these stakeholders is equally delicate. For instance, should user and sectoral groups be given a privileged position by a majority in number as is the case with the RACs? Importantly, the MSFD has further enhanced the legitimacy of the stakeholder role of environmental NGOs in marine policy and management. Therefore the criticism from these groups regarding the fisheries sector's dominance in the RACs is likely to gain in political importance. The IMP's cross-sectoral approach brings more consumer interests into play than just those related to food production and consumption. How should these context conditions be accounted for in determining the proportion of the membership to be assigned to groups with environmental, conservation, consumer or other concerns in a marine advisory body? In addressing such questions, the particular resource constraints (in terms of staff, time, money) facing these stakeholders require consideration (Tamm Hallström and Boström 2010). For example, scholars of fisheries governance have explained inadequate representation of NGOs in the RACs in terms of their lack of manpower (Sissenwine and Symes 2007: 67, see also COM 2008: 5).

Furthermore, the question of whether or not 'non-members' holding relevant decision-making power or knowledge could be invited to participate in the advisory body's work (as it is the case for the RACs; EC 2004, Art. 6) would have to be addressed. This would open the door to national and regional administrations of the coastal countries concerned, the competent EU authorities, representatives of other relevant advisory bodies, representatives of stakeholders from third countries and scientific experts.

What to Include on the Basis of which Mandate?

Inclusion is also a critical issue in terms of what the advisory body is asked to provide an input on. If policy or management options were the targets of advice, the advisory bodies could be asked to evaluate a range of pre-defined policy or management options. For instance, this could be options of marine spatial planning aimed at solving conflicts in an ecologically and socio-economically sensible manner between sectors pressing for as much space as possible in a marine region (cp. De Santo 2011). Alternatively, the task could be confined to providing feedback on a single pre-defined option (such as the multi-annual recovery or management plans that the RACs are consulted about) or partial aspects of such an option. Or the body might be tasked – additionally rather than solely – to the interpretations of data and scientific assessments serving option development.

All other choices with regard to inclusion and closure selection of the object(s) of consultation need to be considered in relation to the particular rationale(s) for stakeholder involvement. This is an important factor for internal and external legitimacy of the participation exercise, as is illustrated by critical comments on a mismatch of participation purpose and participation practice in the case of the RACs (Linke et al. 2011). While the RACs should enable the CFP to benefit from the knowledge and experience of the various stakeholders (EC 2002, Recital (27)), they are only very peripherally involved in the formal processes of knowledge generation and production of advice which inform the selection of the management measure that the RACs are ultimately consulted about. It is questionable whether inclusion of only pre-defined policy or management options would be acknowledged as an appropriate approach for a marine advisory body.

There are, furthermore, fundamental questions about the basic objectives and criteria for performance assessment of an integrated marine management based around an eco-system approach. Overarching basic objectives and criteria might reasonably be defined by official politics at supranational level with the use of established mechanisms of stakeholder consultation. Implementation in a regionalized framework would require that these general guidelines are elaborated through more specific objectives and targets that are tailored to the particular socio-economic, political, cultural conditions and ecological circumstances of the marine regions. This task should involve input from stakeholders that has been produced in a communication process that is based on mutual exchange of arguments and reflections. The marine advisory body could be an appropriate forum for such a deliberation process (Renn 2008: 333) when geared towards developing a shared vision of integrated marine management in a particular region.

Reaching an agreement on what constitutes an appealing vision may prove a difficult task in view of the numerous and disparate social groups that are affected by or have a strong interest in the regional marine management. However, the exchanges among stakeholders might be more effective if they conveyed an accurate picture of areas of convergence and divergence between their views to the policy and decision-makers. Inclusion of this information could be a decisive factor in the regional long-term strategy being implemented.

Being part of such a heterogeneous advisory body would be particularly testing. It is difficult to assess whether stakeholders would be willing to invest the necessary time and energy, especially if the body worked in a purely advisory function meaning that exertion of influence on political decision-making was highly uncertain. It would need at least a formal commitment from the decision-making bodies to give reasons for their decisions in relation to the stakeholders' advice. Otherwise, incentives to participate might be too low. It has been noted that at least a number of the RAC members were increasingly frustrated about the lack or minimal extent of influence that they could exert on actual decision-making (Raakjær et al. 2010: 14). If the RACs' advice was almost always overruled and the participants did not feel that they were being heard, stakeholders would have decreasing motivation to stay engaged in the advisory process.

There are differences in the allocation of competences for the policies included in integrated marine management implies. This is a source of complication in establishing provisions for feedback on the stakeholders' views from the political implementation level. For instance, while the European Community retains exclusive jurisdiction over fisheries management, Member States are responsible for nature conservation within their borders (De Santo 2010). Hence, the stakeholders' advice would concern and need to be geared towards different political levels: the national level (i.e. the countries bordering the marine region), the supranational level (EU), and ideally also the regional level in terms of the collectivity of riparian states.

Effective management of a marine region requires cooperation between the bordering countries and these could use the marine advisory body as their principal stakeholder advisory mechanism. Establishing such cooperation would be difficult, without a statement of responsibilities that the national actors and stakeholders could adhere to, particularly in those regions where collaborative relationships between the riparian states are only poorly developed or exclude non-EU coastal countries. In regions such as the Baltic Sea, the North Sea and North-East Atlantic already existing regional-level organizations such as HELCOM (the Baltic Marine Environmental Protection Commission), and OSPAR (Commission for protecting and conserving the North-East Atlantic and its resources) might play an important role in building up or further expanding such collaboration (Kern and Löffelsend 2008).

What Counts in Producing the Outcome of the Advisory Process?

'Closure' refers to the rules of when and how to close a debate (Renn and Schweizer 2009). These rules include determining what counts as the basis on which the final product of the advisory process is to be generated. Consideration and processing of the concerns and interests of all participating stakeholders might be determined as the basis for closure, if the body's mandate was to compare a range of possible management options in regard to the acceptability or desirability of their consequences. This might include the deliberate attempt to evaluate trade-offs that the different options may imply and reach an agreement on which trade-offs would be preferable over others. As has been emphasized by scholars of marine environmental management, trade-offs between multiple objectives (often corresponding with socio-economic sectors and ecosystem services) are inevitable in such comprehensive management as envisioned by IMP and ecosystem-based marine management (McLeod and Leslie, 2009).

Obviously, evaluation of the consequences of policy options requires insights into the nature of these consequences. There is no doubt that scientific knowledge is of major importance to produce such insights. However, in view of the enormous complexity and scientific uncertainty facing integrated marine management, scientific knowledge should be connected to the practical and experiential knowledge that stakeholders can provide. Therefore, the advisory body may be entrusted with more than one task. The product related to the first task (delivery of input into the characterization of the consequences of policy options) would ideally be based on the processing of systematic, experiential and practical knowledge in an exchange between members of the advisory body and invited scientists. The product related to the second task (statement on what options are preferable) would need to be based on the consideration of potential violations of interests and values caused by these (jointly characterized) consequences.

What Level of Agreement is to be Reached?

Reaching 'consensus advice' may be in the interest of the members of the advisory body. There is more pressure on decision-makers to seriously consider following the advice if this is consensual. For decision-makers the consensus-seeking efforts of the advisory body may be a way to delegate the act of balancing and aggregating various interests and concerns (Dreyer et al. 2011). In the case of the marine advisory body, however, producing consensus advice is likely to be an insurmountable task given the diverse perspectives, interests and values of the numerous actors involved, many of whom may have no experience in expressing common views.

The greater the number of actors and the heterogeneity of the membership, the more difficult it is to reach either a consensus or some other kind of joint agreement. Even though the RACs are not cross-sectoral, they also face considerable difficulties in adopting recommendations through consensus that they are formally called upon to strive for (EC 2004, Art. 7(3)). The important dividing line here is between the fisheries sector and the environmental community (Linke et al. 2011). If no consensus can be reached, dissenting opinions expressed by members of the RACs shall be recorded in the recommendations adopted by the majority of the members (EC 2004, Art. 7(3)). If the membership is as heterogeneous as in the envisioned marine advisory body, more than one dissenting opinion is likely to be the rule rather than the exception.

An advisory body does not necessarily risk losing all of its advisory capacity, if there are several dissenting opinions. This risk would in any case be lower, if these opinions took the form of consistent positions (agreed among the promoters of the respective views) offered as a set of possible courses of action to the political decisions-maker(s) who would then make the final selection. For example, these could be a small set of reasonable options to deal with conflicts about spatial use between socio-economic sectors which perform differently (but none of them optimally) relative to pre-defined environmental, economic and social objectives. Such plural advice (Stirling 2003: 61) may present a minimum consensus among the stakeholders in terms of a 'consensus about dissent' (Renn and Schweizer 2009: 182), if agreement on a single best solution is not achievable. This would presuppose that the positions were clarified or generated in a deliberative process through which mutual understanding was achieved regarding the reasons the opposing parties took a particular view. In this case, the stakeholder exchanges may result in increased levels of trust in the intentions and competence of the other (Boström 2006). This second-order effect could help to keep stakeholders engaged in the advisory body even if disagreement in regard to what recommendation should be adopted was the rule rather than the exception.

Table 7.2 Main issues of inclusion and closure for marine advisory councils

Inclusion	Main issues/options
Whom to include?	Who qualifies as stakeholder? What is a balanced stakeholder representation? Should scientific experts be involved as non-members? How to reconcile broad-based involvement and practical feasibility?
What to include?	Single policy/management option for feedback? Set of options for comparative evaluation? Data basis and interpretation serving option development for review? Basic objectives/criteria of an integrated marine management as a basis for developing a vision for region-specific adaptation/implementation?
Closure	**Main issues/options**
What counts in outcome production?	Processing of knowledge (systematic, experiential, practical) for characterization of the consequences of policy options? and/or Consideration of all interests, concerns and value preferences in evaluation of options?
What level of agreement?	Consensus advice? Majority recommendation and minority statements? Plural advice?

Drawing on: Renn and Schweizer 2009.

Possible Ways to Address the Specified Challenges

The EU has become an important political player in Europe's regional sea areas, in some even the main one. Since the turn of the millennium, the Europeanization of regional seas has been accompanied by growing efforts to develop and introduce a more regionalized approach to EU marine governance. The basic argument of this chapter is that a 'third tier of governance – at the level of the regional sea' (Symes 2009: 101) also needs to include appropriate mechanisms of stakeholder involvement at this level (cf. Jentoft and Chuenpagdee 2015 in this volume). We have dealt with the option of setting up a stakeholder advisory body which works across marine sectors and sustainability dimensions (i.e. ecological, economic, social). This focus takes up the recently emerging idea to drastically extend the RACs in response to the ecological and integration objectives of the new EU marine policies.

We have shown that setting up an Inclusive Marine Advisory Body implies addressing demanding issues related to inclusion and closure. The issues that we have highlighted are not specific to the envisioned stakeholder body. They also pertain to the RACs and continue to give cause for critical reflections of these bodies' design. They are, however, even more critical when the advisory body is to provide input on how to design and/or implement a holistic approach such as integrated marine management. This requires consideration of various economic, social and environmental aspects which have strong links to particular interests which would need to be represented in the body – this produces a major 'dilemma of numbers' (Symes 2005b: 94-95).

It would be worth considering whether giving the advisory body a sophisticated structure would be a possible way of coping with this dilemma. The idea would be to design a structure that minimizes the risk that appropriately broad participation is achieved at the expense of quality of deliberation and effectiveness of reaching joint products. This could involve a combination of sub-divisions and an overarching integrating forum. The sub-divisions could be panels that deal with all issues concerning a specific sector (involving representatives of this sector) or particular cross-sectoral issues (involving stakeholder representatives particularly affected by or interested in these issues). In the overarching integrating forum (drawing on representatives of each of the sub-forums) discussion and decision-making would then be carried out on the basis of the input by all panels. A tiered structure that allows working in smaller groups could possibly increase the likelihood that the advisory body would also serve as an arena for fruitful deliberation, rapprochement and bridge-building among the disparate social groups. Most importantly, sufficient care would need to be taken to ensure that the role of each division and the way in which the different divisions are connected are clearly defined and that transparency of the whole process of advice production is warranted. Discussions on what could be appropriate structural designs are only emerging (Dreyer et al. 2011).

Essentially, integrated marine management requires finding the most appropriate way to deal with divergent interests and associated values and to set efficient and fair trade-offs between conflicting goals (cf. Jentoft and Chuenpagdee 2015 in this volume). Therefore, structures that can facilitate the building up of trustful relationships and constructive deliberation among representatives of the individual socio-economic sectors and related civil society organizations and between representatives of different sectors and related civil society organizations would be crucial. Pure bargaining would probably not be sufficient for reconciliation of the diverse interests and preferences. Deliberation could initiate a social learning process within which preferences are reflected and modified and an argumentation basis created that is in large parts shared by all parties involved. On that basis win-win solutions, reasonable compensation packages or acceptable trade-offs might be more easily generated (Renn 2008: 290-313). As pointed out above, it could also serve as a basis on which plural advice is produced in terms of a set of possible courses of action to be proposed to the decision-makers. Given the diversity of interests, concerns and value preferences a formal mandate to seek consensus could actually have a negative effect on the stakeholders' motivation to engage with the advisory body. Although likely to be a controversial issue, moderation of the deliberations by trained facilitators with skills such as conflict management should be considered.

The Inclusive Marine Advisory Body as outlined in this chapter is probably not the model of the near future. This chapter has, however, served to highlight that regionalization, if it is to improve the process of EU marine governance, needs to also address difficult issues that are involved in the task of devising stakeholder involvement at the regional level. We hope that these reflections help to promote debates on the prospects and challenges of making the regional level a third tier of stakeholder involvement in EU marine governance.

References

Andersson, H. (NSRAC). *The North Sea Regional Advisory Council: Future Governance within a Reformed Common Fisheries Policy.* [Online] Available at: http://www.nsrac.org/wp-content/uploads/2010/08/Statement-on-governance-from-NSRAC-060710.pdf [accessed: 13 February 2012].

Beierle, T.C. and Cayford, J. 2002. *Democracy in Practice: Public Participation in Environmental Decisions*. Washington, DC: Resources for the Future.

Berghöfer, A., Wittmer, H. and Rauschmayer, F. 2008. Stakeholder participation in ecosystem-based approaches to fisheries management: A synthesis from European research projects. *Marine Policy*, 32, 243-253.

Boström, M. 2006. Establishing credibility: Practising standard-setting ideals in a Swedish seafood-labelling case. *Journal of Environmental Policy & Planning*, 8, 135-58.

Commission of the European Communities (COM) 2001a. *Green Paper on the Future of the Common Fisheries Policy*. COM(2001) 135 final, Brussels, 20.3.2001.

Commission of the European Communities (COM) 2001b. *European Governance: A White Paper.* COM 428 final, Brussels, 25.7.2001.

Commission of the European Communities (COM). 2007. *Communication from the Commission to the European Parliament, the Council, the European Economic and Social Committee and the Committee of the Regions: An Integrated Maritime Policy for the European Union*. COM(2007) 575 final, Brussels, 10.10.2007.

Commission of the European Communities (COM). 2008. *Communication from the Commission to the Council and the European Parliament: Review of the functioning of the Regional Advisory Councils*. COM(2008) 364 final, Brussels, 17.6.2008.

Commission of the European Communities (COM) 2009. *The Common Fisheries Policy: A User's Guide*. Luxembourg: Office for Official Publications of the European Communities.

Commission of the European Communities (COM) 2011a. *Communication from the Commission to the European Parliament, the Council, the European Economic and Social Committee and the Committee of the Regions: Reform of the Common Fisheries Policy*. COM(2011) 417 final, Brussels, 13.7.2011.

Commission of the European Communities (COM) 2011b. *Proposal for a Regulation of the European Parliament and of the Council on the Common Fisheries Policy*, {SEC(2011) 891 final} {SEC(2011) 892 final}. COM(2011) 425 final, 2011/0195 (COD), Brussels, 13.7.2011.

De Santo, E.M. 2010. 'Whose science?' Precaution and power-play in European marine environmental decision-making. *Marine Policy*, 34, 414-420.

De Santo, E.M. 2011. Environmental justice implications of Maritime Spatial Planning in the European Union. *Marine Policy*, 35, 34-38.

Dreyer, M., Sellke, P. and Renn, O. 2011. *Summary Report: RISKGOV Round Table on 'Stakeholder Participation and Communication in Baltic Sea Environmental Risk Governance'* (14-15 February 2011, Stuttgart, Germany), Deliverable 'Round Table 3' of the ERANET BONUS project Bonus-79: RISKGOV. Stuttgart: DIALOGIK.

Dreyer, M., Sellke, P., Boström, M. and Jönsson, AM. 2011. *Structures and Processes of Stakeholder and Public Communication on Baltic Sea Environmental Risks*. Deliverable 10 of the ERANET BONUS project RISKGOV (contract no. 217246). DIALOGIK: Stuttgart. Available at: www.sh.se/riskgov. [accessed 13 July 2014].

European Community (EC) 2002. Council Regulation (EC) No 2371/2002 of 20 December 2002 on the conservation and sustainable exploitation of fisheries resources under the Common Fisheries Policy. *Official Journal of the European Communities*, L 358/59, 31.12.2002.

European Community (EC) 2004. Council Decision of 19 July (2004) establishing Regional Advisory Councils under the Common Fisheries Policy, 2004/585/EC. *Official Journal of the European Union*, L 56/17, Brussels, 3.8.2004.

European Community (EC) 2008. Directive 2008/56/EC of the European Parliament and of the Council of 17 June 2008 establishing a framework for community action in the field of marine environmental policy (Marine Strategy Framework Directive) (Text with EEA relevance). *Official Journal of the European Union*, L 164/19, 25.6.2008.

Fact Sheet: Regional Advisory Councils. [Online]. Available at: http://ec.europa.eu/fisheries/documentation/publications/cfp_factsheets/racs_en.pdf [accessed: 15 March 2012].

Gray, T.S. 2005. Theorising about participatory fisheries governance, in *Participation in Fisheries Governance*, edited by T.S. Gray. Dordrecht: Springer, 1-25.

Hajer, M. and Wagenaar, H. 2003. *Deliberative Policy Analysis: Understanding Governance in the Network Society*. Boston, MA: Cambridge University Press.

Inter-RAC Conference 2009. *Decision-Making in the Reform of the Common Fisheries Policy: Report of an Inter-RAC Conference hosted by the Scottish*

Government & jointly funded by Marine Scotland & DEFRA. The Merchants' Hall, Edinburgh, November 3rd & 4th 2009. (Summary). [Online]. Available at: http://www.nsrac.org/wp-content/uploads/2010/03/Final-Report-of-the-Edinburgh-Conference.pdf [accessed: 27 February 2012].

Jentoft, S., Mikalsen, K.H. and Hernes, H.-K. 2003. Representation in fisheries co-management, in *The Fisheries Co-management Experience: Accomplishments, Challenges and Prospects*, edited by D.C. Wilson, J. Raakjær and P. Degnbol. Dordrecht: Kluwer Academic, 281-292.

Jentoft, S. and Chuenpagdee, R. 2015. The 'New' Marine Governance: assessing governability, in *Governing Europe's Marine Environment: Europeanization of Regional Seas or Regionalization of EU Policies*?, edited by M. Gilek and K. Kern. Farnham, UK: Ashgate Publishing.

Kern, K. and Löffelsend, T. 2008. Governance beyond the nation state: Transnationalization and Europeanization of the Baltic Sea Region, in *Governing a Common Sea: Environmental Policies in the Baltic Sea Region*, edited by M. Joas, D. Jahn and K. Kern. London: Earthscan, 115-141.

Linke, S., Dreyer, M. and Sellke, P. 2011. The Regional Advisory Councils: What is their potential to incorporate stakeholder knowledge into fisheries governance? *Ambio*, 40(12), 133-143.

Linnerooth-Bayer, J., Löfstedt, R.E. and Sjöstedt, G. (eds) 2001. *Transboundary Risk Management*. London: Earthscan.

Long, R. 2010. The role of Regional Advisory Councils in the European Common Fisheries Policy: Legal constraints and future options. *The International Journal of Marine and Coastal Law*, 25, 289-346.

Long, R. 2011. Legal aspects of ecosystem-based marine management in Europe. *Ocean Yearbook*, 26, 417-484.

McLeod, K. and Leslie, H. (eds) 2009. *Ecosystem-based Management for the Oceans*. Washington, DC: Island Press.

Mikalsen, K.H. and Jentoft, S. 2001. From user-groups to stakeholders? The public interest in fisheries management. *Marine Policy*, 25, 281-292.

Raakjær, J., Abreu, H., Armstrong, C., Hegland, T.J., Van Hoof, L., Ounanian, K., Ramirez, P., Röckmann, C. and Zetterholm, S. 2010. *Exploring the Option of Regionalising the Common Fisheries Policy. Making the European Fisheries Ecosystem Plan Operatio*nal (MEFEPO): Work Package 4, Technical Document. [Online]. Available at: http://vbn.aau.dk/files/44028562/Work_Package_4_report.pdf [accessed 4 January 2012].

Renn, O. 2006. Participatory processes for designing environmental policies. *Land Use Policy*, 23(1), 34-43.

Renn, O. 2008. *Risk Governance: Coping with Uncertainty in a Complex World*. London: Earthscan.

Renn, O. and Schweizer, P.-J. 2009. Inclusive risk governance: concepts and application to environmental policy making. *Environmental Policy and Governance*, 19(3), 174-185.

Renn, O., Webler, T. and Wiedemann, P. (eds) 1995. *Fairness & Competence in Citizen Participation: Evaluating Models for Environmental Discourse*. Dordrecht: Kluwer.

Sellke, P., Dreyer, M. and Renn, O. 2010. Fisheries: A case study of environmental risk governance in the Baltic Sea. Deliverable 2 of the ERANET BONUS project Bonus-79: RISKGOV. Stuttgart: DIALOGIK.

Sissenwine, M. and Symes, D. 2007. *Reflections on the Common Fisheries Policy. Report to the General Directorate for Fisheries and Maritime Affairs of the European Commission*, July 2007. [Online]. Available at: http://www.seas-at-risk.org/1mages/Midterm%20review%20Sissenwine%20and%20Symes%20 2007.pdf [accessed 4 January 2012].

Steffek, J. and Ferretti, M.P. 2009. Accountability or 'good decisions'? The competing goals of civil society participation in international governance. *Global Society*, 23(1), 37-57.

Stirling, A. 2003. Risk, uncertainty and precaution: Some instrumental implications from the social sciences, in *Negotiating Environmental Change: New Perspectives from Social Sciences*, edited by F. Berkhout, M. Leach and I. Scoones. Cheltenham: Edward Elgar, 33-76.

Stirling, A. 2008. 'Opening up' and 'Closing down'. Power, participation and pluralism in the social appraisal of technology. *Science, Technology & Human Values*, 33(2), 262-294.

Symes, D. 2005a. *Marine Spatial Planning: A Fisheries Perspective. Report to English Nature*. Unpublished. [Online]. Available at: http://ioc3.unesco.org/marinesp/files/Marine%20Spatial%20Planning_Fisheries%20Perspective.pdf [accessed: 17 January 2012].

Symes, D. 2005b. Regionalization of fisheries governance: An empty vessel or a cornucopia of opportunity?, in *Participation in Fisheries Governance*, edited by T.S. Gray. Dordrecht: Springer, 85-102.

Symes, D. 2009. *Regionalising the Common Fisheries Policy: What kind of Institutional Solution?* Nordic Council of Ministers' Conference 'Regionalization of the EU's Common Fisheries Policy' (Copenhagen, 13 October 2009). University of Hull. [Online]. Available at: http://www.nsrac.org/wp-content/uploads/2009/11/NSRAC-DWG-2-David-Symes-Regionalising-CFP-13-10-09-final-_Wo.pdf [accessed: 11 January 2012].

Tamm Hallström, K. and Boström, M. 2010. *Transnational Multi-Stakeholder Standardization: Organizing Fragile Non-State Authority*. Cheltenham: Edward Elgar.

Van Hoof, L. and Van Tatenhove, J. 2009. EU marine policy on the move: The tension between fisheries and maritime policy. *Marine Policy*, 33(4), 726-732.

Van Tatenhove, J. 2011. Integrated marine governance. Questions of legitimacy. *Maritime Studies*, 10(1), 87-113.

Varjopuro, R., Gray, T.S., Hatchard, J., Rauschmayer, F. and Wittmer, H. 2008. Introduction: Interaction between environment and fisheries – The role of stakeholder participation. *Marine Policy*, 32(2), 147-157.

Webler, T. 1999. The craft and theory of public participation: A dialectical process. *Journal of Risk Research*, 2(1), 55-71.

Willets, P. 2011. *Non-Governmental Organizations in World Politics: The Construction of Global Governance*. London: Routledge.

Wilson, D.C. 2009. *The Paradoxes of Transparency: Science and the Ecosystem Approach to Fisheries Management in Europe*. Amsterdam: Amsterdam University Press.

Chapter 8

Science and Policy in the Governance of Europe's Marine Environment: The Impact of Europeanization, Regionalization and the Ecosystem Approach to Management

Michael Gilek, Mikael Karlsson,
Oksana Udovyk and Sebastian Linke

Introduction

The governance of Europe's marine environment concerns the relationship between two systems: a 'system-to-be-governed' made up of the natural system and a 'governing system' made up of institutions and organizations with a functional responsibility to steer the system-to-be-governed towards a set of goals (see Jentoft and Chuenpagdee 2015 in this volume). Both are complex in the sense that they are often diverse, multifaceted, dynamic and vulnerable. Science and policy meet at the interface between the two systems, but the traditional ideal that science, e.g. via scientific committees, speaks objective truth to directly responsive politicians has been questioned (e.g. Nowotny et al. 2001). This is not least the case when it comes to the governance of large-scale marine environmental risks such as overfishing, eutrophication and hazardous chemicals, where the demarcation between the two domains of science and policy is far from clear-cut due to scientific uncertainty and disagreements among stakeholders (Wilson 2009, Karlsson et al. 2011, Linke et al. 2014).

European marine governance is currently adapting to three interconnected processes driven by regulatory reforms both within and outside the European Union, all of which entail challenges and possibilities for policy as well as science (Kern and Gilek 2015 in this volume). First, Europeanization through, for example, expansion of EU-wide regulatory frameworks such as the Common Fisheries Policy (CFP) challenges institutional arrangements as well as science support at both EU and domestic levels (cf. Linke et al. 2014). Second, regionalization through, for example, strengthening of strategies at the level of regional seas such as the Black Sea Strategic Action Plan (BSSAP 2009) may potentially improve the efficiency of marine environmental governance over time (European Commission 2011). However, it is also possible that differences among regional seas in terms of mandate, resources, path dependency, etc. will lead to differences in efficiency and outcomes of environmental governance (cf. Van Leeuwen et al. 2012). Finally, the so-called Ecosystem Approach to Management (EAM), incorporated in marine policies both in Europe and elsewhere, imposes new challenges on science-policy interactions with its deliberate aim to facilitate integration over multiple, often conflicting, management objectives linked to environmental and socio-economic dimensions of sustainable development (Arkema et al. 2006, Hammer 2015 in this volume).

This chapter focuses on these three trends and investigates how they influence science and policy and their interactions: Will Europeanization, regionalization and EAM implementation facilitate the development of a more credible scientific knowledge base and enhanced legitimacy in science-based advice, and thereby reduce tensions and the probability of conflicts, rather than exacerbate scientific uncertainty and disagreements in European marine environmental governance? By exploring this question, we seek to improve the understanding of science-policy interactions and to identify strategies for improving the governance of Europe's marine environment.

Considering the scope of this objective we focus our investigation on the EU Marine Strategy Framework Directive (MSFD), which aims at achieving good environmental status (GES) for a wide set of descriptors linked to e.g. commercial fish and chemical contaminants.[1] The MSFD does not, however, cover all science-policy interactions linked to marine issues. For example, environmental risks linked to maritime transports are covered mainly in other frameworks (Söderström et al. 2015 in this volume). Still, the directive is fundamental to EU marine environmental governance and it has been developed and is implemented in parallel with the three trends outlined above. The MSFD is therefore a relevant and logical case for the concern of this chapter. Considering the MSFD's broad-ranging character, our results and conclusions are of value also for other cases such as fisheries and chemicals not necessarily restricted to European settings.

The main part of the chapter consists of an analysis of how the trends of Europeanization, regionalization and EAM-implementation have influenced the design and implementation of the MSFD, including its impact on scientific activities, as well as on policy measures and stakeholder relations. We also discuss how the three trends influence each other within the scope of the MSFD and compare the findings with the development in the two interconnected policy areas of fisheries and chemicals.

This introduction is followed by a conceptual overview of the key topics of concern (i.e. science-policy interactions, Europeanization, regionalization and

1 Consequently, for particular GES descriptors there is a strong interconnection between the MSFD and other regulatory frameworks such the Common Fisheries Policy (CFP) and the Regulation on Registration, Evaluation, Authorization and Restriction of Chemicals (REACH) (Karlsson et al. 2011).

EAM-implementation). After a brief introduction of the MSFD, we analyse and relate the MSFD to Europeanization, regionalization and the EAM in three respective sections. The final discussion section addresses our findings in relation to the key question and overall aim of the study.

Background to the Analysed Interactions and Trends

This section gives a background to our study in terms of a conceptual overview of science-policy interactions, followed by a description of the trends of Europeanization, regionalization and the EAM. Finally, we provide a description of the case study in focus – the MSFD.

Science-Policy Interactions and Marine Environmental Governance

Science has a prominent role in society and has long since been used to guide policy-making, particularly when managing environmental risks stemming from industrial technologies. Traditionally, science is perceived not only as the cornerstone for developing policies, but often also as the sole legitimate source of knowledge for decision-making – a view that is still very common. Over the last decades, however, scholars in social sciences as well as practitioners have increasingly questioned the elevated position of science on both normative and empirical grounds (e.g. Jasanoff 1990, Nowotny et al. 2001). In the field of environmental governance, a simultaneous politicization of science and scientification of politics has been identified (cf. Weingart 1999, Eriksson et al. 2010, Linke et al. 2014). This has resulted in lowered public trust in science and the cracks in the wall of objective science have enabled recognition of other knowledge sources, such as experiential, laymen and local knowledge (Irwin and Michael 2003). Furthermore, scientific uncertainty and disagreements between stakeholders, easily opening for stakeholders to fight over the privilege of interpretation, have gradually become more acknowledged as key parameters to consider in environmental governance arrangements. According to Stirling (1999),[2] issues characterized by uncertainty, ambiguity or ignorance require an expansion of traditional approaches, to include precautionary and participative methods in both the assessment and management of risks.

As a consequence, the relationship between science and policy is changing on both the theoretical and practical level, particularly with regard to complex environmental issues, such as marine governance. The present chapter will further explore if and how these changes may be influenced by the three trends in focus.

2 Stirling (1999) differentiates between four types of scientific incertitude: risk (quantitative data and knowledge exist), uncertainty (qualitative understanding of outcome, but not probabilities), ambiguity (poor knowledge about potential outcome) and ignorance.

Europeanization and Marine Environmental Governance

In parallel to the changing relations between science and policy, environmental policies have increasingly been Europeanized. During its first three decades, the European Community had no mandate to explicitly legislate in the field of environmental protection, even though some market harmonization laws as well as the CAP (Common Agricultural Policy) and the CFP (Common Fisheries Policy) were of importance from an environmental point of view. With the Single European Act in 1986, protection of the environment was explicitly included in the Treaty and the scope of EU environmental law has since then been gradually widened, including being capped in the late 1990s by the objective of sustainable development in the Amsterdam Treaty (Jans and Vedder 2012). Over time, many consensus-based EC directives, charging Member States with implementation, have been replaced with majority-voting procedures and, in some cases, directly binding EU regulations, e.g. on chemicals (Karlsson 2010). Moreover, the European Parliament has been given a much stronger role over time, also concerning marine environmental governance.

In the academic debate, a common definition of 'Europeanization' is still missing (Olsen 2002), but studies have traditionally concentrated on the impact of European politics on Member States. However, considering that the impact of Member States' actions on EU institutions is also relevant, studies on top-down Europeanization have increasingly been complemented with a bottom-up perspective (Radaelli 2006). This fact, that processes of Europeanization are more interactive than unidirectional, implies that Europeanization can be regarded as a 'co-evolution between the domestic and the European level' (Radaelli 2006). The present chapter will investigate this development in the field of marine environmental governance, with a focus on the MSFD.

Regionalization and the Governance of Europe's Marine Environment

Yet another trend concerns increasing regionalization of responsibilities and power in various policy fields, motivated by e.g. a wish for improving economic or environmental efficiency (e.g. European Commission 2011). In a Europe-wide perspective, regional efforts to improve the marine environment started quite early with the Helsinki Convention on the protection of the marine environment of the Baltic Sea, signed in 1974, as the first regional seas convention.[3] During the last decade, this development has been manifested in so-called 'good governance' approaches in EU fisheries policy, e.g. via the Regional Advisory Councils (Linke et al. 2011), in the EU strategies for the Baltic Sea Region and the Danube

3 The emergence of the Helsinki Convention triggered the creation of UNEP's Regional Seas Programme, which now covers 18 regions in the world, including the Mediterranean Sea (Barcelona Convention 1976), the North-East Atlantic (OSPAR Convention 1992), and the Black Sea (Bucharest Convention 1992).

Region (European Commission 2009, 2010a), and in transnational governance networks consisting of, for example, NGOs (Joas et al. 2008). These examples of more regionalized approaches are assumed to strengthen marine environmental governance over time.

Research on macro-regionalization is still limited, but, as discussed by Kern and Gilek (2015 in this volume), it is possible to define at least two paths for studying 'macro-regionalization'. In the first, macro-regionalization is considered as a process of political and economic interactions among a group of neighbouring states at an intermediary level between the national and the European level (Söderström et al. 2015 in this volume). Along the second path, macro-regionalization is regarded as part of the EU's territorial cohesion policy (Söderström et al. 2015 in this volume). Our study primarily applies the latter perspective when investigating the consequences of EU regionalization through the MSFD on science-policy interactions in marine environmental governance.

The EAM and Marine Environmental Governance

The third trend – implementation of the EAM – has emerged from the Convention of Biological Diversity and is nowadays widely supported in policy and science as a means of facilitating sustainable development, for example, in marine and coastal areas (e.g. Curtin and Prellezo 2010, ESF et al. 2010). According to this place-based and holistic approach, sustainable management of human activities and pressures should take account of the sensitivity and complexity of each particular ecosystem, considering cumulative pressures from various sources of pollution and resource extraction, as well as social aspects (McLeod and Leslie 2009). This necessitates generating knowledge about integrated pressures, ecosystem impacts and societal concerns found in relation to particular ecosystems, which often relate to the scale of marine regions and thus to regionally based organizations, such as the HELCOM and the OSPAR Commission.

The EAM is clearly ambitious (Hammer 2015 in this volume) and particularly challenging for marine environmental issues, owing to the complex nature of the ecosystems and social systems concerned[4] (e.g. Österblom et al. 2010), which results in several practical and scientific challenges. First, the holistic approach opens for diverging definitions and interpretations among and within different organizations and stakeholder groups (Udovyk et al. 2010). Second, differences in terms of mandate, resources and path dependency between regionally based organizations may cause institutional barriers that influence EAM implementation capacity (cf. Hammer 2015 in this volume). Third, the broad set-up of the EAM requires bridging between scientific disciplines and other knowledge sources (Arkema et al. 2006, Barnes and McFadden 2008). These challenges will be further investigated here in relation to the MSFD and the three trends in focus.

4 For example, marine eutrophication is mainly caused by human activities such as agriculture in terrestrial watersheds draining into distant coastal estuaries.

Our Case – the MSFD

The European Union has long since developed laws and policies on single marine environmental issues, for instance on fisheries and chemicals since around 1970. Broader issues came on the agenda much later, including Integrated Coastal Zone Management, but truly comprehensive approaches emerged first with the development of the Marine Thematic Strategy (European Commission 2005) under the 6th EU Environmental Action Programme, and the consultation 'Green Paper' on a Maritime Policy (European Commission 2006) with the resulting Communication on the same theme (European Commission 2007). The Integrated Maritime Policy covers a number of sectors in the marine field and expresses the need for an environmental pillar. The latter emerged in the same period and was enacted a year later as the Marine Strategy Framework Directive (MSFD), aiming at achieving and maintaining 'good environmental status in the marine environment by the year 2020' (EC 2008, Article 1).

Member States are legally obliged to achieve this requirement, but since it is a framework directive the MSFD as such does not define specific targets or detailed management measures. Instead, in a preparatory phase up to 2014, Member States are required to complete an initial environmental and socio-economic assessment, based on 11 descriptors of good marine environmental status (GES),[5] determine 'good environmental status', establish environmental targets and indicators for specific marine environments and implement a monitoring programme (Article 5.2a) (De Santo 2015 in this volume). Forthcoming phases stipulate the development of a programme of measures by 2015, and its implementation from 2016 at the latest (Article 5.2b), aiming at enabling reaching the 2020 objective.

Europeanization and the MSFD

The MSFD has emerged in an area where previous policies were largely national, although EU-wide laws governed some marine issues and regional conventions others. Rather than only coordinating previous national efforts, the directive has broadened and streamlined them in an EU common framework, and thereafter charged primarily Members States with the implementation (Article 28) – albeit in a collaborative manner. The union level played its key role foremost during the first preparatory phase when e.g. GES descriptors were

5 Descriptor 1: Biological diversity; Descriptor 2: Non-indigenous species; Descriptor 3: Population of commercial fish and shell fish; Descriptor 4: Elements of marine food webs; Descriptor 5: Eutrophication; Descriptor 6: Sea floor integrity; Descriptor 7: Alteration of hydrographical conditions; Descriptor 8: Contaminants; Descriptor 9: Contaminants in fish and seafood for human consumption; Descriptor 10: Marine litter; Descriptor 11: Introduction of energy, including underwater noise.

defined and methodological standards and reporting guidelines were elaborated by the European Commission in cooperation with and between Member States[6] (see Article 9.3). This work was done in three expert working groups on good environmental status (WG GES), data information and knowledge exchange (WG DIKE[7]), and economic and social assessment (WG ESA), respectively. WG GES, for example, was responsible for the preparation of the Commission Decision on criteria and methodological standards for assessing GES (European Commission 2010b, WG GES 2011a). In the subsequent implementation – i.e. assessment, and the establishment and implementation of a measurement programme – the Member States themselves have the key responsibility, both individually and in collaboration with each other through e.g. regional forums.

In summary, the MSFD represents a clear case of Europeanization. However, after enactment of the directive and the preparatory phase, with its definitions of frames for action, the potential power at the union level to push for coordination and information exchange is quite weak (see e.g. Van Leeuwen et al. 2012). The latter is done in, for example, the committee structure with the aforementioned working groups, assisted by the Commission's Joint Research Centre (JRC), with e.g. reviews on methodological standards relating to GES as well as monitoring requirements (Piha and Zampoukas 2011, Zampoukas et al. 2012).

Although the MSFD is still in its early days of implementation, some revealing observations relating to science-policy interactions in Member States are possible to discern. First, different strategies and mechanisms for organizing assessment linked to MSFD implementation can be observed among Member States (e.g. in terms of the set-up of competent authorities,[8] the organization of science support or regarding participation). In terms of participation it can be observed that, although several countries (e.g. UK, Finland and others) demonstrated attempts to involve stakeholders already during the earliest phases of MSFD development, some countries (e.g. Greece and Ireland) did not publish the documents on public consultation procedures required (Article 19) by July 2012 (European Commission 2012). Second, it is already evident that knowledge availability is a major challenge for implementing the broad GES approach of the MSFD and that there is a need for additional scientific information linked to the descriptors (see e.g. DEFRA 2012, Nature Agency 2012), and for improving the efficiency of the

6 Linked to this process, eight reports focussing mainly on natural science perspectives linked to GES Descriptors were prepared by groups of independent experts coordinated by JRC and ICES. In addition, the reports for Descriptor 9 and Descriptor 10 were written by expert groups coordinated by DG SANCO and IFREMER, respectively.

7 WG DIKE works on a marine version of WISE (Water Information System for Europe), i.e. for a harmonized data reporting process and an information exchange system (WG DIKE 2012).

8 For example, in Sweden and Denmark reporting under MSFD will be the responsibility of a single competent authority, whereas in e.g. the Netherlands several existing bodies will share this reporting responsibility.

approach by prioritizing sensitive indicators (e.g. Jennings and Le Quesne 2012). As an example, lack of data on e.g. the deep sea environment in the Mediterranean region was emphasized by several Member States during a meeting of the Marine Strategy Coordination Group in February 2012 (MSCG 2012). In some Member States, insufficient capacity for developing marine science and knowledge has also been considered as a major bottleneck for MSFD implementation. For example, several Member States did not meet the July 2012 deadline for reporting environmental targets and associated indicators for GES (e.g. Bulgaria, Greece and Malta). In the case of Bulgaria, Knudsen (2015 in this volume) argues that insufficient capacity for science support is a key reason. Since the MSFD as such does not define specific targets or management measures, Member States have ample room to manoeuvre, which is practical on the one hand, but may cause institutional ambiguity at the EU level on the other (cf. Van Leeuwen et al. 2012). Moreover, mechanisms for coping with the uncertainty following lack of knowledge are largely missing.

To conclude, the Europeanization process has so far not sufficiently taken account of the need to cope with the uncertainty at hand. Even though union level coordination takes place, some Member States still experience severe bottlenecks with regard to the uncertainties involved. Without Europeanization, however, Member States would probably have even less chance of coping with the challenges. Regarding disagreements, the Europeanization process has led to closer collaboration between Member States and other actors, which may help overcoming potential controversies. This kind of cooperation and responses to bottlenecks at the national level are also influenced by regionalization as presented in the next section.

Regionalization and the MSFD

The MSFD requires Member States to coordinate their marine strategies through regional cooperation structures, including those under the regional sea conventions, as well as make every effort to coordinate their actions with those of third countries in the same region or sub-region (Article 6). Baltic Member States, such as Poland and Finland, are required to coordinate their marine strategies through the Helsinki Convention, as well as with the non-member Russian Federation also bordering the Baltic Sea. This coordination (consultation and collaboration) should take place throughout the implementation (see e.g. Article 19.1), for example during the assessment phase, in determination of GES, and in the formulation of the programme of measures. So far, substantial differences are apparent in terms of the degree to which and how the various regional seas conventions have responded to these regional coordination requirements. It is clear that measures to improve coordination of methodology and monitoring (e.g. Piha and Zampoukas 2011, Zampoukas et al. 2012), data and modelling resources, and scientific expertise and infrastructure occur to some extent for all regional European sea areas, e.g.

via EU financed research projects and research networks.[9] For example, UNEP and the Black Sea Commission are participating in the Working Group on Data, Information and Knowledge Exchange (WG DIKE) to articulate what information is being generated and might be shared, and to address gaps identified (MSCG 2011). Nevertheless, only the Helsinki and OSPAR Conventions have developed significant degrees of support through, for example, regional coordination of environmental quality aims, GES indicators, monitoring and information exchange (OSPAR 2012, HELCOM 2012a). For example, the environmental quality aims of the Baltic Sea Action Plan (HELCOM 2007) and the OSPAR Environmental Strategy (OSPAR 2010) are well in line with the GES approach of the MSFD. HELCOM has also published a series of thematic and integrated environmental assessments (HELCOM 2010), which has contributed to Member States work on initial assessments, and has launched several projects for knowledge exchange and coordination of MSFD activities in the Baltic Sea region. For example, the TARGREV project focussed on providing a scientific basis for the HELCOM's eutrophication targets and indicators, the CORESET project aims to develop GES indicators and targets, and the MORE project develops guidelines for a well-coordinated joint HELCOM monitoring programme in the Baltic Sea.[10] Similarly, an Inter-sessional Correspondence Group on the Implementation of the MSFD (ICG-MSFD) has been established and linked to the OSPAR Convention. Even for these two regions, however, some Member States argue that regional coordination of MSFD implementation is challenging. For example, at the time the UK initial assessment and GES indicators were being developed, there was still relatively limited information from other countries, and it was claimed that this complicated the process of coordination (DEFRA 2012).

Besides coordination within regions, the MSFD has catalysed measures for improved coordination and knowledge exchange between marine regions. For example, in a recent project financed by the European Commission, Baltic2Black,[11] the aim has been to transfer know-how on environmental assessment of eutrophication and monitoring of nutrient loads between the HELCOM and the Black Sea Commission. In line with this, Romania has confirmed positive use of expertise with regards to the Baltic Sea (WG GES 2011b). Similarly, scientific coordination and knowledge exchange among regional seas is a key goal of the SEAS-ERA research programme, which brings together national authorities, funding agencies and marine research institutes from several Member States and non-Member States, bordering the Black Sea, the Mediterranean and the North East Atlantic.

---

9 Regional science coordination occurs through intergovernmental organizations (e.g. ICES, CIESM), regional marine research programmes and infrastructures (Black Sea ERA-NET, Black Sea SCENE, KnowSeas, SEAS-ERA, BONUS) and regional research networks (e.g. BMB).

10 Information about these projects can be found at www.helcom.fi/projects.

11 http://www.blacksea-commission.org/_projects_Baltic2Black.asp.

All these regionalization processes clearly promote production, dissemination and sharing of knowledge, thus helping to cope with uncertainty in both science and policy. Clearly, regionalization has also lead to the gradual development of an increasingly institutionalized collaboration within and between science and policy actors, which has the potential to improve conflict mitigation.

EAM implementation and the MSFD

Traditionally, policies for the marine environment have focused on specific pressures and individual pollutants (Karlsson et al. 2011). The MSFD, however, requires that '*marine strategies shall apply an ecosystem-based approach to the management of human activities*' (Article 1.3), thus positioning the EAM at the core of implementation obligations. Even though much has been done at various levels in order to achieve this, several implementation challenges remain, of which four merit discussion here.

First, with respect to interpretation, substantial effort has been put on reaching an operational understanding of how to define the EAM in terms of governing Europe's marine environment at various levels. This began already before the emergence of the MSFD, with a joint OSPAR and HELCOM Ministerial Declaration defining the EAM (HELCOM and OSPAR 2003). In spite of this, experts and scientists linked to HELCOM still have divergent opinions on how to understand the EAM (Udovyk et al. 2010). For example, several ecologists working with GES Descriptor 5 (eutrophication) were of the opinion that the EAM is just a new word for what they have been doing their entire professional life. Other experts, particularly those working on GES Descriptor 3 (commercial fish), identified new requirements and challenges in terms of integration of knowledge, cumulative pressures and socio-economic assessments. This means that EAM seems to have the potential to act as 'communication facilitator' between science, policy and other stakeholders in some situations as seen, for example, in relation to eutrophication in the Baltic Sea, whereas in fisheries management EAM may rather be a source of disagreement (Linke et al. 2014). Although it remains to be seen exactly how EAM will be implemented for various GES Descriptors and in other marine regions, it does not seem far-fetched to assume that differences in interpretation and implementation will remain.

Second, in terms of institutional cooperation it can be observed that when the EAM has been applied in the general GES and socio-economical assessment guidelines of the MSFD, a number of scientific expert groups have provided support, e.g. WG GES, WG ESA, as well as JRC and ICES (e.g. Cardoso et al. 2010). However, this EU level scientific support and coordination is quite generic in nature, compared to the more specific coordination of GES indicators and monitoring observed at the regional level, at least in the Baltic Sea and the North East Atlantic.

Third, looking closer at different marine regions, great variation becomes visible. The HELCOM and the OSPAR Commission have developed a vision, strategic goals, ecological objectives and road maps based on EAM, thus placing EAM implementation at the heart of their work (Backer and Leppänen 2008, Heslenfeld and Enserink 2008). The MSFD was in fact not even the driving force behind EAM implementation in the Baltic Sea and the North East Atlantic. Rather the emergence of the MSFD was to a large extent influenced by earlier developments connected with EAM through HELCOM and the OSPAR Commission, even though the legal strength of the MSFD subsequently reinforced the trend. This development can be exemplified by, for example, the HELCOM work group GEAR,[12] which recently has been established to further strengthen regional coordination and information exchange linked to implementation of EAM, the Baltic Sea Action Plan and the MSFD (HELCOM 2012b).

Regarding the southern marine regions, the Black Sea Commission and the Barcelona Convention secretariat seek ways to incorporate the EAM into their conventions. This process has been complex and has been running at a slower pace than in the northern marine regions. Lately, several developments relating to EAM can be observed. The 2009 Black Sea Strategic Action Plan (BSSAP 2009), for example, contains long-term ecosystem quality objectives, with management targets and indicators, and envisages the EAM as a framework for regional coordination, thereby seeking coherence with the MSFD. However, although the MSFD will be taken into account during further elaboration of targets and indicators for the Black Sea environment, the BSSAP does not contain specific references to the MSFD yet (Van Leeuwen et al. 2012). In the Mediterranean Sea, the synergies between the Barcelona Convention action plan and the MSFD were further elaborated during the 17th Meeting of Contracting Parties of the Barcelona Convention (COP 17) held in February 2012. In particular, Decision 20/4 on 'Implementing the Ecosystems Approach Roadmap' proposed 11 ecological objectives, operational objectives and indicators for the Mediterranean (UNEP 2012). Although some of these operational objectives are related to the implementation of the ICZM Protocol, the majority of the objectives are relevant to the MSFD GES descriptors (WG GES 2011b). Still, despite this common EAM roadmap and indications for collaboration between EU MS and third countries as well as with OSPAR and HELCOM (WG GES 2011b), the actual practical implementation of EAM may still be hampered by scientific uncertainty on ecosystem descriptors (MSCG 2012) and institutional ambiguity linked to the 21 contracting countries of the Barcelona Convention (Van Leeuwen et al. 2012). These challenges are also likely to become important for the practical implementation of the ecosystem approach in the Black Sea (cf. Knudsen 2015 in this volume).

Fourth, since individual Member States are ultimately responsible for the implementation of the MSFD, they can choose their own EAM approaches. Sweden

---

12 The HELCOM Group for Implementation of Ecosystem Approach (HELCOM GEAR).

for example, despite of being a member of both the HELCOM and the OSPAR Commission, has decided to use its own GES eutrophication indicators for both the east and west coast (SwAM 2012). The UK chooses to have one marine strategy covering its marine waters, with exceptions made for significant biogeographical differences (DEFRA 2012). Around the Black Sea, each bordering country sets up targets according to national legislation (WG GES 2011b). Consequently, the practical EAM implementation may often depend on national and not regional selection.

Discussion

Our main question is if the three processes of Europeanization, regionalization and implementation of EAM facilitate marine environmental governance by helping to develop a more credible knowledge base and legitimate science-based advice, and to prevent tensions and conflicts, rather than increase the well-known problems with scientific uncertainty and stakeholder disagreements related to the MSFD. Our general answer is yes. The Europeanization process following the MSFD forces Member States to increasingly collaborate and to apply the EAM, both being necessary (but not sufficient) for linking science to policy in a manner that mitigates controversies and recognizes uncertainty. Hypothetically, one might have expected a tension between the processes of Europeanization and regionalization since they seem, at first glance, to point in opposite directions. However, since the Europeanization process following the MSFD includes a requirement to develop and coordinate a regional dimension, we have not identified any striking conflicts between Europeanization and regionalization in practice. On the contrary, they seem to mutually support each other, perhaps even in a co-evolutionary manner, as far as noticeable at this stage. It must be remembered though, that MSFD implementation has just begun. Moreover, the positive result on this point is based primarily on the developments in the Baltic Sea and the North East Atlantic regions. However, we have not seen anything in the practical implementation in the Mediterranean and the Black Sea regions that would speak against the overall conclusion that Europeanization and regionalization processes facilitate each other interdependently. We rather discover that the development of marine governance in general in the south of Europe is lagging behind the processes underway in the north.

From a theoretical perspective, the MSFD set-up acknowledges scientific uncertainty and potential controversies among stakeholders in complex and context-dependent environmental governance issues, for example by requiring the EAM and regional collaboration. In that sense the directive is going beyond the traditional view of science-policy relations, according to which certain scientific knowledge (often based on a reductionist analysis of reality) defines what needs to be done, assuming that agencies and stakeholders carry out what has been politically decided in a rational and harmonious way. The MSFD, on the contrary, recognizes the need for holistic approaches, underlines uncertainties and the need for precaution, and stimulates stakeholders (both Member States, regionally-based organizations, EU institutions and others) to participate in iterative processes and collaborative learning. In doing so, the MSFD fits well with a modernized understanding of the blurred nature of science-policy interfaces, thus opening opportunities for enhancing trust in the relationship between the 'governing system' and the 'system-to-be-governed' (cf. Jentoft and Chuenpagdee 2015 in this volume).

This statement is based on the analysis of the design of the MSFD as such, and on the limited implementation experiences so far, meaning that it will take a number of years before a richer picture of the situation can be painted. When we elsewhere[13] have analysed subsets of EU marine environmental governance issues, however, we see similar tendencies in policies for e.g. hazardous chemicals (Karlsson et al. 2011) and fisheries (Linke et al. 2014).

In the field of chemicals policy, scientists and expert agencies have for decades underlined the vast uncertainties regarding risks and inherent properties of chemical substances on the market. However, it was not until the last decades that EU policies and laws recognized the need for precautionary assessment and management. A clear example is the stipulation in the central REACH regulation that substances identified to be of 'very high concern' – irrespective of the risks at hand, and sometimes even without necessarily being toxic – ought to be authorized (Karlsson et al. 2011). Still, this is a rare example and comprehensive precautionary policies are in general absent for chemicals.

An example from fisheries policy concerns one of the most sustained outcomes of the 2002 CFP reform, the so-called Regional Advisory Councils (RACs), which aim to include stakeholders at the regional sea level in the policy process by taking account of various interests and knowledge claims within the sector (Linke et al. 2011, EC 2004). Regional cross-sector cooperation and integration of environmental perspectives, such as the HELCOM Fisheries and Environment Forum, are, however, still weakly developed, although numerous efforts can be seen to strengthen these on Member State level, regionally as well as through further reform of the CFP. Furthermore, the science support system in fisheries management is evolving quickly in response to the new challenges posed by the MSFD and EAM. For example, ICES, the scientific advisory organization for fisheries management mainly working in northern Europe, acknowledges the cross-cutting nature of the MSFD and has established a new steering group related to the MSFD (ICES 2011). Linked to this development, a recent report (ICES 2012a) sets out to provide guidance in support for the EU Member States to implement the MSFD, in particular with regard to Descriptor 3 (commercial fish and shellfish). In this work, ICES aims to identify and describe the role of potential ecosystem indicators by using the EU's data collection framework (DCF) to support all MSFD descriptors. One positive interpretation of these developments

13 See more examples in the RISKGOV project (www.sh.se/riskgov).

is that the MSFD offers a kind of 'window of opportunity', which might have the capacity to integrate the long separated sectors of fisheries and ecosystem management on a concrete practical level through ICES' assessment and advisory processes (ICES 2012b).

Taken together, much speaks for a gradually changing paradigm in marine environmental governance, at least in the European context (cf. Linke and Jentoft 2013). What we observe resembles a shift from a highly sector-based science-policy interaction, often complicated by stakeholder conflicts and the unclear role of scientific uncertainty, towards a more open relationship between science, politics and other actors in society. This is based on an increasingly harmonized understanding of overarching ecosystem perspectives provided within the EAM lens. Scientific and other sources of uncertainty might in this mode be addressed in conjunction with social aspects, thus providing improved governance of the marine environment. More specifically, since we aimed to identify strategies for improving the governance of Europe's marine environment, we would like to highlight the following three recommendations in the light of this specific study:

- Europeanization: The observed differences in the degree of MSFD implementation between various marine regions (with slower progress in the Mediterranean and Black Sea) seem to necessitate an enhanced level of support and intervention at the common EU level. In doing so, the European Commission with its agencies should take the leading role and a way forward could be to stimulate learning between different regional seas within the European context, such as seen from the Baltic Sea to the Black Sea in the Baltic2Black project. Such 'cross-regional' learning could potentially even be indicated or required in the MSFD directive as such.

- Regionalization: Much speaks for the importance of further strengthening the environmental and socio-economic knowledge base, as well as of available collaborative forums, in particular in the Mediterranean and Black Sea regions. The current institutional set-up in these areas is far from the most appropriate and effective, and in particular the EU and European-wide ownership for the Barcelona Convention should be strengthened, preferably in continued collaboration with UNEP.

- EAM implementation: The holistic EAM concept is central to governing the complex socio-ecological interactions associated with Europe's marine environment. Sectoral and fragmented management measures have little chance of coping with the critical challenges at hand. Successful realization of EAM will most likely require an improved common European understanding of the approach, both within and between disciplines, institutions and stakeholders. This in turn can promote enhanced knowledge integration between various fields and allow for well-elaborated trade-off discussions, thereby supporting mutual respect for critical decisions.

Furthermore, the place-based nature of EAM implies that there is a need to allow for continuous reflections on the appropriate spatial scales of assessments and management measures. Clearly, improved capabilities and cooperation structures are vital at the level of both individual countries and regional seas. However, it is equally important to acknowledge that ecosystem properties and human pressures may vary from local to Europe-wide scales. This means that, in spite of ambitious holistic aspirations, successful implementation of EAM will require context-dependent considerations and scale-dependent adjustments.

How these recommendations should be implemented and followed up in more detail falls outside the scope of this study. We are, however, confident that these measures, taken in one way or another, would improve the relationship between the marine system-to-be-governed and the social system governing it.

Acknowledgements

The research leading to these results was funded by the European Community's Seventh Framework Programme (2007-2013) under grant agreement n° 217246 made with the joint Baltic Sea research and development programme BONUS, as well as from the Swedish Environmental Protection Agency, the Swedish Research Council FORMAS, the Foundation for Baltic and East European Studies, the Swedish Research Council and the Bank of Sweden Tercentenary Foundation.

References

Arkema, K.K., Abramson, S.C., and Dewsbury, B.M. 2006. Marine ecosystem-based management: from characterization to implementation. *Frontiers in Ecology and the Environment*, 4, 525-532.

Backer, H. and Leppänen, J. 2008. The HELCOM system of a vision, strategic goals and ecological objectives: implementing an ecosystem approach to the management of human activities in the Baltic Sea. *Aquatic Conservation: Marine and Freshwater Ecosystems*, 18, 321-334.

Barnes, C. and McFadden, K.W. 2007. Marine ecosystem approaches to management: challenges and lessons in the United States. *Marine Policy*, 32, 387-392.

BSSAP. 2009. *Strategic Action Plan for the Environmental Protection and Rehabilitation of the Black Sea*. Black Sea Commission. Adopted in Sofia, Bulgaria, 17 April 2009.

Cardoso, A.C., Cochrane, S., Doerner, H., Ferreira, J.G., Galgani, F., Hagebro, C., Hanke, G., Hoepffner, N., Keizer, P.D., Law, R., Olenin, S., Piet, G.J., Rice, J., Rogers, S.I., Swartenbroux, F., Tasker, M.L. and van de Bund, W. 2010. Scientific Support to the European Commission on the Marine Strategy

Framework Directive: management group report. JRC Scientific and Technical Reports. Luxembourg: Office for Official Publications of the European Communities.

Curtin, R. and Prellezo, R. 2010. Understanding marine ecosystem based management: A literature review. *Marine Policy*, 34, 821-830.

DEFRA. 2012. Marine Strategy Framework Directive consultation. UK Initial Assessment and Proposals for Good Environmental Status. Consultation document, prepared by DEFRA for HM Government. London.

De Santo, E. 2015. The Marine Strategy Framework Directive as a Catalyst for Maritime Spatial Planning: internal dimensions and institutional tensions, in *Governing Europe's Marine Environment. Europeanization of Regional Seas or Regionalization of EU Policies?*, edited by M. Gilek and K. Kern. Farnham, UK: Ashgate Publishing.

EC. 2004. Council Decision of 19 July 2004 establishing Regional Advisory Councils under the Common Fisheries Policy, 2004/585/EC. Official Journal, L 256, 17.

EC. 2008. Marine Strategy Framework Directive, 2008/56/EC. Official Journal of the EU, L164, 19-40.

Eriksson, J., Karlsson, M. and Reuter, M. 2010. Technocracy, politicization, and non-involvement: politics of expertise in the European regulation of chemicals. *Review of Policy Research*, 27, 167-185.

ESF, ICES, EFARO. 2010. Science dimensions of an Ecosystem Approach to Management of Biotic Ocean Resources (SEAMBOR). Strasbourg: IREG.

European Commission. 2005. Thematic strategy on the protection and conservation of the marine environment. Communication from the Commission to the Council and the European Parliament. COM(2005) 504 FINAL.

European Commission. 2006. Towards a future Maritime Policy for the Union: A European Vision for the Oceans and the Seas. Green Paper. COM(2006) 275 FINAL.

European Commission. 2007. An Integrated Maritime Policy for the European Union. Communication from the Commission to the European Parliament, the Council, the European Economic and Social Committee and the Committee of the Regions. COM(2007) 575 FINAL.

European Commission. 2009. European Union Strategy for the Baltic Sea Region. Communication from the Commission to the European Parliament, the Council, the European Economic and Social Committee and the Committee of the Regions. COM(2009) 248 FINAL.

European Commission. 2010a. European Union Strategy for the Danube Region. Communication from the Commission to the European Parliament, the Council, the European Economic and Social Committee and the Committee of the Regions. COM(2010) 715 FINAL.

European Commission. 2010b. Commission Decision of 1 September 2010 on criteria and methodological standards on good environmental status of marine waters 2010/477/EU.

European Commission. 2011. Regional Policy Contributing to Sustainable Growth in Europe 2020. Communication from the Commission to the European Parliament, the Council, the European Economic and Social Committee and the Committee of the Regions. COM(2011) 17 FINAL.

European Commission. 2012. Commission Decision of 1 September 2010 on criteria and methodological standards on good environmental status of marine waters, 2010/477/EU. Official Journal of the European Union, L 232, 14-24.

Hammer, M. 2015. The ecosystem management approach. Implications for marine governance, in *Governing Europe's Marine Environment: Europeanization of Regional Seas or Regionalization of EU Policies?*, edited by M. Gilek and K. Kern. Farnham, UK: Ashgate Publishing.

HELCOM and OSPAR 2003. Declaration of the First Joint Ministerial Meeting of the Helsinki and OSPAR Commissions, Bremen 25-26 June 2003.

HELCOM. 2007. HELCOM Baltic Sea Action Plan. Helsinki HELCOM.

HELCOM. 2010. Ecosystem Health of the Baltic Sea 2003-2007: HELCOM Initial Holistic Assessment. Baltic Sea Environmental Proceedings No. 122.

HELCOM. 2012a. Development of a set of core indicators: Interim report of the HELCOM CORESET project. PART B: Descriptions of the indicators. Baltic Sea Environment Proceedings No. 129 B.

HELCOM. 2012b. Terms of reference of the HELCOM group for the implementation of the ecosystem approach (HELCOM GEAR). Helsinki: HELCOM. 4 pp.

Heslenfeld, P. and Enserink, E.L. 2008. OSPAR Ecological Quality Objectives: the utility of health indicators for the North Sea. *ICES Journal of Marine Science*, 65, 1392 1397.

ICES 2011. DRAFT Overview of ICES work in relation to Marine Strategy Framework Directive. ACOM Meeting November 2011 Doc 10. Available at: http://www.ices.dk/news-and-events/Documents/Themes/MSFD/Draft%20 MSFD%20Overview%20Report.pdf [accessed: 13 July 2014].

ICES 2012a ICES MSFD D3 REPORT 2012. ICES Advisory Committee. ICES CM 2012/ACOM: 62. Available at: http://www.ices.dk/sites/pub/Publication%20 Reports/Expert%20Group%20Report/acom/2012/HAWG/HAWG%202012. pdf [accessed: 13 July 2014].

ICES 2012b. ICES scientific and advisory services of relevance to the EU Marine Strategy Framework Directive. Available at: http://www.ices.dk/news-and-events/Documents/Themes/MSFD/ICES_scientific_and_advisory_services_of_relevance_to_the_EU_MSFD.pdf [accessed: 13 July 2014].

Irwin, A. and Michael, M. 2003. *Science, Social Theory and Public Knowledge*. Maidenhead: Open University Press.

Jans, J.H. and Vedder, H.H.B. 2012. *European Environmental Law: After Lisbon*. Fourth edition. Amsterdam: Europa Law Publishing.

Jasanoff, S. 1990. *The Fifth Branch: Science Advisors as Policymakers*. Cambridge, MA: Harvard University Press.

Jennings, S. and Le Quesne, W.J.F. 2012. Integration of environmental and fishery management in Europe. *ICES Journal of Marine Science*, 69, 1329-1332.

Jentoft, S. and Chuenpagdee, R. 2015. The 'New' Marine Governance: assessing governability, in *Governing Europe's Marine Environment: Europeanization of Regional Seas or Regionalization of EU Policies?*, edited by M. Gilek and K. Kern. Farnham, UK: Ashgate Publishing.

Joas, M., Jahn, D. and Kern, K. 2008. *Governing a Common Sea: Environmental Policies in the Baltic Sea Region*. London: Earthscan.

Karlsson, M. 2010. The Precautionary Principle in EU and U.S. Chemicals Policy: A Comparison of Industrial Chemicals Legislation, in *Regulating Chemical Risks: European and Global Challenges*, edited by J. Eriksson, M. Gilek, and C. Rudén. Dordrecht: Springer.

Karlsson, M., Gilek, M. and Udovyk, O. 2011. Governance of Complex Socio-Environmental Risks: The Case of Hazardous Chemicals in the Baltic Sea. *Ambio*, 40, 144-157.

Kern, K. and Gilek, M. 2015. Governing Europe's Marine Environment: key topics and challenges, in *Governing Europe's Marine Environment: Europeanization of Regional Seas or Regionalization of EU Policies?*, edited by M. Gilek and K. Kern. Farnham, UK: Ashgate Publishing.

Knudsen, S. 2015. Marine Governance in the Black Sea, in *Governing Europe's Marine Environment: Europeanization of Regional Seas or Regionalization of EU Policies?*, edited by M. Gilek and K. Kern. Farnham, UK: Ashgate Publishing.

Linke, S., Dreyer, M. and Sellke, P. 2011. The Regional Advisory Councils: What is their potential to incorporate stakeholder knowledge into fisheries governance? *Ambio*, 40, 133-143.

Linke, S., Gilek, M., Karlsson, M. and Udovyk, O. 2014. Unravelling science-policy interactions in environmental risk governance of the Baltic Sea: comparing fisheries and eutrophication. *Journal of Risk Research*, 17(4), 505-523.

Linke, S. and Jentoft, S. 2013. A communicative turnaround: Shifting the burden of proof in European fisheries governance. *Marine Policy*, 38, 337-345.

McLeod, K. and Leslie, H. (eds) 2009. *Ecosystem-Based Management for the Oceans*. Washington, DC: Island Press.

MSCG. 2011. Minutes of the Second MSCG Meeting, 14 November 2011, Marine Strategy Coordination Group (MSCG), Brussels.

MSCG. 2012. Minutes of the Sixth MSCG Meeting, 21-22 February 2012, Marine Strategy Coordination Group (MSCG), Brussels.

Nature Agency. 2012. The Danish Marine Strategy. Good Environmental Status, Targets and Indicators. Danish Ministry of the Environment. Available at: http://www.naturstyrelsen.dk/Lovstof/Hoeringer/Havstrategi.htm [accessed 1 August 2012].

Nowotny, H., Scott, P. and Gibbons, M. 2001. *Re-thinking Science: Knowledge and the Public in an Age of Uncertainty*. Cambridge: Polity Press.

Olsen, J. 2002. The Many Faces of Europeanization. *Journal of Common Market Studies*, 40(5), 921-952.

OSPAR. 2010. The North East Atlantic Environment Strategy. Strategy of the OSPAR Commission for the Protection of the Marine Environment of the North-East Atlantic 2010-2020 (OSPAR Agreement 2010-3). London.

OSPAR. 2012. *Finding common ground – Towards regional coherence in implementing the Marine Strategy Framework Directive in the North-East Atlantic region through the work of the OSPAR Commission*. London: OSPAR.

Österblom, H., Gårdmark, A., Bergström, L., Müller-Karulis, B., Folke, C., Lindegren, M., Casini, M., et al. 2010. Making the ecosystem approach operational. Can regime shifts in ecological and governance systems facilitate the transitions? *Marine Policy*, 34, 1290-1299.

Piha, H. and Zampoukas, N. 2011. *Review of Methodological Standards Related to the Marine Strategy Framework Directive Criteria on Good Environmental Status*. JRC Scientific and Technical Reports. Luxembourg: Office for Official Publications of the European Communities.

Radaelli, C. 2006. Europeanization: Solution or Problem?, in *Palgrave Advances in European Union Studies*, edited by M. Cini and A. Bourne. Basingstoke, UK: Palgrave.

Stirling, A. 1999. Risk at a turning point? *Journal of Environmental Medicine*, 1, 119-126.

Söderström, S., Kern, K. and Hassler, B. 2015. Marine governance in the Baltic Sea: current trends of Europeanization and regionalization, in *Governing Europe's Marine Environment: Europeanization of Regional Seas or Regionalization of EU Policies?*, edited by M. Gilek and K. Kern. Farnham, UK: Ashgate Publishing.

SwAM. 2012. God havsmiljö 2020. *Marin strategi för Nordsjön och Östersjön. Del 1: Inledande bedömning och socioekonomisk analys, and Del 2: God miljöstatus och miljökvalitetsnormer*. Göteborg: The Swedish Agency for Marine and Water Management.

Udovyk, O., Rabilloud, L., Gilek, M. and Karlsson, M. 2010. Hazardous Substances: a Case Study of Environmental Risk Governance in the Baltic Sea Region. Deliverable 5, RISKGOV project. Available at http://webappl.web.sh.se/p3/ext/res.nsf/vRes/forskning_1320238597406_case_study_chemical_pollution_pdf/$File/Case%20Study%20Chemical%20Pollution.pdf [accessed: 13 July 2014].

UNEP. 2012. Support to the Barcelona Convention for the Implementation of the ecosystem approach, including the Establishment of MPAs in open seas areas, including deep Sea. Final report, April 2012. Rome: United Nations Environment Program (UNEP).

Van Leeuwen, J., Van Hoof, L. and Van Tatenhove, J. 2012. Institutional ambiguity in implementing the European Union Marine Strategy Framework Directive. *Marine Policy*, 36, 636-643.

Weingart, P. 1999. Scientific Expertise and Political Accountability: Paradoxes of Science in Politics. *Science and Public Policy*, 26, 151-61.

WG DIKE. 2012. Minutes of the Fifth Meeting of WG DIKE. DIKE 5/2012/21.

WG GES. 2011a. Common Understanding of (Initial) Assessment, Determination of Good Environmental Status (GES) & Establishment of Environmental Targets (Articles 8, 9 & 10 MSFD).

WG GES. 2011b. Minutes of the Meeting of Working Group on Good Environmental Status (GES), 27-28 September 2011, DOC 10. Brussels.

Wilson, D.C. 2009. *The Paradoxes of Transparency: Science and the Ecosystem Approach to Fisheries Management in Europe*. Amsterdam: Amsterdam University Press.

Zampoukas, N., Piha, N., Bigagli, E., Hoepffner, N., Hanke, G. and Cardoso, A.C. 2012. Monitoring for the Marine Strategy Framework Directive: Requirements and Options. JRC Scientific and Technical Reports. Office for Official Publications of the European Communities: Luxembourg.

PART 3:
Marine Governance of Europe's Regional Seas

Chapter 9
Marine Governance in the Baltic Sea: Current Trends of Europeanization and Regionalization

Sara Söderström, Kristine Kern and Björn Hassler

Introduction

Just as the Baltic Sea region has gone through dramatic changes over the last 25 years, marine governance in the Baltic Sea has also changed substantially during this period. Not only have the political preconditions for collaboration on marine policy among the littoral states been fundamentally altered, but so have the perspectives on what to protect and how to protect it, from abatement of point sources and natural science perspectives to an emphasis on diffuse pollution sources, sustainability and ecosystem approaches to management. Historically, collaboration between people in the region has been prominent, in particular in the area of trade and commerce, but the region also has a long history of war, power struggles and problems caused by the iron curtain and the East-West divide (Karlsson 2004, Salines 2010). Thus, the sea itself has been a physical divide separating the north-western from the south-eastern part. There is still a rift in many areas between the Nordic countries and Germany on the one hand and the former socialist states on the other, both in terms of wealth but also social systems. In this region we find some of the richest as well as some of the poorest countries within the European Union (Vangas 2010).

However, the collapse of the Soviet Union in the late 1980s and the following re-establishment of four independent states – Estonia, Latvia, Lithuania and Poland – together with the re-unification of Germany sparked off a plethora of interactions between, in particular, the Nordic countries and the newly independent states. Since the mid-1990s two waves of EU enlargement have strengthened the integration of the whole region and created preconditions for developing an innovative approach to marine governance. Recently, the macro-regionalization of EU policy-making, which led to the development of the EU Strategy for the Baltic Sea Region (EUSBSR), has re-enforced the perceptions of the Baltic Sea region as a relevant arena for policy-making and has altered the framework for joint decision-making, monitoring and enforcement.

Traditionally, nation-states have been the dominant actors in marine governance in the Baltic Sea region. However, the historical, decisive events in the late 1980s and early 1990s pushed marine governance in the region far beyond the boundaries of the nation-state. Although the Convention of the Protection of the Marine Environment of the Baltic Sea Area (Helsinki Convention) had already been introduced in 1974, it gained even more importance in the region after the end of the Cold War, after which it was substantially revised in 1992. Likewise it can be argued that EU influence in the Baltic Sea area was very limited until the early 1990s in comparison to today's situation. In addition, new governance arrangements such as transnational networks have emerged and contributed to the dynamic development of marine governance in the region. Today, marine governance in the Baltic Sea region is a complex combination of national, international, European and transnational governance arrangements (Kern 2011).

Starting from the current state of the marine environment in the Baltic Sea region, this chapter describes and analyses the changing governance arrangements and their problem solving capacities. The article is based mainly on existing and ongoing research (including own research projects), a literature review and relevant policy documents such as EU publications. As an empirical basis for our analysis we have examined policy documents, EU directives as well as reviewed relevant research. This chapter concentrates on HELCOM, the governing body of the Helsinki Convention, and the European Union because these actors have been most important in this policy area. It is assumed that the success of multi-level governance arrangements depends on both horizontal and vertical interplay as well as the integration of non-member states, in particular Russia.

This chapter analyses the relationship between the Europeanization and regionalization of marine governance in the Baltic Sea by concentrating on three phases of development: (i) regionalization through the Helsinki Convention; (ii) Europeanization through EU legislation; and (iii) macro-regionalization through the EU Strategy for the Baltic Sea Region. Section 2 gives a brief overview of the various environmental problem areas in the Baltic Sea, followed by a description and analysis of the three above mentioned governance arrangements (section 3). Subsequently, some conclusions with respect to the success of these arrangements are drawn in the final section 4.

Main Problems in the Marine Environment

The Baltic Sea is a semi-enclosed inland sea in the north-eastern part of Europe bordered by Sweden, Finland, Russia, Estonia, Latvia, Lithuania, Poland, Germany and Denmark (see Figure 9.1). The water is brackish and the average depth rather shallow in comparison to the other European regional seas (with an average of 52 meters and a maximum of 459 meters). The size of the surface area of the Baltic Sea, the Belt Sea and the Kattegat is 415 000 km^2 with a total water volume of approximately 20 000 km^3, making the sea one of the largest brackish water bodies worldwide. The Baltic Sea ecosystem contains comparably few species and since the sea is rather young in a geological perspective (approximately 13,000-13,500 years old, and where the current marine-brackish state occurred some 10,000-8,000 years ago) there are few endemic species.

Around 85 million people live in the drainage basin of the Baltic Sea which is four times the size of the Baltic Sea itself. Sweden (25.3%) and Russia (19%) are the countries with the largest shares of the catchment area, which, apart from the fringing states, also includes (parts) of Norway, Belarus, Ukraine, the Czech Republic and Slovakia. The saline water inflow to the Baltic Sea comes from the North Sea through the Danish straits in irregular intervals of five to ten years, and fresh water is flowing in continuously from several European rivers as well as via snow and rain. Since the water exchange is relatively slow, the Baltic Sea is rather vulnerable to pollution and different types of environmental degradation. Therefore, the region is, despite all efforts, still regarded as one of the most polluted marine areas in the world (Vlasov 2010).

Eutrophication, over-fishing, chemical pollution, invasive alien species, pollution from marine transportation and climate change are the most important threats to the integrity of the Baltic Sea ecosystems. First, eutrophication can be briefly summarized as nutrient enrichment and is regarded as one of the major threats to the marine environment. It is caused by human activities through which nutrients enter the water through the deposition from air emissions and discharges from both point sources and diffuse sources. Eutrophication contributes to detrimental effects such as *hypoxia* ('dead sea-beds') and excessive algae blooms (HELCOM 2009a, HELCOM 2013).

Second, the impact of over-fishing is another major threat to the entire Baltic Sea ecosystem (Linke et al. 2011). The pressure from fishing in the Baltic Sea affects different parts of the ecosystem, not only the targeted fish stocks. By-catches and the removal of top-predators are pressing issues (HELCOM 2009b). Even though the fisheries sector is very science-dependent and efforts have been launched to achieve sustainable fisheries, most commercial fish stocks have declined due to over-fishing (Linke et al. 2011).

Third, there are numerous hazardous substances entering the Baltic Sea, from a wide variety of sources. The so-called cocktail effect (i.e. the combined toxicity of the large number of contaminating substances) is to a large extent unknown, and new chemicals are rapidly introduced. Although national, regional and international initiatives aim to reduce the toxic levels in the marine environment, the Baltic Sea must still be considered one of the most polluted areas worldwide with regard to toxic substances (HELCOM 2010).

Fourth, invasive alien species may alter marine ecosystems at local, regional or even higher scales. However, the impact varies and is often characterized by a lack of knowledge. New species may enter the Baltic Sea through natural migration in water corridors as well as through transportation via marine vessels' ballast water. Experiments on purification of ballast water have been conducted, but so far no adequate method to solve this problem has been found. Although severe disturbances by invasive alien species have not yet taken place in the Baltic Sea, this may happen in the future (HELCOM 2009b).

Figure 9.1 The Baltic Sea region with drainage basin and political borders

Source: GRID-Arendal 2014.

Fifth, oil pollution from marine transportation emanates from two sources, accidental oil spills and intentional pollution, which lead to approximately the same magnitude of oil pollution in the Baltic Sea. Large oil spills cause negative effects on the ecosystems and harm economic interests. The intentional oil spills are harder to assess and their long-term consequences are largely unknown. These spills are typically caused by cleaning oil tanks at sea. Although this is not allowed, incentives to avoid costs by cleaning tanks *en voyage* rather than in ports are substantial drivers for this behaviour (Hassler 2011).

Sixth, climate mitigation and adaptation are overarching problems with severe repercussions on most of the above mentioned problem areas. Therefore, climate-related hazards need to be addressed in various ways. Apart from climate mitigation efforts at national and sub-national scales, in particular in the Nordic countries and Germany, climate adaptation has gained a prominent status in all the countries around the Baltic Sea. This is because the effects of climate change, such as heavy rains and flooding, have already started to cause severe problems in the region (HELCOM 2012).

Due to the complex structure of the main environmental threats to the ecological integrity of the Baltic Sea region, marine governance has become a real challenge. A better integrated and inclusive approach is currently under development, at least in some areas (cf. Gilek et al. in this volume). This development is driven by the two main actors for marine governance in the region, HELCOM and the European Union.

The Marine Governance Architecture in the Baltic Sea Region

Two parallel trends can be identified in the Baltic Sea region: (i) the emergence of a Baltic Sea region with its own institutions, such as HELCOM and the Council of Baltic Sea States (CBSS), and an (ii) increasing Europeanization of the region since the end of the Cold War. Despite all the differences among the political and social systems, the region has not only a common heritage and culture, dating back to the Middle Ages when it was dominated by the Hanseatic League, but was also the first region worldwide with a regional sea convention for the protection of the marine environment. Today, the region is characterized by multi-sector, multi-actor and multi-level governance arrangements. New forms of environmental governance are based on the ecosystem approach to management and involve a combination of public and private actors at different levels. Macro-regions extend the scope of national policy-making because they establish functional regions which serve as a basis for inter-governmental and trans-national cooperation. Macro-regional institutions may constitute a layer of governance between the European Union on the one hand and the member states and partner countries on the other (Salines 2010, Schymik 2011).

Three aspects are of particular importance for the multi-level governance arrangements in the Baltic Sea region (Kern and Gänzle 2013a). First, it can be assumed that multi-level governance works best if horizontal interplay between institutions leads to synergies and avoids disruptions (see Oberthühr and Stokke 2011, Van Leeuwen and Kern 2013). In the Baltic Sea region, horizontal interplay exists between EU institutions and the Helsinki Convention with HELCOM as its secretariat.

Second, policy success also depends on vertical interplay, i.e. relationships between institutions at different levels. Apart from relationships between national, macro-regional and European institutions, vertical interplay also includes new institutional arrangements which provide new opportunities for sub-national governments and civil society organizations. Both types of organizations may start trans-national networks which can become constitutive elements of macro-regions. Such networks aim for (i) representation and lobbying in the macro-region but also in Brussels; (ii) funding of common activities, for example through membership fees or EU funding; and (iii) best/good practice transfer and learning among their members in the macro-region (Kern and Bulkeley 2009, Kern 2013).

Third, multi-level governance involves both EU member and non-member states because macro-regions extend the borders of the European Union and usually include (parts of) non-member states. The situation in the Baltic Sea region has been influenced by the role of the Soviet Union in the south-eastern part of the region during the Cold War period and the Russian Federation, in particular North-West Russia, since the end of the 1990s. Cooperation with non-member states is also supported by the Northern Dimension, a framework for cooperation of the EU with the Russian Federation, Norway and Iceland (European Commission 2013b: 31).

The three dimensions of multi-level governance in the Baltic Sea region will now be discussed for the different phases of marine governance in the region. Three phases of regionalization and Europeanization can be distinguished here: (i) the Helsinki Convention as a first step towards the regionalization of marine governance in the region; (ii) the Europeanization of marine governance in the region through EU directives such as the Water Framework Directive (WFD) and the Marine Strategy Framework Directive (MSFD); (iii) the macro-regionalization of the Baltic Sea region through the EU Strategy for the Baltic Sea Region (EUSBSR). The following section thus describes and analyses the changing governance arrangements in the area of marine governance that have emerged in the region since the 1970s.

Regionalization of Marine Governance through the Helsinki Convention

As early as 1974, the Helsinki Convention, which aimed for an improvement of environmental conditions throughout the region, was signed by all the states around the Baltic Sea at that time. The convention, which entered into force in 1980, was a forerunner for a more integrated perspective on the protection of the marine environment (Kern 2011). The Helsinki Convention was amended in 1992 and entered into force in 2000, after being ratified by all (new) signatories, including the now nine Baltic Sea countries and the European Community. The revised convention also covers land-based sources of pollution and the inner waters of all member countries. Starting from a regional perspective, policies are shaped by the perspective that environmental degradation is a trans-boundary and cross-sectoral phenomenon. HELCOM, the governing body of the Helsinki Convention, was established in a world that was still divided by the Cold War. It facilitated regional cooperation in the area of environmental policy even during this period, and thus HELCOM is not only the oldest but also the most experienced institution in the area of marine governance in the Baltic Sea region (cf. Hjorth 1994).

The Baltic Sea Joint Comprehensive Environmental Action Programme (JCP) was an early regional attempt at developing environmental protection. This was established in 1992 as a regional cooperative initiative identifying and targeting sources of pollution in the Baltic Sea region (HELCOM 1999). After years of negotiations and stakeholder participation, the Baltic Sea Action Plan (BSAP) was finally adopted in November 2007. The BSAP represents a new approach in the history of HELCOM in the sense that it introduces 'ecological objectives' in order to reach improved environmental status. This innovative initiative pursues more holistic and cross-sectoral ends based on the ecosystem approach to management (Kern 2011, Hammer 2015 in this volume). The BSAP, which is funded through the signatories' national budgets and EU funds (Backer et al. 2010), covers several target areas recognized as the main issues of importance, namely eutrophication, hazardous substances, biodiversity and marine activities. The overall goal is to reach a 'good environmental status' in the Baltic Sea by the year 2021. Signatories are obliged to provide national implementation plans and status reports that show how the reduction targets will be achieved and how the situation improves over time.

The development of HELCOM since the mid-1970s until today has been marked by an increase of horizontal and vertical interplay. Horizontal interplay was restricted to horizontal interaction among the nation-states in the region and the consolidation of HELCOM as the major institution of marine governance in the Baltic Sea region. The EU was not really present in the region before the late 1990s since Germany and Denmark were the only EU member states before Finland and Sweden joined the Union in 1995.

Vertical interplay has also increased over time. In the early phase of HELCOM, vertical interplay was restricted to the relationship between HELCOM and its signatories. Today, HELCOM not only interacts far more with the European Union (see next section), but also involves sub-national authorities and civil society organizations, at least as observers or organizers of stakeholder forums. The BSAP, for example, acknowledges the need to solve existing problems through a multi-level approach because it states that actions at various operating levels are necessary, i.e. it identifies measures that should be taken at the local, regional, EU or global levels.

Finally, interaction with Russia has changed considerably over time, and HELCOM (together with the Council of Baltic Sea States; CBSS) has certainly contributed to this development. Thus, it can be argued that with respect to Russia the establishment and consolidation of the Baltic Sea region may have supported the Soviet Union's and Russia's socialization within the Baltic Sea region. In contrast, the situation in the Black Sea is characterized by rivalry between Russia and Turkey as the most important geopolitical powers in the region. The role of the European Union, however, is rather weak because Bulgaria and Romania are the only member states in the region. Russia has even prevented the EU becoming a party to the Bucharest Convention for the Protection of the Marine Environment in the Black Sea Region (see Knudsen 2015 in this volume).

Europeanization of Marine Governance through EU Legislation

Despite HELCOM's long-standing authority, the European Union has become a very important actor in marine governance in the Baltic Sea region. The Europeanization of the Baltic Sea region started with German re-unification in 1990 and increased with the EU enlargements in 1995 (Sweden, Finland) and 2004 (Poland, Lithuania, Latvia, Estonia). Since then the Baltic Sea has become an almost internal sea of the European Union because all the border countries, except the Russian Federation, are EU member states. Even HELCOM has become 'Europeanized' because the European Union became a party to the Helsinki Convention after its revision in 1994.

Apart from the EU Common Fisheries Policy, which regulates fisheries in all EU waters in a quite centralized manner, two major Directives are most important for the regulation of the marine environment in the region: (i) the Water Framework Directive (WFD) and (ii) the Marine Strategy Framework Directive (MSFD). The WFD (Directive 2000/60/EC) was adopted in October 2000 and entered into force in December 2000. The main aim of this directive is to protect, sustain and enhance water quality in European waters, with a clear focus on reaching a 'Good Ecological Status'. It was the result of several years of consultation which led to a growing insight that the traditional perspective on water issues was too narrowly focused and that there was an urgent need for a more comprehensive perspective. Thus, a new approach was launched, based on geographical boundaries instead of administrative borders (river-basin management). The European waters were divided into River Basin Districts (RBD), consisting of one larger river basin or a combination of several smaller basins with connecting ground and coastal waters. There are 14 larger international river basins in the Baltic Sea region, covering more than 50% of the Baltic Sea Drainage Basin itself. The member states are now obliged to produce river basin management plans (RBMP) for all these river basins (Nilsson and Langaas 2006, Hedin et al. 2007). The WFD has enhanced river basin management in the region and helped with harmonization of classifications and monitoring methods. Since the adoption of the Directive the scientific knowledge on European waters has increased substantially (Hering et al. 2010).

Another EU Directive that affects the marine environment of the Baltic Sea directly is the Marine Strategy Framework Directive (MSFD) which was adopted in 2008 after several years of negotiations. The MSFD divides the European waters into four European marine regions based on geographical and ecological criteria (the Baltic Sea, the North-East Atlantic Ocean, the Mediterranean Sea and the Black Sea). These areas are further divided into sub-regions. The overall aim of the MSFD (Directive 2008/56/EC, paragraph 5) is to achieve 'Good Environmental Status' in all marine areas, which entails

> ... environmental status of marine waters where these provide ecologically diverse and dynamic oceans and seas which are clean, healthy and productive within their intrinsic conditions, and the use of the marine environment is at a level that is sustainable, thus safeguarding the potential for uses and activities by current and future generations [...].

Similar to the approach chosen by the WFD the member countries need to assess the current situation, determine criteria for good environmental status and initiate monitoring schemes and measuring programmes. The MSFD is supposed to complement the WFD by connecting the inland water bodies with the open sea. The MSFD goal of 'good environmental status' draws upon eleven quality indicators, while the WFD's aim of reaching a 'good ecological status' is based on five biological quality elements (Borja et al. 2010).

Since the WFD and the MSFD were developed to govern ecosystems (such as a specific river basin) that cross regional, national and EU borders, both directives require new modes of EU governance. They differ considerably from traditional nationally-oriented governance approaches. Starting from an ecosystem approach to management requires the development of multi-sectoral, multi-actor and multi-level arrangements which may need to cross national borders. Thus, these EU directives clearly aim to solve regional environmental problems through cross-border arrangements.

Horizontal interplay between EU and macro-regional institutions is most obvious with regard to the relationship between the BSAP and the Marine Strategy Framework Directive since they have been developed during the same time frame and by the same countries (with the exception of Russia). Since the MSFD was not yet finalized when the BSAP was adopted in 2007, there is evidence that the BSAP influenced the development of the MSFD with respect to the problem definition and objective (Good Environmental Status), the methods (ecosystem approach) and the scientific and technological knowledge basis (Wenzel 2011: 36); *vice versa* the MSFD requires the utilization of existing regional governance architectures, including regional sea conventions (MSFD, article 6). Therefore, in 2010 HELCOM was established as a platform for the MSFD implementation in the Baltic Sea, coordinating the national assessments and facilitating the exchange of information.

Vertical interplay involving sub-national authorities and civil society is supported by EU institutions, in particular the Committee of the Regions. This body has published a White Paper on Multi-level Governance, which calls for 'coordinated actions by the European Union, the Member States and local and regional authorities, based on partnership and aimed at drawing up and implementing EU policies' (CdR 89/2009). The White Paper states that the EU should develop a governance approach which allows bottom-up processes. Apart from this White Paper, there is also a need to involve sub-national authorities and local stakeholders when it comes to the implementation of EU legislation such as the WFD which requires the active involvement of local and regional stakeholders, often organized around the authorities in charge of river basin management (Hedin et al. 2007: 33).

There are considerable differences among neighbouring non-EU countries, in particular between Norway on the one hand and Russia, Belarus and Ukraine on the other because Norway implements EU directives in the framework of its EEA agreement (Hedin et al. 2007: 116). In contrast, the regulations in Belarus and the Russian Federation differ considerably from EU Directives. There are nonetheless some impacts on these countries, for example with respect to agreements on transboundary waters between the Russian Federation and the EU member states Estonia and Finland. In addition, the main principles of the WFD were included in the Russian water management concept and some objectives and actions are consistent with the WFD (Tynkkynen 2007: 136). However, problems remain with respect to the governance of river basins which are shared between EU countries and non-EU countries. Although the directive encourages cooperation (i.e. signing treaties and starting joint efforts to create RBMPs), this approach seems to work well only if river basins are shared among EU member states, but its implementation can lead to considerable problems when river basins cross EU borders (Nilsson and Langaas 2006).

Macro-Regionalization of Marine Governance through the EU Strategy for the Baltic Sea Region (EUSBSR)

In addition to binding EU Directives, the EU may also influence marine governance in the Baltic Sea region through policy programmes which are not legally binding, in particular the EU Strategy for the Baltic Sea Region (EUSBSR). This strategy was initiated by the European Commission in 2009 as the EU's first macro-regional strategy, based on the hope that it will be successful in the Baltic Sea region and can then serve as a model for other European macro-regions. According to Bengtsson (2009), the strategy displays a clear example of the regionalization of the EU because it led to the development of a macro-regional vision and regional targets for the Baltic Sea region. Although macro-regionalization requires the support of all EU member states, macro-regional strategies provide new options for more flexible approaches which allow adaptation to changing conditions (Bengtsson 2009).

Macro-regionalization is driven by the new objective of territorial cohesion, enshrined in the Treaty of Lisbon alongside social and economic cohesion; the need to increase the efficient use of financial resources as a result of the economic and financial crisis of the EU; and the growing heterogeneity of the member states due to EU enlargement. Moreover, the emergence of macro-regions throughout Europe[1] is also supported by the characteristics of the regions, in particular their biophysical features (regional seas, river systems, mountain areas); increasing economic interdependencies between the territories within the macro-region; and a common historical and cultural heritage such as the Hanseatic tradition in the Baltic Sea region (Kern and Gänzle 2013a).

The strategy aims for enhanced cooperation among the countries (in particular the EU member states) in the region. The original version of the EUSBSR consisted of four pillars: (i) environment; (ii) economic development; (iii) accessibility and attractiveness; (iv) safety and security. These areas were broken down into so-called Priority Areas (PAs) and complemented by flagship projects. The Action Plan was revised in 2010 and 2013 in order to quickly absorb the 'lessons learnt' (European Commission 2013a). As a result the original four pillars were transformed into three objectives: (i) Save the Sea; (ii) Connect the Region; and (iii) Increase Prosperity. Although the strategy encompasses three objectives, it can be regarded as an important initiative for improving the marine environment of the Baltic Sea since environmental protection is a prominent issue of the strategy. Among the 17 Priority Areas (PAs)[2] and 5 Horizontal Action (HAs)[3] (cross-cutting themes) 7 Priority Areas refer to the objective 'Save the Sea', and there are also two Horizontal Actions which directly affect environmental issues (cf. European Commission 2013b: 42f.).

The strategy treats the region as a coherent macro-region and aims to strengthen already existing cooperation schemes instead of developing new forms of cooperation (Bengtsson 2009). From the outset there has been an emphasis on the so-called three NOs, meaning that no new institutions should be created, no new legislation should be generated and no new funding schemes should be set up by the EUSBSR (see for example Stocchiero 2010). After four years of implementation, it can be argued that the EUSBSR has changed existing institutions such as HELCOM, affected the implementation of existing legislation such as the WFD and the MSFD and transformed existing funding schemes due to

1 Apart from the EUSBSR the EU has already decided on two other macro-regional strategies, the EU Strategy for the Danube Region and the EU Strategy for the Adriatic and Ionian Region. Besides there are also plans to start an EU Strategy in the Alpine and North Sea Regions.

2 (1) PA Agri – Reinforcing sustainability of agriculture, forestry and fisheries; (2) PA Bio – Preserving natural zones, including fisheries; (3) PA Hazards – Reducing the use and impact of hazardous substances; (4) PA Nutri – Reducing nutrient input to the sea to acceptable levels; (5) PA Safe – to become a leading region in maritime safety and security; (6) PA Secure – Protection from emergencies and accidents on land; and (7) PA Ship – Becoming a model region for clean shipping.

3 (1) HA Spatial Planning – Encouraging the use of maritime and land-based spatial planning in all member states around the Baltic Sea and developing a common approach to cross-border cooperation; (2) HA Sustainable development and bio-energy.

the need to align already existing funds, for example projects funded under the EU Baltic Sea Region Programme (Kern and Gänzle 2013a).

After the enthusiasm of the initial phase of the strategy a more pragmatic perspective now prevails (Ozolina 2010). First, there seems to be different perspectives among the member states with respect to the overall aim of the strategy. While the Nordic countries and Germany put environmental issues high on the agenda, the Baltic States and Poland emphasize economic cohesion and competitiveness (Rostocks 2010, Salines 2010). Therefore, it has become a real challenge to keep all actors focused on a set of common goals (Reinholde 2010). Second, there is an ongoing debate on the added value of the strategy (European Commission 2013b). This has led to a refinement of the macro-regional concept, which is now based on five principles (integration, coordination, cooperation, multi-level governance and partnership), an assessment of the preliminary results and suggestions as to how the remaining challenges can be overcome. Overall, the European Commission concludes that 'clear results are already evident in terms of projects and more integrated policy making, although further improvements are essential in implementation and planning' (European Commission 2013c: 11). Third, there are still open questions because there is an evident lack of leadership (Ozolina 2010, European Commission 2013c) and challenges with respect to the implementation of the strategy (Laizāne-Jurkāne 2010). The EUSBSR was thus complemented by its own monitoring system with indicators and targets for individual Priority Areas (European Commission 2013c: 8-9). For the objective 'Save the Sea' the indicators and targets refer not only to EU legislation (in particular the MSFD) but also to HELCOM's BSAP and targets to be set by HELCOM (European Commission 2012).

Although new institutions where not established within the framework of the EUSBSR, the strategy does affect existing institutions and stimulates new forms of institutional interplay (Kern and Gänzle 2013b). For the implementation of the Priority Area 'Natural Zones and Biodiversity', for example, HELCOM provides the technical and scientific framework (indicators and targets) for the implementation of EU Directives (EUSBSR News, May 2012: 5). This shows a new phase of horizontal interplay, linking (i) HELCOM; (ii) EU legislation; and (iii) the EUSBSR; in other words the EUSBSR utilizes HELCOM (and its BSAP) as an institutional basis for the implementation of EU legislation (such as the WFD and MSFD).

Vertical interplay has also increased because the European Commission sought legitimacy via a wide consultation process with a considerable number of stakeholders (Rostocks 2010). Macro-regionalization provides new political opportunities for subnational authorities and civil society actors in the region. The commitment of the stakeholders is essential because the strategy is built around soft values and voluntary cooperation (Reinholde 2010). The annual stakeholder meetings, which took place in Tallinn (2010), Gdansk (2011) and Copenhagen (2012), are seen as an opportunity for all actors to gather and express opinions. However, the involvement of stakeholders depends on their commitments and capacities because not all affected groups have enough capacities to participate in such events (cf. Dreyer and Sellke 2015 in this volume).

It is a characteristic feature of macro-regional strategies that they aim for the cooperation of old member states, new member states, candidate countries and non-member states. Although the EUSBSR does not commit non-member states, the implementation of the EUSBSR requires close cooperation with the Russian Federation (European Commission 2013b: 31), such as joint maritime surveillance in the Gulf of Finland (European Commission 2012: 8). Though Russia's involvement in the strategy is still limited, cooperation with Russia has not only a long history, it has also improved through the EUSBSR. Russia has launched a North-West Strategy which provides an interface with the EUSBSR. Moreover the so-called Turku Process, which was launched as part of the HA 'Neighbours' directly addresses practical cooperation with Russian partners at the subnational level (EUSBSR News, March 2013). Such projects are often based on long-standing twin city partnerships and include a variety of actors, ranging from cities and regional authorities to companies and their representative bodies as well as civil society actors and research organizations.

Discussion and Conclusions

The Baltic Sea region is a highly polluted and sensitive marine area with an intricate set of entangled environmental issues. Physical conditions increase the complexities of both the environmental problems and governance architecture. This chapter described the current situation regarding environmental governance in the Baltic Sea region, depicting a system with two strong institutions, HELCOM and the EU. It went on to examine three phases of regionalization and Europeanization of marine governance in the Baltic Sea region and their problem solving capacities: regionalization through the Helsinki Convention; Europeanization through EU legislation; and macro-regionalization through the EU Strategy of the Baltic Sea Region.

HELCOM is still the main actor in the area of marine governance. Through the work of HELCOM, the Baltic Sea countries have established directions for the protection of the marine environment, learnt to join forces and when a consensus is reached HELCOM is a strong regional actor in voicing demands within, for example, a UN setting. Despite the fact that the Baltic Sea has almost become an internal sea of the EU, HELCOM still plays an essential role for marine governance in the region. The interplay between HELCOM and the EU may even strengthen HELCOM's position, especially since Russia is a party to the Helsinki Convention but stands outside the EU.

Traditionally, Europeanization of the Baltic Sea region has been limited to EU legislation which is implemented by the member states (cf. Bohman and Langlet 2015 in this volume). This type of Europeanization requires a certain degree of cross-boundary cooperation only, for example, in the case of trans-boundary river basin management. The EUSBSR differs from this national paradigm because it contributes to the construction of the Baltic Sea as a macro-region. However, the regionalization of the area has been ongoing for a long time and a multitude of regional institutions, networks and partnerships have emerged, in particular since the end of the Cold War.

The institutional interplay between the EU and HELCOM has led to important synergies. Horizontal interplay between HELCOM and the BSAP on the one hand and the EU and the MSFD on the other has led to synergies which strengthen HELCOM and support the implementation of the MSFD. Since the MSFD has been built on the experience of HELCOM's Baltic Sea Action Plan, HELCOM is in a position to influence decision-making in Brussels. The European Commission, in turn, utilizes HELCOM as a sort of regional environmental protection agency, which supports the implementation of EU legislation in the macro-region. Synergies have increased through the EUSBSR because it combines HELCOM, EU legislation and the EUSBSR. This may lead to more effective governance because HELCOM recommendations require a consensus among the cooperating countries and lack formal enforcement powers, while most EU directives are decided on the basis of a qualified majority, are binding after transposition into national law and are also subject to the infringement procedure for the EU member states (Wenzel 2011: 30ff., Van Leeuwen and Kern 2013). This creates new features of institutional interplay which facilitate and stabilize the development of a functional space and thus creates a new macro-regional level of governance which transcends both the borders of the nation-state and the external borders of the EU. In the Baltic Sea region we find a rather unique governance architecture combining existing regional institutions with trends towards Europeanization through EU legislation and macro-regionalization through the EUSBSR.

Vertical interplay has also increased over time. Today, HELCOM's Baltic Sea Action Plan is based on a multi-level governance approach and the EUSBSR provides new political opportunities for sub-national authorities and civil society. The strategy differs from traditional forms of Europeanization because it pursues a macro-regional approach through the inclusion of a variety of national and trans-national actors and the organization of stakeholder meetings during the creation of the strategy and its implementation. However, it can be argued that there is still a lack of legitimacy because the process appears to be driven mainly by proactive actors with adequate capacities, even though the official channels are open to everyone.

The role of the Soviet Union and, since the end of the Cold War, the Russian Federation has always been decisive for the success of marine governance in the Baltic Sea region. Protecting and cleaning up the sea depends on cooperation with this important partner. Despite considerable shortcomings, the relationship with Russia has changed considerably over the last forty years, mainly due to collapse of the Soviet Union and the reestablishment of the Baltic States and Poland, but also based on various institutional arrangements and programmes such as the

Helsinki Convention, the Northern Dimension and the European Neighbourhood Policy. This has led to a certain degree of policy convergence between North-West Russia and the member states in the region. As the recent macro-regionalization transcends EU borders, multi-level governance is not restricted to member states; instead macro-regionalization is strongly intertwined with EU enlargement and the role of non-member states.

There are many challenges ahead, for example how to even better include non-EU countries in the EU-dominated setting in the Baltic Sea region, but the cross-sectoral approach, the improved participation at the macro-regional scale and the dynamic development of regional institutions and their interplay are novel. Although it is yet to be seen whether the new initiatives will be successful and sustainable in the long run, the emerging governance arrangements, which combine (i) HELCOM and its BSAP; (ii) EU legislation; and (iii) the EUSBSR in innovative ways, lead to synergies and seem to provide an adequate basis for marine governance in the Baltic Sea region. The new macro-regional approach in particular could be an option to overcome many shortcomings. It may, for instance, help to develop more democratic processes with high inclusiveness and legitimacy at the macro-regional level. However, constructing a coherent macro-region in the Baltic Sea area based on nation-states which show great differences in terms of wealth, culture and historical heritage might prove difficult. It will thus be necessary to reach compromises between countries with varying interests and preferences. Marine governance in the region will to a high degree depend on developing a coherent approach balancing national interests, Europeanization and macro-regionalization.

References

Backer, H., Leppänen, J.M., Brusendorff, A.C., Forsius, K., Stankiewicz, M., Methonen, J., Pyhälä, M., Laamanen, M., Paulomäki, H. and Vlasov, N. 2010. HELCOM Baltic Sea Action Plan – A Regional Programme of Measures for the Marine Environment Based on the Ecosystem Approach. *Marine Pollution Bulletin*, 60(5), 642-649.

Bengtsson, R. 2009. *An EU Strategy for the Baltic Sea Region: Good Intentions Meet Complex Challenges*. Stockholm: Swedish Institute for European Policy Studies.

Bohman, B. and Langlet, D. 2015. Float or Sinker for Europe's Seas? The role of law in marine governance, in *Governing Europe's Marine Environment: Europeanization of Regional Seas or Regionalization of EU Policies?*, edited by M. Gilek and K. Kern. Farnham, UK: Ashgate Publishing.

Borja, Á., Elliot, M., Carstensen, J., Heiskanen, A.S. and van de Bund, W. 2010. Marine Management – Towards an Integrated Implementation of the European Marine Strategy Framework and the Water Framework Directives. *Marine Pollution Bulletin*, 60(12), 2175-2186.

CDR 2009. *The Committee of the Regions' White Paper on Multilevel Governance,* Committee of the Regions 89/2009.

Dreyer, M. and Sellke, P. 2015. The Regional Advisory Councils in European Fisheries: An appropriate approach to stakeholder involvement in an EU integrated marine governance?, in *Governing Europe's Marine Environment: Europeanization of Regional Seas or Regionalization of EU Policies?*, edited by M. Gilek and K. Kern. Farnham, UK: Ashgate Publishing.

European Commission 2009. Commission Staff Working Document Accompanying the Communication from the Commission to the European Parliament, the Council, the European Economic and Social Committee and the Committee of the Regions Concerning the European Union Strategy for the Baltic Sea Region Action Plan.

European Commission 2012. Communication from the Commission to the European Parliament, the Council, the European Economic and Social Committee and the Committee of the Regions Concerning the European Union Strategy for the Baltic Sea Region, COM(2012) 128 final.

European Commission 2013a. Commission Staff Working Document Accompanying the Communication from the Commission to the European Parliament, the Council, the European Economic and Social Committee and the Committee of the Regions Concerning the European Union Strategy for the Baltic Sea Region, Action Plan, February 2013 Version, SEC(2009) 712-2.

European Commission 2013b. Commission Staff Working Document Accompanying the Report from the Commission to the European Parliament, the Council, the European Economic and Social Committee and the Committee of the Regions Concerning the Added Value of Macro-regional Strategies, SWD(2013) 233 final.

European Commission 2013c. Report from the Commission to the European Parliament, the Council, The European Economic and Social Committee and the Committee of the Regions Concerning the Added Value of Macro-regional Strategies, COM(2013) 468 final.

Gilek, M., Karlsson, M., Udovyk, O. and Linke, S. 2015. Science and Policy in the Governance of Europe's Marine Environment: The impact of Europeanization, regionalization and the ecosystem approach to management, in *Governing Europe's Marine Environment: Europeanization of Regional Seas or Regionalization of EU Policies?*, edited by M. Gilek and K. Kern. Farnham, UK: Ashgate Publishing.

GRID-Arendal. 2014. UNEP.

Hammer, M. 2015. The ecosystem management approach – implications for marine governance, in *Governing Europe's Marine Environment: Europeanization of Regional Seas or Regionalization of EU Policies?*, edited by M. Gilek and K. Kern. Farnham, UK: Ashgate Publishing.

Hassler, B. 2011. Accidential versus Operational Oil Spills from Shipping in the Baltic Sea: Risk Governance and Management Strategies. *Ambio*, 40(2), 170-178.

Hedin, S., Dubois, A., Ikonen, R., Lindblom, P., Nilsson, S., Tynkkynen, V.-P., Viehhauser, M., Leisk, Ü. and Veidemane, K. 2007. *The Water Framework Directive in the Baltic Sea Region Countries: Vertical Implementation, Horizontal Integration and Transnational Cooperation*. Stockholm: Nordregio.

HELCOM 1999. HELCOM Programme Implementation Task Force (HELCOM PITF), The Baltic Sea Joint Comprehensive Environmental Action Programme (JCP) Annual Report 1999.

HELCOM 2009a. Eutrophication in the Baltic Sea: An Integrated Thematic Assessment of the Effects of Nutrient Enrichment and Eutrophication in the Baltic Sea Region, Baltic Sea Environmental Proceedings no. 115B.

HELCOM 2009b. Biodiversity in the Baltic Sea: An Integrated Thematic Assessment on Biodiversity and Nature Conservation in the Baltic Sea, Baltic Sea Environment Proceedings no. 116B.

HELCOM 2010. Hazardous Substances in the Baltic Sea: An Integrated Thematic Assessment of Hazardous Substances in the Baltic Sea Region.

HELCOM 2012. Activities Report 2012. Baltic Sea Environment Proceedings no. 134.

HELCOM 2013. Approaches and Methods for Eutrophication Target Setting in the Baltic Sea Region, Baltic Sea Environment Proceedings no. 133.

Hering, D., Borja, A., Carstensen, J., Carvalho, L., Elliot, M., Feld, C.K., Heiskanen, A.S., Johnson, R.K., Moe, J. and Pont, D. 2010. The European Water Framework Directive at the Age of 10: A Critical Review of the Achievements with Recommendations for the Future, *Science of the Total Environment*, 408(19), 4007-4019.

Hjorth, R. 1994. Baltic Sea Environmental Cooperation. *Cooperation & Conflict*, 29(1), 11-31.

Karlsson, M. 2004. *Transnational Relations in the Baltic Sea Region*. Huddinge: Södertörns högskola.

Kern, K. 2011. Governance for sustainable development in the Baltic Sea region. *Journal of Baltic Studies*, 42(1), 21-35.

Kern, K. 2014, Climate governance in the European Union multilevel system: the role of cities, in *Multilevel Environmental Governance: Managing Water and Climate Change in Europe and North America*, edited by I. Weibust and J. Meadowcroft. Cheltenham: Edward Elgar, 111-130.

Kern, K. and Bulkeley, H. 2009. Cities, Europeanization and multi-level governance: governing climate change through transnational municipal networks. *Journal of Common Market Studies*, 47(2), 309-332.

Kern, K. and Gänzle, S. 2013a. 'Macro-regionalization' as a new form of European governance: the case of the European Union's strategies for the Baltic Sea and the Danube regions, *ISL Working Paper* 2013(3). University of Adger.

Kern, K. and Gänzle, S. 2013b. Towards CruSng Speed? Assessing the European Union's Strategy for the Baltic Sea Region. *European Policy Analysis*, 17, 1-20.

Knudsen, S. 2015. Marine Governance in the Black Sea, in *Governing Europe's Marine Environment: Europeanization of Regional Seas or Regionalization of EU Policies?*, edited by M. Gilek and K. Kern. Farnham, UK: Ashgate Publishing.

Laizāne-Jurkāne, M. 2010. The Baltic Sea Strategy: illusions and perils, in *EU Strategy for the Baltic Sea Region: A Year after and beyond*, edited by Z. Ozolina, I. Reinholde and T. Rostocks. Riga: Zinātne, 233-247.

Linke, S., Dreyer, M. and Sellke, P. 2011. The Regional Advisory Councils: What is their potential to incorporate stakeholder knowledge into fisheries governance? *Ambio*, 40(2), 133-143.

Nilsson, S. and Langaas, S. 2006. International river Basins management under the EU Water Framework Directive: an assessment of cooperation and water quality in the Baltic Sea Drainage Basin. *Ambio*, 35(6), 304-311.

Oberthür, S. and Schram Stokke, O. 2011. *Managing Institutional Complexity: Regime Interplay and Global Environmental Change*. Cambridge, MA and London: The MIT Press.

Ozolina, Ž. 2010. Designing national governance for macro-regional strategy, in *EU Strategy for the Baltic Sea Region: A Year After and Beyond*, edited by Z. Ozolina, I. Reinholde and T. Rostocks. Riga: Zinātne, 59-89.

Reinholde, I. 2010. How to govern the strategy? Whether to govern at all …?, in *EU Strategy for the Baltic Sea Region: A Year After and Beyond*, edited by Z. Ozolina, I. Reinholde and T. Rostocks. Riga: Zinātne, 41-58.

Rostocks, T. 2010. In place of an introduction: why the Baltic Sea Strategy?, in *EU Strategy for the Baltic Sea Region: A Year After and Beyond*, edited by Z. Ozolina, I. Reinholde and T. Rostocks. Riga: Zinātne, 9-38.

Salines, M. 2010. *Success Factors of Macro-regional Cooperation: The Example of the Baltic Sea Region*, Bruges Political Research Papers no. 12, March 2010.

Schymik, C. 2011. *‚Modellversuch' Makroregion. Die EU-Strategien für den Ostsee- und den Donauraum*. Berlin: Stiftung Wissenschaft und Politik.

Stocchiero, A. 2010. *Macro-regions of Europe: Old Wine in a New Bottle. Background Paper*, Centre Studi di Politica Internazionale, Working Papers 65.

Tynkkynen, V.-P. 2007. Russia, in *The Water Framework Directive in the Baltic Sea Region Countries: Vertical Implementation, Horizontal Integration and Transnational Cooperation*, S. Hedin, A. Dubois, R. Ikonen, P. Lindblom, S. Nilsson, V.-P. Tynkkynen, M. Viehhauser, Ü. Leisk and K. Veidemane. Stockholm: Nordregio, 131-137.

Vangas, A. 2010. Can the EU Strategy for the Baltic Sea Region Bridge the 'Great Divide'?, in *EU Strategy for the Baltic Sea Region: A Year After and Beyond*, edited by Z. Ozolina, I. Reinholde and T. Rostocks. Riga: Zinātne, 103-119.

Van Leeuwen, J. and Kern, K. 2013. The external dimension of EU Marine Governance: institutional interplay between the European Union and the

International Maritime Organization. *Global Environmental Politics*, 13(1), 69-87.

Vlasov, N. (ed.) 2010. *HELCOM Atlas of the Baltic Sea*. HELCOM.

Wenzel, B. 2011. *Environmental Governance and Institutional Interaction in the Baltic Sea Region: Effective Governance System or Institutional Entanglement?* Masters thesis, Philipps University Marbur.

Chapter 10
Marine Governance of the North Sea: Patterns of Regionalization

Jan P.M. van Tatenhove and Judith van Leeuwen

History of Marine Governance of the North Sea

Marine governance of the North Sea refers to the sharing of policy-making competences of governments, international organizations, the European Union (EU), non-governmental organizations (NGOs) and market parties to govern activities in the North Sea and to control their consequences, such as environmental or spatial problems and conflicts (cf. Van Leeuwen and Van Tatenhove 2010, Van Tatenhove 2013). Marine governance of the North Sea became a transnational endeavour as early as the 1970s. Crucial to this development was the adoption of the Oslo and Paris Conventions in 1972 and 1974 respectively. These two conventions complement each other because the Paris Convention focused on pollution by land-based sources, while the Oslo Convention focused on dumping practices. In addition, the EU developed its first rules in fisheries management in 1970, while the Common Fisheries Policy (CFP) was created in 1983 and is at the heart of management of North Sea fish stocks. Finally, a series of North Sea Ministerial Conferences (NSMCs) were organized between 1984 and 2006 to show political will in dealing with marine pollution. One of the main changes in marine governance of the North Sea is the emergence of the EU as a key player. Several new marine issue areas have been added to the policy spectrum of the EU, such as shipping, marine nature, environmental protection and sustainable economic use of marine space.

The objective of this chapter is to understand these recent developments in marine governance of the North Sea as different patterns of regionalization. In general, regionalization refers to the shift of administrative responsibilities from a central (national) level to the regional or local levels. According to Symes (2012), 'for regionalization to add value to the system of governance, it must not be limited to bureaucratic decentralization involving the relocation of central government's decision-making apparatus to regional offices. Some element of devolved responsibility is necessary'. Devolution is the moving of power or responsibility from a main organization to a lower level, or from a central government to a regional government (Cambridge Dictionary Online, visited 11-02-2012). In general, devolution and the granting of greater autonomy to the regions can be seen as a means whereby the state is able to further democratize decision-making while retaining hegemony over all its territory (Stacey 2001 in Symes 2012). Regionalization encompasses both processes of decentralization and devolution, but is also broader than that as it is as much about the shift of responsibilities between layers of government as it is about the empowerment of governmental and non-governmental actors in decision-making processes at the regional level (in this case the North Sea). In this chapter, we distinguish between three patterns of regionalization: (1) regionalization through cooperation of governmental actors at the level of the North Sea; (2) regionalization through the empowerment of non-governmental actors at the level of the North Sea and (3) regionalization as an organizing principle for activities and planning on the North Sea.

The key questions for this chapter are:

- What are the main environmental and spatial problems in the North Sea?
- What kind of governance initiatives have been taken to deal with these problems in the North Sea?
- Which patterns of regionalization have emerged in marine governance for the North Sea as a result of the Europeanization of marine governance?

In section 2, we give an overview of the environmental and spatial problems in the North Sea, followed by an overview of recent developments in marine governance of the North Sea (section 3). In section 4, we examine the Europeanization of marine governance of the North Sea. Since 2007, the EU has become a central player in marine policies. However, marine governance is characterized by different forms of Europeanization, which show a tension between the initiatives of Member States, OSPAR and the EU for the whole of the North Sea. The result is a patchwork of institutions, fragmented policies and regulations (Van Tatenhove 2013). A possible way out of this situation of institutional ambiguity (Van Leeuwen et al. 2012) is different forms of regionalization of marine governance. In section 5, we describe three patterns of regionalization of marine governance. In section 6, we illustrate the patterns with examples: the Dogger Bank and the implementation of the Marine Strategy Framework Directive (MSFD) as examples of regional cooperation; the establishment of Regional Advisory Councils (RACs) as an example of empowerment; and the plans to develop a network of MPAs and an Offshore Power Grid as examples of regionalization as an organizing principle. In section 7, we formulate conclusions.

Main Environmental Problems and Challenges for the North Sea

The North Sea is a relatively shallow marginal sea (average depth 95 meters) located between the United Kingdom, France, Belgium, Netherlands, Germany, Denmark and Norway. It is one of the seas most affected by human impact

(Halpern et al. 2008). The high population density of the neighbouring countries in the eastern and southern parts of the region results in pressures from human activities. In some coastal areas, the population density amounts to more than 500 people per km^2, while intensive farming covers up to 70% of the land with run-offs into this part of the North Sea prevalent. There is also an increase of coastal structures and tourism. The North Sea is one of the busiest seas in the world in terms of oil and gas production and navigation. Some of the busiest shipping lanes in the world are located in the North Sea and maritime transport to the ports of Rotterdam, Amsterdam, Antwerp, Hamburg and London continues to increase. Wind farms are increasingly taking up space as several North Sea countries have expressed interest in meeting their renewable energy targets through offshore wind farms. While the overall amount of fishing is decreasing (reduced by 25% between 2000 and 2006), around 30 different commercial fish stocks are still fished.

Extensive mudflats and estuaries line the coast of the southern North Sea, while other important ecosystems comprise fjords and sandy beaches. The Wadden Sea is the largest area of intertidal mudflats in the world, hosting 10-12 million migrating birds every year. In total 5.4 % of the North Sea covers Marine Protected Areas (MPAs).

Currently, the main environmental problems that threaten biodiversity in the North Sea are (Knights et al. 2011, OSPAR, 2011):

- The introduction of non-indigenous species through shipping;
- Pressure on commercial fish stocks, food webs and habitats because of overfishing of commercial fish stocks, with progress towards sustainable fishing slow;
- Sea floor integrity is under threat because of a variety of activities, such as agriculture, aquaculture, coastal infrastructure, fishing, non-renewable energy (oil and gas), military and research activities and shipping;
- Marine litter generated by shipping, tourism and fisheries (90% of fulmars have microscopic plastic particles in their stomachs and 45% to 60% have more than the Ecological Quality Objective (EcoQO) set by OSPAR;
- Underwater noise through offshore renewable energy resources (wind mill farms) and shipping;
- Eutrophication on the coasts caused by nitrogen (and phosphorus) inputs from agriculture and point sources (such as sewage plants and industry);
- Pollution with hazardous substances such as metals (cadmium, mercury and lead) and persistent organic pollutants. Monitored sites with unacceptable status: Mercury 37% and PAHs 55%.

Taken together these threats have a potentially detrimental effect on biodiversity. For example, seabed habitats are damaged in especially shallow areas and seabirds have suffered from a long-term failure to breed. According to the OSPAR Quality Status of 2010, 29 species and 10 habitats are already under threat. In addition, the effects of climate change (1°to 2°C over the last 25 years) and pressure from responses to climate change on biodiversity are still unknown. The increase in human population and activities in the North Sea area and climate change will continue to pose a threat to the marine environment for the foreseeable future.

Recent Developments in Marine Governance of the North Sea

Marine governance of the North Sea is currently in a turbulent state. The relatively intergovernmental nature of marine governance through the Oslo and Paris Conventions and the NSMCs has been replaced by new EU developments. The Oslo and Paris Conventions merged into the OSPAR Convention in the 1990s, though the NSMCs have ceased to exist since the last one of 2006. The conclusion was that the efforts of other international organizations, including OSPAR, but also the EU, made the NSMCs redundant. One of the intergovernmental arenas of decision-making for marine governance therefore no longer exists. At the same time, new multi-level arenas with intergovernmental, supranational and informal characteristics have emerged within marine governance of the North Sea. This has changed the institutional setting in which policies for the North Sea are shaped, the type of actors involved, the dynamics between different layers of governance and the range of available policy and enforcement instruments.

In this section, we provide an overview of the institutional setting of marine governance of the North Sea. According to Skjærseth (2006: 158) the 'history of international cooperation among countries bordering the North Sea/North East Atlantic is the story of evolution from a state of water and marine pollution 'anarchy' to domestic and international 'governance'. Environmental problems in the North Sea have been dealt with by three types of international institutions: legal conventions on marine pollution, the NSMCs and the EU.

A Short History of OSPAR

In 1972, the Convention for the Prevention of Marine Pollution by Dumping from Ships and Aircraft (Oslo Convention) was signed by all 13 West European maritime states. In 1974, the Convention for the Prevention of Marine Pollution from Land-based Sources (Paris Convention) was signed. The Oslo and Paris Conventions were supported by a joint secretariat, executive commissions (Oslo and Paris Commissions) and several standing and ad hoc scientific/technical bodies.[1] On 22

1 'Two executive commissions – which met annually – were set up in order to implement and review the functioning of the Conventions. The Oslo Commission (OSCOM)

September 1992, The Convention for the protection of the Marine Environment of the North-East Atlantic was signed in Paris. The OSPAR Convention[2] replaced the Oslo and the Paris Convention. The purpose of the OSPAR Convention was to create a comprehensive regime in a single legal instrument for the protection of the marine environment of the North-east Atlantic and Arctic oceans from pollution by the previously covered sources,[3] as well as from other adverse effects on human activities (De la Fayette 1999: 250). General obligations formulated in the OSPAR Convention are the precautionary principle, the application of Best Available Techniques and Best Environmental Practice and the polluter pays principle.

The first Ministerial Meeting of the OSPAR Commission after the coming into force of the 1992 OSPAR Convention was held in Sintra in July 1998. At this meeting, besides a non-binding political declaration (the 'Sintra Statement'), the Ministers and the EU Environment Commissioner adopted several significant legal instruments and enunciated OSPAR policy for the next two decades (De La Fayette 1999: 248). For example, several OSPAR strategies were adopted to set out long-term policy goals for OSPAR's main issue areas: eutrophication, hazardous substances, radioactive substances and biodiversity. The adoption of the strategy for the offshore industry followed in 2003.

The North Sea Ministerial Conferences

Spurred by dissatisfaction with existing international institutions, Germany took the initiative to arrange the first North Sea Ministerial Conference in Bremen in 1984. The aim of the conference was not to create a new set of international agreements, but to provide political impetus for an intensification of the work of the competent commissions and international bodies, and to ensure more efficient and effective implementation of the existing international rules in all the North Sea States (Annex 1 to the Progress Report to the 5th North Sea Conference). The Bremen conference was followed by 5 conferences (London 1987, The Hague 1990, Esbjerg (Denmark) 1995, Bergen (Norway) 2002 and Gothenburg 2006).[4] The NSMCs have led to political commitments, which have

---

and the Paris Commission (PARCOM) were assisted by the Standing Advisory Committee for Scientific Advice (SACSA) and the Technical Working Group (TWG), respectively, by ad hoc working groups and by the Joint Monitoring Group (JMG)' Skjærseth (2006: 158).

2 The parties to the OSPAR Convention are Belgium, Denmark, the European Community (now European Union), Finland, France, Germany, Iceland, Ireland, Luxembourg, the Netherlands, Norway, Portugal, Spain, Sweden, Switzerland and the United Kingdom.

3 Dumping and land-based sources, including offshore installations. Ship-source pollution is covered by IMO.

4 The North Sea Conferences focused on: the protection of species and habitats, fisheries, hazardous substances, nutrients inputs and eutrophication, pollution form ships, pollution from offshore installations, radioactive substance, dumping of waste at sea and incineration of industrial waste at sea.

been adopted in national regulations as well as within the framework of legally binding conventions (Skjærseth 2006). Important agreements emanating from the NSMCs are the adoption of the precautionary principle (London 1987) and the development and commitment to an ecosystem approach (Bergen 2002). After the Gothenburg Conference (2006) there was no plan for another North Sea Conference or Ministerial Meeting. The Ministers declared that many of the issues that had been discussed over the years were now being treated in other forums. With a view to safeguarding the fulfilment of the commitments from the various NSMCs, the North Sea Ministers invited OSPAR, in cooperation with the EU, to facilitate a periodic follow-up to this effect (www.ospar.org, visited 06/02/2012). The OSPAR Commission regularly reviews progress in the implementation of commitments from the NSMCs.[5]

The European Union

In recent years, the EU has undertaken several new initiatives and has, as a result, become a key political arena for marine governance of the North Sea. Since the 1990s, the EU has been developing a set of environmental policies for shipping. This development accelerated after the sinking of the Erika (1999) and Prestige (2002) tankers (Urrutia 2006, Van Leeuwen 2010). The EU adopted a recommendation for Integrated Coastal Zone Management in 2002 to improve the sustainable development of Europe's coastal zones. In 2007, the Integrated Maritime Policy (IMP) was adopted to support sustainable (economic) development of the European Seas. The EC's goal is for an integrated maritime policy that covers all aspects of our relationship with the oceans and seas. This innovative and holistic approach will provide a coherent policy framework that will allow for the optimal development of all sea-related activities in a sustainable manner (EC 2007b). In other words, the IMP seeks integration between sectors at the EU level. One of the tools of IMP is Marine Spatial Planning (MSP) (cf. De Santo 2015 in this volume).

The environmental pillar of the IMP, which ensures the sustainable ecological use of the seas, is the Marine Strategy Framework Directive (MSFD) of 2008. The MSFD sets out a common framework based on cooperation between Member States to ensure the sustainable use of marine goods and services by current and future generations. Member States must achieve, or maintain, Good Environmental Status in the marine environment by the year 2020 at the latest. New in this framework directive are the introduction of 'marine region' and 'regional cooperation' (Long 2011, Van Tatenhove 2013). According to the MSFD, Member States bordering the North Sea (marine region) should cooperate

5 OSPAR has published a comprehensive general report to North Sea Ministers on follow-up to the 2002 Bergen Declaration and a special report on implementation of the Ecological Quality Objectives for the North Sea. A second comprehensive review of progress in implementing North Sea Conference commitments was published in 2009 to inform the North Sea Ministers prior to the OSPAR Ministerial Meeting in 2010.

and coordinate their activities to define Good Environmental Status and to develop and implement marine strategies. Member states can make use of existing regional institutional cooperation structures, including the Regional Sea Conventions, or develop new institutions. In addition, Natura 2000 aims to protect important bird species and habitat types at the European level. Since 2005, implementation of the Bird and Habitat Directive under Natura 2000 is required for the North Sea. States bordering the North Sea have to designate Marine Protected Areas to protect marine habitats and bird species (either as Special Protection Areas or as Special Areas of Conservation).

By developing Regional Advisory Councils in the 2002 reform of the CFP, forums of stakeholder participation in fisheries management were created at the regional level. It is expected that the 2012 reform will result in a further process of regionalization of fisheries management and an operationalization of the ecosystem approach towards fisheries.

The interdependencies between these policy initiatives are strong, although it is still unclear how coordination between them will be organized. For example, the IMP has to take existing shipping and fisheries policies into account. Similarly, achieving the aims of the MSFD will partly depend on the implementation of Marine Protected Areas under Natura 2000. How to avoid inconsistencies between these policy instruments remains to be seen. A challenging factor in this regard is the fact that different Directorate-Generals (DG) are responsible for these policy developments, i.e. DG Mobility and Transport for shipping, DG of Maritime Affairs and Fisheries for the IMP and CFP and DG Environment for the MSFD and Natura 2000 (Ounanian et al. 2012).

Europeanization of Marine Governance for the North Sea

With the emergence of EU policies, the influence of the EU on the marine governance of the North Sea is growing. However, EU policy-making is characterized by multi-level interactions between Member States, EU institutions and stakeholders. It is therefore important to take a closer look at what the Europeanization of marine governance of the North Sea specifically entails.

There is no consensus on the concept of Europeanization. On the one hand, traditional definitions of Europeanization refer to causal mechanisms through which EU policies, institutions and political processes impact upon the domestic structures of the Member States (Börzel and Risse 2012). On the other hand, scholars define Europeanization as the institutionalization at the European level of a distinct system of governance with common institutions and the authority to make, implement and enforce European-wide binding policies[6] (Olson 2001).

6 This view is illustrated by Risse et al. (2001: 3), who define Europeanization as: (a) the emergence and development at the European level of distinct structures of governance, that is, of political, legal, and social institutions associated with problem solving, which

Olson (2002: 923-924) also points to another use of the concept Europeanization, namely the increasing reach of the EU governance system through enlargement (i.e. new Member States), the division of responsibilities and powers between different levels of governance and export of forms of political organization and governance to countries outside Europe. Europeanization of marine governance for the North Sea is a multi-dimensional form of Europeanization, combining the development of institutions both at the European level and the regional sea level. It was initiated by the European supranational institutions and changes in core domestic institutions of governance and politics, as a consequence of the development of European-level marine institutions, identities and policies. The increasing reach of EU marine governance lies in the need and wish for cooperation with non-EU states bordering European Seas (e.g. Norway in the North Sea, Russia in the Baltic Sea, etc.) to ensure sustainable use and protection of the marine environment. In addition, the EU is seeking cooperation with the Regional Sea Conventions to support the implementation of some of its policies, while at the same time it has been building institutional linkages with the IMO through its shipping policies (Van Leeuwen and Kern 2013).

The multi-dimensional processes of Europeanization provided a new dynamic in marine governance. What is more, Europeanization of marine governance has caused an exceptionally high level of regionalization. For example, the implementation of the MSFD has introduced a strong regional focus as coordination between Member States is not only required at the EU level, but also at the level of the marine region. Regional Sea Conventions are a first starting point for doing this. Although this process is in some regional seas clouded by a considerable degree of institutional ambiguity (Van Leeuwen et al. 2012), it has certainly created a new dynamic in marine governance of the North Sea. The political reach of the EU is increasing into new institutions and non-EU states because of the MSFD.

The Integrated Maritime Policy provides another example of how the Europeanization of marine governance creates a high level of regionalization. The most important tool at the moment, i.e. Marine Spatial Planning, is developed and implemented nationally. The European Commission (EC) defines the steps to follow in order to realize a marine spatial planning process, but the EC leaves the development and implementation of Marine Spatial Plans to the Member States (Van Tatenhove 2013). Of course, in implementing it at the national level, Member States are faced with cross-boundary issues, such as the designation of the Doggers Bank as an MPA, the development of the Eems harbour at the Dutch and German border or the planning of windmill parks by the Belgium government at the border of the Dutch Exclusive Economic Zone, where the Dutch planned Special Protection Areas according to the Bird Directive. Regional coordination is therefore also needed in implementing MSP.

---

formalize interactions among the actors, and (b) of policy networks specializing in the creation of authoritative European rules.

While Europeanization of marine governance has always been characterized by EU and national dynamics, marine governance for the North Sea has become more complex because of the regional dynamics between the EU, Member and non-Member States and OSPAR. This has resulted in a situation characterized by institutional ambiguity, i.e. a mismatch between the institutional settings of the European Union and the level of the North Sea (Van Leeuwen et al. 2012). To overcome this mismatch, different forms of regionalization have emerged in EU marine governance.

Regionalization of Marine Governance for the North Sea

The development of different EU marine policies for the North Sea not only affects the policies and institutions of the bordering countries, but also forces the EC and Member States to think about how to develop marine governance at the level of the North Sea itself. Regionalization of marine governance of a regional sea, in this case the North Sea concerns the geographical aspect of the ecosystem and the maritime activities, crossing boundaries.

We distinguish three different forms of regionalization of marine governance.

1. **Regionalization as cooperation of governmental actors at the level of the North Sea.** Regionalization refers to the need for neighbouring countries and governmental actors on the supra and international level to cooperate at a regional scale in order to coordinate and implement policy (Van Hoof et al. 2012). Regional cooperation is an important element in the MSFD and IMP. A specific form of this kind of regionalization is trans-boundary cooperation to deal with conflicting spatial claims in areas which belong to the Exclusive Economic Zones of different states. Both IMP and MSFD formulate the regional level as that at which both activities and policies should be integrated. In its progress report on the IMP the EC stressed the importance of regionalization. According to the report the implementation of the MSFD and the development of sea-basin strategies[7] play an important role. Regionalization in the MSFD refers to regional seas basins and to the need for Member States to cooperate in implementing the MSFD. The discourse on regionalization in the MSFD is closely related to the existing Regional Sea Conventions, their historical role and their ability to integrate the EU Member States

7 The sea-basin strategies allow for the priorities and the tools of the policy to be adapted to the specific geographic, economic and political contexts of each large maritime region. Co-operation with and among Member States and regions sharing a sea basin is a crucial element of success and, whenever necessary, this should be accompanied by proper dialogue with third countries sharing a sea basin with the EU (Commission of the European Communities 2009).

at a regional sea level. Hence the MSFD attempts to bring together a physical regional boundary of the ecosystem with the several political administrative boundaries of Member States and non-EU states.

2. **Regionalization as the empowerment of non-governmental actors on the level of the North Sea**. Another form of regionalization is to create institutions on the regional level for stakeholder involvement. An example is the 2002 reform of the CFP and the establishment of Regional Advisory Councils (cf. Dreyer and Sellke 2015 in this volume). The seven RACs are stakeholder forums consisting predominantly of representatives of the fisheries sector (see Hegland et al. 2012, Council of the European Communities, 2004). The RACs are primarily meant to function as advisory bodies to the EC but the Member States can also draw on the RACs for resolutions.

3. **Regionalization as an organizing principle of maritime activities.** Examples of this form of regionalization of marine governance of the North Sea are the establishment of networks of Marine Protected Areas and the development of an offshore Power Grid. This kind of regionalization is about the regionalization of maritime activities and takes the regional sea as a starting point of planning and policy-making.

Patterns of Regionalization of Marine Governance of the North Sea

In this section, we illustrate each of the three forms of regionalization with examples in the North Sea area.

Regionalization as Cooperation

Dogger Bank

The Dogger Bank is a shallow sea area in the southern central North Sea. It is about 300 km in extension and ranges in depth between 18 m to more than 40 m. 'The bank is a huge moraine that was deposited at the southern limit of the last glaciation. For centuries, it has been a well-known fishing ground. The large amounts of food available to the fish result in the catch of sizable quantities of plaice, cod, haddock, turbot, dabs, and herring. (…) The lines demarcating the international rights of Great Britain, the Netherlands, Germany, Denmark, and Norway to the North Sea intersect just north of the Dogger Bank; all but Norway have rights to the bank itself'.[8]

8 http://www.britannica.com/EBchecked/topic/167941/Dogger-Bank, visited March 14, 2012

The Dogger Bank is a highly contested marine sub-region in the North Sea. This area meets the Natura 2000 (Habitat and Birds Directive) conditions to be assigned as a Marine Protected Area. However, the Dogger Bank is faced with different claims, ranging from Site of Community Importance (Germany), possible Special Areas of Conservation (Netherlands, UK), developing offshore windmill parks (UK, The boundary of Tranche A (Dogger Bank project One) of the Forewind Dogger Bank Wind farm Zone) and fisheries (the Netherlands, Denmark and Germany). To resolve these conflicting claims one marine spatial plan for the whole Dogger Bank should be developed. However, the problem is that there is neither a planning organization nor maritime planning instruments at the level of the regional sea. Integrated planning for the Dogger Bank depends on the initiatives of the four countries involved, but also on OSPAR and, for example, the North Sea RAC. In other words, there is a tension between EU MSP initiatives and the interests of MS. To overcome this tension, regionalization as cooperation is needed. This could be organized in different ways. One possibility is to set up a new institution to develop and implement a trans-boundary marine spatial plan for the Dogger Bank. However, this could conflict with the different national management frameworks and the initiatives of existing institutions (OSPAR, North Sea RAC, etc.). Another possibility is to develop together with governments and stakeholders a participatory, trans-boundary plan. An example is the MASPNOSE project (Preparatory Action on Maritime Spatial Planning in the North Sea), which aims to facilitate cross-border cooperation between European countries on ecosystem-based MSP. It explores opportunities and constrains for cooperation among the North Sea states by creating a common agenda. For the Dogger Bank, 4 activities are formulated to improve ongoing and planned trans-boundary spatial planning processes: (1) a workshop with stakeholders organized by the North Sea RAC (NSRAC) to develop management proposals about fisheries management in relation to nature conservation; (2) a comparison of national plans; (3) the investigation of two trans-boundary issues: sand eel fisheries and renewable energy production (wind energy); and (4) an analysis of the different national and trans-boundary spatial management processes. The first activity not only supports regionalization as cooperation between governmental actors, but can also be considered as regionalization as empowerment. We will discuss the empowerment of non-governmental actors through RACs in more detail below.

The Implementation of the Marine Strategy Framework Directive

The implementation of the MSFD occurs both nationally and regionally. At the regional level, the OSPAR Convention adopted a North-East Atlantic Environmental Strategy in 2010, which emphasizes that the Directive's objective to achieve or maintain Good Environmental Status in the marine environment by 2020 concurs with and supports the aims of OSPAR, and that OSPAR will facilitate the coordinated and coherent implementation of this Directive (OSPAR 2010a).

Besides its commitment to accommodate the MSFD, the institutional structure of OSPAR has changed considerably and is reflected in its focus, scope, structure and strategies (OSPAR 2010b). First, an Intersessional Correspondence Group on implementation of the MSFD was set up to discuss progress and coordination of the implementation of the MSFD. While the Intersessional Correspondence Group on MSFD provides strategic direction, several of the existing working groups cover technical work on the various descriptors of Good Environmental Status. Second, the Quality Status Report of 2010 provides a detailed evidence base for the initial assessment (Van Leeuwen et al. 2012). OSPAR also provides input to the initial assessment by coordinating a socio-economic analysis for the OSPAR area.

The prospects for regional coordination in the implementation of the MSFD do not only depend on the strategy and institutional structure. The willingness and preferences of the North Sea States also influence the level of coordination and the strength of the regional level in marine governance. Some differences between Member States will impede decision making at the regional level, for example, states set different targets related to the most urgent problems at the national level, they have different financial budgets available for marine conservation and they use different monitoring programs.[9] In general, 'the aims of the OSPAR Convention are in line with the MSFD and the institutional structure of OSPAR allows coordination in implementing the MSFD. On the other hand, there is some institutional ambiguity[10] about the desired level of regional coordination for national tasks in implementing MSFD (i.e. status assessment and defining GES)' (Van Leeuwen et al. 2012: 639-640).

Regionalization as Empowerment

RACs (CFP)

Seven Regional Advisory Councils were set up.[11] The RACs are stakeholder forums: representatives of the fisheries sector[12] make up two thirds and representatives of

9 Ministry of Infrastructure and Environment (Netherlands). Interview. 2011; Federal Public Service Health; Food chain safety and Environment (Belgium). Interview. 2010.

10 Institutional ambiguity describes the mismatch between the institutional setting and the specific territorial locations (in this case the North Sea) in which they are operating (Van Leeuwen et al. 2012, Van Tatenhove 2013).

11 The RACs are predominately organized along specific sea areas (corresponding to large marine ecosystems/regional seas), though two are based on a specific type of fishery (Council of the European Communities, 2004): The North Sea RAC, the Baltic RAC, the Mediterranean Sea RAC, the North-western waters RAC, the South-Western Waters RAC, the Pelagic Stocks RAC and the Long Distance RAC.

12 The fisheries sector is defined as 'the catching sub-sector, including ship owners, small-scale fishermen, employed fishermen, producer organizations and women's networks' (Council, 2004, art.1).

other interest groups[13] the remaining third. The RACs were proposed by the EC as purely advisory bodies, providing recommendations to the DG for Maritime Affairs and Fisheries or to national authorities of involved member states. The Commission or Member States are not obliged to follow the advice recommended by the RAC. The North Sea RAC is an example of the empowerment of representatives of fisheries and interest groups at the regional level of the North Sea. 'The principal objective of the NSRAC is to prepare and provide advice on the management of the fisheries of the North Sea on behalf of stakeholders in order to promote the objectives of the Common Fisheries Policy. This will be done within the general aim of attaining the sustainable management of fisheries, incorporating an ecosystem-based approach and based on the precautionary principle' (http://www.nsrac.org/).

Although the RAC links the fisheries constituency (fishermen, processors, traders, environmental NGOs) to fisheries management at the regional level, it neglects a particular aspect of the ecosystem approach, i.e. integration with other sectors, activities and policies (Van Hoof et al., 2012). Ounanian and Hegland (2012) showed that 53% of the NSRAC participants find that their organization's participation in the RAC resulted in 'very little' impact on the course of fisheries management in the EU. In another study, Hegland et al. (2012) asked members of RACs what kind of regionalization they preferred. The participants could approve or disapprove of five regionalization models (nationalism, Regional Fisheries Management Organizations; Regional Fisheries Co-management Organizations; Regional Marine Management Organizations and Cooperative Member State Councils). The results of the survey showed that the NSRAC disapproves of the present structure and is most in favour of the Regional Fisheries Co-Management Organization. Under this model of regionalization, the Member States would be given wide authority for fisheries conservation on the condition that the Member States with fishing interests in a regional sea area establish a regional fisheries co-management organization to deal with fisheries management issues specific to that area. These studies show the desire to develop new institutional arrangements at the regional sea level to empower non-governmental actors. The EU should provide a general framework for these institutional arrangements, in which stakeholders, scientists, and Member States work together to determine the best strategies for the North Sea.

Regionalization as Organizing Principle

A Network of MPAs in the North Sea

Marine Protected Areas (MPAs) are important place-bound management tools for marine environmental protection and nature conservation (cf. Jentoft and Chuenpagdee 2015 in this volume). The selection and designation of MPAs is the

---

13 'Amongst others, environmental organizations and groups, aquaculture producers, consumers and recreational or sport fishermen' (Council 2004, art. 1).

responsibility of states. Every country is responsible for the quality and size of MPAs in their Exclusive Economic Zone. With Natura 2000, the EU has formulated ecological criteria for the selection of MPAs. Recently, the governance of MPAs has been taken a step further; OSPAR and some environmental NGOs want to develop a network of MPAs for the North Sea. This is a form of regionalization as organizing principle.

Already at the fifth North Sea Ministerial Conference in Bergen (Norway, 2002,) the North Sea Ministers formulated the target of creating an MPA network within the North Sea by 2010 (Dotinga and Trouwborst 2009). It was agreed that the Natura 2000 network of Special Areas of Conservation and Special Protection Areas should serve as a legal framework. At the First Joint Ministerial Meeting of the Helsinki and OSPAR Commissions in Bremen (Germany) in 2003, Recommendation 2003/3 was adopted. This aims to establish an ecologically coherent network of well-managed MPAs in the North-East Atlantic by 2010. Central to the OSPAR definition of a network of MPAs is the concept of ecological coherence. Although there is no formally agreed definition of this concept, OSPAR and HELCOM have generally agreed that an ecologically coherent network of MPAs 'interacts with and supports the wider environment; maintains the processes, functions and structures of the intended protected features across their natural range; and functions synergistically as a whole, such that the individual protected sites benefit from each other to achieve the two objectives above' (OSPAR 2011: 25). By 31 December 2010, the OSPAR Network of MPAs compromises a total of 181 sites, including 175 MPAs situated within national waters of Contracting Parties and six MPAs in Areas beyond National Jurisdiction. OSPAR works on the basis of lists of species and habitats that partly link up to Natura 2000. Almost all of the MPAs reported to OSPAR by EU Member States largely overlap existing Natura 2000 sites (OSPAR 2011). Member States play a central role in the governance of MPAs in the North Sea. They are key players in OSPAR and have a large autonomous role in the designation of Nature 2000 areas (as the practical compliance of the Bird and Habitat Directives).

Offshore Power Grid

The point of departure for a European energy policy is to combat climate change, to limit the EU's external vulnerability to imported hydrocarbons, and to promote growth and jobs, thereby providing secure and affordable energy to consumers (EC, COM(2007)1final). To make this a reality, the EU has committed to the '20-20-20' initiative: reducing greenhouse gas emissions by 20%, increasing the share of renewables in the energy consumption to 20% and improving energy efficiency by 20% in 2020. In doing so, the EU 'needs to tap the full potential of its oceans and seas for energy generation, rapidly evolve its transport system and make real progress in terms of the interconnection of the European energy market' (EC 2008a: 3). One of the six priority infrastructural actions in the Second Strategic Energy Review is the development of a Blueprint for a North Sea offshore grid to interconnect national electricity grids in North-West Europe together and plug-in the numerous planned offshore wind projects. It should become, together with the Mediterranean Ring and the Baltic Interconnection project, one of the building blocks of a future European super-grid, to be developed by the Member States and regional actors involved and facilitated where necessary by action at Community level (EC 2008a: 5-6).

The development of renewable energy is seen by the EC as EU's greatest potential source of indigenous energy. In its Communication about Offshore Wind Energy, the EC stresses the synergy between Europe's energy policy and IMP. According to the EC both aim for an integration of economic development and environmental protection (EC 2008b: 3). One of the key areas for special attention, as formulated by the EC,[14] is the lack of integrated strategic planning and cross-border coordination: '(…) the absence of points of access to the electricity grids at sea leads to uncertainties about the ability to, or costs of, connecting to the grid and creates additional risks for offshore projects' (EC 2008b: 5). '(…) (P)otential synergies between offshore projects and cross-border inter-connectors are currently not being exploited. One reason for this is the additional complexities that cross-border cooperation entails because of the need to deal with different planning and regulatory regimes. (…) The need for better cross-border cooperation is not only limited to network planning and development, but also related to system operation and management. Increasing offshore wind penetration may have consequences which need to be reflected in power congestion management strategies and generation/demand balancing plans, and in improved mechanisms for cross-border trade and balancing power markets'(EC 2008b: 5). In this case, it is suggested that regionalization as organizing principle should be supported by regionalization as cooperation between governmental actors. In order to organize an offshore power grid at the regional level, cross-border coordination is needed on several fronts.

For the EC one of the ways forward is to adopt a 'more strategic, coordinated approach to offshore developments'. In this approach, a range of planning instruments and forums at EU or regional level may play a role, such as the development of National Action Plans, regional cooperation within the new European Network of Transmission System Operators, the move to integrated maritime spatial planning and the development of best practices (NORSEWIND and WINDSPEED (www.windspeed.eu).

---

14 The other key areas are: the sector faces particular industrial and technological challenges; lack of knowledge and information sharing hampers a smooth application of EU environmental legislation. The developers of offshore projects face uncertainties because there is no experience in applying EU environmental legislation (Birds Directive, Habitats Directive and Environmental Impact Assessment) in respect of these projects. Offshore projects are frustrated by the delays in MS' designation of protected areas under the HD and BD in the marine environment and dealing with bottlenecks and power balancing in the onshore electricity grids.

Initiatives to develop an offshore wind power grid in the North Sea are the Intergovernmental North Seas Countries' Offshore Grid Initiative (NSCOGI) and the 3E report 'A North Sea Electricity [R]evolution' commissioned by Greenpeace. On 3 December 2010, the Ministers of NSCOGI[15] and the European Commissioner for Energy signed a Memorandum of Understanding. In this Memorandum of Understanding[16] the signatories declare that they 'will facilitate a strategic, coordinated development of the offshore and onshore grids to ensure more cost-effective and sustainable investment, and will identify and tackle barriers to grid development at both national, regional and EU level, in particular regulatory, legal, market, planning, authorisation and technical issues' (MoU 2010: 2).

Conclusions

Marine governance of the North Sea has become a complex multi-level system comprised of EU, regional and national dynamics. In this chapter, we started with the main environmental and spatial problems of the North Sea. Initiatives to overcome these problems are taken at different levels by different institutions, such as OSPAR, North Sea Ministerial Conferences and more recently the EU.

Characteristic for marine governance is a patchwork of policies and institutions and a specific form of Europeanization stressing the level of the North Sea to develop institutions and policies. This specific form of Europeanization is characterized by 3 forms of regionalization. The regional level is emphasized by various European initiatives, but regionalization plays a role in these initiatives in different ways. In some cases, the regional level is institutionalized through cooperation between governmental actors, in other cases by empowering non-governmental actors at the regional level and finally, the regional level can be important as an organizing principle. We illustrated these forms of regionalization with several examples of recent initiatives from the EU.

We believe that these different forms of regionalization are in the first instance intended to be complementary to each other. Cooperation is needed to make binding and non-binding agreements and to coordinate national policy plans. At the same time, non-governmental actors should participate in these processes. New and empowering institutions should be developed to realize this. Finally, in order to achieve policy objectives, activities and plans have to be organized at the

15 The NSCOGI consists of the Ministers from Germany, France, Belgium, the Netherlands, Luxemburg, Denmark, Sweden, Ireland and the UK (7 December 2009), and Norway (2 February 2010). The aim of the NSCOGI is to develop their offshore wind energy grids in an integrated and coordinated fashion in the North and Irish Seas. It also offers a framework for regional cooperation, to find common solutions to questions related to current and possible future grid infrastructure developments in the North Seas.

16 http://ec.europa.eu/energy/renewables/grid/doc/north_sea_countries_offshore_grid_initiative_mou.pdf (last visit, March, 19, 2012).

regional level as well (cf. Jentoft and Chuenpagdee 2015 in this volume). Whether conflicts between these forms or regionalization in the marine governance of the North Sea can be avoided remains to be seen.

The overall conclusion is that to realize marine governance of the North Sea different patterns of regionalization should be combined. In this regard, additional research is needed to understand how the different patterns of regionalization complement and support each other, and to what extent the regional level will become further institutionalized in marine governance of the North Sea.

References

Börzel, T.A. and Risse, T. 2012. When Europeanization meets diffusion: exploring new territory. *West European Politics*, 35(1), 192-207.

Christie, P. and White, A.T. 2006. *Best Practices in Governance and Enforcement of Marine Protected Areas: An Overview*. Rome: FAO.

European Council. 2004. Council Decision (EC) of 19 July 2004 establishing Regional Advisory Councils under the Common Fisheries Policy (2004/585/EC), in *Official Journal of the European Communities*, L 256 (3.8.2004), 17-22.

Cowles, M.G., Caporaso, J.A. and Risse, T. (eds) 2001. *Transforming Europe: Europeanization and Domestic Change*. Ithaca, NY: Cornell University Press.

De la Fayette, L. 1999. The OSPA Convention Comes into Force: Continuity and Progress. *The International Journal of Marine and Coastal Law*, 14(2), 247-297.

De Santo, E. 2015. The Marine Strategy Framework Directive as a Catalyst for Maritime Spatial Planning: internal dimensions and institutional tensions, in *Governing Europe's Marine Environment: Europeanization of Regional Seas or Regionalization of EU Policies?*, edited by M. Gilek and K. Kern. Farnham, UK: Ashgate Publishing.

Dotinga, H. and Trouwborst, A. 2009. The Netherlands and the designation of marine protected areas in the North Sea: Implementing international and European law. *Utrecht Law Review*, 5, 21-43.

Douvere, F. and Ehler, C. 2009. New perspectives on sea use management: initial findings from European experience with marine spatial planning. *Journal for Environmental Management*, 90, 77-88.

Dreyer, M. and Sellke, P. 2015. The Regional Advisory Councils in European fisheries: an appropriate approach to stakeholder involvement in an EU integrated marine governance?, in *Governing Europe's Marine Environment: Europeanization of Regional Seas or Regionalization of EU Policies?*, edited by M. Gilek and K. Kern. Farnham, UK: Ashgate Publishing.

Halpern, B.S., Walbridge, S., Selkoe, K.A., Kappel, C.V., Micheli, F., D'Agrosa, C., Bruno, J.F., et al. 2008. A Global Map of Human Impact on Marine Ecosystems. *Science*, 319, 948-952.

Heglan, T.J., Ounanian, K. and Raakjaer, J. 2012. What does 'regionalization' mean? An exploratory mapping of opinions on reform of the Common Fisheries Policy. *Maritime Studies* (*Mast*), 11, 8.

Jentoft, S. and Chuenpagdee, R. 2015. The 'New' Marine Governance: assessing governability, in *Governing Europe's Marine Environment: Europeanization of Regional Seas or Regionalization of EU Policies?*, edited by M. Gilek and K. Kern. Farnham, UK: Ashgate Publishing.

Knights, A.M., Koss, R.S., Papadopoulou, N., Cooper, L.H. and Robinson, L.A. 2011. Sustainable Use of European Seas and the role of the Marine Strategy Framework Directive. Deliverable 1, EC FP7 Project (244273) 'Options for Delivering Ecosystem-based Marine Management'.

Long, R. 2011. The Marine Strategy Framework Directive: A new European approach to the regulation of the marine environment, marine natural resources and marine ecological services. *Journal of Energy & Natural Resources Law*, 29(1), 1-44.

Olson, J.P. 2002. The many faces of Europeanization. *Journal of Common Market Studies*, 40(5), 921-952.

OSPAR Commission. 2010a. The North-East Atlantic Environment Strategy; Strategy of the OSPAR Commission for the Protection of the Marine Environment of the North-East Atlantic 2010-2020 (OSPAR Agreement 2010-3). London: OSPAR Commission; 2010.

OSPAR Commission. 2010b. OSPAR Regional Implementation Framework for the EU Marine Strategy Framework Directive; MSFD Road Map. London: OSPAR Commission; 2010.

OSPAR Commission. 2011. 2010 Status Report on the OSPAR Network of Marine Protected Areas, Biodiversity Series. Available at: www.ospar.org [accessed: 13 July 2014].

Ounanian, K. and Hegland, T.J. 2012. The Regional Advisory Councils' current capacities and unforeseen benefits. *Maritime Studies* (*Mast*), 11, 10.

Risse, T., Green Cowles, M. and Caporaso, J. 2001. Europeanization and Domestic Change: Introduction, in *Transforming Europe: Europeanization and Domestic Change*, edited by M. Green Cowles, J. Caporaso and T. Risse. Ithaca, NY: Cornell University Press, 1-20.

Skjærseth, J.B. 2006. Protecting the North-East Atlantic: enhancing synergies by institutional interplay. *Marine Policy*, 30, 157-166.

St. Martin, K. and Hall-Arber, M. 2008. The missing layer: Geo-technologies, communities. And implication for marine spatial planning. *Marine Policy*, 32(5), 779-786.

Symes, D. 2012. Regionalising the Common Fisheries Policy. Context, Content and Controversy, *Maritime Studies* (*Mast*), 11, 6.

Urrutia, B. 2006. The EU regulatory action in the shipping sector: a historical perspective. *Maritime Economics and Logistics*, 8(2), 202-221.

Van Leeuwen, J. and Kern, K. 2013. The external dimension of European Union marine governance: institutional interplay between the European Union and the International Maritime Organization. *Global Environmental Politics*, 13(1), 69-87.

Van Hoof, L., Van Leeuwen, J. and Van Tatenhove, J. 2012. All at sea; regionalization and integration of marine policy in Europe. *Maritime Studies* (*Mast*) 11, 9.

Van Leeuwen, J. 2010. *Who Greens the Waves? Changing Authority in the Environmental Governance of Shipping and Offshore Oil and Gas Production.* Wageningen: Wageningen Academic Publishers.

Van Leeuwen, J. and Van Tatenhove, J. 2010. The triangle of marine governance in the environmental governance of Dutch offshore platforms. *Marine Policy*, 34(3), 590-597.

Van Leeuwen, J., Van Hoof, L. and Van Tatenhove, J. 2012. Institutional ambiguity in implementing the European Union Marine Strategy Framework Directive. *Marine Policy*, 36(3), 636-643.

Van Tatenhove, J. 2013. How to turn the tide: developing legitimate marine governance arrangements at the level of the regional seas. *Ocean & Coastal Management*, 71, 296-304.

Chapter 11

Marine Governance in the Mediterranean Sea

Juan Luís Suárez de Vivero and Juan Carlos Rodríguez Mateos

Introduction

Governance in the Mediterranean Sea is marked by two major processes: the first, has been ongoing since the 1970s and consists of the regionalization of intervention/protection actions in the marine environment; the second, which is more recent, is the Europeanization of some marine policies in the Mediterranean (such as fisheries, the environment, or coastal management).

As we shall try to demonstrate in this chapter, at the time when the Mediterranean Action Plan (MAP) was launched, the focus was more multilateral and cooperative, whereas today it is more driven and conditioned by the EU. Both these key elements of regional marine governance, the Action Plan (Convention and protocols) and the European Union (EU policies), will be analysed in the following.

Of the European regional seas, the Mediterranean possesses a series of features that make it unique: it is both the largest[1] and the sea with the greatest number of countries along its banks. The Mediterranean basin is the point where three continents converge and is traversed by one of the world's principal trade flows, connecting the Straits of Gibraltar with the Suez Canal, the Panama Canal and the Asian straits. Its two shores (northern and southern) are separated by one of the most marked economic divides on the planet and at their eastern end are home to one of the most intricate and dangerous geopolitical conflicts in modern international relations. From a jurisdictional point-of-view, its waters are both rare and exceptional: (30%) still come under the high seas regime. Marine governance is conditioned by this set of geographical, legal, economic and political circumstances which, individually or in combination, both hamper and encourage coordinated initiatives.

One aspect of the Mediterranean that must be highlighted is that it is the region that pioneered the adoption of the UNEP Regional Seas Programme

1 Its surface area is 2,509,000 million square kilometres; the North Sea, 570,000 million square kilometres; the Black Sea, 466,200 million square kilometres; the Baltic Sea, 422,300 million square kilometres (Merriam-Webster's Geographical Dictionary 2001).

(the Mediterranean Action Plan [MAP, 1975]).[2] Over this period of time, the last third of the 20th century, a new international maritime paradigm has been shaped with the appearance of new strategic vectors defining the way that states determine their new maritime policies and redefine their strategies: energy security has displaced food security (fishing), bioprospecting has diverted interest away from mineral to biogenetic resources and in the political domain it has culminated in the most far-reaching overhaul of the coding of the Law of the Sea (UNCLOS) with the beginning of an era of new maritime powers (the emerging economies). In this new scenario, the Mediterranean can count on the drive of European Union initiatives (Integrated Maritime Policy and the Marine Strategy Directive). Although these cover a significant part of the Mediterranean (section 3), the complexity of the region and uncertainties about one or the other of these initiatives[3] do not presage developments that effectively contend with the problems of environmental decline being experienced in some of its waters (UNEP/MAP 2009).

However, in the Mediterranean Sea there is a wide and diverse range of maritime governance structures that involve the large majority of the coastal states. These instruments combine with actions taken by states and the regional political bodies. The former are the fundamental actors and therefore have maximum responsibility. Whilst the maritime legal dimension can be considered to be sufficiently developed, the political and economic dimensions are the weak points of the governance system. This translates into insufficient regional political integration (i.e. only the EU has any significant degree of cohesion and executive capacity). There are marked differences in economic development making this a differentiating feature in a region with a North-South imbalance. This strongly limits the effective management of marine affairs, with only a small number of coastal states having financial and technical capacity.

To summarize, the profile of marine governance in the Mediterranean Sea is characterized by the existence of an adequate legal-institutional structure that exists alongside weak political integration and marked economic differences. Although the regional instruments have developed in recent decades, the state, as the key actor in implementing the norms, lacks (with the exception of some of the

2 The Mediterranean Action Plan was signed in 1975; the Barcelona Convention was signed in 1976, but did not enter into force until 1978. The UNEP Regional Seas Programme was launched in 1972. In 1993 the Black Sea Environment Programme and the Strategic Action Plan were set up within UNEP. Out of the thirteen Regional Seas programmes, which include 143 countries, these are the only two initiatives in Europe. A programme has also been set up in the Baltic Sea (signed in 1974; in force in 1980), not under the auspices of UNEP, but as an independent programme. In 1992 the Baltic Sea Joint Comprehensive Environmental Action Programme was created and coordinated by HELCOM (http://www.unep.org/regionalseas/about/default.asp).

3 The Integrated Maritime Policy especially, and some of its developments, such as maritime spatial planning, which may not be accompanied by a binding regulation (directive) as had been envisaged.

EU members) financial and technical capacity, with there being no single authority nor any supranational executive power in the region.

These issues are developed in four sections in this chapter. Firstly, the geographical, jurisdictional and political factors that shape the region are set out (section 2), followed by a description of the main marine uses and environmental conflicts. All these factors – the geopolitical framework, uses and conflicts – have a bearing on and explain the nature of marine governance that has been constructed over recent decades (section 3). The chapter concludes with a brief section summarizing the key points (section 4).

Geographical, Political and Jurisdictional Factors

This section describes the basic features that shape marine governance of the Mediterranean basin. The aim is to set out the geographical, political and jurisdictional components that have a bearing on marine governance on the state, regional and sub-regional scales. These three dimensions (geographical, political and jurisdictional) can be considered structuring elements, although geographical features define and determine to a greater extent than political and jurisdictional circumstances, which are subject to change and alterations.

Geographical Features

Covering an area of 2.5 million km^2, the Mediterranean stretches 3,860 km from east to west and is 1,600 km across at its widest point, although states that face each other (including their islands) are never actually more than 720 km (400 nautical miles) apart. The Mediterranean is not generally very deep (1,500 m average), with a maximum depth of 5,150 m along the southern coast of Greece.

The morphology of the northern coast of the Mediterranean is made up of numerous bays, peninsulas and islands. In the basin as a whole there are more than 5,000 islands and islets; 4,000 of these islands are less than 10 km^2 in size and 162 of them are larger (IUCN 2009). Corsica, Sardinia and the Balearics are the most well-known in the west, and Cyprus, Crete and Rhodes in the east. Sicily and Malta are located in the centre. The Aegean Sea contains more than 700 islands and islets, forming a large archipelago.

The Mediterranean coast, including the coasts of the only archipelagic state (Malta), along with the coasts of the islands that form part of continental states, measures approximately 45,000 km. This coast is, however, unevenly distributed among the coastal states, with four (Greece, Italy, Croatia and Turkey) accounting for approximately 75% of the whole coast. Croatia is particularly notable due to the large number of islands that make up the country. In contrast, ten states, including Bosnia-Herzegovina, Monaco and Lebanon, have very small coastlines (González Giménez 2007).

The Mediterranean forms a concentration basin in which the amount of water evaporating is greater than the inflowing rain and river water. The consequent concentration of salts increases the density of the water, causing it to sink to the depths and flow into the Atlantic Ocean through the Straits of Gibraltar. This outflow of deep water from the Mediterranean is compensated for by the entry of surface water from the Atlantic. This continual exchange prevents a saturation of the ecosystem (IEO 2008). In addition, the water in the Mediterranean is completely renewed every eighty years.

Due to its hydrological and climatic features, the biological productivity of the Mediterranean as a whole, measured in terms of its primary production, is less than that of most oceanic areas. There are some exceptions, such as the Adriatic, the Gulf of Lion and the southern Aegean which are of greater primary productivity due to the magnitude of average concentrations of nutrients (AEM 2000).

Maritime Jurisdictions

The Mediterranean had traditionally been regarded as an exception from a jurisdictional perspective because coastal states have desisted from declaring new jurisdictions. In recent years, and particularly since 2002, the process of nationalizing maritime space has quickened with the result that the high seas has been reduced to approximately 29% of the basin (Figure 11.1). Although the majority of states might eventually extend their jurisdictions beyond the territorial sea,[4] for various reasons several coastal states in the Mediterranean have abstained from declaring exclusive economic zones (or fisheries protection zones or ecological protection zones), which explains the existence of High Seas status. Only lately, from the 1990s onwards, have jurisdictions started to be declared that are reducing the size of the High Seas.[5] This is a significant circumstance from the perspective of marine management as, for the moment, there is free access to almost a third of the waters in the basin for all states, including non-coastal states. Nevertheless, in accordance with the Convention regulations, the continental shelf does not need to be expressly claimed by coastal states,[6] whereby, due to the above-stated reasons regarding the width of the basin, all the seabed and subsoil come under the jurisdiction of one coastal state or another. This means that while there is free access to the waters of the High Seas, the seabed and the underlying subsoil are part of the national jurisdiction of one state or another (cf. Bohman and Langlet 2015 in this volume).

---

4 To date (2012) 20 States or territories have declared the different widths for the territorial sea (3, 6 and 12 NM).

5 The High Seas are defined by exclusion: '... all parts of the sea that are not included in the exclusive economic zone, in the territorial sea or in the internal waters of a State, or in the archipelagic waters of an archipelagic State' (art. 86 UNCLOS).

6 'The rights of the coastal State over the continental shelf do not depend on occupation, effective or notional, or on any express proclamation' (art. 77.3 UNCLOS).

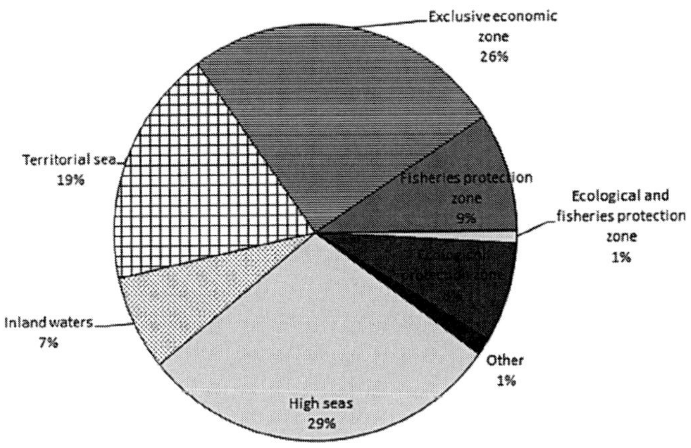

Figure 11.1 Distribution of maritime jurisdictions

A second circumstance that contributes to the exceptional nature of the Mediterranean could be termed its jurisdictional asymmetry or the contiguity of water masses (Figure 11.2) under different jurisdictional regimes: exclusive economic zone, fisheries protection zone and ecological protection zone. In a semi-enclosed basin such as the Mediterranean Sea, where the mechanism envisaged in the Convention (Art. 122 UNCLOS) is cross-border cooperation, the wide range of jurisdictional regimes does not make it easy for joint actions to be undertaken, which is, nevertheless, one of the Principles in the EU's Integrated Maritime Policy and in Directive 2008/56/CE. It is precisely the geographical constrictions that result in a geopolitical scenario characterized by a high concentration of border contacts[7] and an abundance of borders. And these in turn are a source of territorial conflicts that restrict the required inter-coastal state cooperation. The weight of the European Union in Mediterranean Sea waters can be seen in terms of the

7 Between them, the coastal states of the Mediterranean basin generate 29 boundary contacts which, in turn, give rise to different kinds of delimitations between the maritime jurisdictions (basically territorial sea and contiguous zone, exclusive economic zone and continental shelf). To date, 16 delimitation agreements have resulted from these interactions between adjacent and facing states (including borders that emerged following the breakup of the former Yugoslavia), nine of which are between opposite, and four between adjacent States. The longest-standing agreement dates back to 1960 (Cyprus-United Kingdom [Akrotiri and Dhekelia]) and the most recent was signed in 2011 (Cyprus-Israel), thus forming the first EEZ delimitation agreement. Over the 40-year period between the two, 50% of the 16 boundary agreements were signed in the 1970s and 80s, nine in relation to the continental shelf. (Suárez de Vivero 2010).

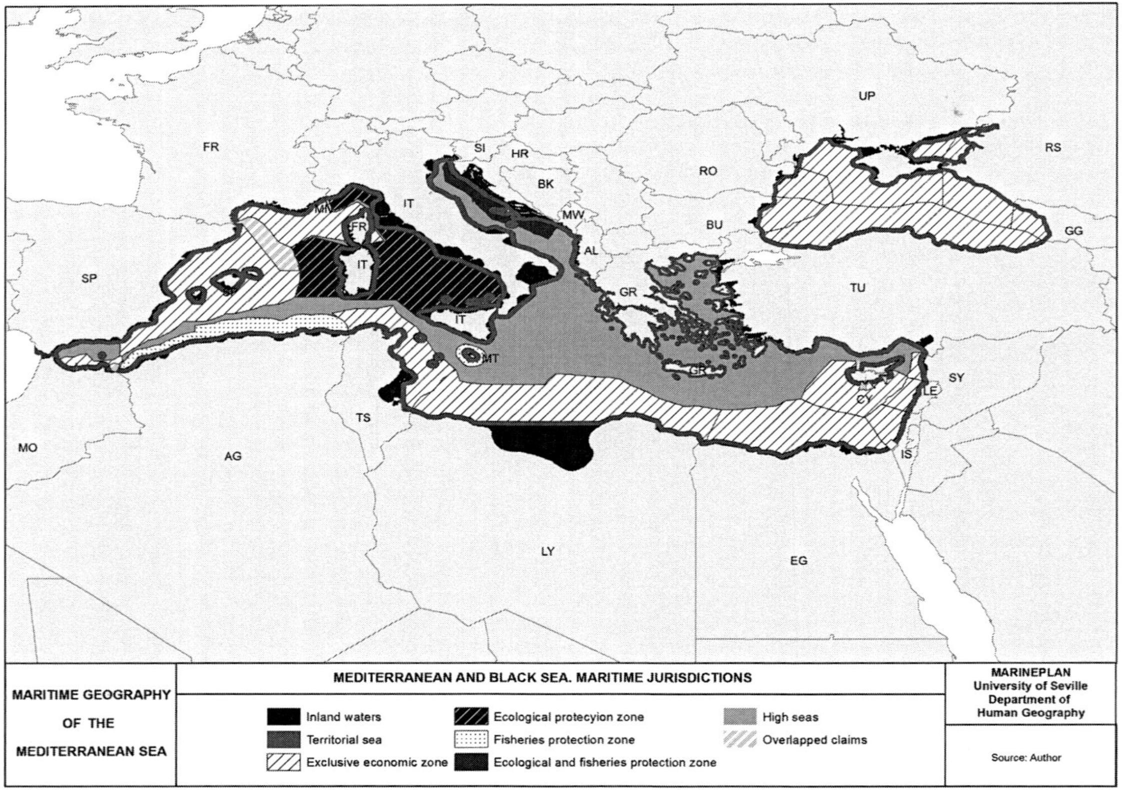

Figure 11.2 Maritime jurisdictions in the Mediterranean

surface area of Member States' jurisdictional waters (Spain, France, Italy, Slovenia, Malta, Greece, Cyprus and Croatia). In the Mediterranean, the area of EU Member States' jurisdictional waters totals 945,564 km^2 and represents approximately 53% of all national jurisdictions over these waters.[8] In quantitative terms, the jurisdictional waters of candidate countries like Turkey (38,929 km^2) can be added to this figure.

Political Framework

There are a number of different levels of political organization existing within the above geographical context. The political framework of the Mediterranean Sea is the result of the interaction of different levels of political activity and organization: supranational, transnational, national and sub national. This structure is important insofar as each of these levels has tasks and responsibilities for managing and governing the maritime coastal space. The states play a central role in the political configuration of these basins. Of the 21 Mediterranean coastal states, 11 are in Europe, five are in Africa and five in Asia (Figure 11.3). It is interesting to note that apart from the role of the state, on the supranational level Mediterranean countries are part of a regional area (South Europe/North Africa/Asia Minor; Mediterranean Arc) where supranational and transnational organizations also play a major role (EU, Arab Maghreb Union, Arab League, Union for the Mediterranean, etc.) and where instruments and strategies that could be referred to as being of a macro-regional type (e.g. EU strategies for certain regional areas, such as the Adriatic). Also, to use the terminology of the EASES project,[9] there is also a meso-regional level (coastal regions), a sub national level (NUTS 2, regions, federations) and a local level (NUTS 3, Local Administrative Units 1, Local Administrative Units 2, municipalities).

In addition to the states, various supranational bodies have become increasingly important players with management roles in the maritime space. In the Mediterranean, there are obvious differences between the north and south coasts (Figure 11.3); the former comprises mostly EU Member States, while political cohesion on the south coast, with its organizations like the Arab League and the Arab Maghreb Union, is weak (Table 11.1).

On the supranational level, the recent (2008) creation in Paris of the Union for the Mediterranean (the official name of which is the Barcelona Process: Union for the Mediterranean – BP: UFM) must be noted. This consists of 43 countries, 28 of them from the EU plus countries along the south coast of the

8 Should Italy bring its ecological protection area law (2006) into effect, EU member States would then exercise jurisdiction rights over 40% of Mediterranean waters. For the jurisdictional aspects of the Mediterranean, see Suárez de Vivero (2010).

9 Resilience in the European Atlantic social–ecological system (EASES). Coastal & Marine Resources Centre; ERI; University College Cork.

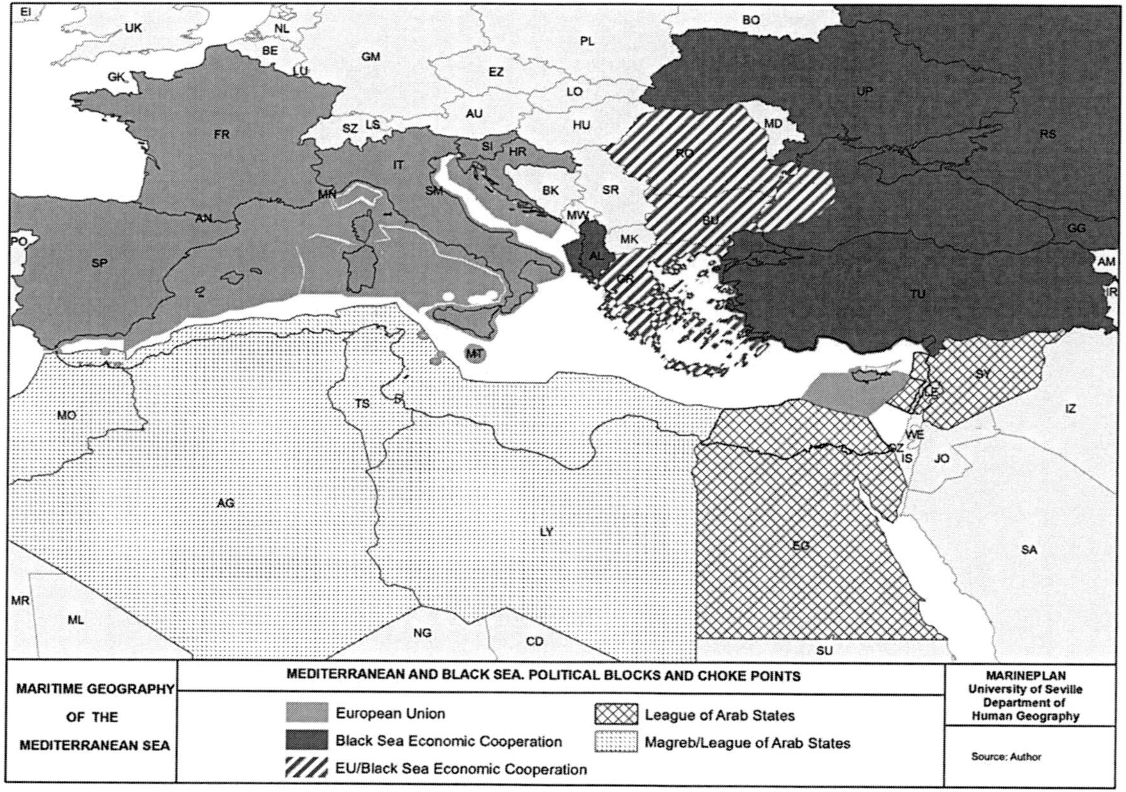

Figure 11.3 Political blocks

Table 11.1 Supranational political organizations in the Mediterranean Sea

Supranational organizations	Purpose	Nº. of countries	Location
EU	Political-economic	8	Europe
EEA*	Economic	9 (4 associated)	Europe/Asia/Africa
Union for the Mediterranean**	Political-social-economic	43	Europe/Asia/Africa
Arab League	Political	7	Africa/Asia
Arab Maghreb Union	Economic	4	Africa

* EEA: European Economic Area.

** Union for the Mediterranean: former EUROMED (Euro-Mediterranean Partnership, was re-launched in 2008 as Union for the Mediterranean).

Source: Author.

Mediterranean (with the exception of Libya) and some of the Balkan states. This body has improved political, economic and social relations between the EU and the rest of the Mediterranean countries (Blue Book 2009). The expansion and consolidation of the European Union has encouraged the creation of a web of intermediary-level political structures in the northern arc of the Mediterranean, for example the Intermediterranean Commission. The interaction and dialogue between institutions like the Intermediterranean Commission and other levels of government generates a more organized governance system. This contrasts with the south coast of the Mediterranean (North Africa), which is less structured at this intermediary political level (Table 11.2). This increases the gap between the two coasts in terms of their capacity to manage the marine environment.

The European Union has promoted cooperation programmes and policies aimed at encouraging the region's development and cohesion, among which the Neighbourhood Policy (COM(2004) 373 final) stands out. Apart from this initiative, there is no other kind of intermediary-level political entity in the region, and this results in a lack of cohesion between the coastal states, diminishing their capacity to jointly manage the maritime spaces adjoining their waters. The sub-national and local political levels are represented in the Mediterranean Sea by the coastal regions, provinces and local authorities. These bodies, by virtue of their number (there are 45 coastal regions in Europe alone) and their tasks in relation to maritime coastal space management and administration, are ensuring a growing role for the sub-state level in the

Table 11.2 Other supranational political entities in the Mediterranean

Transnational organizations	Purpose	N° of countries	Location
Intermediterranean Commission (CPMR)	Regional political	4	Europe
Islands Commission (CPMR)	Regional political	6	–

Source: Author.

political structure of the basin[10] and are consolidating the idea of multi-level governance in the region.

Marine Uses and Environmental Conflicts

The purpose of this section is to present the main forms of use and activity in the Mediterranean basin including some brief remarks alluding to the historical weight of this region, then to highlight the environmental impacts generated by the activities of both maritime and terrestrial origin.

Since antiquity, the banks of the Mediterranean have been densely populated[11] and put to intense use in maritime terms: commercial navigation, fishing, military-naval activity, etc. Today, other more innovative activities of major economic importance coexist alongside these more traditional ones, including energy-production and research into biogenetic resources. Another interesting dimension of the Mediterranean marine area in the scientific-technological sphere must also be added to these emerging marine uses, which is heritage, both natural (Mediterranean marine ecosystems) and historic-cultural (maritime cultural heritage). The last of these refers to what could be called the 'postmodern oceanic phase', in which a representation of the maritime space is construed with greater links to (cultural and environmental) heritage and maintaining quality of life within some sustainable parameters (Vallega 2001a, 2001b).

10 Taking into consideration the importance of these levels of government, the Euro-Mediterranean Assembly of Local and Regional Authorities (ARLEM) was created in 2010. This is a Union for the Mediterranean institution with the objective of strengthening the territorial dimension of Euro-Mediterranean relations.

11 The population of the coastal states, which stood at around 246 million inhabitants in 1960, has now reached about 450 million. The Blue Plan estimates that this figure could rise to 520-570 million in 2030. Population density is greater in the coastal regions and more so around major cities, some of which have a population of over a million (Barcelona, Marseilles, Naples, Algiers, Alexandria, etc.).

In general terms, the Mediterranean region's economy possesses a major maritime component and this is demonstrated, among other aspects, by the establishment of large towns and cities along its shores as part of growing tourist activity; the intense maritime traffic that often relies on large-scale port infrastructure system; and the appearance some years ago of numerous North-South connections that use the sea as their priority route: gas-pipelines, short sea shipping, motorways of the sea, the Straits of Gibraltar fixed link project, and so on.

Of all these uses of the coastal-marine area, perhaps the one which has the greatest economic and environmental impact is sea transport. Before the current economic crisis, there was a 50% increase in Mediterranean Sea transport between 1997 and 2006. This increase in maritime traffic through the basin was due for the most part to the transport of energy resources and containers (whose flows generally originate and terminate in ports on the northern shore). This traffic has undoubted economic and technical consequences (increased vessel size, need for ports to be expanded, etc.), but above all they are accompanied by major environmental harm to coastal-marine ecosystems (UNEP-MAP 2009). The magnitude of the impacts of Mediterranean Sea transport is directly proportional to the importance of the triple role that the basin plays, as it takes global traffic (it is one of the main E-W routes in the world), connects three continents (Europe, Asia, Africa) and is an area of growing intraregional exchange (especially between EU-Med countries and countries on the southern shore) (Reynaud 2009).

Fishing is another age-old Mediterranean activity, and one which has seen a decrease in the contribution it makes to both the economy and to food supply, given that the level of fish catches has gradually fallen due to the exhaustion of the fishing grounds and the impact that other marine uses have had on fishery resources. According to FAO (2010) statistics, in 2008 around 1.5 million tonnes of different species of fish, crustaceans and molluscs were caught in the Mediterranean-Black Sea area,[12] which represents only 1.66% of the world total. Also, according to GFCM-FAO data, aquaculture in the Mediterranean and the Black Sea only accounted for a little over 400,000 tonnes in 2009. This is twice the figure for the mid-1990s, but only 1.14% of the world total.

An extremely interesting contribution to the economy of coastal countries is undoubtedly made by tourism. According to the Blue Plan, the number of tourists in Mediterranean coastal regions stood at almost 176 million in 2000 and could reach 312 million in 2025 (UNEP-MAP-Blue Plan 2005). One of the most significant aspects of this activity is the impact that tourists have on the coastal segment, as in some sectors (particular European coasts and most

12 If we exclude the Black, Azov and Marmara Seas, the figure is around one million tonnes of catches. General Fisheries Commission for the Mediterranean (GFCM) information can be consulted at: http://www.gfcm.org/fishery/statistics/GFCM-capture-production/query/en.

of the islands) population densities during high tourist influx periods can be many times more than during other months of the year. Also, tourist activities require communication infrastructure to be built, a large number of trips to be made and urban and real-estate development that almost always impact negatively on the environment (UNEP-MAP-Blue Plan 2005).

Environmental reports prepared by some international and European organizations[13] since the 1990s outline certain trends that will affect coastal-marine systems in the Mediterranean basin in the short-, medium- and long-term. The human pressures cited in some of these reports (UNEP-MAP 1996 and 2009) highlight above all population growth and distribution and economic activities associated with the coast (urban growth, industry, transport, tourism and recreational activities, agriculture, fishing and aquaculture, exploitation of water resources, exploration/exploitation of hydrocarbons and other minerals, energy production). The environmental situation has therefore been highlighted by (UNEP-MAP 1996 and 2009):

- Impacts and problems in the coastal area (urban development, industrial and urban waste, soil erosion and desertification processes);
- Problems in the marine environment (pollution from certain sources and to differing degrees, destruction of habitats and species, reduced biodiversity, overfishing, eutrophication, a rise in sea-level due to climate change, etc.);
- Impacts on natural (areas of ecological interest) and cultural (historic-archaeological) heritage.

The effects of environmental problems in the Mediterranean are both great in size and important enough for a list of 'environmental priorities' to be included on political agendas – pollution, eutrophication, the proliferation of harmful algae, invasion by exotic species, the over-exploitation of living resources (European Environment Agency 2006, Hoballah 2006). The effects that climate change will foreseeably have in the region should also be mentioned: increased coastal erosion (and the attendant fall in soil fertility), the flooding of coastal plains, the loss of wetlands and the salinization of coastal lagoons. The Mediterranean basin's vulnerability, especially to rises in sea-level and increased numbers of storms, tides and waves (Jeftic et al. 1992, Jeftic et al. 1996, European Environment Agency 1999, Georgas 2000), will be even more patent in areas like coastal towns and cities (Venice, Alexandria, etc.), deltas and islands (Nicholls and Hoozemans 1996).

---

13 As well as UNEP-MAP (1996, 2009) reports, MEDPOL programme and Blue Plan data, and reports and bibliography published by FAO and by the European Environmental Agency (1999, 2006) can be highlighted.

Marine Governance

There is a wide range and variety of maritime governance structures in the Mediterranean Sea involving most of the coastal states. These instruments combine with actions taken by states and the regional political bodies. States are the key actors and therefore hold maximum responsibility.

The Mediterranean Sea is characterized by the existence of an adequate legal-institutional structure alongside weak political integration and marked economic differences. Although the regional instruments have developed in recent decades, the state, as the key actor in implementing legislation, lacks (with the exception of some of the EU members) financial and technical capacity, with there being no single authority or any supranational executive power in the region.

Background

There is a history of cooperative actions on the regional level going back to at least the beginning of the 20th century. The regional marine concept arose early with the International Commission for the Scientific Exploration of the Mediterranean Sea (CIESM) being set up in 1908. Other regional initiatives include the Treaty of Montreux (1936), the Nyon Arrangement (1937) on the freedom and security of navigation, and the General Fisheries Council for the Mediterranean (1948)[14] set up by FAO. More recently the so-called 1975 Mediterranean Action Plan (MAP)[15] laid down a complex network of policies, arrangements, programmes, institutions and activities for the protection of the marine environment, and which aims in the long-term to achieve the necessary understanding that could serve as a basis for broader cooperation agreements (Chircop 1989). Apart from its legal and technical apparatus, MAP also includes research and pollution monitoring – the MEDPOL programme and other integrated planning – and development-linked aspects – set out in the Blue Plan.

This Action Plan has evolved (Table 11.3), having been reviewed and given a change of direction in the 1990s (MAP-Phase II). The new Action Plan and the new Barcelona Convention lay more emphasis on sustainable development, integrated management and regional cooperation as key elements.[16]

---

14 Called the General Fisheries Commission for the Mediterranean since the end of the 1990s onwards.

15 Although there had been a number of interesting endeavours in the field of environmental protection in the Mediterranean, such as the so-called Euro-Mediterranean Charter (1973) and the Inter-parliamentary Conference of Coastal States on the Control of Pollution in the Mediterranean Sea, the Mediterranean Action Plan (1975) was undoubtedly the first major milestone among all the regional actions for protecting the sea.

16 For further information, vid. Pavasovic (1996).

Table 11.3 Evolution of Mediterranean Action Plan

Period	Most relevant facts	Strategies and focuses
1970s (Initial phase)	– Intergovernmental meeting for protection of Mediterranean: MAP adopted (1975) – Conference of Plenipotentiaries (1976): Barcelona Convention, Protocols on waste, Emergency Protocol – Split Conference (1978): Blue Plan and Priority Action Plan	– Conservationism – Eco-development – Protection of marine environment and combating pollution – Integrated planning of environmental development and protection
1980s (Development phase)	– Protocol on Land-based Sources of Pollution (1980) – Development of MEDPOL programme – Protocol concerning Specially-Protected Areas (1982) – 4th Ordinary Meeting of the Contracting Parties (1985): Genoa Declaration	– Protection extended to coastal areas – Definition of major environmental protection strategies
Beginning of 1990s (Maturity phase)	– 6th Ordinary Meeting of the Contracting Parties (1989): Adoption of UNEP Directorate General report – Nicosia Charter* (1990) – Coastal Zone Management Programme (1990)	– Change in direction of MAP towards integrated coastal management – Reconciliation of environment and sustainable development.
1990-1995 (Maturity and adaption to UNCED postulations)	– Preparation of MAP report for presentation at UNCED (1991) – 8th Ordinary Meeting in Antalya (1993): Change of MAP direction – Tunis Conference (1994): Declaration on Sustainable Development in the Mediterranean; Med Agenda 21 – 9th Ordinary Meeting in Barcelona (1995): New MAP and New Convention, Amendments to Protocols	– Sustainable development – Change in direction of legal protection instruments – Application of Agenda 21

Table 11.3 *Continued*

Period	Most relevant facts	Strategies and focuses
1995-present (recent modifications to the system)	– Establishment of the Mediterranean Commission on Sustainable Development (MCSD) (2005) – Conference of Plenipotentiaries (2008): signature of Protocol on Integrated Coastal Zone Management in the Mediterranean (2008); in force from 2011 – 17th Ordinary Meeting in Paris (2012): adoption of the Action Plan for the implementation of the ICZM Protocol	– Sustainability – Participation and governance (states, local authorities, business community, NGOs) – Promotion of the integrated coastal zone management

* Charter on Euro-Mediterranean Cooperation concerning the Environment in the Mediterranean Basin.

Source: Author.

The 2008 formulation of a protocol on integrated coastal management (in force since March, 2011) was one of the most recent milestones in the evolution of Mediterranean marine governance.

Legal-Institutional Framework

In recent years, several phenomena in the marine environment scenario (Figure 11.4) have been subject to such rapid change that management instruments have not always been able to respond effectively. In large part, this is due to the fact that these instruments are usually created by international organizations and their action mechanisms require broad consensus among countries. This is difficult to achieve in a region like the Mediterranean, where there are still sharp economic, demographic, and political contrasts. However, if the action that comes from international organizations does not seem to be very effective, the unilateral action taken by some states is even less so, especially that taken by the weakest in economic and technological terms. Be that as it may, in the Mediterranean international/regional institutions and legislation coexist alongside the various coastal states' own legal frameworks, Regional cooperation instruments sometimes appear to take precedent while at other times national instruments prevail. When the latter occurs, the inequality between countries' capacities and the varying degree of interest that they show in Mediterranean affairs could lead to lack of unanimity over issues that affect them collectively.

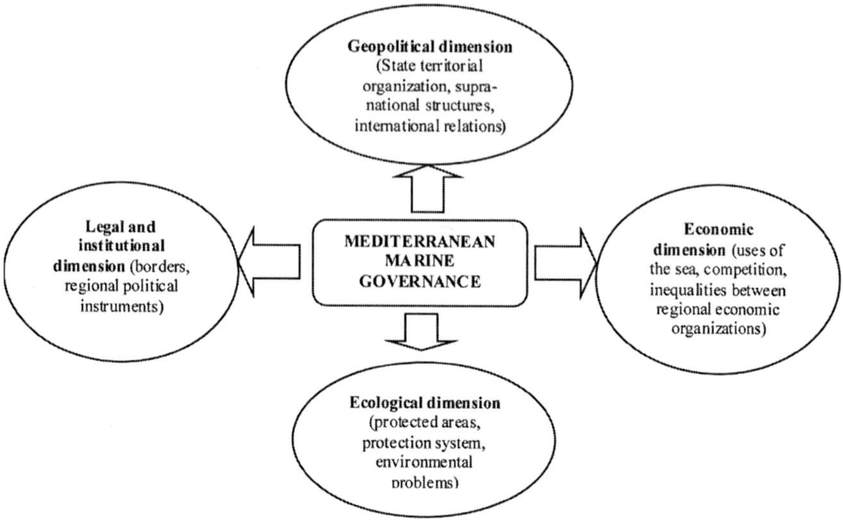

Figure 11.4 Dimensions of marine governance in the Mediterranean

Mediterranean marine governance should be unfailingly multilateral and concerted, both because of the basin's peculiar geographical constraints and the nature and size of the problems shared by those along its coasts. However, it is also evident that each of the dimensions of Mediterranean marine governance (Figure 11.4) is framed in a variety of regulations, legislation and institutions. Legal issues, maritime borders and the navigation regime are regulated by UNCLOS – and binding only for the states that have endorsed it. Meanwhile, environmental protection issues are, as is obvious, regulated by the states themselves, UNCLOS and also by an intricate regional web that revolves around the Mediterranean Action Plan and complemented by other (EU, World Bank, NGOs', etc.) institutions and actions.

There is a therefore a wide variety of concerted actions in this region (navigation, piracy, exploitation of resources, migrations, etc.), although the greatest efforts are made in the area of environmental protection (Table 11.4). Unlike in the field of the environment, where over time a regional spirit of cooperation has taken hold, more purely economic and, especially, geopolitical actions remain the domain of state sovereignty. Nevertheless, being aware of how complex and intertwined the problems that afflict the region are, the Mediterranean states have put a number of regional cooperation strategies in place both in the field of the environment (Barcelona Convention) and other areas (the Euro-Mediterranean Partnership, for example),[17] seeking the most suitable solution through dialogue and consensus,

17 Political initiatives that can be highlighted along with the Euro-Mediterranean Partnership include the Conference for Security and Cooperation in the Mediterranean

Table 11.4 Legal-institutional marine governance forms in the Mediterranean

International initiatives	– UNCLOS – Conservation agreements – Fishing treaties – Agreements on dumping of waste and pollutants – UNEP-Regional Seas Programme
Regional initiatives	– Mediterranean Action Plan: Barcelona Convention and protocols; Blue Plan; MEDPOL Programme – General Fisheries Council for the Mediterranean – EU initiatives – Other initiatives: METAP (World Bank); NGOs (IUCN); sub regional initiatives (Declaration on the Conservation and Sustainable Development of the Alboran Sea, Pelagos Sanctuary, RAMOGE Agreement, etc.)
National initiatives	– Transposition of international law – General environmental legislation (natural spaces, pollution prevention, coastal protection and coastal and marine environment protection, etc.) – Legislation on marine aspects (fishing, protected marine areas, navigation, exploitation of non-living resources, etc.)

Source: Prepared by author.

regional integration, agreements and the participation of multiple actors (states, international organizations, all types of NGOs, economic associations, clusters, etc.).

To recapitulate, it can be said that there are some favourable aspects to the framework of action in the Mediterranean Sea, especially in the field of the environment. However, it is also true that there are some partial or incomplete aspects that have been at the root of most of the problems that continue to exist (or are worsening). Among the strong points of the protection system we can highlight: a) the wide range of actions (national, regional, international) due to deep concern and recognition of the environmental problems; b) the environmental instruments that have traditionally been the most important means for intervening in the regions have acted as drivers of international cooperation and dialogue and of other political and economic actions; c) the presence at the core of the system of the Action Plan, which has been the catalyst for other complementary actions to its benefit and, especially, for attracting institutional

(CSCM), economic cooperation agreements, the European Neighbourhood Policy and the Union for the Mediterranean (Table. UE Med.).

and financial support from bodies such as the World Bank and the European Investment Bank and the very significant political support of the EU; d) the shaping within MAP of a suitable set of protocols, rules and measures (legal mechanism) conducive to achieving a better environmental state despite non-compliance with said legislation.

In spite of this, and although it is true that the system organized around the Action Plan is the oldest and probably the most effective way of protecting the Mediterranean marine environment, it also suffers from a number of short-comings. The instruments of environmental protection are not adequately taken into consideration (and are on occasion simply accepted as partial corrections and not interventions in the problems at root level); international protection rules and regulations are not fully accepted and complied with, a problem which is not caused by the instruments themselves, but by a lack of general awareness; the lack of a defined common state strategy to at last abandon the search for fast economic growth and aim for balanced development respectful of the environment (this should also involve the rethinking of major Mediterranean and Euro-Mediterranean policies); the lack of widespread awareness of environmental problems and their consequences could be a major motive for regional conflict and insecurity; the decoupling of some international/regional initiatives and each state's own policies because they can only intervene on the basis of their own immediate priorities, without taking into account the more general problems in the region; the unilateral character of certain actions, which means that they are less effective and do not consider the cross-border nature of marine ecosystems; the financial weakness of the Action Plan; a variety of situations regarding the implementation and effectiveness of the different protection instruments, as some are partial and not coordinated with the others.

The Mediterranean and the EU

EU action in the Mediterranean can be analysed on two different but complementary levels. The geopolitical and international policy level (bilateral EU-Mediterranean third country agreements, Neighbourhood Policy, Euro-Mediterranean Partnership, Union for the Mediterranean) which, although devoted to making international cooperation proposals for the whole of the Mediterranean region, could be a good political and institutional framework for advancing other more specific initiatives. One example is the fresh impulse that various EU institutions (European Commission, EIB) seek to give Mediterranean maritime cooperation in fields related to social issues (employment), security and maritime surveillance (to combat environmental problems, illegal immigration and illicit trafficking) and maritime infrastructure (basically transport-linked)[18] through the Facility for Euro-Mediterranean Investment and Partnership (FEMIP).

18 See website: http://www.enpi-info.eu/mainmed.php?id=24624&id_type=1&lang_id=450.

Table 11.5 Ways that the EU participates in Mediterranean marine governance

Management policies concerning European marine space	– EU environmental strategies; Strategy for the protection and conservation of the marine environment; Proposal of European environmental strategy for the Mediterranean; funding instruments for the environmental protection (MEDSPA Programme/LIFE Programme) – European Territorial Strategy – Common coastal strategy – Integrated Maritime Policy; Integrated maritime policy for the Mediterranean – Common Fisheries Policy; Fishery regulations in Mediterranean waters; EU Action Plan for the conservation and sustainable exploitation of fishery resources in the Mediterranean Sea
Euro-Mediterranean management policies	– Participation in MAP and Barcelona Convention – Scientific projects in cooperation with third countries – Support for environmental programmes in the region – Cooperation in the field of underwater cultural heritage – Euro-Mediterranean environmental and fishery cooperation (Nicosia Charter, Cairo Declaration, Heraklion Declaration)

Source: Prepared by author.

On a more strictly maritime level (Table 11.5), the EU has been playing a very active role in developing multilateral regional policies and approaches (such as in the MAP system,[19] in the General Fisheries Commission for the Mediterranean and in the Mediterranean Strategy for Sustainable Development) and in proposing a variety of initiatives of its own (sometimes in cooperation with other countries in the region) both on fisheries[20] and environmental issues (environment strategy for the Mediterranean [COM(2006) 475 final]) and marine management (proposal for the application of the Integrated Maritime Policy to the Mediterranean [COM(2009) 466 final]).

19 In this context it is interesting to refer to the 1990 Nicosia Charter and the 1992 Cairo Declaration on Euro-Mediterranean cooperation on environmental issues in the Mediterranean basin.

20 2002 EU Action Plan for the conservation and sustainable exploitation of fishery resources in the Mediterranean Sea in the framework of the Common Fisheries Policy [COM(2002) 535 final]; Council Regulation (EC) No. 1967/2006 of 21st December, 2006, concerning management measures for the sustainable exploitation of fishery resources in the Mediterranean Sea, European Union Official Journal, L 409, 30.12.2006.

The EU's incursion into the Mediterranean took the shape of EU legislation being implemented by the Member States: the assumption and transposition of fisheries regulations for the area, the conducting of COPEMED sub-regional projects and the major transposition of Marine Strategy Framework Directive in EU-Med countries.

The EU is to a certain extent driving the 'Europeanization' of the Mediterranean's regional system, especially due to its leading role and also because many coastal states often concur with its legal approaches and take them on board as their own. However, despite there being a degree of unilateral projection of EU law towards Mediterranean countries, it is also true that this occurs within a complex political system of bilateral or multilateral relations and legislation on different levels (global, European, regional), which result in European leadership that is watered down and limited by the region's climate of complexity and interaction (Barbé 2010).

Conclusions

The most relevant conclusions of this paper are as follows:

- In the Mediterranean there is a wide and diverse range of maritime governance structures that involve the large majority of the coastal states. These instruments combine with actions taken by states and the regional political bodies. The former are the fundamental actors and therefore have maximum responsibility.

- The presence of this legal and institutional architecture does not guarantee an acceptable ecological state (objective of Directive 2008/56/CE) which plainly shows that the existence of said architecture is a necessary requirement, but not sufficient on its own.

- The degree of internationalization of the Mediterranean Sea is still relevant (29.2 of the waters are high seas) and this translates into a theoretical limitation on intervention in environmental affairs by coastal states. At the same time, it should be noted that there is no marine bottom or subsoil outside national jurisdiction. The political and security aspects can be considered to be subject to control by international norms.

- Whilst the maritime legal dimension can be considered to be sufficiently developed, the political and economic dimensions are the weak points of the governance. This translates into insufficient regional political integration (only the EU has any significant degree of cohesion with executive capacity). There are marked differences in economic development making this a differentiating feature in the region with a North-South imbalance.

This strongly limits the implementation of the management of marine affairs, with only a small number of coastal states having financial and technical capacity.

In general terms, the Mediterranean Sea is characterized by the existence of an adequate legal-institutional structure that exists alongside weak political integration and marked economic differences. Although the regional instruments have developed in recent decades, the state, as the key actor in implementing the norms, lacks (with the exception of some of the EU members) financial and technical capacity, with there being no single authority nor any supranational executive power in the region.

References

Barbé, E. (Dir.) 2010. *La Unión Europea más allá de sus fronteras. ¿Hacia la transformación del Mediterráneo y Europa Oriental?* Madrid: Tecnos.

Bohman, B. and Langlet, D. 2015. Float or sinker for Europe's seas? The role of law in marine governance, in *Governing Europe's Marine Environment: Europeanization of Regional Seas or Regionalization of EU Policies?*, edited by M. Gilek and K. Kern. Farnham, UK: Ashgate Publishing.

Chircop, A.E. 1989. Participation in Marine Regionalism: An Appraisal in a Mediterranean Context. *Ocean Yearbook*, 8, 402-404.

COM(2004)373 FINAL, Communication from the Commission, European Neighbourhood Policy. Strategy Paper.

European Environment Agency 1999. State and pressures of the marine and coastal Mediterranean environment. Environmental issues series, N° 5. Luxembourg: Office for Official Publications of the European Communities.

European Environment Agency. 2000. State and pressure of the marine and coastal Mediterranean environment. Luxembourg: European Communities Official Publications Office.

European Environment Agency 2006. Priority issues in the Mediterranean environment, EEA Report, N° 4/2006. Luxembourg: Office for Official Publications of the European Communities.

FAO 2010. FAO Yearbook 2008, Fishery and Aquaculture Statistics. Rome: FAO.

Georgas, D. 2000. Assessment of Climate Change Impacts on Coastal Zones in the Mediterranean. UNEP's Vulnerability Assessment Methodology and Evidence from Case Studies. Fondazione Eni Enrico Mattei.

IUCN 2009. The Status and Distribution of Dragonflies of the Mediterranean basin, compiled by Elisa Riservato, J. et al. Gland, Switzerland and Malaga, Spain.

González Jiménez, J. 2007. La evolución del derecho del mar desde el punto de vista de un mar semicerrado como el Mediterráneo. Revista electrónica de Estudios Internacionales [Online], No 14. Available at: http://www.reei.org/

index.php/revista/num14/articulos/evolucion-derecho-mar-desde-punto-vista-mar-semicerrado-como-mediterraneo [accessed: 5 of March 2010].

Hoballah, A. 2006. La Estrategia Mediterránea para el Desarrollo Sostenible: marco para la asociación regional, in *Anuari de la Mediterrània 2006.* Barcelona: Institut Europeu de la Mediterrània, 176-179.

Instituto Español de Oceanografía (IEO) 2008. *Cambio climático en el Mediterráneo español.* Madrid: Instituto Español de Oceanografía, Ministerio de Educación y Ciencia.

Jeftic, L., Milliman, J.D. and Sestini, G. 1992. *Climatic Change and the Mediterranean.* London: Arnold.

Jeftic, L., Keckes, S. and Pernetta, J. 1996. *Climatic Change and the Mediterranean. Volume 2.* London: Arnold.

Merriam-Webster's Geographical Dictionary Third Edition. 2001. Springfield, MA: Merriam-Webster, Inc.

Nicholls, R.J., Hoozemans, F.M.J. 1996. The Mediterranean: vulnerability to coastal implications of climate change. *Ocean and Coastal Management*, 31(2-3), 105-132.

Pavasovic, A. 1996. The Mediterranean Action Plan phase II and the revised Barcelona Convention: new prospective for integrated coastal management in the Mediterranean region. *Ocean and Coastal Management*, 31(2-3) Special Issue: Sustainable Development at the regional level: the Mediterranean, 133-182.

Reynaud, C. 2009. *Los componentes del transporte marítimo en el Mediterráneo in Anuari de la Mediterrània 2009.* Barcelona: Institut Europeu de la Mediterrània, 275-279.

Suárez de Vivero, J.L. 2012. Fisheries cooperation in the Mediterranean and the Black Sea, Brussels: European Parliament, Directorate General for Internal Policies, Policy Department, Fisheries [online]. http://www.europarl.europa.eu/committees/en/studiesdownload.html?languageDocument=EN&file=78711 [accessed: 19 of November 2012].

UNEP-MAP 1996. The State of the Marine and Coastal Environment in the Mediterranean Region. MAP Technical Reports Series, N° 100. Athens: UNEP/MAP.

UNEP-MAP-Blue Plan 2005. Dossier on Tourism and Sustainable Development in the Mediterranean. MAP Technical Report Series No. 159. Athens: UNEP/MAP.

UNEP-MAP 2009. *State of the Environment and Development in the Mediterranean.* Athens: UNEP/MAP-Plan Bleu.

Vallega, A. 2001a. *Sustainable Ocean Governance: A Geographical Perspective*, London and New York: Routledge.

Vallega, A. 2001b. Ocean governance in post-modern society – a geographical perspective. *Marine Policy*, 25(6), 399-414.

Chapter 12
Marine Governance in the Black Sea

Ståle Knudsen

Introduction

It is sometimes claimed that the Black Sea is the most degraded sea in the world (see e.g. Griffin 1993). Whatever the merits and grounds for such statements, it is clear that the Black Sea has undergone dramatic and probably irreversible environmental change since the 1960s. The years around 1990 saw important turning points both in environment and governance. Hypoxia events were at their most extreme, and new species and overfishing brought dramatic changes to the ecosystem, together resulting in overall ecosystem regime change. At the same time the USSR and the Warsaw Pact disintegrated and a series of new Black Sea states emerged, opening the way for regional cooperation on the Black Sea environment. Yet, the geopolitical situation around the Black Sea remains diffuse and tense, constraining regional cooperation on environmental issues. Recent enlargement of the EU to the shores of the Black Sea has further changed the context for management of Black Sea environmental issues.[1] What is now the character of Black Sea marine governance? To what extent is the current governance structure of the Black Sea able to tackle environmental issues of the sea? What role does the EU play in Black Sea marine governance and can the EU and other supra-national bodies contribute to strengthened environmental management of the Black Sea? To what extent has Black Sea regionalization around environmental issues been successful? A relevant policy related issue is whether a strategic choice to focus on Black Sea regional cooperation on environmental issues, being 'soft', fosters or stimulates regional integration. Or is successful cooperation on marine environmental issues difficult to achieve without the existence of deeper political cooperation and integration, without a lessening of geopolitical tension and the emergence of 'bottom up' regionalization?

To exemplify the particular challenges of environmental policy making in the Black Sea, and the character of EU involvement in this, I will provide a detailed survey of the quite different experiences with efforts at transboundary cooperation in fisheries management and nutrient inflow reduction. I shall argue that there is a disjunction between a very progressive environmental policy agenda and a significant lack of ability or willingness to implement policies that would significantly

1 This article was written before the Maydan protests in Ukraine and the Russian annexation of Crimea in 2014.

improve the environment of the Black Sea. EU policies and EU legal instruments seem to constitute the soundest and most realistic road towards effective regional cooperation, but they encounter considerable geopolitical challenges as particularly Russia and Turkey claim stronger and more independent roles in the region.[2]

The article has the following structure. First I review the history, character and causes of environmental problems in the Black Sea. Second, I discuss processes of regionalization, especially intergovernmental legal and institutional structures as well as NGO cooperation. This section also includes a consideration of the emerging regional environmental cooperation. Third, I survey EU influence on Black Sea environmental policies, focusing in particular on EU-guided policies to reduce Danube nutrient flows. The challenges to regionalization and EU influence are addressed in the fifth section where I discuss geopolitical tensions. Lastly, challenges to regionalization and EU influence are exemplified in a detailed examination of one particular case: the attempt to agree on a legally binding document that could form the basis for transboundary Black Sea fisheries management.

Short History of Environmental Problems

There is at present no overall agreement among scientists about the reasons for and dynamics of the shifts in the Black Sea ecosystem since the 1960s. Caddy (2008) identifies several different approaches, all of which, to a certain extent, seek to give primacy to one causal factor. In some models, fishing has constituted a major pressure on the environment, resulting in dwindling stocks and changed trophic structure among target species. Other models stress the importance of different pressures, primarily eutrophication and the introduction of alien species. The upheavals in the ecology of the Black Sea are probably best understood as the complex interaction of qualitatively very different pressures and processes – the salient ones being eutrophication, removal of top predators through fishing, and the establishment of introduced species. There has been considerable concern about maritime transport – accidents and oil spills – but this has been related primarily to Istanbul and the straits. Apart from some localized concentrations (Istanbul, Socci, Danube river mouth), chemical contamination in the Black Sea is considered 'low' or 'moderate' (Readman 2002). However, pollution in the form of nutrient inflow has caused one of the major environmental problems in the Black Sea. From the mid-1970s until the early 1980s the North-western shelf of the Black Sea experienced hypoxia (serious oxygen depletion) as a result of eutrophication

2 This study is primarily based on desktop studies of relevant reports and academic articles, but also on interviews and some ethnographic fieldwork. The writing of this chapter has been supported by and contributes to the FP7 project KnowSeas where I am a partner in a work package focusing on governance and institutions in the management of Europe's seas. I am also a leader of the Black Sea work package within the same project.

caused by heavy nutrient inflow, especially though the Danube (Mee 2006, McQuatters-Gollop and Mee 2007). Removal of top predators by heavy fishing probably contributed to this. The ecological changes also opened the way for establishment of invasive non-indigenous species (such as the comb jelly *Mnemniopsis leidyi*). While it was primarily the NW-shelf that experienced hypoxia – at its maximum covering an area up to the size of Switzerland – overfishing and the spread of new species contributed to irreversible regime changes in the Black Sea as a whole. The early 1990s saw a dramatic decline in catches of small pelagic species (anchovy and horse mackerel) since stocks were decimated by overfishing and the impact of the comb jelly.

It is now considered impossible to return to some (undefined) pristine state of the sea. Yet, the Black Sea ecosystem has seen some recovery over the last 10-15 years. A 2007 assessment of the Black Sea ecosystem (BS-TDA 2007) concluded that the ecosystem was in a better condition than in the 1980s and 1990s. There are signs of increased biodiversity, hypoxia occurrences have decreased on the NW-shelf, and stocks of anchovy and sprat are to some extent recovering. However, stocks of large pelagic species as well as benthic species are in serious trouble, and the Black Sea provides a classic example of 'fishing down the food chain' (Ulman et al. 2013). The benthic system is being transformed by the spread of the invasive top predator the Japanese sea snail *Rapana venosa*. Some important species – such as sturgeon and the endogenous salmon *Labrax* are threatened by extinction. While there generally has been a removal of top predators, dolphin species, however, seem to have fared quite well since hunting them became illegal during the 1970s and early 1980s.

Overall, the Black Sea ecosystem is characterized by ecological instability and recovery is non-linear, with different opportunistic and invasive species now dominating the benthic and pelagic realms. Climate change, to which the Black Sea is supposed to be very sensitive, adds to this instability. The recovery of areas previously affected by hypoxia may be problematic, Mee (2006) warns, as different kinds of resistances exist in the new, often quite stable state of the north-western shelf. It should also be mentioned that the relative recovery of the Black Sea was not primarily a result of improved transnational environmental management. The main causes were (1) economic change in East Europe resulting in less use of fertilizer and consequently reduced nutrient inflow to the Black Sea, and (2) the accidental introduction of a jelly species (*Beroe ovata*) that was a natural predator on and checked the invasiveness of the comb jelly.

The major pressures affecting negatively the Black Sea environment are thus fishing, nutrient inflow, introduction of new species (through maritime transport and aquaculture), and habitats destruction. Management to address most of these requires transboundary cooperation to be successful. There is now also increasing concern over possible consequences of massive infrastructure and energy projects around the coasts of the Black Sea (tourism in Bulgaria, road construction and energy projects in Turkey, Olympics infrastructure in Sochi etc.), but the effects of these have not been addressed systematically by science.

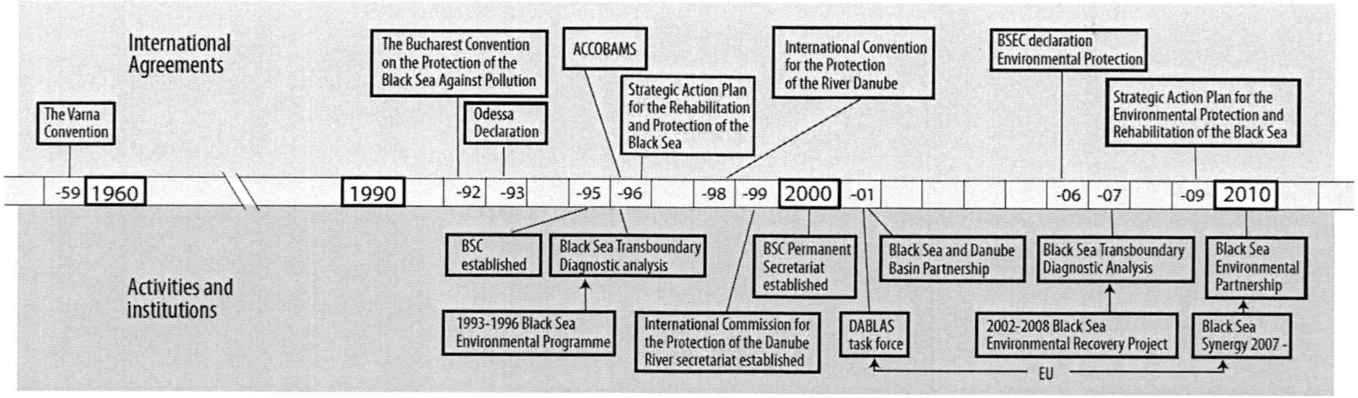

Figure 12.1 International agreements, activities and institutions pertaining to Black Sea environmental management

Regional Governance Systems

Moves Towards Regional Environmental Law and a Commission

The Varna Convention on Black Sea fisheries, signed in 1959 by the Soviet Union, Romania and Bulgaria, was the only international instrument regulating issues of environmental relevance in the Black Sea before the early 1990s (Figure 12.1). While the convention was ambitious, and had tangible results in research and information dissemination among signatories, the relevance and effect gradually decreased as Turkish Black Sea fisheries developed quickly during the 1980s (Reynolds 1987). Later, with the geopolitical shifts the foundation for this convention was eroded. The disintegration of the USSR, the establishment of the new independent states and the political changes in Romania and Bulgaria around 1990 dramatically changed the framework for cooperation among Black Sea countries. New initiatives were quickly taken, first with the Bucharest Convention on the Protection of Black Sea Against Pollution (1992), and soon after with the Odessa Declaration (Ministerial Declaration on the Protection of the Black Sea, 1993) which, relative to the Convention, broadened the scope beyond pollution and also more explicitly developed a common policy/regulatory framework (GEF 2004: 11, Mee 2002: 95). Protocols on a range of issues (land-based pollution, oil spill, dumping, biodiversity and landscape conservation)[3] were developed, and the legal framework further elaborated with the Sofia Declaration (2002), Bucharest Declaration (2007) and the (second) Sofia Declaration (2009).

While the initiatives for these agreements were taken by (the primarily new) Black Sea states, international assistance from funding bodies such as UN, the World Bank (through the newly established GEF), the EU as well as individual governments in Europe was instrumental in transforming these into actual activities and institutions.[4] The Odessa Declaration thus resulted in the establishment of the Black Sea Environmental Programme (BSEP) in 1993, with

3 For details, see BSC website http://www.blacksea-commission.org/_convention-protocols.asp, or Velikova and Oral 2012.

4 The Global Environmental Facility (GEF) has been a core instrument for WB and UN support to regional/transboundary environmental projects in the Black Sea region, such as DABLAS and projects in support of the BSC. More recently GEF has sought to develop and support initiatives for the establishment of MPAs in the Black Sea. During the 1990s NATO was relatively active in sponsoring scientific studies on various aspects of Black Sea oceanography, ecology and fish stock assessments and in promoting closer interaction between scientists in the region. A few other international agreements potentially apply to the Black Sea. The BSC is working with IMO on BS countries' ballast water policies. The states are intent on signing the convention, which will hopefully be implemented within 4-5 years. ACCOBAMS (Agreement on the Conservation of Cetaceans of the Black Sea, Mediterranean Sea and Contiguous Atlantic Area) ideally applies to the Black Sea, but since it is as yet not signed and ratified by Russia and Turkey, it has little effect on actual management in the Black Sea.

a Program Coordinating Unit (PCU) in Istanbul. A major task and achievement of this programme was the production of the Black Sea Transboundary Diagnostic Analysis which paved the way for a negotiated Strategic Action Plan (SAP) adopted by Black Sea states at a Ministerial Conference in Istanbul in 1996. The Bucharest Convention foresaw the establishment of a Commission with a secretariat in Istanbul. While the Commission had its first meeting in 1995, the establishment of the secretariat was delayed due to the non-payment of some national governments. Although the BSEP was formally ended in 1996, funding from various sources kept the activities going at the PCU in Istanbul until the Commission secretariat became operational in 2000.

The Bucharest Convention, the Odessa Declaration, the BSEP and the BSC have resulted in some significant achievements, especially in identification of issues, agenda setting, regional networking, monitoring etc. Like most of the already existing marine conventions the Bucharest convention focused on pollution. During the last decade the BSC has seemingly had most success in establishing databases and in bringing together scientists and bureaucrats in the Black Sea region within the context of six advisory groups and three large scientific conferences (even getting Georgians and Russians together when tensions between the countries were high). However, at balance, implementation of the Convention and declarations has been relatively poor.

The Sofia Declaration of 2002 was developed partly as a response to the lack of progress and paved the way for a redrafting of the timetable dates (Velikova and Oral 2012). Renewed funding from GEF facilitated the operation of a project in support of the BSC, especially in producing a new Transboudary Diagnostic Analysis (TDA) and in a revision of the SAP. However, the 'Final Report' produced by Black Sea Environmental Recovery Project (BSERP), which ran until 2007, was not overtly optimistic about the future of the BSC and noted that, overall, '[t]he materials produced by the Advisory Groups [of the BSC] are not generally used by the decision makers in the Black Sea countries because they are not seen as being relevant to policy making' (BSERP 2006: 9).

In addition to the BSERP evaluations (BSERP 2006, 2007, GEF 2004) and the most recent Transboundary Diagnostic Analysis (BS-TDA 2007: 137-140), scholars – many of whom have at some stage and in various capacities been directly involved themselves in the work of BSEP or the BSC secretariat – have at various times lamented the 'lack of progress' (see e.g. DiMento 2001: 248, Sezer 2001: 59-60, Mee 2002, Dimadama and Timotheou 2010: 8-9, Velikova and Oral 2012: 166-167). Specifically, implementation of the SAPs at national level and coordinated action at regional level had been very limited. The immediate reasons for this are primarily found within two fields: funding and law.

Funding by member states has been a continuous challenge, both before and after the establishment of the secretariat. In its exit strategy, external donors to the BSERP noted that '[t]he current situation is not sustainable in that the organizational and financial programme mandate given to the BSC cannot be achieved with the existing resource base, in fact it cannot be maintained at even a minimal level'

(BSERP 2007: 16-17). The activities of the secretariat have partly been maintained by support from external donors, in particular GEF and EU. Although the secretariat has now been in operation for 12 years, it has continuously struggled with lack of funding and staff, and the situation at present is the most difficult thus far. In 2012 it was staffed by 7 people, including supporting personnel (e.g. technical assistance). Approximately half of the staff is sponsored by externally funded projects. The Black Sea Environmental Fund that was originally planned has never materialized.

Although the Commission has had some success in cooperation with various Danube initiatives in reducing pollution and euthrophication, it has seemingly been relatively ineffective in carrying through the measures foreseen in the Bucharest Convention and the Odessa Declaration. First, the Odessa Declaration (and later amendments/additions) is considered a 'soft' law (Sezer 2001: 59, McQuarter-Gollop and Mee 2007: 7): it is not binding in the same way as e.g. the EU directives. Therefore, the level of legal compliance has been low (Dimadama and Timotheou 2010), and even though the SAP resulted in national action plans being drafted, they were never implemented (Sezer 2001: 60). Furthermore, several of the protocols have not been ratified and momentum has been lost in development of new legal documents. One case in point is the unsuccessful attempt to approve a regional fisheries agreement/convention, to be discussed in more detail below.

Beyond efforts at cooperation on environmental issues between Black Sea states, it has been acknowledged that international cooperation in management of the Black Sea should also include the extensive drainage areas of rivers emptying into the Black Sea, especially of the Danube that carries approximately half of the nutrient loads to the Black Sea (McQuatters-Gollop and Mee 2007). These issues were included and addressed in the Bucharest Convention and the Odessa Declaration. Yet, an independent convention and commission were created to address water treatment issues. The International Commission for Protection of the Danube River (*ICPDR*) was set up in 1994, and the Danube River Protection Convention ratified in 1998. The EC played a central role in this work, but UNDP and GEF were also important supporters. In 2001 the EU took the initiative to establish the Danube-Black Sea Task Force (*DABLAS*) for the protection of water and water-related ecosystems in the Danube and Black Sea region. This initiative will be discussed in more detail below.

Other Attempts at Regional Environmental Cooperation

Beyond the BSC and the Convention and declarations underlying it, some other initiatives at regional cooperation to address environmental issues have emerged. Although cooperation between states, such as in the Black Sea Economic Cooperation (BSEC), and regional NGO cooperation supposedly have very different character, there are some strong linkages.

Following a Turkish initiative, the BSEC was established in 1992, primarily to facilitate economic development in its member countries. BSEC had from the start a Working Group on Environmental Protection, and has since 2006 developed an environmental policy based on a declaration and an action plan on environmental protection (Velikova and Oral 2012). Since membership of the BSEC includes many states with no border to the Black Sea, cooperation is sought for a range of environmental issues. Yet, in addition to climate change, one main focus of this initiative seems to be on the Black Sea marine environment. Cooperation with BSC has been sought, but except for joint, but rather limited, participation in each others' meetings, little concrete seems to have come out of this. In sum, progress has been made in incorporating the environment at the political – some may perhaps like to say the rhetorical – level of the work of the BSEC, but implementation has not been forthcoming (Stribis 2009: 10, Dimadama and Timotheou 2010: 21, Velikova and Oral 2012: 163).

It might be questionable to what extent an organization set up primarily to foster economic cooperation and development in the region is capable of implementing measures for environmental protection, particularly when protection will often be seen as a limitation on economic growth in a region where few national governments give the environment a high priority (see e.g. Dimadama and Timotheou 2010). In Russia, for instance, '... the 'environment sector' was considerably downgraded within the state bureaucracy during the 1990s' (Mee 2002: 93). Russia has been reluctant to fund the BSC headquarters and make annual payments, but has willingly helped to fund expensive international energy projects. In Turkey the Ministry of Environment has generally supported the BSC, while the Ministry of Foreign Affairs has held that there are other issues of higher importance.

In 2002 the BSEC Permanent Secretariat advised the Turkish NGO TURMEPA to set up a NGO with an international character (Stribis 2009: 29). TURMEPA, as a NGO established by the Koç family – one of the richest private business families in Turkey – and with business leaders and private companies as members (esp. in the maritime sector), has little problems with funding. They primarily focus on marine pollution, as well as awareness and education activities, but have recently cooperated with GEF and the BSC in promoting MPAs in Turkey. Under the umbrella of INTERMEPA they have established branches abroad, including in Ukraine. They have responded to the BSEC request by establishing a branch in the Turkish Black Sea port city of Samsun, and the new director of the INTERMEPA stresses that in the future they intend to focus especially on Black Sea activities. However, thus far there has not really been any Black Sea wide INTERMEPA activity. With the kind of sponsors and focus the TURMEPA has (see members list at http://www.turmepa.org.tr/icerik.aspx?id=659), an important aspect of their activity is arguably 'green-washing' of maritime businesses. Ultimately there seems to be little scope for this organization to form the gravitational centre for ENGO activity in the Black Sea region. That the BSEC asked this particular NGO to take responsibility for ENGO activity in the region is also indicative of what kind of environmental NGO activity they would like to see develop.

An earlier attempt at regional cooperation between Black Sea environmental NGOs was sponsored by another regional body. During the mid-1990s the BSEP actively supported the establishment and activities of a *Black Sea NGO Forum* (http://www.bsnn.org/index.html). Formally established in 1998 after the BSEP had first sponsored a directory of and meetings between ENGOs in the region, this was at the time seen as a great success. However, after the BSC established its secretariat the forum lost some of its momentum. With a membership of 62 it is today renamed *The Black Sea NGO Network* and is coordinated from its regional office in Varna, Bulgaria. They seem to be strongly attached to the BSEP/BSERP agendas (TDA and SAP) and mostly focus on raising awareness. The activities of the network are to a large extent financed by international sponsors and projects. They are observers to the BSC, but overall seem to be relatively inactive as a network, and out of 14 Bulgarian member organizations, only one can be considered really engaged. The members of the Black Sea NGO Network make up an odd list. Many of the major marine environmental NGOs (such as TURMEPA and TÜDAV in Turkey, both close to business and government) are not members. On the other side, neither are the more activist, political and critical organizations members of the network. For instance, in Turkey there has recently emerged a range of place-based social movements, NGOs and networks that oppose the current wide-ranging and active energy development policy of the authorities. Most of these organizations are careful not to be seen cooperating with international organizations, and particularly distance themselves from anything related to the EU.

With the EU's launch of the Black Sea Synergy in 2007,[5] the WWF together with the Heinrich Böll Stiftung undertook a new initiative to coordinate ENGO activities in the region. This may signal a significant change, since – except for Greenpeace's support for protests against planned nuclear and thermal power stations in Sinop, Turkey – it is the first time an international ENGO has shown interest for the Black Sea.

In summary, ENGOs in the Black Sea region, with the exception of some international ENGOs that have recently engaged in the region, are 'very disperse and dispose of limited resources' (Stribis 2009: 27). Overall, most regional networking and coordinating activities of Black Sea ENGOs have been top-down, stimulated by funding from outside of the region. ENGOs have had little impact on actual policies and have not contributed much to the setting of the regional environmental agenda. Most Black Sea countries have very hierarchical political systems, allowing for little participation of NGOs and citizens. With the current outlook, poor funding and often lack or relevant language skills, powerful regionalization of Black Sea ENGOs is not likely without more active involvement of some larger international ENGOs.

5 Related to the BSS Romania took the initiative to form the Black Sea NGO Forum, which is not to be confused with the NGO Forum established by the BSEP during the 1990s. This new forum seems to focus primarily on human right issues etc., and pays little attention to environmental issues (Delcour and Manoli 2010, http://blackseango.org/new/, [accessed 16.01.2012]).

Perspectives and Visions

In contrast to the relatively insignificant role of regional cooperation among environmental NGOs in the Black Sea region, the various initiatives that have addressed environmental issues in the Black Sea since the early 1990s have articulated the very 'last fashions' in environmental policy. In particular, the focus on a holistic approach was central from the start, especially in the work of the BSEP (Mee 2002: 100). Also, it has been claimed that the Odessa Declaration '... was the first policy agreement on regional seas to reflect the philosophy of UNCED, Agenda 21 ...' (Mee 2002: 95, GEF 2004: 11). This thinking was also articulated in the work and documents produced by the BSEP during the 1990s, for instance in a desire to stimulate 'participation' (through the support of a Black Sea Environmental NGO Forum) and raising 'environmental awareness'. Furthermore, 'the Black Sea regime recognizes new principles of international law', exemplified by the SAP's statement that the concept of sustainable development is to be applied (DiMento 2001: 255). The first draft Black Sea fisheries convention explicitly made reference to Agenda 21 and set up 'sustainable development' as a general aim and notes that reaching this goal would need new approaches such as the 'precautionary' principle.

There are several interconnected reasons for this progressive environmental agenda. First, experts that staffed the BSEP offices in Istanbul and who developed the TDA, authored the Transboundary Action Plan and provided 'technical advice' in the drafting of the Odessa Declaration (Sezer 2001: 59) were international experts, many educated in the US. These experts brought with them new, progressive ideas for environmental management. I paid several visits to the BSEP secretariat in 1996 and 1997 when I was contracted by the BSEP to conduct a comparative study of fisheries and, notably, 'public awareness' in Turkey and Ukraine. The informal conversations among the young and highly trained international experts abounded, according to my notebook, with references to the 'precautionary principle', to 'life support system', and, most fundamentally, to a distinction between 'utilitarian' and 'eco-centric' perspectives on the environment. One should, obviously, be the latter, and not 'anthropocentric'. Some considered it a problem that many in the Black Sea region, especially the Turks, were unable to realize that the environment has inherent value. This group of people made a significant imprint on the environmental discourse on the Black Sea during the 1990s. The influence of these experts was, of course, an effect and articulation of the impact GEF, UNEP and the other funding institutions had on the work of the BSEP.

Second, the new political situation in the early 1990s opened up new possibilities in a context where the partners had probably found themselves quite constrained by vested interests in previous paradigms. For this reason they may have been, initially, open to more progressive approaches to the environmental issues of the Black Sea. Although the 'eco-friendly' rhetoric has been toned down to some extent since the BSC secretariat was established, the agenda of the BSC and other initiatives has remained relatively comprehensive and progressive. The

DABLAS Task Force based their approach on 'adaptive management' (McGollop and Mee 2007), and recent developments in the work of the BSC has identified new management approaches such as Integrated Coastal Zone Management (ICZM), The Ecosystem Approach, and Integrated River Basin Management (IRBM). According to Velikova, who until recently worked at the BSC secretariat, the overall '... intention is to reach "Good environmental status" of the whole Black Sea and to sustain it as likewise stated in the EC Marine Strategy Framework Directive' (Velikova and Oral 2012: 168).

Third, engaging progressive environmental agendas and terminology like ICZM, IRBM etc., may have been a strategic choice by Black Sea states to attract international funding. Further, the desire to comply with EU environmental legislation was an increasing concern of Bulgaria, Romania and to some extent Turkey during the first decade of the 2000s. It has been argued that the multiplicity of activities in the Black Sea environmental field demonstrates '... the need of the Black Sea countries to showcase their problems and seek for [*sic*] solutions not internally, but internationally' (Dimadamana and Timotheou 2010: 10). In the case of DABLAS and the ICPDR the 'progressive' agendas of e.g. IRBM was more a direct result of the active and leading role of the EU.

Europeanization and EU Influence: The DABLAS Task Force

The wider Black Sea region has been considered a 'neighbour' region by the EU since the 1990s, both because of its strategic importance (energy, trade, geopolitics) and because it could be (partially) integrated within the EU itself. The European Community was one of the sponsors of the development of institutional structures for environmental protection during the 1990s. Yet before 2007 the EU tended to be reluctant to become involved directly in any Black Sea regional structures (Emerson 2008). With Bulgarian and Romanian membership this changed. EU directives and policies with implications for marine environmental management, such as WFD, MSFD, CFP and Natura 2000, have to be implemented in the new member states. Some of these policies and directives can be implemented by Romania and Bulgaria without consulting other Black Sea states. While the legal adjustment has been smooth, actual implementation of new policies has been difficult. For example, some criteria and measures for specifying Good Environmental Status (GES), required by the MSFD, could be adopted from work elsewhere in the EU. However operationalization of these indicators requires adaptation to the special environmental conditions of the Black Sea. This has proved to be a challenge in Bulgaria at least, where initiatives have been taken belatedly and the capacity of marine science is insufficient. The establishment of environmental targets and associated indicators for GES in Bulgaria, due by July 2012, is therefore considerably delayed in Bulgaria.

In some instances effective environmental policies, e.g. related to fish stocks, will require cooperation with other Black Sea states. Thus, the EU would like to sign up to the Bucharest Convention. This would facilitate cooperation on fisheries issues, for instance, and allow a legally binding document to be created that could clarify the relation between the CFP and regional cooperation on fisheries management. However, resistance from some of the signatory countries, primarily Russia, has hindered EU membership in the BSC and the prospects for future membership are not good.

The DABLAS Task Force is the first example of a regional institutional structure initiated and led by the EU in the Black Sea region. Its experiences are therefore of particular interest when exploring both EU-influence and regionalization. One reason for the formation of DABLAS was the need for EU to find ways to cooperate on the implementation of the WFD in the Danube watershed. DABLAS thus aimed to provide a platform for co-operation for the protection of water and water-related ecosystems in the Danube and Black Sea Region. Accordingly, this initiative focussed on various kinds of water pollution and did not explicitly address the eutrophication challenge. But since the majority of the projects it supported related to urban wastewater treatment, one should expect reduction in nutrient input to be a major result. Other initiatives have also addressed the nutrient input issue. In particular, the Black Sea Strategic Partnership, coordinated by the WB and funded in cooperation with UNEP/UNDP has sought to enhance regional capacity to deal with eutrophication. I will, however, focus on the DABLAS Task Force since this has been considered the most successful attempt by the EU to work with states in the region to address regional environmental issues.

The DABLAS Task Force was comprised of representatives from the countries in the Danube and Black Sea region, from ICPDR, BSC, International Financing Institutions (IFIs), the EC and interested EU Member States and other bilateral donors and regional/international organizations. The European Commission DG Environment controlled the Secretariat. 'The main function of the DABLAS process was to encourage a more strategic focus to the use of available financing, and to ensure coordinated action between all financial instruments operating in the region'.[6] The task force primarily targeted urban wastewater treatment in the Danube watershed but also other river basins connected to the Black Sea, with many of the major projects undertaken in the accession country Turkey.

Through DABLAS the necessary stakeholders – including IFIs – were brought together to realize projects for water improvement. This relied on a pipeline methodology whereby potential projects to be sponsored move up a priorities list as they develop through preparatory stages. States and organizations were thus able to cooperate and fund relevant projects, e.g. on sewage and municipal waste treatment. The DABLAS priority pipeline was also intended to reflect the best practice principles of Integrated Water Resource Management.

DABLAS was considered a very effective instrument. On its own webpage it claims that 'in terms of facilitating additional technical assistance for investment

6 European Commission – Environment DABLAS web pages, http://ec.europa.eu/environment/enlarg/dablas/index_en.htm, [accessed 6. January 2012].

support DABLAS has been particularly successful'.[7] By 2009, 113 municipal sector projects were evaluated and considered for funding, resulting in total funding of 2.5 billion Euros (Stribis 2009: 12). Since the focus was on creating a mechanism for securing successful financing of water cleaning projects, little attention has been paid to the (positive) effects of DABLAS's projects on the environment. The major reason for the declared success is that DABLAS managed to bring together the BSC, the Danube Commission and Danube countries to implement projects related to the EU WFD (Tassinari 2006). It has arguably been the most effective governance tool for transboundary environmental management in the Black Sea region (Vahl and Celac 2006: 184),[8] and it has been argued that it could be a model for how other transboundary environmental issues could be addressed in the region (ibid.).

Yet, DABLAS ceased work in 2011 and there are currently no plans to re-start. Why? Apparently, DABLAS experienced '... increasing disengagement of Member States, beneficiary countries and IFIs ...' (DABLAS 2009: 5). With changes in the EU's relation to the Black Sea and Danube states – some becoming members or accession states – and geopolitical shifts in the region, especially with Russia and Turkey becoming more assertive, the EU has developed new tools and instruments to deal with states in the Black Sea region. It was felt that there was too much overlap between DABLAS and these other instruments and that there was a need to build better synergies and increase efficiency. IFIs, in particular, seem to have become increasingly unsure about the role of DABLAS in this rapidly changing political context.

Two different strategic initiatives were taken by the EU Commission during the second part of the 2000s: the formulation of the Black Sea Synergy (BSS) policy, and the development of an EU Strategy for the Danube Region (SDR) (EC 2010). The instruments earlier embedded within the DABLAS have been redistributed between these two strategies. While the Strategy for the Danube Region, among a wide range of topics, also includes environmental issues, the Black Sea is clearly outside of the focus area: positive effects for the Black Sea of reduced nutrient loads carried by the Danube are mentioned, but more as a welcome side-effect than a policy aim of the strategy. The SDR may likely result in less direct interaction between EU and non-EU states concerning policies to combat eutrophication and hypoxia in the Black Sea.

Within the overall umbrella of the European Neighbourhood Policy there had developed different forms of cooperation (TACIS, PHARE, European

7 http://ec.europa.eu/environment/enlarg/dablas/overview_en.htm, [accessed 9. January 2012].

8 However, it remains unclear to what extent the DABLAS task force has made a major difference when it comes to actually reducing the pressures resulting in eutrophication. A WWF/Henrich Böll Stiftung (2008: 47) publication claims the DABLAS Task Force to be '... the most useful coordination structure in terms of results achieved (i.e. pollution reduction) ...', but provides no source or evidence for its claim.

Neighbourhood and Partnership Instrument – East, RENA) on a range of issues (not only environmental) between the EU and individual or groups of Black Sea countries. In 2007 the EU made an effort to coordinate these activities through the launching of the ambitious Black Sea Synergy initiative. The BSS policy signals that the EU has started to consider the Black Sea as an EU sea. By supporting regional development in the Black Sea region the BSS seems to go further than previous EU initiatives towards stimulating BS regionalization. However, since the regionalization ambition of the BSS can also be seen as an attempt by the EU to increase its influence in the region, the BSS has met with some caution, especially from Russia. It has therefore achieved much less than first intended and expected (Berindan 2010, Delcour and Manoli 2010). For instance, despite the clearly stated ambition of the EU to become a signatory to the Bucharest Convention, considered particularly relevant to the adoption of the Marine Strategy Framework Directive (COM 2008: 391), this has not been achieved – probably due to Russia blocking EU membership. Although it has been the intention of the BSS to help establish sectoral partnerships in the areas of environment, transport and energy, The Black Sea Environment Partnership has been the only one launched thus far (Delcour and Manoli 2010: 8). However, this partnership has resulted only in the formation of an administrative unit within the European Union External Action service. Since 'environmental protection is the most developed area of cooperation within the Black Sea Region' (Aydın 2005: 66) and is one of the'… widely accepted and easier areas of cooperation' (Berindan 2010: 5), the BSS synergy chose this 'soft' issue as their first priority focus. It is also likely that this was some of the rationale behind WB and UN support for environmental projects during the 1990s. Laurence Mee (personal communication) relates how the Bucharest Convention initiative actually had its roots in the final years of the Soviet Union, and its further development was undertaken by the new independent states Russia and Ukraine in particular. At the time there was a tension between these two states concerning the Black Sea fleet, and the environment, being a 'soft' issue, was considered something on which agreement could be found.

It is difficult to really assess the success of treating environmental concerns 'soft' issues. However, it is doubtful that starting regional cooperation on the 'soft' sector of environmental issues has improved trust, set a good example, opened up cooperation in other fields and thereby facilitated deeper regional integration.[9] In the Black Sea region geopolitical concerns related to energy in particular have largely inhibited attempts at cooperation in the supposedly less contentious field of environmental management.

---

9 Yet, a certain basis has been established in international law, in scientific and bureaucratic interaction, in establishment of data monitoring and databases that will make implementation much easier when the political situation allows for progress in this field. On the other hand, lack of funds, scientific training and competence, variable language skills, lack of continuity in data monitoring demonstrate the weak fundament for cooperation.

Geopolitics and Regionalization

Several developments since 1990 might be expected to have stimulated intraregional Black Sea environmental cooperation: the dissolution of the Soviet Union and the rapprochement between the new independent states and Turkey as well as the EU, the willingness of international bodies to support environmental regionalization, the progressive environmental agenda that was pursued, and the gradual inclusion of the Black Sea in EU environmental policies. However, cooperation has been fraught with complications and implementation of the progressive agenda has been difficult. This discrepancy can only be understood in the context of the geopolitics of the wider Black Sea region.

The 'region' itself is elusive. It is not a consolidated region, and the foremost 'regional' institution, the BSEC, itself articulates two different visions: the 'Black Sea Region' and the 'Wider Black Sea Region' (Berindan 2010). Berindan even argues that the way the EU develops its environmental policy under the flag of BSS '... actually discards the concept of region altogether replacing it with what it truly is: a space that connects other regions among them ...' (Berindan 2010: 11). The Black Sea may be more a contact zone than a region. There has been little bottom up regionalization in the field of environment. There is no strong internal force for integration, as with the Nordic countries or the Council of Baltic Sea States (WWF 2008: 48). Security concern is the major issue shaping interaction around the sea, including recent armed conflict (Russia-Georgia 2008). It is a contact zone where the geopolitical interests of three major regional powers meet: the EU, Russia and Turkey, and all of these have increased their relative claim to and power over the 'region' during the last decade, and EU influence is made difficult by the emerging partnership between Russia and Turkey (Emerson 2008, Berindan 2010, Delcour and Manoli 2010). Especially Russia tends to resist EU influence in the Black Sea area (Emerson 2008, Delcour and Manoli 2010: 12). Thus, the international agenda concerning the Black Sea focuses on energy policies, transport, political stability, human rights, etc. While major environmental issues are clearly apparent in the region, these are seen as being of minor importance in relation to these other issues in the international realm.

There are several reasons for the relatively high geopolitical tension between the EU and Russia in the Black Sea region. First, the Black Sea has long been considered by Russia as a 'Russian' sea, or a sea where Russian (imperial) interests should be protected and articulated by a strong Russian Black Sea navy (see e.g. King 2004: 192ff). Russia has during the last years played forcefully, by several means, to retain influence in/over Georgia and Ukraine. The significance for Russia of retaining the navy base at Sevastopol in Ukraine – now extended beyond the initial 2017 deadline (Winrow 2007) – attests to the continued military-strategic importance of the Black Sea to Russia.

Second, even more than military-security issues, energy security and energy policies have emerged as the major issue around which Russia-EU relations turn. Here stakes are high: a significant proportion of EU's energy consumption will for the foreseeable future have to be met from Russia and its 'backyard' – the Caucasus and Central Asia – and the oil and gas will have to pass the Black Sea region. It is in Russia's interest to control and direct as much as possible of the flow of oil and gas from this region into Europe to maximize its revenues and to retain a certain degree of political influence in its 'backyard' to ensure its own security.

Until approximately 2000 EU's strategy towards Russia in the Black Sea and the Caucasus regions was largely to seek a partnership. After that, Lussac (2010) argues, EU has become increasingly concerned about its energy security and sought ways to bypass Russian oil and gas deliveries and infrastructures. Russia's 'loss of credibility as a reliable partner' (Lussac 2010: 621) was a result of (1) the enlargement of EU in 2004 to include several eastern post-communist states with a critical stance towards Russia, and (2) the conflict between Russia and Ukraine over Russian gas transport across Ukraine. The change in policy signalled that the EU was becoming more willing to challenge Russia and work unilaterally in Russia's 'backyard'. That the overriding concern of EU in the region, especially the Caucasus, is now energy security is demonstrated by the fact that 'according to Brussels, [Azerbaijan] must become an EU strategic partner, both as a [gas] producer and a transit state. That is why it was integrated within the Black Sea Synergy initiative' (Lussac 2010: 618). There is now 'straightforward competition between Brussels and Moscow on the export of Caspian oil and gas' (ibid.: 621). That energy security is driving EU policy towards the Caucasus, if not the whole wider Black Sea region, is demonstrated by the fact that 'DG Energy has been able to take solely the lead of the external energy policy of the EU' (ibid.: 622).

Thus, Russian resistance to EU involvement in the Black Sea region, such as opposing its inclusion in the Bucharest Convention, can likely be read as a reaction to EU assertiveness concerning energy issues in the region. This is a clear demonstration of the geopolitics related to energy prevailing over regional environmental issues in the Black Sea region. This is very different from the Baltic, where Russia is more eager to cooperate with the EU. DG Environment tries to draw on this difference and negotiate Russia's interests in the Baltic to gain EU influence in the environmental field in the Black Sea (personal communication, DGEnv officer).

Regionalization Failure: The Fisheries Convention That Never Came To Be

Around 1990 the geopolitical shifts made the Varna convention obsolete. At the same time a severe resource crisis (in 1900/91 fishery season Turkish anchovy catches fell to 10% of previous season) convinced most states and stakeholders of the need for transnational cooperation to ensure sustainable fisheries in the Black Sea. There really seemed to be a good opportunity for regionalization around an important environmental and economic issue, and work on a legally binding document and the formation of some kind of Black Sea fisheries commission started in the early 1990s. However, to this day almost no degree of regional cooperation on fisheries management has emerged. Why? And what does this teach us about regionalization and EU-influence?

While Turkish Black Sea fisheries were for various reasons quite resilient during the crisis years (see Knudsen 1997), the combined effect of resource crisis and changed economic and political conditions for fisheries in Ukraine and Russia resulted in a dramatic decline in the catch capacity of their fleets (Knudsen and Toje 2008). Fisheries in Bulgaria, Romania and Georgia are of little importance regionally, and Turkey emerged as the most important fishery nation in the Black Sea. Although the number of Turkish purse seiners has remained stable during the last two decades, their total catch capacity has continued to increase due to investments in larger boats, more powerful engines, and more sophisticated electronic equipment. There are also signs that Ukrainian and Russian fisheries sectors are now slightly increasing their catch capacity again. Overall, there seems to be consensus among experts as well as among actors within the sector that there is overcapacity in Black Sea fisheries, especially on the Turkish side. Many of the most important commercial species, such as anchovy, sprat, turbot and bonito, are shared among several or all Black Sea countries, and there has been widespread conflict over cross border fishing activities, occasionally resulting in aggression, arrest or sinking of vessels and death of fishermen.

Fisheries management has very different traditions in the various Black Sea countries. There is some tradition of applying TACs and vessel quotas in Russia and Ukraine, while Turkey uses a range of different regulatory mechanisms, but does not favour TACs/quotas. Except for some bilateral (commercial) agreements (e.g. Turkish anchovy fishing in Georgian waters) there is no overall agreement about regional management of Black Sea fish stocks. A further challenge to regional management has been the lack of coordinated data collection and research. No ICES-like scientific body exists for the Black Sea. The establishment of the BSC Advisory Group on the Environmental Aspects of the Management of Fisheries and other Marine Living Resources has partly helped to address this, but science is still poorly funded, and international cooperation made difficult by different traditions of research and the lack of skills in a common language.

The Bucharest Convention and its protocols do not directly address fisheries. The Black Sea Biodiversity and Landscape Conservation Protocol to the Convention on the Protection of the Black Sea Against Pollution (signed in Sofia, Bulgaria 2002), should have some relevance for fisheries management, but is only ratified by Turkey and Ukraine. The Black Sea SAP, however, repeatedly stresses the need for restoration of commercial fisheries and makes reference to the future Black Sea fisheries commission.

Deliberations between the states on a Legally Binding Document on Fisheries and Conservation of Living Resources (LBDFCLR) started in 1993, and the first draft convention was prepared by Turkish authorities in 1994, sponsored by the WB and assisted by foreign expertise. However, disagreement hindered progress. A new draft was discussed at a meeting in Ankara in June 1997, but differences, especially between Turkey and Russia, continued to stop the convention from being signed. The BSEC established a fisheries sub-group to try to complete negotiations, but because of the commission's wide geographical scope it was decided that the BSEC was not a suitable host, and it asked the secretariat of the BSC to take responsibility for finalizing the deliberations on the fishery convention/LBDFCLR (Mee 2002: 126). A new text on LBDFCLR was approved by BSC in 2005, and in 2007 the Black Sea countries were very close to reaching agreement on a fishery convention. Yet, it now confronted a new challenge: Since Romania and Bulgaria had become Member States of the EU, jurisdiction lay with the EU which wanted to become a partner to the Bucharest Convention. But since Russia did not approve of having the EU in the BSC, agreement on the LBDFCLR could not be signed. Recently Turkey has also become more sceptical about the EU and has therefore also changed position on EU participation in the BSC.

With Bulgarian and Romanian EU-membership EU CFP was for the first time applied to parts of the Black Sea. In Romania and Bulgaria the transfer to CFP has seemingly met with little resistance as they have basically accepted and met all legal and technical requirements for joining the CFP and are now eligible for support from the European Fisheries Fund. However, with so little of the Black Sea covered by the CFP, the EU has – unlike the other seas where the CFP applies – decided not to establish a Regional Advisory Council. However, a Scientific, Technical and Economic Committee for Black Sea Fisheries (STECF) has been established, and in 2008 it made the first recommendations for TACs for sprat and turbot in Bulgarian and Romanian waters. Other Black Sea countries have since been invited and, except for Russia, participated in the annual meetings of the STECF. As an accession country Turkey has received EU assistance to conform to CFP through a twinning project and a technical assistance project (2004 – 2007) to improve scientific, technical and managerial capacity (Knudsen et al. 2007). However, due to the new draft of the fisheries law being rejected by the Turkish Parliament, many of the foreseen changes have not taken place.

The EU can obviously not effectively manage migrating and shared stocks in the Black Sea alone, and DG-Mare has sought ways to facilitate regional cooperation. When the BSC-based option stalled, a new initiative was taken through the European Parliament (EP), and within the frame of the BSS, to form an independent Regional Fisheries Management Organization (RFMO) (EP Committee on Fisheries 2011). In the new initiative by the EU the BSC is side-lined.[10] The EP notes that all Black Sea states as well as the EU should be members, and that it should be '… based on the example of the body that exists in the Baltic Sea' (ibid.: 12).

The General Fisheries Council of the Mediterranean (GFCM) had not been involved in the work on the draft LBDFCLR, but with the potential of EU

10 When I talked to the BSC director and the head of the fisheries advisory group in September 2011, several months after the EP initiative, they did not even know about the initiative!

participation and financial support for a fisheries convention, it tried in 2008 to position itself to cooperate with the BSC to establish a 'BLACKFISH' project (Knudsen 2008). The Black Sea has been within the scope of GFCM work since its establishment, but its involvement has not been continuous, and its ability to act in the region has been limited due to the fact that Turkey, Bulgaria and Romania are the only Black Sea states that are members. The BLACKFISH project never materialized. Yet, on Turkey's initiative the GFCM is now somehow involved in EC's RFMO initiative (GFCM 2011a, 2011b). This seems to fit with the BSS approach where the EC 'promotes bilateral cooperation with third countries ... and the General Fisheries Commission for the Mediterranean ...' (Delcour and Manoli 2010: 19). GFCM organized a Black Sea Working Group scientific meeting in Constanta in 2012 with some participation from the EC and minimal involvement from the BSC. Russian scientists attended, but were unwilling to provide data. They insist on the necessity of the establishment of large regional projects that can contribute to fund their work before they can consider submitting data. That this foot-dragging is not the result of individual whims or desire for economic gain is attested to by the fact that when Russian scientists were invited to the STECF meetings and had agreed to come, they simply did not show up. Most likely their attendance had been stopped for political reasons. It is unclear how the GFCM Black Sea Working Group initiative will be taken further beyond the intention to organize a joint meeting with the STECF. Thus, whether the RFMO will actually be established probably depends on Russia's position. At the time of writing the prospects are not good.

Regional cooperation on fishery management has this far been overruled by more important political and/or economic interests, such as energy policies and general geopolitical considerations. And, at least in Turkey, the state fisheries authorities have not always considered a LBDFCLR advantageous to the interests of the fishery sector. This case demonstrates how weak Black Sea regionalization has been around environmental issues. The failure to agree on a fisheries convention also shows that even a legal framework has not always been achieved. EU efforts might now seem to be the best chance to finally achieve regional management of Black Sea fisheries, but paradoxically EU's involvement may also be the primary challenge to progress as Russia continues to resist EU-influence in the region.

Conclusions

Although it has been argued that the legal basis for environmental cooperation in the Black Sea is partly 'outdated' (BS-TDA 2007: 140) and ratification is sometimes missing, a fairly comprehensive legal framework and conceptualization of issues and procedures exist (cf. Bohman and Langlet 2015 in this volume). Considered at this level, marine environmental governance in the Black Sea region has primarily been influenced by the Bucharest Convention. However, lack of personnel and funding has limited the ability of the BSC to act.

The political driving force (and main sources for funding) for transboundary environmental policy in the Black Sea has been external institutions: The World Bank and UN organizations (often jointly through GEF) taking the lead during the 1990s, The EU being more active after 2000. However, although EU's influence has become stronger, it is still striving to find its sea legs in Black Sea environmental policies. Integration of Black Sea environmental management within EU policies has been limited to the cooperation in the Danube region (DABLAS), the role of EU as a funding agency, and the implementation of EU-directives (CFP, WFD, MSFD) in Romania and Bulgaria. Instruments to address nutrient inflow have been relatively more successful than e.g. attempts at regional cooperation on fisheries management, most likely because these have been embedded within the more politically and economic stable framework of the EU Commission. Thus, EU policies have had some limited success. Beyond this, EU has recently sought more actively to foster regional cooperation, primarily through the BSS and the effort to establish a regional fisheries management organization. Outcomes of these efforts seem, however, to be very volatile. The dilemma is that stronger EU involvement may actually also hamper regionalization.

Together with lack of funding and a general de-prioritization of environmental issues by Black Sea riparian countries, geopolitical tensions have made progress on transboundary environmental cooperation very difficult. One analyst holds that '… one goal should be to work on harmonizing the DABLAS managerial model with the inter-sectoral BS-SAP approach and to contribute in this way to translate the BS-SAP into actual projects' (Tassinari 2006: 6). However, I find it slightly naïve to think that the DABLAS approach can be easily transferred to other areas or issues. This thinking ignores the geopolitical realities, including the emerging partnership between Turkey and Russia, and especially the tension between Russia and the EU. Thus, there may be no real change in prospects for transboundary cooperation on marine environmental issues in the Black Sea before more national governments prioritize environmental issues higher, and before the geopolitical situation makes regional cooperation overall easier. It is doubtful whether considering the environment a 'soft' issue has benefited either the environment or regionalization.

References

Aydin, M. 2005. Regional cooperation in the Black Sea and the role of institutions. *Perceptions*, 57-83.

Berindan, I. 2010. 'Black Sea Synergy': Looking at the sea … from the shore. An appraisal of the EU policy towards the Black Sea Region three years after. *European Standing Group on International Relations*. Stockholm.

Bohman, B. and Langlet, D. 2015. Float or Sinker for Europe's Seas? The role of law in marine governance, in *Governing Europe's Marine Environment:*

Europeanization of Regional Seas or Regionalization of EU Policies?, edited by M. Gilek and K. Kern. Farnham, UK: Ashgate Publishing.

BSERP 2006. Final report. Project component Black Sea Commission Institutional Review. UNDP/GEF Black Sea Ecosystems Recovery Project.

BSERP 2007. Exit strategy. UNDP/GEF Black Sea Ecosystem Recovery Project.

BS-TDA 2007. Black Sea Transboundary Analysis. Black Sea Environmental Recovery Project, Black Sea Commission, GEF, UNDP, UNOPS.

Caddy, J. 2008. Recent experience and future options for fisheries assessment and management in the Black Sea: A GFCM perspective. *GFCM internal report*.

DABLAS 2009. Meeting report Eight Meeting of DABLAS Task Force, Brussels, 17 November 2009. The DABLAS Task Force, EC-DG Environment.

Delcour, L. and Manoli, P. 2010. The EU's Black Sea Synergy: Results and possible ways forward. *Standard Briefing*. Brussels: European Parliament Directorate-General for external policies of the union.

Dimadama, Z. and Timotheou, A. 2010. Greening the Black Sea: Overcoming inefficiency and fragmentation through environmental governance. *ICBSS Policy Brief*. Athens: International Centre for Black Sea Studies.

Dimento, J.F. 2001. Black Sea environmental management: Prospects for new paradigms in transnational contexts, in *Reflections on Water: New Approaches to Transboundary Conflicts and Cooperation*, edited by J. Blatter and H. Ingram. Cambridge, MA: The MIT Press.

EC 2010. European Union Strategy for Danube Region. European Commission Communication, COM (2010) 715 final.

Emerson, M. 2008. The EU's new Black Sea policy. What kind of regionalism is this? *CEPS Working Document*. Brussels: Centre for European Policy Studies.

EP Committee on Fisheries. 2011. REPORT on current and future management of Black Sea fisheries (2010/2113(INI)). European Parliament Committee on Fisheries.

FAO 1993. Report on the technical consultation on stock assessment of the Black Sea, Ankara, Turkey, 15-19 February 1993. *FAO Fisheries Report*. Rome: FAO – General Fisheries Council for the Mediterranean.

GEF 2004. Control of eutrophication, hazardous substances and related measures for rehabilitating the Black Sea ecosystem: Phase 2. Washington: UNDP – Global Environmental Facility.

GFCM 2011. Identification and formulation of a project to strengthen scientific, technical and institutional cooperation to support responsible fisheries in the Black Sea. Rome: General Fishery Commission for the Mediterranean.

GFCM 2011. Status of the GFCM actions in the Black Sea. Rome: General Fisheries Commission for the Mediterranean.

Griffin, M. 1993. 'It's collapsing completely'. Two ecosystems, both (mostly) dead: Hope is faint that the Black Sea anchovy fishery can recover. *Ceres, The FAO Review*, 28-31.

King, C. 2004. *The Black Sea: A History*. Oxford, Oxford University Press.

Knudsen, S. 1997. *A Comparative Study of Fishing Communities and Public Awareness in Turkey and Ukraine*. Istanbul: Black Sea Environmental Programme.

Knudsen, S. 2008. *GFCM Black Sea Programme: Preliminary Elements for a Project Framework*. Rome: GFCM.

Knudsen, S., Pelczarski, W. and Brown, J. 2007. *Joining the EU: The Impacts on Fisheries*. Bergen, Gdynia, London: European Lifestyles and Marine Ecosystems.

Lussac, S.J. 2010. Ensuring European energy security in Russian 'Near Abroad': the case of the South Caucasus. *European Security*, 19, 607-625.

Mcquatters-Gollop, A. and Mee, L. 2007. Eutrophication in the Black Sea. World Resources Institute.

Mee, L.D. 2002. Protecting the Black Sea environment: A challenge for cooperation and sustainable development in Europe, in *Europe's Black Sea Dimension,* edited by T. Adams, M. Emerson, L. Mee and M. Vahl. Brussels: Centre for European Policy Studies, 77-133.

Readman, J.W., Fillmann, G., Tolosa, I., Bartocci, J., Villeneuve, J.-P., Catinni, C. and Mee, L.D. 2002. Petroleum and PAH contamination of the Black Sea. *Marine Pollution Bulletin*, 44, 48-62.

Reynolds, A.E. 1987. The Varna Convention: a regional response to fisheries conservation and management. *International Journal of Estuarine and Coastal Law*, 2, 154-170.

Sezer, S. The role of international environmental institutions in protecting regional seas: A focus on the Black Sea, in *International Symposium on the Problems of Regional Seas*, edited by B. Öztürk and N. Algan. 12-14 May 2001 Istanbul.

Stribis, I. 2009. Pooling forces in protecting the Black Sea marine environment: Actors and actions. *ICBBS Policy Brief*. Athens: International Centre for Black Sea Studies.

Tassinari, F. 2006. A synergy for Black Sea Regional Cooperation: Guidelines for an EU Initiative. *CEPS Policy Brief*. Brussels: Centre for European Policy Studies.

Knudsen, S. and Toje, H. 2008. Post-Soviet Transformations in Russian and Ukrainian Black Sea Fisheries: Socio-economic Dynamics and Property Relations. *Southeast European and Black Sea Studies*, 8, 17-32.

Ulman, A., Zengin, M., Bekişoğlu, Ş., Knudsen, S., Ünal, V., Mathews, C., Harper, S., Zeller, D. and Pauly, D. 2013. From Bonito to Anchovy: A Reconstruction of Turkey's Marine Fishery Catches (1950-2010). *Mediterranean Marine Science*, 14, 309-342.

Vahl, M. and Celac, S. 2006. Ready for a Breakthrough: Elements for a European Union Strategy Towards the Black Sea Region. *Southeast European and Black Sea Studies*, 6, 269-191.

Velikova, V. and Oral, N. 2012. Governance of the protection of the Black Sea: A model for regional cooperation, in *Environmental Security in Watersheds: The Sea of Azov*, edited by V. Lagutov. Dordrecht: Springer.

Winrow, G. 2007. Geopolitics and Energy Security in the Wider Black Sea Region. *Southeast European and Black Sea Studies*, 7, 217-235.

WWF 2008. *Greening the Black Sea Synergy*. Brussels: World Wide Fund for Nature and Heinrich Böll Foundation

Chapter 13

Marine Environmental Governance in Europe: Problems and Opportunities

Michael Gilek, Björn Hassler and Svein Jentoft

Introduction

We set out in this book project with the ambitious aim of achieving a better and more comprehensive understanding of the fragmented architecture of marine environmental governance in Europe, focussing on tensions between the Europeanization of regional seas and regionalization of EU policies. The question is – have we learnt anything about the identified key multi-level, multi-sector and multi-actor integration challenges (Kern and Gilek 2015 in this volume), or is the overall understanding of core problems still obscured by the complexity of the interactions? Furthermore, if in fact something has been learnt, can opportunities for improvements in practice be identified?

The answers to such questions can never be simple. As argued by Jentoft and Chuenpagdee (2015 in this volume), the governing system must somehow reflect the complexity and dynamics of the marine social and ecological systems, as well as the anthropogenic and natural pressures put on these systems. This means that contextual factors and temporal dynamics must always be part of our understanding of marine environmental governance and 'silver-bullet' type solutions to governance shortcomings will never be fully achievable. Still, we do believe that the in-depth analyses provided by the authors of the individual chapters have made a significant contribution to unravelling and clarifying the complexities of marine environmental governance in Europe. In this concluding chapter we thus highlight and discuss what we perceive to be the main empirical and analytical conclusions of the book in terms of key problems and opportunities of marine environmental governance in Europe.

The structure of the chapter follows a reversal of the logic found in the introductory chapter in that we identify and explore problems and opportunities linked to multi-level, multi-sector and multi-actor integration. This is done through a discussion of similarities and differences in preconditions and governance problems related to Europe's regional seas. Finally, we reflect on possible pathways for addressing the analysed integration challenges and thereby improving governance structures and processes.

Problems and Opportunities in the Governance of Europe's Marine Environment

The complex marine governance structures and many institutions in contemporary Europe can be viewed from different perspectives. Taking a rear-view look at systems to be governed and preconditions for effective governance in an attempt to better understand why things are the way they are today, it is clear that history matters, as do biophysical, social, cultural and political preconditions. As regards those regional seas where there have been strong and long-standing cooperative structures, relative economic affluence and stable democratic systems, institutions have had opportunities to become stronger. Hence, institutional systems are more developed in the Baltic and North Sea than in the Mediterranean and Black Sea, where differences in these dimensions are considerable. Additionally, the fact that almost all Contracting Parties to the Helsinki and OSPAR Conventions are also EU members means that the EU regulatory machinery can play a much more powerful role in these parts of Europe, compared to the Mediterranean Sea and especially the Black Sea, where the EU has thus far been less influential. However, despite the many differences, there are also important similarities, which might mean that potentials for learning between the regions could be substantial. Above all, the types of environmental problems threatening the integrity of the marine ecosystems are quite similar in all four regions, although their severity differs somewhat. Chemical pollution is a serious threat in all marine regions, although the situation in the Black Sea seems to be somewhat less grave (Knudsen 2015 in this volume). Eutrophication is a serious problem for all, as are the introduction of alien species and negative environmental effects from shipping. Over-fishing of many commercial fish stocks is another problem area in all regions that, furthermore, tends to interact negatively with eutrophication, creating even larger marine areas with anoxic sea floors.

In the following sections we will depart from observed differences and similarities in the four regional seas to discuss problems and opportunities in the governance of Europe's marine environment. One of the most interesting and crucial issues that has emerged in several of the chapters of this volume concerns the extent to which EU regulation, Europeanization and regionalization impede each other and the extent to which they are, or could be, complementary and synergistic. It is to this issue that we now turn.

Coping with Changing Institutional Arrangements at Regional and EU Level

Although the UNEP Regional Seas Programme has been important in establishing regional environmental conventions in the four EU macro regions discussed in this volume, it is fair to state that these conventions have mainly influenced governance outcomes through bottom-up processes and engaged countries in the respective regions. The Helsinki, Oslo/Paris and Barcelona Conventions were set up already in the 1970s, while the Bucharest Convention was not signed until 1992. They all provide what could be called rudimentary regulatory structures based on what practically amounts to soft law. However, although the updated versions of these structures all adhere to contemporary environmental principles and approaches, such as the Precautionary Principle and the Ecosystem Approach to Management, their actual impact varies considerably between the regions, where more has been achieved in the North than in the South. Based on the findings of this volume, an important factor behind this variation in impact is the extent to which comprehensive action plans such as the Baltic Sea Action Plan (BSAP) and the North-East Atlantic Environment Strategy (NEA Strategy) have been elaborated and agreed upon and – crucially – whether these plans have been sufficiently anchored in the individual member states' political and administrative systems.

In parallel with the Regional Seas development, EU authority has expanded both in regard to *reach* (number of member states in these regions) and *scope* (comprehensive framework directives). The directives – especially the Marine Strategy Framework Directive (MSFD), but also the Water Framework Directive (WFD) in combination with the Common Implementation Strategy (CIS) – provide a level regulatory framework for all EU member states. However, the scope dimension varies considerably, where the Baltic Sea and the North Sea are heavily dominated by EU member states and therefore by EU regulatory structures (Söderström et al. 2015 in this volume, Van Tatenhove and Van Leeuwen 2015 in this volume), while this only holds for the northern shores of the Mediterranean Sea (Suárez de Vivero and Rodríguez 2015 in this volume) and just for an even smaller part of the Black Sea (Knudsen 2015 in this volume). Thus, the scope of EU influence is much more restricted in the latter cases.

Institutional interaction is a topic that has been extensively discussed in the contemporary scholarly literature on international environmental cooperation (Oberthür and Stokke 2011, Van Leeuwen and Kern 2013). It has been shown that international environmental conventions such as the Convention on Biological Diversity and the Climate Convention as well as EU directives may interact in varying synergistic or contradictory ways, either inadvertently or as a result of states promoting national interests by, for example, forum shopping (Gillespie 2002). One of the major conclusions that might be drawn from this volume concerns institutional interaction between, on the one hand, Regional Seas Conventions and the accompanying Regional Commissions and, on the other hand, mainly the MSFD, and how this interaction has shaped governance outcomes. How the interactions between institutions play out in various contexts is an important issue from a policy perspective, since contradictory, overlapping or redundant regulatory structures can cause substantial inefficiencies and lead to institutional tensions (De Santo 2015 in this volume) and so-called *regulatory overload* (Knudsen and Hassler 2013). However, when institutions are adapted to each other, important synergism may evolve that can empower governance structures. Somewhat to our surprise, since most scholarly interest so far has been placed on conflicting interactions, the case studies in this volume indicate that bottom-up initiatives such as regional action plans can serve as providers of much needed detail in the more general EU framework directives, regarding biophysical indicators as well as coordination, monitoring and implementation facilitation. However, for such synergistic processes to emerge, regional conditions have to be favourable. Comparing the Northern Regional Seas of Europe with the Southern, we see that although rudimentary regulatory structures are largely in place in both, key elements such as regional economic capacity, political will, expertise and geopolitical stability are much more prominent in the Northern Regional Seas. This means that so far, it is primarily the jurisdictional strength of binding directives that have been given additional momentum by regional ambitions to turn words into action.

Before leaving this theme, two additional aspects related to interactions between Regional Seas initiatives, EU directives and global conventions are important to note. First, a powerful opportunity to turn regional conventions into mandatory national law emerges when the EU becomes a full member of these conventions. Depending on circumstances, EU membership in formally binding regional conventions can mean that not only the EU becomes obliged to follow this convention when signed and ratified, but all EU members (not only those who have ratified the Convention) become obliged to follow suit through the mechanism of an immediately binding EU Regulation (Bohman and Langlet 2015 in this volume). This powerful mechanism can become a double-edged sword as 'laggard' states certainly realize what consequences may follow from EU membership in a Regional Convention. Since unanimous decision-making is required in the regional conventions, any member can stop the EU from becoming a full partner to the convention if tighter regulations are perceived to negatively affect national interests. Hence, the non-EU members Russia and Turkey have, presumably to some extent because of these factors, been unwilling to allow the EU to become a full Contracting Party of the Bucharest Convention (Knudsen 2015 in this volume).

Second, depending on where the main regulatory competence resides, individual states, or smaller groups of allied states, can adopt strategies that considerably empower soft laws in regional or global conventions. In issue-areas where the EU has full competence such as in fisheries management, bottom-up government influence is limited. The type of regionalization we see here is rather in the form of Regional Advisory Councils (RACs), where primarily stakeholders and sectoral organizations have a voice. Whether the scope of the RACs will be expanded to cover wider issues within the fisheries/environment domain, and possibly other environmental problems, is an open question (Dreyer and Sellke 2015 in this volume). However, an argument could be made that expansion into areas where the EU does not have full competence would be more problematic. In contrast, in areas where important regulatory mandates remain with the individual states (e.g. marine pollution from land sources), proactive states may use so-called *upload* strategies in attempts to promote specific interests of various kinds by turning them into binding EU directives or high-impact EU strategies such as the EU Strategy for the Baltic Sea Region (EUSBSR) (Söderström et al. 2015 in this volume). This uploading strategy takes place when countries use regional or sub-regional agreements to empower biding EU directives. For example, it has been an outspoken ambition of HELCOM to upload the Baltic Sea Action Plan to the level of the MSFD in order to increase regulatory clout (Hassler et al. 2013).

Summing up the problems and opportunities linked to multi-level challenges in the governance of Europe's marine environment, it is clear that although much has been achieved, conditions differ substantially between the four regions, most prominently, the multi-faceted differences between the North and South. Fairly similar institutional frameworks have been established by Regional Seas Conventions with accompanying Commissions and crucial EU directives and strategies. However, it is only in the North that synergies have strengthened between comprehensive bottom-up regional initiatives and, particularly, the MSFD. The prospects for positive development in the South are mixed. All four regional seas share similar environmental problems and thus preconditions for fruitful knowledge sharing and institutional learning between North and South are already in place. Nonetheless, a further expansion of the EU to include additional Mediterranean or Black Sea countries does not seem likely in the near future and geopolitical tensions, as well as internal political strife in Northern Africa and parts of the Black Sea region, certainly make successful bottom-up environmental strategies difficult to achieve.

Combining Sectoral with Integrative Approaches: EAM and New Science-policy Interfaces

Several chapters in this volume confirm an ongoing shift from a traditional, sector-based approach focussed on handling particular resources (e.g. commercial fish) or sources of contamination (e.g. hazardous chemical substances), towards a more integrative and ecosystem based approach (e.g. De Santo 2015 in this volume, Gilek et al. 2015 in this volume, Hammer 2015 in this volume). However, opinions on the degree of shift that has occurred, and, in particular, on the associated problems and opportunities of the contrasting approaches, differ somewhat between chapters. For example, Gilek et al. (2015) and Hammer (2015) argue that implementation of the MSFD has already promoted a significant shift towards sector integration and an ecosystem-based approach to management (at least in the Baltic and North Seas). These authors also argue that the opportunities of such a sector-integrated approach, in terms of coping with uncertainties and stakeholder conflicts, as well as promoting a 'new' and more 'integrative' role for science, are already considerable as exemplified by recent developments in the International Council for the Exploration of the Sea, ICES (even though several enduring challenges and possible improvements also are identified). Similarly, Gilek et al. (2015) contend that recent developments in the EU Common Fisheries Policy (CFP) and in the EU chemicals regulation REACH also exhibit indications of institutional reforms promoting wider knowledge and stakeholder inclusion at the science-policy interface (in the case of the CFP) as well as improved coping with uncertainties (REACH and CFP). In contrast, whilst agreeing that the MSFD provides the foundation for an ecosystem-based approach, De Santo (2015) identifies and explores several significant integration challenges and tensions that need to be addressed for the MSFD to realize its potential to catalyse the development of more integrative approaches such as Marine Spatial Planning (MSP). Examples of such challenges include tensions between policy objectives (e.g. economic development and environmental management) and between various institutions linked to the EU, Member States, Regional Seas Conventions and non-EU members, as well as undeveloped integrated science support, especially in the Mediterranean and Black Seas.

It is not surprising that different studies of complex multi-sector governance arrangements give rise to slightly diverging pictures. Still, in relation to the aim of this section to identify problems and opportunities with sector integration in European marine governance, several recurring issues can be distinguished in the chapters of this volume.

First, the inclusion of the *Ecosystem Approach to Management (EAM)* as a core requirement in the implementation of several important EU Directives (e.g. MSFD, WFD), as well as regional seas action plans (e.g. in the Baltic and North Seas), has clearly been instrumental in placing specific knowledge about the marine environment and its sensitivity at the heart of marine governance. However, a closer look at the action plans presents a more nuanced picture with many lasting scientific, legal and institutional challenges, as well as clear indications of a slower rate of EAM implementation in the South (Black Sea and Mediterranean) than in the North (Baltic Sea and North Sea) (Bohman and Langlet 2015 in this volume, Gilek et al. 2015 in this volume). Furthermore, when looking specifically at progress in terms of sector integration, even more challenges and problems can be observed. To begin with, even though definitions of EAM usually include a reference to necessary trade-offs between societal use of the ecosystem and ecosystem integrity, the main implementation tools are firmly based on the ecological dimension of sustainability, thus more or less neglecting social and economic dimensions of sustainability (as e.g. observed for the HELCOM BSAP by Gilek et al. 2013). Linked to this is the observation that many of the eleven descriptors for Good Environmental Status (GES) in the MSFD can be seen as still largely building on a sectoral approach with their focus on, for example, commercial fish, eutrophication, chemical contaminants and energy (e.g. De Santo 2015 in this volume). This questions the extent to which interdependencies among environmental risks and pressures can be considered in current marine governance arrangements in Europe. Hence, there is clearly a need to further develop forums for cross-sectoral cooperation addressing not only environmental management, but also the social and economic dimensions of sustainability and interdependencies between environmental pressures. Some positive developments in this direction can be observed, for example in the Baltic Sea through the recently established HELCOM stakeholder forums on fisheries/environment and agriculture/environment as well as the joint HELCOM VASAB working group on MSP. However, it is too early to tell whether or not these initiatives will positively shape governance outcomes (Hassler et al. 2013), while progress in relation to the other European Seas (especially in the South) is even less evident (Gilek et al. 2015 in this volume).

Second, *Marine Spatial Planning (MSP)* has recently been given increased prominence in Europe and world-wide in response to the problems of fragmentation of marine regulation, increasing pressures upon the seas and tensions between sectoral and stakeholder interests and knowledge claims (e.g. Jentoft and Chuenpagdee 2015 in this volume). MSP has also been identified as the central approach to give effect to the EU Integrated Marine Policy and the associated Blue Growth Strategy that promotes more intensive utilization of marine resources to facilitate the growth of maritime economies, while improving ecological conditions in line with the MSFD. However, while policy documents on a conceptual level explain Blue Growth as building on the related foundations of sustainable development and the ecosystem approach, it remains to be seen how it can be implemented in practice (e.g. Van Tatenhove 2015 in this volume). A fundamental question linked to this is whether or not policy approaches and mechanisms can be developed to facilitate higher degrees of multi-sector integration, and if win-win outcomes in terms of Blue Growth and good environmental standards are achievable.

Some progress in developing marine spatial plans and implementing MSP can be seen in a number of countries (e.g. Germany and the Netherlands) (e.g. Van Tatenhove and Van Leeuwen 2015 in this volume). However, development of transboundary and regional sea level MSP is still in its infancy in Europe, although there are, for example, processes apparent in the Baltic Sea to develop pan-Baltic coordination of MSP in line with the HELCOM MSP roadmap from December 2013. Furthermore, while optimizing sector and policy integration is a laudable ambition in MSP, knowing the limits of integration and the different and specific forms it takes may be equally important, since MSP can be seen as a 'wicked' problem where consensual outcomes among stakeholders are likely to be elusive and where problem definitions are contested, solutions are less than ideal, always preliminary, and never given (Rittel and Webber 1973, Jentoft and Chuenpagdee 2009, Jentoft and Knol 2014).

Several interesting ideas on how to address these MSP challenges and thereby increase opportunities for sector and policy integration are identified and explored in this volume. Jentoft and Chuenpagdee (2015), for example, develop a general framework based on the idea of interactive governance proposing that identification of potential improvements relating to MSP processes and outcomes (i.e. governability using their terminology) should be based on a three-step process considering system properties, institutional capabilities and stakeholder interactions. Essentially their argument is that all of these aspects need to be considered to develop a context-specific MSP approach. In this way, they maintain that MSP should be seen rather as an approach or catalyst that triggers interactive learning and not a strictly defined tool or solution. The issue of institutional capacity building is further developed by Van Tatenhove (2015), who, based on a thorough analysis of the scientific literature, outlines a typology of the dimensions of institutional capacity building, and subsequently uses this to explore integration opportunities for MSP in European marine governance. A key conclusion in this analysis is that further development of MSP in Europe requires a particular focus on institutional design and capacity building at the regional seas level. For example, as argued above for EAM, there is a need to further strengthen integrated marine governance arrangements consisting of coalitions of governmental and sector representatives, scientists and a range of NGOs and other interest groups. The challenge is to establish governance arrangements that promote constructive decision-making processes that involve interested parties in a way that is democratic and legitimate. How this can be accomplished, is a wicked problem in itself, always easier said than done, also because it is a sensitive issue, as Dreyer and Sellke (2015 in this volume) point out in their chapter 'Who qualifies as legitimate stakeholders? And how urgent are their concerns?' MSP is therefore deemed to remain a work in progress where such questions must be clarified even before the planning process starts.

Finally, linked to the development of integrative policy approaches such as EAM and MSP, there is a push towards developing a *new and more 'integrative' role for science and the use of science-based advice*. In line with this 'policy push', several scholars argue from a theoretical perspective that complex and uncertain risks and pressures linked to environmental governance, such as contamination and resource use, require new forms of science support built on wider knowledge inclusion and extended peer review, as well as coping with irreducible uncertainties (cf. Udovyk and Gilek 2013). In their analysis of science-policy interfaces linked to the MSFD and the CFP, Gilek et al. (2015) and Linke et al. (2014) also observe what appears to be a shift from highly sector-based science-policy interaction, often complicated by stakeholder conflicts and the contested status of scientific uncertainty, towards a more open relationship between science, politics and other actors in society (at least in the Baltic and North Seas). This shift is exemplified by recent developments in the international scientific organization ICES. It can be seen to be expanding its traditional role as a key provider of science-based advice for commercial fisheries in Northern Europe (e.g. Baltic and North Seas) to also address scientific issues relating to MSFD implementation and associated integrative approaches such as EAM and MSP. Despite this general trend connected to the MSFD, a more detailed analysis also reveals a parallel occurrence of almost sector-specific expert communities in several sectors (such as chemicals management, maritime risks etc.), as well as a general lack of state-of-the-art treatment of uncertainties. Clearly, even though such parallel scientific support structures linked to specific GES Descriptors in the MSFD and specific EU regulations on, for example, chemicals or fisheries can ensure that the best available scientific evidence is used, there is certainly also a risk that scientific disagreements can aggravate stakeholder conflicts. This means that, in order to provide more integrated scientific support for implementing EAM and MSP, there is a need to further develop interdisciplinary and cross-sectoral collaboration forums for achieving integrated science-based advice, preferably at the regional seas level. As previously concluded, addressing this requirement is particularly pertinent in the Mediterranean and Black Sea where scientific support is still comparatively undeveloped and fragmented (Knudsen 2015 in this volume, Suárez de Vivero and Rodríguez 2015 in this volume).

Towards New Actor Constellations: Increasing Influence of Stakeholders and the Public?

There is no simple way to involve stakeholders, particularly at higher scales of organization such as regions and macro-regions, in a process that is deliberative, representative and democratic. This is a classic challenge in democratic theory and practice, expressed as a conflict between integration and aggregation (March and Olsen 1989); the former referring to a process that involves exchange and deliberation, the latter a process of summation, as when votes are cast and counted. This is a problem that is felt within, for example, the RAC system in fisheries management, where representatives from both industry and civil society are supposed to deliberate and reach consensus on issues where they all have different and to a large extent diverging interests. An additional challenge, no less complicated, is that in situations of conflict where decisions need to be made, some have more at stake than others, which is to be addressed by weighing of representation. In this particular case of stakeholder involvement, the fishing industry is represented more strongly in the RACs and hence has a louder voice and more votes than other stakeholders. Therefore, other stakeholder groups often find the process unfair (Linke and Jentoft 2013). Given this, and other reasons related to representation and power, consensus on matters up for discussion and decision-making may be unrealistic, as Dreyer and Sellke (2015 in this volume) argue. Instead, it may be more realistic and fruitful in the long term to focus less on consensus and more on developing inclusive arenas promoting learning through exchange of stakeholder critique, input and advice (Voss et al. 2006).

Inclusive marine governance unavoidably raises issues related to social justice, both with regard to distribution and procedure. There is a real danger that differences in power between sectors and actors may impact on the distribution of resources and spatial opportunities. A consequence being that some stakeholder groups risk further marginalization. For example, traditional small-scale fishers may have reasons to fear the power of the oil and wind energy industries in the context of MSP. They might not have the requisite resources to effectively pursue their claims to particular spaces, even if they can claim to have had made much longer use of those spaces. Creating a level playing field in marine governance under such conditions is a governability problem as far as justice is concerned, something that institutional designs for participation and decision-making must plan for. This suggests that marine governance and MSP are not only technical issues, but also highly political ones, where conflicting stakeholder interests and power differentials matter in determining outcomes. Consequently, advisory councils, marine spatial planning processes and the co-production of knowledge do not ensure justice unless they are designed and exercised with the necessary built-in checks and balances.

Furthermore, what makes governability and increasing stakeholder influence extremely challenging to achieve in the move from government to governance are, apart from a not uncommon democratic deficit at all scales and institutions, the complex differences in preconditions, system properties and stakeholder interactions among countries, regions and sectors (Jentoft and Chuenpagdee 2015 in this volume). As described in the chapters of this book, there are considerable variations between countries and sectors, since governing systems and practices have roots in different regimes and ideologies. Europeanization, through the EU inclusion of Eastern European countries, has almost certainly significantly counteracted this heterogeneity, but major differences and institutional tensions remain among countries, regions and sectors (e.g. Van Leeuwen et al. 2012, De Santo 2015 in this volume). For instance, one would assume that stakeholder inclusion and deliberation in marine governance would be much easier in the context of the North Sea than in, for example, the Baltic Sea or the Mediterranean areas. The countries that share this ocean space exhibit similar political cultures and participate in common institutional frameworks linked to various EU directives. Nonetheless, differences in governance cultures and practices have also here hampered coordination and stakeholder cooperation in, for example, MSP (Van Tatenhove and Van Leeuwen 2015 in this volume). A pessimistic interpretation of these observations would be that, if inclusive and deliberative marine governance is extremely hard to achieve even for the North Sea, it is quite unlikely that this could be realized for other regional seas, at least in a foreseeable future (cf. Jentoft and Knol 2014). Still, based on the chapters of this book, it is possible to identify some signs of progress as well as opportunities for improvements linked to stakeholder involvement and influence. These are discussed below.

Given the complexities and the multiple and conflicting stakes that together make problems and challenges inherently 'wicked', marine governance in Europe (and elsewhere) is deemed to be a work in progress where outcomes are unpredictable. Goals often lack the clarity and precision that can provide the direction needed. The planning process is going to be one of incremental change or even a process of 'muddling through' (Lindblom 1959) because a strictly technical/scientific process is not possible. Goals are never given once and for all but are rather subject to ongoing negotiation among public and private stakeholders from various sectors and at different scales. What was originally envisioned is not necessarily what one ends up with as the operative goals, i.e. those that are actually acted upon. Rather, goals are likely to be introduced, deliberated, scrapped and replaced by new goals throughout the planning process as experiences are gained and ambitions adjusted to better fit what is accomplished. This lack of linearity within marine governance should not come as a surprise. Organization theorists have been highlighting it for decades (see for example Cyert and March 1992), while it has been empirically validated in the case of MPAs (Marine Protected Areas) (Jentoft et al. 2011). In fact, rather than indicating a flawed process ridden by conflict and indecisiveness, 'muddling through' may be the outcome of a rational process adaptive to shifting circumstances and influenced by interactions and experiential learning. The evolvement of RACs in fisheries management can, despite continuing problems of representation, power dynamics and limited mandates, exemplify such an incremental development process (Dreyer and Sellke 2015 in this volume). Hence, in spite of the fundamental challenges, adaptive processes, as observed in the RAC development, indicate that there are opportunities to facilitate the creation of forums that cut across sectors and scale in a way that allows for the proactive participation of public and private stakeholders.

How to create such a constructive and integrated deliberation process is, however, a fundamental challenge in need of more focussed attention by all interested parties, especially if the EU, as it has suggested, gets more serious in 'shifting the burden of proof' (Linke and Jentoft 2013). The mandates and roles of deliberative forums and processes are also in need of significant clarification. For example, the question is to what extent the RACs should remain in a strictly advisory role or if mandates should be expanded to involve deeper responsibilities. Associated to this is a clear risk that stakeholders will end up frustrated, to the extent that they might see their efforts as a waste of time, if they cannot see the impact of their advice on decisions made at EU levels or by national governments. But the RACs are just for one sector, whereas the real difficulties in implementing a holistic ecosystem approach to management (EAM) as required by the MSFD involve relationships and interactions between sectors that require some form of integration (e.g. Hammer 2015 in this volume). It is hard today to envisage institutions that are 'all-inclusive', that integrate everything and everyone at the same time, especially if built on bottom-up mechanisms that involve stakeholders from all relevant sectors. The transaction costs of representation and negotiation may simply be too high. An alternative, as explored by Dreyer and Sellke (2015 in this volume), could be to develop a more inclusive and deliberative advisory function in European marine governance through a 'tiered' structure combining sectoral sub-divisions and overarching integrating forums. This set-up could possibly increase the likelihood for fruitful deliberation, rapprochement and bridge-building among disparate social groups. At the same time it might allow for the required incremental learning, context-dependent considerations and scale-dependent adjustments (cf. Gilek et al. 2015 in this volume). Clearly, development and coordination of governance arrangements at the level of Europe's regional seas (i.e. regionalization) could nurture opportunities for moving towards more inclusive and deliberative marine governance (Söderström et al. 2015 in this volume, Van Tatenhove and Van Leeuwen 2015 in this volume). Ultimately, in line with the EU principle of subsidiarity, this regionalization could provide a means for achieving a higher degree of congruence between the 'system-to-be-governed' and the 'governing system' (Jentoft and Chuenpagdee 2015 in this volume). However, as was also explained in several of the chapters, the development and outcomes of such regional-level marine governance forms will always be dependent on multi-level interactions where EU institutions as well as national governance structures and processes are of importance.

The different chapters of this book have adopted rather different perspectives on European marine governance. This is not surprising, given the different political, administrative, social, economic and cultural settings in the Regional Seas covered. However, a common theme that has emerged is the perceived need for improved integration as a vehicle to increased effectiveness and efficiency as well as better-adapted institutional structures for stakeholder deliberation to facilitate institutional coordination and learning. We close the book by addressing this issue.

The Importance of Integration in Future European Marine Governance

Based on the findings of this book, we conclude that several dimensions of integration linked to multi-level, multi-sector and multi-actor governance challenges will most likely play a key role if future European marine governance is going to be effective, efficient, democratic and sustainable. As explained in this chapter, the complexities of both the 'system-to-be governed' and the 'governance system' imply that 'silver bullet' types of solutions to governance shortcomings will never by fully achievable. Rather, the required integrative turn identified in this volume needs to be adaptive and incremental rather than radical, in order to allow for necessary adjustments, adaptation, reflexivity and institutional learning between the regional seas of Europe. It is, however, equally important to identify the context-dependent limits of integration and the different and specific forms it takes. The basic argument here is that 'forced' integration may obfuscate rather than resolve differences, among important actors such as governments, sectoral organizations, stakeholders and providers of scientific support.

Despite the fundamental challenges, several opportunities for improved integration have been identified. In relation to multi-sector challenges we have, for example, identified situations where EAM and MSP have fostered improved integration of knowledge and sectoral perspectives. The optimistic observer can also interpret the setting up of the RACs in fisheries management as a potential first step towards developing more inclusive and deliberative marine governance in Europe.

Returning to the key objective of this book – to investigate the tensions between the Europeanization of regional seas and the regionalization of EU policies – it is clear that there are opportunities for synergies despite tensions. In fact, integration between, on the one hand, regional initiatives such as HELCOM and OSPAR and, on the other, EU directives and strategies identifying potential synergies could increase governance efficiency and effectiveness. This means that such regional organizations could play even more important roles than they do today in elaborating how EU directives could be adapted to local conditions as well as strengthening monitoring and compliance. At the same time, the EU could provide well-needed coherence at the pan-European level. However, it should also be noted, that conditions for institutional learning between North and South need to be improved to stimulate this development. Comparing North and South, it is clear that there are substantial differences between the regions. To effectively reduce the sizes of these inconsistencies, institutional learning needs to be interactive and adapted to regional contexts rather than unidirectional and predetermined. Even though HELCOM and OSPAR may serve as valuable examples, conditions in the South are far too different from those in the North to make the application of blueprints possible. By making institutional learning reflexive, governance can be improved in all four regions.

In this reflexive learning process we believe that the 'good governance' concept (European Commission 2001), with its set of meta-principles (on e.g. openness, participation and accountability) is useful in setting standards for what governing institutions at various scales should strive for. Similarly, well-established and commonly accepted principles in environmental policy such as those addressing precaution, polluter pays and equity offer additional criteria for assessing governance systems and needs for reform (e.g. Karlsson 2006). Our argument here is that, even though contexts between the Northern and Southern seas in Europe differ to the extent that institutional designs cannot be replicas of each other, good governance and environmental policy principles would apply generally and equally in both contexts. The fact that these principles are perhaps more challenging and would be more time consuming to realize in the Mediterranean and Black Sea in comparison to the Baltic and North Sea does not make them irrelevant. One should of course be flexible and adaptive with regard to institutional design and how to operationalize these principles, but not with respect to their adoption. Thus, if strived for in both settings, one may over time see that governance systems will converge while allowing them to remain embedded in regional contexts, which they would have to be in order to be legitimate, just and effective. The former is about their acceptance among stakeholders and their willingness to comply. Justice is about distribution of resources and space as well as due process. Effectiveness concerns the basic governance concerns, one of them being good environmental status and the way to realize it most cost-effectively. Thus, marine governance must be multipurpose and multidimensional. It must be able to realize many things at the same time, things that are not necessarily compatible but require choices that are hard and where science can only help a bit of the way. This is also why marine governance is as much about process as about outcome. Indeed the two are intimately linked and must be thought of in parallel.

References

Bohman, B. and Langlet, D. 2015. Float or Sinker for Europe's Seas? The role of law in marine governance, in *Governing Europe's Marine Environment: Europeanization of Regional Seas or Regionalization of EU Policies?*, edited by M. Gilek and K. Kern. Farnham, UK: Ashgate Publishing.

Cyert, R. and March, J.G. 1992. *A Behavioral Theory of the Firm*. Second edition. Oxford: Wiley-Blackwell.

Dahl, R.A. 1991. *Democracy and its Critics*. New Haven, CT: Yale University Press.

De Santo, E. 2015. The Marine Strategy Framework Directive as a Catalyst for Maritime Spatial Planning: internal dimensions and institutional tensions, in *Governing Europe's Marine Environment: Europeanization of Regional Seas or Regionalization of EU Policies?*, edited by M. Gilek and K. Kern. Farnham, UK: Ashgate Publishing.

Dreyer, M. and Sellke, P. 2015. The Regional Advisory Councils in European Fisheries: An appropriate approach to stakeholder involvement in an EU integrated marine governance?, in *Governing Europe's Marine Environment: Europeanization of Regional Seas or Regionalization of EU Policies?*, edited by M. Gilek and K. Kern. Farnham, UK: Ashgate Publishing.

European Commission. 2001. European Governance: A White Paper, COM(2001) 428.

Gilek, M., Hassler, B., Engkvist, F. and Kern, K. 2013. The HELCOM Baltic Sea Action Plan: challenges of implementing an innovative ecosystem approach, in *Political State of the Region Report 2013 – Trends and Directions in the Baltic Sea Region*, edited by B. Henningsen, T. Etzold and A.-L., Pohl. Copenhagen, Denmark: Political Baltic Development Forum, 58-61.

Gilek, M., Karlsson, M., Udovyk, O. and Linke, S. 2015. Science and Policy in the Governance of Europe's Marine Environment: The impact of Europeanization, regionalization and the ecosystem approach to management, in *Governing Europe's Marine Environment: Europeanization of Regional Seas or Regionalization of EU Policies?*, edited by M. Gilek and K. Kern. Farnham, UK: Ashgate Publishing.

Gillespie, A. 2002. Forum shopping in International Environmental Law: The IWC, CITES, and the management of cetaceans. *Ocean Development & International Law*, 33(1), 17-56.

Hammer, M. 2015. The ecosystem management approach. Implications for marine governance, in *Governing Europe's Marine Environment: Europeanization of Regional Seas or Regionalization of EU Policies?*, edited by M. Gilek and K. Kern. Farnham, UK: Ashgate Publishing.

Hassler, B., Boström, M. and Grönhom, S. 2013. Towards an ecosystem approach to management in regional marine governance? The Baltic Sea context. *Journal of Environmental Policy & Planning*, 15(2), 225-245.

Jentoft, S. and Chuenpagdee, R. 2009. Fisheries and coastal governance as a Wicked Problem. *Marine Policy*, 33, 553-560.

Jentoft, S., Chuenpagdee, R. and Pascual Fernandez, J.J. 2011. What MPAs are for? On goal formation and displacement. *Ocean and Coastal Management*, 54(1), 75-83.

Jentoft, S. and Knol, M. 2014. Marine spatial planning: risk or opportunity for fisheries in the North Sea? *Maritime Studies*, 12(13), 1-16.

Jentoft, S. and Chuenpagdee, R. 2015. The 'New' Marine Governance: assessing governability, in *Governing Europe's Marine Environment: Europeanization of Regional Seas or Regionalization of EU Policies?*, edited by M. Gilek and K. Kern. Farnham, UK: Ashgate Publishing.

Karlsson, M. 2006. Science and norms in policies for sustainable development: Assessing and managing risks of chemical substances and genetically modified organisms in the European Union. *Regulatory Toxicology and Pharmacology*, 44, 49-56.

Kern, K. and Gilek, M. 2015. Governing Europe's Marine Environment: key topics and challenges, in *Governing Europe's Marine Environment: Europeanization of Regional Seas or Regionalization of EU Policies?*, edited by M. Gilek and K. Kern. Farnham, UK: Ashgate Publishing.

Knudsen, O.F. and Hassler, B. 2011. IMO legislation and its implementation: accident risk, vessel deficiencies and national administrative practices, *Marine Policy*, 35(2), 201-207.

Knudsen, S. 2015. Marine Governance in the Black Sea, in *Governing Europe's Marine Environment: Europeanization of Regional Seas or Regionalization of EU Policies?*, edited by M. Gilek and K. Kern. Farnham, UK: Ashgate Publishing.

Lindblom, C.E. 1959. The Science of 'Muddling Through'. *Public Administration Review*, 19, 79-88.

Linke, S. and Jentoft, S. 2013. A communicative turnaround: Shifting the burden of proof in European fisheries governance. *Marine Policy*, 38, 337-345.

Linke, S. and Jentoft, S. 2014. Exploring the Phronetic dimension of stakeholders' knowledge in EU fisheries governance. *Marine Policy*, 47, 153-161.

Linke, S., Gilek, M., Karlsson, M. and Udovyk, O. 2014. Unravelling science-policy interactions in environmental risk governance of the Baltic Sea: comparing fisheries and eutrophication. *Journal of Risk Research*, 17(4), 505-523.

March, J.G. and Olsen, J.P. 1989. *Rediscovering Institutions: The Organizational Basis of Politics*. New York: The Free Press.

Oberthür, S. and Stokke, O.S. (eds) 2011. *Managing Institutional Complexity: Regime Interplay and Global Environmental Change*. Cambridge, MA: The MIT Press.

Rittel, H.W.J. and Webber, M.M. 1973. Dilemmas in a general theory of planning. *Policy Sciences*, 4, 155-169.

Suárez de Vivero, J.L. and Rodríguez, J.C. 2015. Marine Governance in the Mediterranean Sea, in *Governing Europe's Marine Environment: Europeanization of Regional Seas or Regionalization of EU Policies?*, edited by M. Gilek and K. Kern. Farnham, UK: Ashgate Publishing.

Söderström, S., Kern, K. and Hassler, B. 2015. Marine governance in the Baltic Sea: current trends of Europeanization and regionalization, in *Governing Europe's Marine Environment: Europeanization of Regional Seas or Regionalization of EU Policies?*, edited by M. Gilek and K. Kern. Farnham, UK: Ashgate Publishing.

Udovyk, O. and Gilek, M. 2013. Coping with uncertainties in science-based advice informing environmental management of the Baltic Sea. *Environmental Science and Policy*, 29, 12-23.

Van Leeuwen, J., Van Hoof, L. and Van Tatenhove, J. 2012. Institutional ambiguity in implementing the European Union Marine Strategy Framework Directive. *Marine Policy*, 36, 636-643.

Van Leeuwen, J. and Kern, K. 2013. The External Dimension of European Union Marine Governance: institutional interplay between the EU and the International Maritime Organization. *Global Environmental Politics*, 13(1), 69-87.

Van Tatenhove, J. 2015. Marine Governance: institutional capacity building in a multi-level governance setting, in *Governing Europe's Marine Environment: Europeanization of Regional Seas or Regionalization of EU Policies?*, edited by M. Gilek and K. Kern. Farnham, UK: Ashgate Publishing.

Van Tatenhove, J. and Van Leeuwen, J. 2015. Marine Governance of the North Sea: patterns of regionalization, in *Governing Europe's Marine Environment: Europeanization of Regional Seas or Regionalization of EU Policies?*, edited by M. Gilek and K. Kern. Farnham, UK: Ashgate Publishing.

Voss, J.-P., Bauknecht, D. and Kemp, R. (eds). 2006. *Reflexive Governance for Sustainable Development*. Cheltenham: Edward Elgar.

Index